Lifting the Veil

Lifting the Veil

A POLITICAL HISTORY OF STRUGGLES
FOR EMANCIPATION

Richard A. Couto

The University of Tennessee Press / Knoxville

Frontispiece: Elisha Davis and sons, 1940. Courtesy of the Library of Congress.

The paper in this book meets the minimum requirements of the
American National Standard for Permanence of Paper for Printed
Library Materials. ∞ The binding materials have been chosen
for strength and durability.

LIBRARY OF CONGRESS CATALOGING IN PUBLICATION DATA

Couto, Richard A. , 1941–
    Lifting the veil: a political history of struggles for emancipation / Richard Couto.—1st ed.
        p.   cm.
    Includes bibliographical references (p.   ) and index.
    ISBN 0-87049-807-X (cl.: alk. paper)
    ISBN 0-87049-808-8 (pbk.: alk. paper)
1. Civil rights movements—Tennessee—Haywood County—History.
2. Afro-Americans—Civil rights—Tennessee—Haywood County.
3. Haywood County (Tenn.)—Race relations.   I. Title
F443.H4C68   1993
305.8'960730768223—dc20   93-23842
                                            CIP

For Nann Davis and all the other "bleating" voices of protest and hope

If somewhere in this whirl and chaos of things there dwells
Eternal Good, pitiful yet masterful, then anon in His good time
America shall rend the Veil and the prisoned shall go free.

W. E. B. Du Bois
The Souls of Black Folk, 1903

Contents

Illustrations

Preface

The frontispiece of this book portrays Elisha Davis lifting a blindfold from the faces of his two sons. Davis wrote a caption, which he called "A Poem," for this photograph: "Lifting the veil from the faces of the coming generations of Haywood." The camera and the caption captured Davis's awareness that he was part of a historical and political drama. They also express his confidence, and that of his sons, that he was playing his role well. The symbolic blindfold Davis is lifting represents a social, political, and economic system of racial restrictions and limitations referred to as "Jim Crow." The title of this book is taken from Davis's epigram. The body of this volume traces the efforts of Davis and many others like him to lift the veil of racism and to achieve the promise of emancipation over time and in one place.

Davis and his sons posed for this photograph in 1940, when Davis was forming a chapter of the National Association for the Advancement of Colored People (NAACP) in Haywood County, Tennessee. The dramatic role which Davis thought he was playing did not proceed as he had anticipated. After he and other NAACP chapter members inquired about registering to vote in time for the 1940 presidential election, they were threatened, and one man was lynched. Davis and five other NAACP members were banished from the county. Davis went into hiding, separated from his pregnant wife and seven children, who escaped into hiding elsewhere. After several months the family reunited and fled the South. Thus the photograph has become not a mere snapshot in a simple story of registration and voting, as Davis had expected, but a brief scene in a much longer and larger historical drama, the struggle for emancipation of African Americans. That struggle was carried out in many locations and involved many people like Elisha Davis. The photograph does not show what Davis did not understand and what this book explains. Elisha Davis grasped only a segment and not the corners of the veil that so many others, both before and after him, have attempted to raise.

This book reaches beyond Davis's grasp to a time before him, Reconstruction, and a time that followed him, the civil rights movement and its aftermath. Our account locates Davis's experiences within the larger fabric of African-American emancipation efforts. It places him in the company of other African Americans who discreetly maintained their sense of dignity and protested the laws that denied them their civil rights.

Like Davis, national leaders of other emancipation efforts employed the metaphor of the veil. For example, W. E. B. Du Bois explained that to write his classic work, *The Souls of Black Folk*, he had left the white world and "stepped within the Veil" that shrouded the lives and aspirations of African Americans. Once within it, Du Bois sketched "the spiritual world in which ten thousand thousand Americans live and strive."[1] Likewise, Ida B. Wells, an extraordinary champion of racial justice, prefaced the diary she kept as a young woman with a reference to a veil, taken from a Confucian proverb: "There is in every human being, however ignoble, some view of perfection; some one place where—as we may fancy—the veil is thin which hides the divinity behind it."[2]

These three uses of the metaphor of the veil suggest three emphases in American emancipation struggles. People like Davis tried to lift one veil from their faces and the faces of others, to improve these people's vision of their own potential. People like Du Bois tried to lift a veil obscuring groups and races of Americans, to enable them to see each other better. People like Wells peered through a third veil for a glimpse of the dignity and value of the individuals behind it.

Because I intend to make this book as personal an account of emancipation as possible, I have written it with two distinct audiences in mind: those who do not read endnotes and those who do. I wrote it first for people like Nann Davis, Elisha's widow, and other key actors in the events recounted here, such as Robert McElwee and C. P. Boyd, as well as for their children and grandchildren. I sought to convey the experiences of these individuals as directly as possible, the way they described them to me, and in terms relevant to them and people like them. They are people who put more effort into living free than into reflecting on emancipation. It has been difficult to portray them while also offering generalizations, referring to the ideas and writings of others, and addressing the concerns of scholars—the second audience I had in mind.

Different parts of the book have been created with the two different audiences in mind. The preface and the seven chapters speak primarily, directly, and personally of and to people who pursue emancipation. The introduction and the conclusion are directed to those who study and observe the emancipatory efforts of others—historians and social scientists primarily. Such scholars expect more generalization and discussion of other writings than the first audience. These two audiences are not mutually exclusive, of course; their differences are in degree rather than kind. Throughout the book, I explain politics as it is lived, where its analysis is personal rather than abstract. When I reach points that I think might try the patience of my first audience, I resort to the endnotes to satisfy more scholarly readers.[3]

Acknowledgments

It is my pleasure to acknowledge several people who helped me in researching and writing this book. First of all, people whom I interviewed provided information and inspiration. Milmon Mitchell, for example, kept records of some of the events reported in this book in his trunk for over forty years. That trunk was tied to one of the greatest disappointments of his life. He was forced to withdraw from Fisk University for financial reasons. His mother had bought the trunk for him when he left home to begin studies at Fisk; the trunk is the remnant of their dream of a college education for him. The trunk contains memories of the violence and terror he lived through in 1940. Mr. Mitchell is only one person, but he is typical of the many who ushered me into the private spaces of their resistance and their profoundly personal experiences. I did nothing to earn the trust that they gave me. It was their gift. I am grateful but at a loss as to how to go beyond the words "Thank you." In the end, I think those words best express my sentiments, including my frustration at being unable to reciprocate. These people trusted me to share with others what they shared with me. I hope they are gratified by the words with which I have surrounded their own. I mention most of these people in the list of references at the end of this book.

Some of those who helped me I cannot mention. Out of fear of retaliation, they asked that I not give their names. As one said, "There are a some people here who would sooner not have this story known and would be very angry with me for telling you these things. These are the sort who went around in robes before." I realize that some people may take offense at this history, but I sincerely hope that this work will help us all realize the valor of those who resisted and the errors of those who repressed. The path to transforming politics passes through an area in which the majority must find the courage to accept responsibility for the present consequences of past actions that it would prefer to deny or forget.

The staffs of several libraries and archives assisted me in piecing together elements of this story. In particular, Archie Motley, curator of archives and manuscripts at the Chicago Historical Society, and Robert Miller, director of the Vivian G. Harsh Research Collection of the Carter G. Woodson Regional Library in Chicago, pointed me toward recovering the lost history of Samuel A. McElwee. I also depended heavily on the staffs of the Library of Congress, Manuscript Division, and the Tennessee State Library and Archives.

Two research assistants, Neil Wolf and Veronica Lucas, made countless trips to university libraries and the state archives to stare at barely legible microfilmed documents so that you and I would not have to do so. I am deeply indebted to the students, faculty, staff, and administration of Tennessee State University. During most of the time I was writing this book, I was a member of the Institute of Government at TSU. I am grateful for the support of my colleagues there. Clare Sullivan, especially, shouldered many tasks alone that I should have shared. Most of all, however, I benefited from being a white person in a predominantly African-American institution. I know that that experience has made me more sensitive to my own biases and prejudices; as a result, I believe that I am a more complete human being. I owe special thanks to Dorothy Granberry, Andrew Jackson, "Mac" Lipsey, and Marjorie Seward for explaining the complexities of race and the choices we have before us to redress past inequities.

Herbert Aptheker, James MacGregor Burns, Richard C. Cortner, John Hope Franklin, Jan Fritz, Bobby Lovett, Doug McAdam, James C. Scott, Patricia Sullivan, and Jim Summerville contributed to my work with their scholarship and assisted me personally with their kind replies and encouragement. Tana McDonald, then acquisitions editor of the University of Tennessee Press, believed there was a book to be written from this material before I did. She coaxed me into preparing a very preliminary draft that, in the end, hooked me into seeing the project through. Editors Meredith Morgan and Stan Ivester traveled troubled waters with me and kept the book afloat. Mavis Bryant copyedited the manuscript with the friendly competence we have come to expect of her.

Members of my family, and especially my wife, Took, have been very patient with me. I took up this demanding writing project soon after completing another one. I immersed myself so completely in this work that I came to recognize their looks and gentle chiding when I was no longer with them. They did not know to what place or time I had traveled; they only knew that I left them frequently to go to a place where I could not take them, and they forgave me for that. They conjectured that perhaps I was in Haywood County during Reconstruction, on the Fisk campus with W. E. B. Du Bois and Samuel McElwee in the 1880s, visiting among African-American professionals on Cherry Street in downtown Nashville in the 1890s, or on the river bank in Haywood County watching helplessly as angry mobs threatened Elisha Davis and later lynched Elbert Williams. My family welcomed the people of this book into our home when they visited in person. I can only hope that, as a result of many conversations about the resistance of others, our home became a free space and a reservoir of the human spirit of resistance.

TENNESSEE

HAYWOOD
COUNTY

Introduction

The civil rights movement expressed the synergy of myriad, locally organized struggles. It was not a movement carried out by a few charismatic leaders; in fact, it spread among thousands and thousands of participants, most of whom left no record. Also, the civil rights movement was but one episode in a century of protests against racial repression and subordination. What distinguished the civil rights movement from preceding events was, first, the overt expression of protest in thousands of places and by millions of people in a relatively short time; and, second, the attention and support that these local struggles received from the federal government.

In few places were the issues of the civil rights movement of the 1960s in the rural South expressed more clearly than in Haywood County, Tennessee. Located forty-five miles from Memphis, Haywood County has much in common with areas of Alabama, Mississippi, and Arkansas. African Americans have formed a majority of the population since the Civil War. The total population of the county numbered about twenty-six thousand from 1880 to 1950. After that time, outmigration decreased the population. Currently, the total population numbers slightly under twenty thousand. The county's economy is still based on row-crop agriculture, although King Cotton now shares his throne with soybeans and grains. By 1950, sharecropping, and the economic subordination it entailed, had largely disappeared in the county, as in the rest of the rural South. Row-crop agriculture had become increasingly mechanized, and large numbers of poorly paid, unskilled laborers were no longer needed. However, the majority of African Americans who lived in the county were still enmeshed in the legacies of sharecropping—poor people, poor education, and poor prospects for meaningful or well-paying alternative employment.

Political repression within the county was more complete than the economic subordination it enforced and showed fewer signs of change in 1950. In a county whose population was, on average, 60 percent African American, not one African American had served in elected or public office since 1888. Likewise, not one African American had served on a jury or as an officer of the law or courts of the county in the twentieth century.[1] The civil rights movement changed this; beginning in 1968, African Americans began serving on juries and in elected offices in the county. On the other hand, the civil rights movement did not fully realize the promise of emancipation, and people within the county are still working to achieve that goal.

In most accounts of the civil rights movement, Haywood and neighboring Fayette County, Tennessee, earn a brief mention. In 1960, African-American residents there conducted an early, organized, and successful effort to register as voters. Their efforts earned fourteen stories in the *New York Times* in one month. Their efforts are mentioned in accounts of the broader movement because of the severe reprisals taken against those who registered to vote. Scores of sharecropping families were forced from their homes. Some took refuge in hastily constructed tent cities. Other registered African-American voters found that merchants would no longer extend them credit and that bankers would not make loans to them. Without credit and loans, they could not farm.

These reprisals forced leaders of the broader movement to recognize the intimate relationship of economic subordination and political repression of African-American sharecroppers in the rural South. It was this relationship that made the civil rights movement both necessary and traumatic. James Forman worked in Haywood and Fayette counties with the Chicago chapter of the Congress on Racial Equality (CORE). He would later direct the Student Nonviolent Coordinating Committee (SNCC), a major force within the movement. Likewise, through his work for the Justice Department in Haywood and Fayette counties during the Eisenhower administration, John Doar began new procedures of investigation and enforcement of civil rights violations; later he would instruct the Kennedy administration in the lessons he had learned. For their influence on these and other leaders, events in Haywood did find their way, modestly, into most accounts of the civil rights movement.[2]

This book offers a view of the civil rights movement grounded in the history of local efforts undertaken with the goal of emancipation, and in the experiences of specific people over four generations. Thus, rather than explaining events in places like Haywood County in the context of the civil rights movement, the book places the movement in the context of places like Haywood County. Even more than with place, this volume is concerned with time and with people. It locates the civil rights movement in the context of efforts, starting in Reconstruction and including the work of the NAACP, to achieve democratic equality for African Americans in places like Haywood County. Recent scholarly generalizations, applicable to African Americans in the rural South, are expressed here in the flesh, bones, and words of specific, individual human beings.

THE CIVIL RIGHTS MOVEMENT
AND LOCAL EMANCIPATION STRUGGLES

Analysts disassemble the civil rights movement into parts—for example, Montgomery, Selma, or Birmingham—and relate these parts to each other, to a larger whole, and most often to prominent leaders or organizations. This combination of specific events, leadership, and mass participation constitutes for analysts the historical account of the movement. As a consequence of this disassembly and reassembly, we understand the relationship of some parts to the movement better than we do the makeup of the parts themselves. Seldom do we study the unique history of each place to understand how the movement there relates to the resistance to economic subordination and political repression that preceded the movement. Nor do we often return to those places to understand what difference the movement made there.[3] Even less often do we examine local efforts that were not in the path of prominent national leadership of the movement.

It would be impossible, of course, to delineate and document every part of a profound social movement that occurs in a thousand different places and in millions of individual lives. The events in each place and each life have a unique history, most of which is not public or even recorded. In the civil rights movement often that history extends back at least a century, to Reconstruction. Compounding the problem is the continuation of the movement for emancipation in each place and in the lives of thousands of people who live there now. However understandable this inattention may be, it means that we often leave unexamined the significance of the civil rights movement in the lives of people it was intended to benefit most.

A different portrayal of the civil rights movement, as one effort of emancipation in a succession of several in one place such as Haywood County, entails three related tasks, each of which this book takes up. The first task is to depict the economic subordination and political repression that the movement confronted. The second is to connect events of the movement to previous emancipatory efforts in the same place. The third is to connect the ebb and flow of emancipation efforts to the lives of specific individuals.

To undertake these tasks, I have organized the history of emancipation efforts into three periods: legal emancipation, the interregnum of emancipation, and the civil rights movement. Legal emancipation came during the Civil War and more completely with the policies of Reconstruction. No other country enfranchised more former slaves or made more efforts for their education than did the United States during Reconstruction. These and other radical democratic policies of Reconstruction, described in chapter 1, were implemented for only five years in Tennessee. Tennessee proceeded through the policies of Reconstruction sooner and faster than the other former Confederate states. Reconstruction began earlier there than in other states; therefore Tennessee, unlike the other states that had seceded, never came under Congressional Reconstruction policies, which included military government. Because Tennessee was not part of Congressional Reconstruction, the state began revoking Reconstruction policies in 1870, far sooner than other southern states. Nevertheless, Reconstruction in Tennessee, as in other southern states, was a radical experiment in democracy. The end of Reconstruction in Tennessee brought the erosion of democratic achievements before the steady pressure of legal and illegal repression. This sequence of reform and reaction, from 1865 to 1870 in Tennessee, occurred in other former Confederate states between 1867 and 1876.

Civil rights that had been granted to freedpeople in the South during Reconstruction subsequently were denied them, and sporadic efforts to regain a remnant of those rights were suppressed, at times violently. Chapter 2 describes the efforts of African Americans, Samuel A. McElwee in particular, to forestall the retraction of Reconstruction's democratic policies. His and the nation's failure to stem the tide of reaction ushered in a period a repression, an interregnum of emancipation, described in chapter 3. Chapters 3 and 4 describe the covert efforts for modest degrees of emancipation that African Americans made when overt efforts to reclaim the political promise of Reconstruction seemed futile and dangerous.[4] Chapters 4 and 5 detail a modest public effort in 1940 by the Haywood County NAACP chapter to regain some rights of Reconstruction, and the violent repression elicited by that effort. Between overt emancipation efforts, people undertook less public efforts.

This analysis of two periods of emancipation in one place suggests that the third period of emancipation, the civil rights movement, both locally and nationally, was part of a succession of individual and collective efforts by African Americans to participate more completely in the political life of the county, state, and nation. The movement, according to this view, was not a one-time demand for political participation, equality, and opportunity. Rather, it was a crescendo in a continuing chorus of resistance and emancipation that began with the enslavement of Africans and continues today. Chapters 6 and 7 examine the civil rights movement in the county and its relation to past and present efforts at emancipation. The conclusion generalizes about the politics of any form of human emancipation.

MOVEMENTS AND VOICE

Portraying the civil rights movement as part of a continuum of expressions of emancipation offers an alternative perspective on social movements. On the continuum of emancipatory efforts, social movements occur when large numbers of ordinary people, hopeful of achieving some desired change, publicly express long-held convictions with the intent of achieving political and social change. This view suggests that the aspiration for emancipation is constant over time, at least among some people. What varies is how hopeful people feel of success, of achieving some increased degree of emancipation, and how safe they feel in pursuing new forms of emancipation.

All of this is more apparent at the local than at the regional or national level.

To convey this viewpoint clearly, this study relies heavily on the voices of participants. Thus this book can be seen as a political biography of a local part of a social movement. Readers will meet people such as John L. Poston, who was the superintendent of the Freedmen's Bureau, subdistrict of Haywood County, in 1867–68 and county clerk from 1865 to 1874. Samuel A. McElwee, born in slavery, served as representative to the Tennessee General Assembly from Haywood County from 1882 to 1888. Three of McElwee's grandchildren provide accounts of conditions in Haywood County after their grandfather was forced to leave. Members of Elisha Davis's family recount the terror of the 1940 repression. Dr. C. P. Boyd, who helped to start the Haywood County Civic and Welfare League in 1959, recalls the voter registration effort that began that year. William King, who currently coordinates a community organization and serves as a county commissioner in Haywood County, describes some continuing efforts to promote racial equality.

This approach counters, in a modest way, the prevalent tendency to examine social movements as the actions of a few men and women (Dr. Martin Luther King, Jr., for example) or organizations (SNCC, for example). As valuable as these people and organizations are, we should keep in mind that they mobilized people locally. Where they did not find local leaders ready and willing to act, they were unsuccessful. How people in some places and not in others acted for emancipation at different times, including the civil rights movement, is a question that can only be answered in terms of particular local and personal histories. This book offers such a history. Likewise, the impact of a social movement is best measured by the difference it made in the lives of ordinary people living in the places where the movement occurred. This book assesses these changes as well.

On a less personal level, I attempt to go farther than much of the excellent research that already links Reconstruction with the Jim Crow era or Jim Crow with the civil rights movement. I intend to link not only two periods but the time from Reconstruction to the present. Likewise, I intend to move beyond excellent accounts that provide new interpretations of major events that affected the civil rights of African Americans.[5] Grounded in events in one place, this book suggests how large movements, Reconstruction, the Compromise of 1876, the disfranchisement of African Americans, Jim Crow, or the voter registration drives in the rural South varied in particular places. For example, in Haywood County the elections of 1874 and 1888 achieved the party realignment that the election of 1876 established nationally.

MOVEMENTS AND POLITICS

Social movements are extraordinary events in American politics, in part because, to achieve change, they give rise to unique forms of political action. The ordinary responses of Americans to unsatisfactory conditions are loyalty, exit, or voice. In choosing loyalty, we decide that the benefits to be gained in an effort to change are less than its costs, and we remain quietly where we are. In opting to exit, we leave a set of arrangements for another set that better suits our individual needs and preferences. Loyalty and exit are the approaches to problem solving most favored in the United States: "America—love it or leave it."

Social movements exceed the usual bounds of these two options and even the usual bounds of voice. In selecting the third option, voice, people work to change a set of unsatisfactory conditions. Voice is explicitly political. Someone is pressured to make some change to redress a grievance of another person. Voice is more than exit but less than a social movement in terms of political change. Voice becomes a social movement when it demands improvement for a group of people and not merely for individuals within a group. What distinguishes a movement is its demand that the floor, which supports the most disadvantaged members of the group, be raised. Voice may speak to this, or it may speak only to eliminating barriers so that some members of the group may ascend higher. Social movements differ from the ordinary options of change, exit and voice because they propose political solutions to collective problems.[6]

Albert O. Hirschman explained loyalty, exit, and voice in terms that leave a central question for this book to examine. He was concerned primarily to rescue the politics of voice from the seemingly universal preference for exit— that is, for individual, economic solutions to social and economic problems. Specifically, he wrote to counter the erosion of voice that the prevalence of exit brings about. However, exit is not prevalent among all groups with social and economic problems. Sharecroppers in the South, for example, did not have ready exit from their condition. Among groups like share-croppers, voice would appear to be in greater danger of eroding because exit is not available, rather than because it is prevalent. When a social movement expresses the voice of an economically subordinated and politi-cally repressed group, the question arises how voice survived among them. How does voice continue to exist under circumstances where there is nei-ther an available exit nor reason for loyalty?[7]

For the most part, the study of social movements has avoided looking at voice and the politics of social movements. It has mirrored American politics in preferring economic explanations. Resource mobilization theory, for example, emphasizes the availability and management of resources in the creation of a social movement and the functions of groups and organi-zations within a movement.[8] This method mutes the voice of social move-ments—the voice that speaks of values such as human dignity, individual worth, and democracy, and that protests the injustices that spark social movements. Likewise, the economic model pays little attention to the survival of voice in conditions designed to repress it. Hirschman lamented this preference for eco-nomic explanation but accepted its underlying assumption that exit is ubiqui-tous. He overlooked a central aspect of the political nature of voice.

It is more accurate, given the political and social nature of movements, to treat them as spaces in which people, who do not have access to exit, voice their worth and dignity and acquire skills for new forms of political and social participation.[9] This study will view emancipation efforts in this manner and will emphasize their political nature.[10]

Ironically, political science not only has ignored the political nature of social movements, but generally it has ignored the study of movements altogether. It prefers to equate politics with elections and other forms of behavior that can be seen as similar to consumer choice within a market.[11] Of course, studies of community power are exceptions, although they sel-dom examine subordinated groups to see the effects of power on them and the mechanisms of their resistance. Robert Dahl, in his paradigmatic 1961 study of political pluralism, for example, observed that "in local [New Haven, Connecticut] politics and government the barriers are comparatively slight" for African Americans. Dahl continued, "In comparison with whites, therefore, Negroes find no greater obstacles to achieving their goals through political action but very much greater difficulties through activities in the private socioeconomic spheres." Dahl then examined the share of political offices occupied by African Americans and noted the latter's preference for work in city government.[12] We shall treat such outcomes as "the politics of portions" and as only one form of the politics of emancipation.

Believing that African-American political participation was satisfactory, as Dahl found in New Haven, left the majority of Americans poorly prepared to understand the political upheaval of the civil rights movement. Even if most Americans recognized the inequalities within their society, they also believed that American politics was, and should be, open enough to provide disadvantaged groups public means to redress and improve their conditions in steady increments. Consequently, if Americans treated the movement as necessary, they thought it was so only because of the uniqueness of southern politics. It seemed patently absurd when a sheriff in Haywood County declared, amid a 1965 voter registration drive abundantly marked by threats of violence, "Everything is open to Negroes here. We have never tried to discriminate against them."[13] The task of the movement, it seemed then, was to bring the South into the American political mainstream. The smoke of riots in Watts, Newark, and eventually New Haven obscured this vision of pluralist politics and of the adequacy of the American political mainstream. Even in the light of such contradictory evidence, however, Americans, including social scientists, held fast to theories of American politics, much like a southern sheriff. Political science, in particular, most often treats the civil rights movement, and other social movements, as apolitical, extraordinary, or unnecessary.[14]

Studies of community power that are critical of Dahl-style pluralism probe for mechanisms of power over subordinate groups that may explain the groups' seeming acquiescence in their domination. Most often these studies emphasize the control of dominant groups and their power to exclude issues from politics, rather than focusing on the resistance of subordinate groups.[15] Critics of pluralism thus suggest that pluralist theory is insufficiently democratic, since elites are more powerful than the theory accounts for. However important elite power may be, the critique of pluralism overlooks the fact that the seeds of democratic movements are not completely suppressed by elite power and control.

Consequently, the issues raised in this book stretch the ordinary theoretical boundaries of American politics. We are concerned with voice rather than exit, with social movements rather than individual behavior. In addition, within these concerns we focus on voice under domination and on the space within social movements where voice survives. George M. Frederickson has illuminated the complex themes of domination and resistance in the historiography of slavery. Slavery, portrayed as total domination, supposedly produced a "Sambo," a contented, amiable, unskilled black male who was better off in slavery. On the other hand, slave masters justified violent repressive measures because of a belief that black men had a savage nature that had survived slavery. Child or savage; these dichotomous and contradictory stereotypes supported the white institutions of slavery and Jim Crow. Between these extremes, scholars such as John W. Blassingame reclaimed and articulated a tradition of resistance within slavery, which Herbert Guttman explained included the slave family. This approach, as James C. Scott has pointed out, assumes that the survival of voice under domination represents a triumph over, or at least a challenge to, what appears both inevitable to most members of a subordinate group and satisfactory to the majority within dominant elites.[16] I assume that the survival of voice is the central issue for democratic politics.

This book also accepts the invitation of Charles E. Lindbloom to "bring into sight elements of political life now less manifest than the easily observable turbulence of pluralist politics."[17] Our text enters private spaces in which people maintain the pride and dignity to resist mechanisms of economic subordination and political repression. It relates economic subordination and political repression, suggesting that some American political mechanisms may be used to suppress political participation, while others may be used to end repression. Thus the emancipation described in this book is *from* some elements of American politics, and made possible *by* other elements of those politics.

This description of emancipation suggests that there are several forms of American emancipatory politics. There is, first, a politics of protest against political arrangements. In times of severe repression this protest is covert and conducted in private spaces, largely over economic matters. A sharecropper may withhold a portion of his crop from his landlord and sell it secretly, keeping the money, to compensate himself for the cheating that went on in the settlements of debts and income. Such actions may be so covert that, years after they occurred, I was asked not to attribute this instance of political protest to those who described their family's use of it. At times when repression is less stringent, protest becomes more overt.

Beyond the politics of protest is the politics of portions, such as Dahl found in New Haven. In this type of politics, groups previously politically repressed acquire some share of public resources. Protest may continue over the amount of the share, as we shall see.

Finally, there is a politics of transformation, which is the vision that social movements provide us. This is a vision of democratic equality in which the degree of economic subordination and political repression are ended and replaced by higher forms of economic well-being and of political representation and participation.

THEORETICAL FOUNDATIONS

The work of James C. Scott provides the theoretical foundation for this book. For Scott, the important questions concern not overt defiance or repressed compliance, but where and how resistance is expressed. One of his books is grounded in the experience of Malayan peasants; another is theoretical and draws on the experience of a wide range of subordinate groups.[18] This book occupies a space between these two approaches. It is grounded in the experience of a specific group but also examines historically the processes of subordination and emancipation.

The concern of this book with emancipation immediately allies it with critical theory, which proceeds from the assumption that human beings are agents in history, able to establish more equitable social, economic, and political arrangements. This book incorporates the fundamental optimism of critical theory, as well as its attention to mechanisms of domination. Clearly illustrated in this story of emancipation are the imposition of oligarchical political control, political repression instigated under majority rule, and economic subordination of African Americans, as a surplus pool of low-wage laborers with few marketable skills. Like critical theory, this study begins with the assumption that, as a society and a polity, the United States can do more to reduce political repression and economic subordination and to increase freedom. Similarly, along with critical theory, this study assumes that individuals develop more completely as human beings in environments of freedom. With more developed individuals, society benefits.

This book parts company with critical theory by looking for emancipatory efforts even within domination. The fact that our nation has achieved such a limited degree of racial equality since Reconstruction has made it incumbent upon African Americans themselves to reach for emancipation within the limits imposed on them. Circumstances influencing the path to emancipation differed in the times of legal emancipation, Reconstruction, and political emancipation (the civil rights movement). The interregnum of emancipation, when political repression and economic subordination was portrayed as inevitable and natural, presented still different conditions. Even then, however, some people remained emancipated, as free as they could be within their circumstances. The prevalence of domination does not mean the absence of resistance.

Resistance, like emancipation, takes different forms at different times. Individuals seldom act with certainty concerning historical processes. They walk toward progress, making the road as they walk.[19] However clear their goal is, the way to reach it remains unclear. We portray the people in this book, therefore, as agents of history who are themselves embedded in and who embody their history. In addition to being victims of circumstances, they are also agents within circumstances. This amended view of human beings, combined with the concern for emancipation, underlies what Brian Fay calls a critical social science.[20]

As Scott has observed, the political life of subordinate groups lies precisely in the territory between overt defiance of domination and seemingly complete compliance with forms of domination.[21] This "between" sphere of political life expands or contracts for each of us, depending upon our work, income, gender, and other features of our circumstances.

Because of its links to critical theory, this study aims to be more than a case study of one county in Tennessee. It is also a study of qualitative and quantitative differences in expression of emancipation by a subordinate group. To follow the political life of African Americans in Haywood County is to trace, in Clifford Geertz's apt phrase, "a social history of the moral imagination"[22] that has relevance for other subordinate groups in other places and times.

This moral imagination is profound precisely because it belongs to a group that is subordinate and under great pressure to abandon imagination and to comply with the seemingly unavoidable terms of its subordination. If critical theorists are right in stating that social benefit "trickles up" from the development of individuals, then the moral imagination of subordinate groups is a social measure of extreme consequence. The greatest hope of increased emancipation for every member of society is the hope preserved among the most subordinated members, because they are farthest from it. A group within society cannot abandon its longing for emancipation without moving all of society some measure away from emancipation. Conversely, we cannot remove one mark of oppression without moving closer to removing another.

METHODS

Interviewing people in Haywood County showed me the history and present conditions of race relations in the county. Often these interviewees looked beyond Haywood County to generalize about American race relations, past and present. The interviews reveal a realm of discourse that exists within a particular group and that ordinarily is shared only in circumstances of trust. Others who have shared in similar forms of discourse, in other places, refer to them as primary stories or hidden transcripts.[23] Whatever the term, this discourse details the manifestations of domination and the expression of resistance in everyday life. It is the imaginative task of social scientists to render public this private political discourse that expresses the politics of experience and the experience of politics.

The selection of people to include in the social history of a movement is, in practice, circumscribed by the difficulty of finding records of a subordinated group. Social movements protest a set of conditions that includes the systematic underestimation of the severity of the conditions and the importance of the protests. Very often, at times of severe repression, the only record of social movements is in the rebuttal of the powerful to those who protest against them.[24] This is one obvious reason why studies of domination more often focus on the powerful; the latter's power includes the preponderant if not the exclusive ability to leave written records. To exacerbate the problem, in a dangerous time of change, subordinated group members may deliberately avoid writing of their resistance as a precaution against reprisals.[25]

I selected the people in this study, then, in large part because of the historical record they or others left. This process began serendipitously. I was completing research on another book and wanted to illustrate the role of lynching in the repression of political organization with an example from Haywood County. Only one source mentioned the 1940 lynching of Elbert Williams in Haywood County for registering to vote.

I found an extraordinarily complete file on that lynching in the archives of the Library of Congress, which holds the papers of the NAACP. The records explained that Williams's murder was part of the suppression of the Brownsville, Tennessee, chapter of the NAACP and of its effort to register its members to vote in time for the 1940 presidential election. Affidavits and letters carefully documented how mobs, led by police officials, had taken several NAACP members from their homes at night, questioned them, threatened them with death, and then expelled them from the county.

The record was larger and more complete than most other lynching records because Elisha Davis and the NAACP made an intense, eighteen-month effort to prosecute the mob members. By early 1942, that effort had failed. Thereafter, Davis, from his new home in Niles, Michigan, alone continued efforts to gain compensation for the losses he had incurred when he fled from the county to save his life. He also sought to prosecute the people who had banished him and lynched Elbert Williams.

From that written record, I entered the private space of resistance. With the assistance of Dr. C. P. Boyd, I found Davis's widow, children, and grandchildren, who still live in Niles. Our first interview lasted several hours and included more than thirty family members who came by to talk and observe. They acquainted me with other events in Haywood County in 1940 and subsequent events in the family. They also made me aware that there was not a day before Elisha Davis's death, a year before my visit, that he had not tried to undo the injustices he and others had suffered. They assured me that, had he known of my interest, he would have lived another year just to visit with me and that I would not have left the house until the early hours of the morning. I have visited with the family two other times, the last time to discuss a draft of this work. Our visits have been tearful and emotional. Many of the Davis children learned about most of the events recounted here because of this work.

The Davis family introduced me to a close family friend, Milmon Mitchell. Mitchell had been an NAACP leader in West Tennessee in the late 1930s and had encouraged Davis, Williams, and others to begin a chapter in Haywood County. He is now retired and living in Detroit. When he heard of my work on this book, he called and offered me an inch-thick file of correspondence, affidavits, and other material related to the 1940 events. They are brown and brittle from age; water has damaged some of them. Mitchell regards these records as a covenant with the past. He has carried them with him despite the painful memories they trigger when he sees them. He sent them to me in the belief, as he expressed it, that I would be the Moses who would deliver these events from the desert of obscurity. There never was a trial or even a complete exposition of the injustices that Davis, his family, and others had endured. I hope that this book compensates them—belatedly—for that lack of public attention. The extensive records that Davis and Mitchell had gathered provided an unusually complete account of the lynching of Williams and the repression of the NAACP. Interviews with the Davis family, Mitchell, and others brought vividly to life the immediate human experience of those events.

This powerful combination of written record and memory stimulated my search for the records and memories of others involved in an entire succession of emancipation efforts in Haywood County. Naturally, events of the civil rights movement are documented in newspaper accounts. Most older adults in Haywood County remember them.[26] Unfortunately, the records pertaining to civil rights efforts prior to 1940 in the county are not as complete as those provided by Davis and Mitchell.

The written record of a prominent African American from the county, Samuel A. McElwee, who served in the state legislature in the 1880s, served as another starting point. Very little written record of his subsequent life and

career, except for courthouse records of trust deeds and land dealings, remains.[27] By incredible luck, through an elevator conversation that William
King overheard at a high school reunion, I located McElwee's grandson
and two granddaughters. Robert McElwee and his sisters, Ethel McElwee
Black and Julia McElwee Ford, provided much more information about
their "Grandpa Sam." Telling of their own family's experiences, they
graphically depicted individual strategies for coping with the systematic repression of a social movement for freedom. Their grandfather played a
prominent role in that movement. Moreover, these three provided a rich,
detailed account of the life of a sharecropper in Haywood County in the
interregnum of emancipation.

The remainder of the written record is far less complete than I would
have liked. Government hearings and the records of the Freedmen's Bureau provide a written record about the freedpeople in the period just after
emancipation. But this time lies beyond the reach of any living person's
memory. The most direct, though hardly personal, accounts of legal emancipation are those of the Freedmen's Bureau agents and others—mostly
white—with whom they worked.

These records do detail the support that emancipation had among
white people. Studies of domination and power focus on the compliance
of members of the subordinated group, placing less emphasis on dissent
among members of the dominant group. To challenge that focus is one of
the tasks of this book. We shall dispel the myth that white residents of
Haywood County universally complied with the repression of black residents. Just as there were degrees of emancipation, there were also degrees
of repression. Many white residents of the county resisted the repression in
both periods of emancipation and in the interregnum. By overlooking this resistance, social science helps construct a view that overt racial repression was
part of every white person's belief system and conduct. However common the
violence of white people against black people, it was not universally condoned.
Far more common was the acquiescence of a majority of white people in the
violence of a few. Among white as among black people, resistance to racial
oppression was not overt. Even now, such acts of resistance among white
people are not publicly admitted because fear of reprisal continues.

Differences in the sources that were available to portray emancipation
efforts at different times are reflected in the different styles of the three

parts of this book. Part I, which deals primarily with Reconstruction, incorporates archival sources of the Freedmen's Bureau, congressional hearings, legal records, and accounts—some of them blatantly prejudiced—in the white press.

My accounts of events after 1889 depend on newspapers and primary sources of the time. Unfortunately, the period from 1888 to about 1920 constitutes a lacunae in my sources on freedom efforts by Haywood County African Americans. For example, Samuel McElwee published a newspaper briefly in Nashville in the early 1890s, but I could locate no copies of any issues. Nor could I locate any living people with detailed memories stretching back to this time. Consequently, chapters 2 and 3 recount events from the scant remaining historical record.

The memories of some people interviewed extend back to about 1920. It seemed that by the time a grandchild talked about a grandparent without the aid of written material, the account was brief and vague, detail having been lost. But all interviews were useful to assist in a search of the written record and to verify and interpret other accounts. Part II of this book therefore combines primary sources with interviews taken in 1987, 1989, and 1990. Part III depends most heavily on interviews with people who recounted lived experiences and on written records still in the possession of organizations. The three sections exhibit a shift from reliance on official records and secondary material, with modest backup from personal accounts, to dependence on oral accounts supported by documentation.

The methods of this inquiry resemble the logic of naturalistic inquiry, as delineated by Yvonna Lincoln and Egon Guba. These authors outlined a mode of inquiry detailing the axioms and methods of social inquiry consistent with critical theory. I subscribe to their paradigm and used its tenets to direct my inquiry.

This study's design emerged as interviews and information offered new insights and pointed to potentially useful trails. The sampling for the interviews was purposive; qualitative methods and inductive analysis are found here as well. I view research as human interaction and derive great pleasure from approaching collaborators as people rather than as "subjects." Thus I used natural settings—the offices and homes of those who granted me entry to their private worlds.

I trusted the knowledge of the people with whom I spoke and probed it only to understand it more completely. In particular, the reader will find negotiated outcomes here. I have discussed the interviews and often the interpretations of events recounted here with the people who lived them. Thus, I can pinpoint the dates of interviews I conducted (see "Interviews" in the bibliography), but the quotations used in the text evolved in discussions over time. The choice of this procedure reflects assumptions about the nature of social reality and meaning that this book shares with naturalistic inquiry. According to Lincoln and Guba, naturalistic inquiry

> prefers to negotiate meaning and interpretations with the human sources from which the data have chiefly been drawn because it is their constructions of reality that the inquirer seeks to reconstruct; because inquiry outcomes depend upon the nature and quality of the interaction between the knower and the known, epitomized in negotiations about the meaning of the data.[28]

The methodology of this book treats the people within the movements as narrators enacting a dramatic epic.[29] Each narrator constitutes the drama while he or she is in it. Like Elisha Davis, these narrators have only a partial understanding of their current part, the origin of their role, and their impact on subsequent narratives. The narrative they enact begins in the lives of others before they join it and continues after them in the lives of followers who take it up.

MOVEMENTS AND METHODS

The community of a social movement and the dramatic narrative that community enacts introduce outsiders to an unfamiliar realm of American politics. Many white Americans will find events in this narrative incredible. Some young African Americans, distant by time, class, or place from the community that contains the memory of these events, may find the events unfamiliar. Some African Americans who want to assimilate into the white upper classes may contest the accuracy of these events or lament their telling. Among the central elements of the narrative are the next-to-last lynching in Tennessee and the political exile of American families within their own country. In the United States, the political terror and violent denial of civil rights that these events express occur far less frequently now and almost always provoke public response, including investigations and punishment. The terror and repression recounted here did not provoke such responses. This narrative recalls an era when small groups of white people could lynch, beat, and intimidate African Americans with the compliance or acquiescence of police, other authorities, and the overwhelming majority of white society.

The unfamiliar presents a challenge to what we know. Consequently, these dramatic narratives will challenge what most Americans "know" about race relations. The "truth" of a social movement depends on one's place within the sequence of events that makes up the dramatic narrative. In starting with central actors in key events, we begin with a "truth" different from the "truths" of persons starting at other places in the same sequence of events. The "truth" of the present narrative, like all truth, is embedded in the virtues and social purposes that the narrative serves. What distinguishes the truth of this narrative from that of other narratives is the tradition within which events are explained and the particular virtues and purposes involved.

It is not unusual for a study of American race relations to engage in a reflection on truth. Gunnar Myrdal conducted the most comprehensive study of American race relations. His study prompted a long essay in which Myrdal underscored the political nature of American social science, despite the latter's façade of apolitical value-neutrality. Social scientists, Myrdal observed, are part of the culture in which they live and cannot completely separate themselves from the dominant preconceptions and biases of that culture. Myrdal concluded that American social science demonstrated "a common American prejudice against legislation" and political problem solving.[30] In this conclusion, Myrdal preceded Hirschman in lamenting the inattention to "voice" within American social science.

Similarly, in 1934, W. E. B. Du Bois reflected on historical studies of Reconstruction. He judged them to be propaganda for the enforcement of legal segregation, Jim Crow, rather than scholarship.[31] Beginning in the mid-1950s, with the dissolution of Jim Crow laws and barriers, the scholarship on Reconstruction shifted more dramatically than perhaps any other field in American history.[32]

Because this study deals with American race relations, and especially because it deals with social movements to change those relations, it too has a special concern for "truth" and method. The method is narrative, accounts

of lived experience. Like every other method, narrative establishes a relation between fact and truth. Unlike other methods, however, narrative—
drawing on phenomenology—remains aware of its own dependence on a
tradition, of which it is a part, for its claim to truth. Similarly, phenomenology keeps us mindful of the relation of truth and social purpose. The
truth of this book explicates the need of one group of people for emancipation, the means they employed in pursuing it, the limits to its realization, and the virtues of the people who attempted to secure it.

Emancipation from Without

1865–1900

Freedom's Gain
1865–1870

1 The rancorous divisions attendant upon the American Civil War extended down to the state and local level, especially in the South. Like the nation, the white citizens of Haywood County had been divided over secession. Before hostilities broke out, 37 percent of white male voters opposed secession in a referendum. Whigs and small land-owners generally rejected calls for secession. Large land-owners heeded and amplified these calls.[1] Only after fighting began did white sentiment in Haywood County coalesce around secession. Even then, men from the county fought on both sides in the Civil War.

With the end of hostilities, social and political divisions remained at national, state, and local levels. The American Civil War, like all other wars, determined only who would control the postwar relations of the combatants. In many places in the South, guerrilla fighting broke out as defeated ex-Confederates contested federal policies to reconstruct the political system, economy, and society of the secessionist states. The situation of African Americans had been central to the causes and conduct of the Civil War. That concern remained central in these continuing, smaller civil wars over postwar policies. Authorities in Washington, D.C., fashioned the new programs of Reconstruction, but people at the local level lived them. Like similar places in the rural South, Haywood County was a crucible in which the freedom of those newly emancipated and their place in a changed America would be tested.

As part of national Reconstruction policy, Tennessee, and Haywood County in particular, participated in an experiment in radical democracy from 1865 to 1870. State and federal laws granted new political rights to those freed from slavery, established new conditions for their labor, and provided in new ways for their education. Legally, slaves had had the status of property and not of people. Now the ex-slaves had a legal status equal to that of people who previously had been able to buy and sell them. That new legal status, however, was fragile and contested by political terror.

"WE THINK THAT WE HAVE A RIGHT"

Even before emancipation, freedom had been on the minds of some African Americans in Tennessee. In 1856, during the presidential campaign of John C. Fremont, the nominee of the newly formed Republican party, thirty slaves and a white man were arrested in Fayette County, adjoining Haywood, for plotting insurrection. The plot extended to surrounding counties, according to a report in New York's *Weekly Tribune*: "The insurrectionary movement in Tennessee obtained more headway than is known to the public—important facts being suppressed in order to check the spread of the contagion and prevent the true condition of affairs from being understood elsewhere."[2] Slaves continued to pursue their own emancipation during the Civil War. Some escaped from their owners and joined the Union army.

The outcome of the war brought the end of slavery but the meaning of freedom was unclear. Tennessee had been half-Union and half-Confederate during the Civil War. At the end of the war, the state remained divided and immediately entered the bitter postwar disputes over Reconstruction emancipation policies. Several legislative steps began a particularly angry debate in Tennessee. The pro-Union Republican party, in power in 1865, was divided by degrees of animosity towards ex-Confederates, most of whom were Democrats. The Radical wing of the state Republican party gained power and pushed its advantage. Gov. William P. Brownlow and the legislature disfranchised many ex-Confederates. Political power fell into the hands of the minority of whites who had opposed secession, most of whom were from the mountainous, eastern, nonslave, Republican part of the state. Amid the controversy over the civil rights of ex-Confederates, there was little discussion of radical reform in race relations or of the civil rights of free black people. Brownlow, while well known for his antisecessionist views, was not an abolitionist either before or during the war.

Having no representation in the state government, African Americans spoke for themselves to demand representation, the essence of the political change for which they had fought. The Tennessee State Convention of Colored Citizens met in Nashville in mid-August 1865 and resolved "to protest against the Congressional delegation from Tennessee being received into the Congress of the United States." The action of this convention of freedmen interrupted the smooth readmission of Tennessee into the political life of the Union that President Andrew Johnson had proposed. Johnson, following policies set by Lincoln, demanded few explicit political changes in the former Confederate states. Johnson had served as military governor for Tennessee before becoming Lincoln's vice president and eventual successor. While Lincoln was still alive, Tennessee had set a precedent by meeting his conditions for readmission into the Union. As military governor, Johnson had overseen the policies for readmission, which included the now-protested election of representatives and appointment of senators to Congress. Brownlow and the Republican Party of Tennessee had complied with these policies, and in 1865 the state's newly chosen representatives and senators awaited confirmation by Congress.

The protest from the Tennessee State Convention of Colored Citizens raised questions about the readmission policies, opening a breach between Congress and the new president. Charles Sumner, leader of the Republicans most opposed to Johnson's policies, presented the convention's protest to his colleagues in the U. S. Senate, relaying the convention's two reasons for its protest. First, the federal government had acknowledged the "humanity and right to freedom" of African Americans, as well as their claim to citizenship, when it called "for our assistance in putting down the iniquitous rebellion." Second, African Americans' requests to Tennessee authorities for legislation and constitutional provisions to enfranchise them had gone unheeded.

The protest message recalled for Congress that, in January 1865, a meeting of African Americans in Nashville had petitioned the convention drafting the Tennessee constitution of Reconstruction. The petition explained that African Americans

> know the burdens of citizenship and are ready to bear them. We know the duties of the good citizen and are ready to perform them cheerfully, and would ask to be put in a position in which we can discharge them more effectively. We do not ask for the privilege of citizenship, wishing to shun the obligations imposed by it.

The government has asked the colored man to fight for its preservation and gladly has he done it. It could afford to trust him with a vote as safely as it trusted him with a bayonet.

Will you declare in your revised constitution that a pardoned traitor may appear in court and his testimony be heard, but that no colored loyalist shall be believed even upon oath? If this should be so, then will our last state be worse than our first, and we can look for no relief on this side of the grave.[3]

Only when the constitutional convention rejected this petition did the convention members take their case to Congress. They explained to Sumner:

We have respectfully petitioned our Legislature upon the subject, and have failed to get them to do anything for us, saying that it was premature to legislate for the protection of our rights.

We think it premature to admit such a delegation. . . .

. . . The United States Constitution guarantees to every State in the Union a republican form of government, we are at a loss to understand that to be a republican government which does not protect the rights of all citizens, irrespective of color.

. . . The government did not forget to call for our help, and now we think that we have a right to call upon it.[4]

Congress eventually seated the Tennessee delegation, in July 1866, after six months. But Tennessee had had to meet additional, more stringent conditions before Congress was willing to act. For example, the state legislature ratified the Fourteenth Amendment as a condition of Tennessee's readmission to the Union. This amendment required states to enfranchise African Americans or lose a portion of Congressional representation.[5] Despite the Fourteenth Amendment, Tennessee enacted no law enfranchising African Americans until February 1867.[6]

The character of federal policies towards the newly freed people, and the implications of those federal policies for state and local governments (including those in Tennessee), were issues at the heart of the controversies between President Johnson and Congressional Republicans like Sumner. Congress demanded measures, stricter than President Johnson wanted, to insure that the new constitutions of the former Confederate states guaranteed to freedmen the right to vote and other civil liberties. Military governments were established, over the president's vetoes, to oversee the reconstruction of the former Confederate states. Tennessee, already having been readmitted to the Union, was exempted from military government. Part of the conflict between the president and Congress concerned the Freedmen's Bureau. The bureau continued to exist after February 1866 only because Congress overrode the president's veto of the legislation authorizing it. The bureau was to become the primary vehicle of federal policy extending new political freedoms to freedpeople at the state and local levels.

This work of the Freedmen's Bureau and others at the local level responded to the wishes of ordinary freedpeople for democratic change. Immediately after the war, the voice of protest against restrictions on political participation by African Americans was raised primarily by a few African Americans whose circumstances, including freedom before emancipation, were exceptional. The Tennessee State Convention of Colored Citizens exemplified the voice of these early African Americans, who were limited in number. The work of the Freedmen's Bureau, on the other hand, meant a federal presence at the local level and, with it, change efforts for the vast number of ordinary freedpeople who had just left slavery and who lacked preparation for new forms of economic and political participation.[7]

THE FREEDMEN'S BUREAU

For three years, the Freedmen's Bureau maintained a subdistrict office in Haywood County. As the lowest rung on the Freedmen's Bureau organizational ladder, each subdistrict office in West Tennessee (there was approximately one in each county) reported to the sub-assistant commissioner for the Memphis District. All five district sub-assistant commissioners in Tennessee reported to the assistant commissioner for Tennessee and to the superintendent of education, whose offices were in Nashville. The assistant commissioners, one in each of the Confederate states, reported to Maj. Gen. Oliver Otis Howard, commissioner of the Freedmen's Bureau in Washington, D.C., formally named the Bureau of Refugees, Freedmen and Abandoned Lands.

In Tennessee, as in other southern states, the bureau's work fell into three

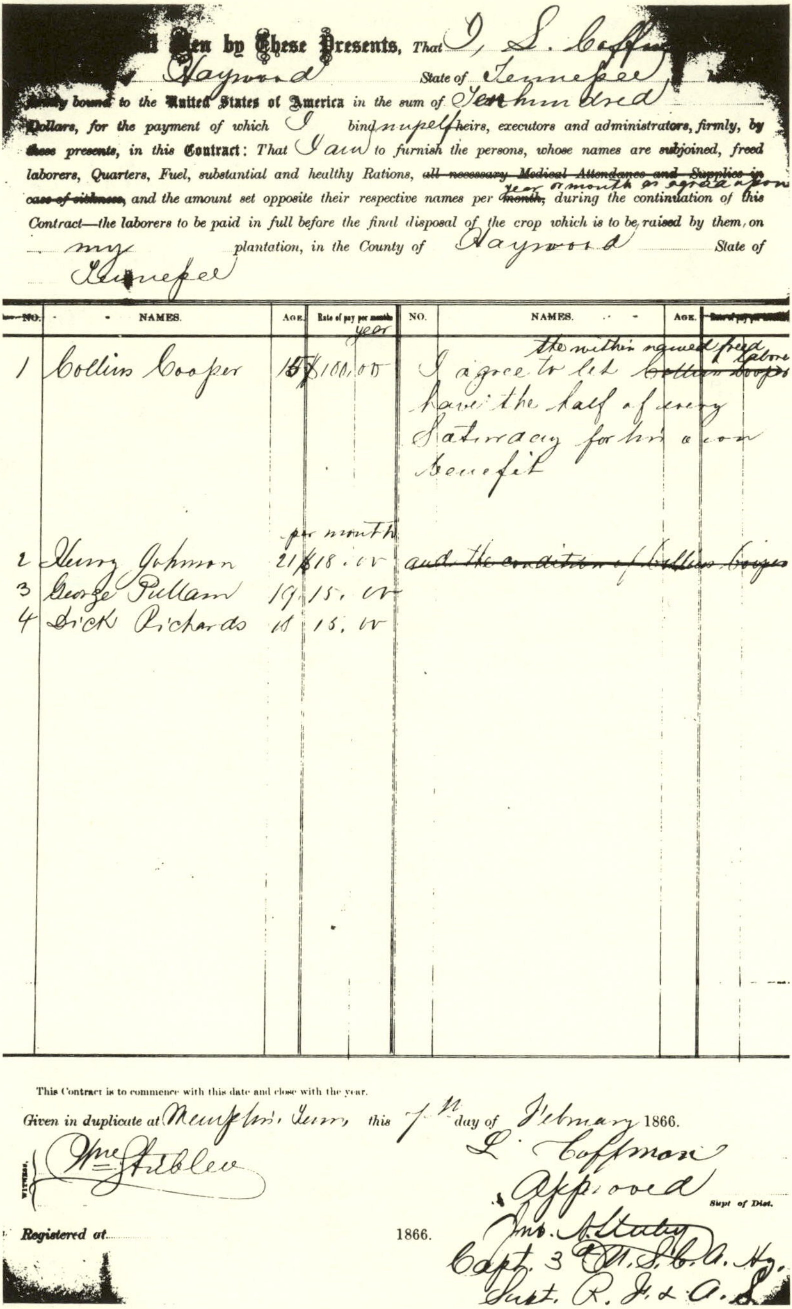

[Know all M]en by These Presents, That I. S. Coffm[an] of Haywood State of Tennessee [am firm]ly bound to the United States of America in the sum of Ten hundred Dollars, for the payment of which I bind myself heirs, executors and administrators, firmly, by these presents, in this Contract: That I am to furnish the persons, whose names are subjoined, freed laborers, Quarters, Fuel, substantial and healthy Rations, ~~all necessary Medical Attendance and Supplies in case of sickness~~, and the amount set opposite their respective names per ~~month~~ year or month as agreed upon, during the continuation of this Contract—the laborers to be paid in full before the final disposal of the crop which is to be raised by them, on my plantation, in the County of Haywood State of Tennessee

NO.	NAMES.	AGE.	Rate of pay per month (year)	NO.	NAMES.	AGE.	Rate of pay per month
1	Collins Cooper	15	$100.00		I agree to let the within named freed laborer ~~Collins Cooper~~ have the half of every Saturday for his own benefit		
2	Henry Johnson	21	per month $18.00		~~and the condition of Collins Cooper~~		
3	George Pullam	19	15.00				
4	Dick Richards	18	15.00				

This Contract is to commence with this date and close with the year.

Given in duplicate at Memphis, Tenn, this 7th day of February 1866.

WITNESS: Wm Stiblee

L. Coffman

Approved Supt of Dist.

Jno. A. Staley
Capt. 3 R. U.S.C.A. Hy.
Supt. R. J. & A. S.

Registered at 1866.

Fig. 1. Standard Freemen's Bureau labor contract. Executed in Haywood County in 1866. Courtesy of the National Archives.

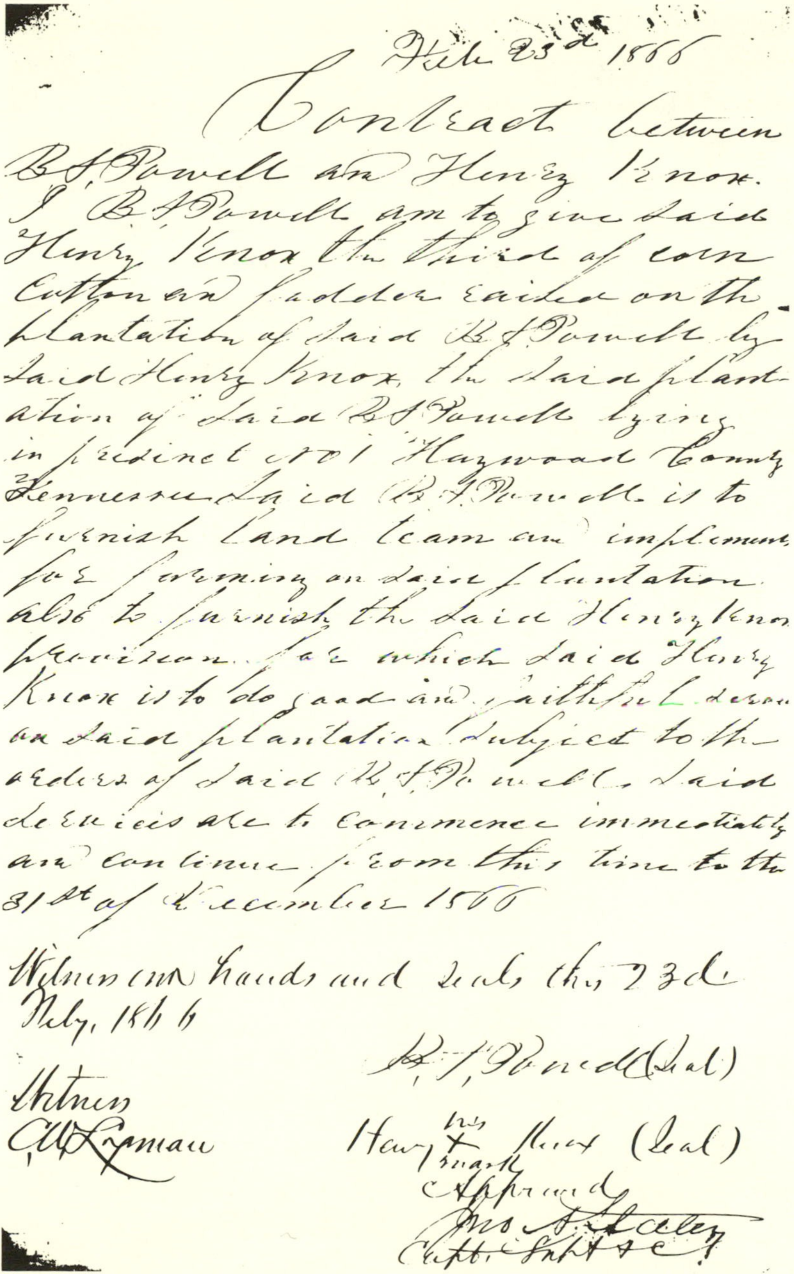

Feb 23d 1866

Contract between B. S. Powell and Henry Knox. I B. S. Powell am to give said Henry Knox the third of corn Cotton and fodder raised on the plantation of said B. S. Powell by said Henry Knox, the said plantation of said B. S. Powell lying in precinct No 1 Haywood County Tennessee. Said B. S. Powell is to furnish land team and implements for farming on said plantation also to furnish the said Henry Knox provision. for which said Henry Knox is to do good and faithful service on said plantation subject to the orders of said B. S. Powell. Said services are to commence immediately and continue from this time to the 31st of December 1866.

Witness our hands and seals this 23d July, 1866

Witness   B. S. Powell (Seal)
C. H. Lyman   Henry Knox (Seal)
*   Approved*
*   Jno. A. Lacey*

Fig. 2. Labor contracts between Henry Knox and B. S. Powell. Executed in Haywood County, 1866. Courtesy of the National Archives.

broad categories. First, the bureau established contract labor for the freed-people to replace the terms of slavery. Second, it assisted the establishment and conduct of schools for these newly freed people as well. And third, the bureau protected the freedpeople's newly established civil and property rights.

The subdistrict officers' official charge was to promote "the physical, intellectual, and moral advantage, improvement, and elevations of the freed-people." Beneath their bureaucratic language, the standard commissioning papers imparted a vision of unprecedented democratic reform for Haywood County and for America:

> You will see that the county authorities discharge their whole duty in mak-ing the proper arrangements for the care and support of all the colored pau-pers of your district, give them to understand that these people have a legal claim upon them for their assistance and insist that this claim must not only be acknowledged by them but that it must be properly met.
>
> Endeavor to impress upon the minds of the colored people that to be successful in this great struggle for personal, political, and social rights they must be industrious economical and temperate. Strive at all times to create and foster a good healthy state of feeling between the whites and blacks be-tween employees and employers.[8]

FROM SLAVERY TO SHARECROPPING

From 27 October 1865 to 30 March 1867, R. C. Scott served as the first Freedmen's Bureau agent in Haywood County. Scott, like other bureau agents, had orders to restore the local economy as quickly as possible.[9] This incredibly difficult task entailed a regional shift from the wageless agricultural economy of slavery to a wage economy at a time when the South had a shortage of capital for wages or for structural change. Quickly the bureau improvised labor contracts that promised but postponed payment for the labor of freed individuals. For example, B. S. Powell, a white planter, prom-ised to give Henry Knox, a freed farmer, "a third of corn, cotton and fodder" raised on Powell's plantation. Powell would provide Knox with land, a team of mules, implements for farming, and provisions for Knox and his family. In exchange, "Henry Knox is to do good and faithful service on said plantation, subject to the orders of said B. S. Powell. Said services are to commence immediately and continue from this time to the 31st of December 1866."[10]

This arrangement provided all participating parties with something they wanted. The bureau recruited workers for the South's agricultural economy and provided the appearance of instituting a new form of labor for the freedpeople. The planters acquired workers without having to expend cash for wages. The freedpeople acquired access to land and labor and the appearance of labor for income.

The bureau's contracts provided only an appearance of labor for income, however. In practice, they instituted sharecropping, an arrangement that would predominate until the middle of the next century, when mechanization of row-crop agriculture made large supplies of cheap, unskilled labor unnecessary. The system of sharecropping remained remarkably unchanged until that time. The end of December remained "settling time." At that time, landlords reported to their laborers the cost of provisions, implements, and other materials which the landlords had lent to make the crop. Landlords and tenants compared that debt with the value of the laborer's share of the crop. The difference between the amount owed and the value of the share of the crop equaled the tenant's income.

The "X" marking the signature of the sharecropper at the bottom of the contracts that Scott arranged for the bureau provided few guarantees of adequate income for the newly freed laborer. The landlord provided the materials and supplies and determined their value. The landlord sold the crop and determined its value. The books recording all transactions were kept exclusively by the landlord. Remarkably and consistently, the debt of the laborer exceeded or equaled the value of his share of the crop. During the first year of the new system, the freedpeople complained about its inequity. The bureau was overwhelmed with complaints but, with thousands of contracts and a staff of one per county, could do nothing. For a laborer to complain, or to keep his own set of books, was to risk reprisal. Landlords not only evicted laborers who voiced their grievances but also agreed not to hire those evicted by other planters. Until the mid-twentieth century, this system, established with alacrity after the war, kept the vast majority of African-American farm laborers, like Henry Knox, dependent and poor.

In this new economy, the freedpeople did acquire more freedom than they had had in slavery. Henry Knox had bargained for a third of the crop. That was better than a quarter share. It was not as good as a half share, which a highly skilled, dependable farmer could negotiate. In addition, a good bargain included the cotton seed as well as the cotton. The seed provided a resource for the next crop that would not have to be borrowed. Eventually, with luck and hard work, an African-American farmer might accumulate draft animals and farming tools and have to borrow less to make a crop. These most successful farmers worked "a third." That is, they paid their landlord one-third of the crop; the inverse of Henry Knox's payment. Naturally, the larger the share a farmer kept and the less one had to borrow, the greater the likelihood that one could escape the bondage of debt. That bondage made the new sharecropping system actually peonage, despite the apparent protection of the contracts.

In rare instances, contracts were made for wages. On 7 February 1866, for example, J. S. Coffman agreed, upon forfeiture of a $1,000 bond, to employ four freedmen for wages. The oldest, Henry Johnson, was twenty-one years old and was to receive $18 a month. George Pullam, aged nineteen, and Dick Richards, aged eighteen, were to receive $15 each a month. Collins Cooper was only fifteen years old, so his wages were less, $100 for the year. The contract specified that Coffman would provide all four men with "Quarters, Fuel, substantial and healthy Rations." The contract's standard language specifying provision of "all necessary Medical Attendance and Supplies in case of sickness" had been crossed out. Coffman did agree to give all four men "the half of every Saturday for [their] own benefit." This provision usually was extended only to younger workers such as Cooper. Such contracts were attractive because they offered cash in return for labor.

Cash contracts were infrequent and often not fulfilled by the employer. In many instances, wage earners were scared into leaving their workplace before time for payment, thus forfeiting their pay.[11] Shortly, wage labor became the least attractive form of labor in the new agricultural economy. It was difficult for the worker to enforce agreed-upon terms and left her or him without any tangible asset, such as a share of the crop, to show for the work. Eventually, wages were extended only to day workers and left them with insufficient resources to provide housing and provisions. Sharecropping, for all its problems, provided a better guarantee of subsistence.[12]

"THE SHORTEST AND MOST DIRECT ROAD TO RIGHTS"

Scott, like other bureau staff members, viewed the inadequacies of sharecropping as a temporary problem that education would eradicate. The greatest and most enduring effort of the bureau went into education. The bureau assisted others to establish and conduct schools for the newly freedpeople. The most deliberate policy at this time was to educate enough freedpeople to establish leaders who would then protect the political rights of others and create new economic roles for them. Scott's commission instructed him, "Interest yourself upon the subject of the education of the colored people. Strive by every means in your power to awaken an interest among the colored people upon this subject. Convince them if possible that the School-house is the shortest and most direct road to all their social and political rights."

The standard commission continued:

> Foster and encourage in every way in your power every effort which they may make in that direction. Urge the colored people to erect Churches and School-houses where ever and when ever possible. Cooperate with such white persons as may take an interest in the education of the colored people and endeavor by all means to overcome the prejudice which some may entertain against the establishment of colored schools.
>
> Visit frequently all the colored schools of your district and keep yourself thoroughly posted in regard to their conditions and wants. These instructions apply to plantation schools as to those conducted in the cities and towns.[13]

At the end of 1866, Scott reported that Harriet McMurray was teaching twenty-seven girls and twenty boys in the one school in Brownsville. Of the girls, two were in the alphabet; thirteen could read and spell easy lessons; and twelve were advanced readers. The Freedmen's Bureau provided forty-seven dollars a month for support for the school. In May 1867, enrollment had dropped to thirty-four—eleven boys and twenty-three girls. Evidently the class had seen some turnover, as only one of the students was beginning the

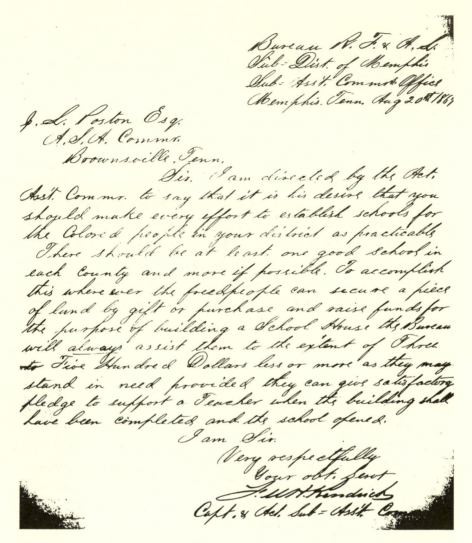

Bureau R. F. & A. L.
Sub-Dist. of Memphis
Sub-Asst. Commr Office
Memphis. Tenn. Aug 20th 1867

J. L. Poston Esq.
  A. S. A. Commr.
  Brownsville. Tenn.

        Sir. I am directed by the Act.
Asst. Commr. to say that it is his desire that you
should make every effort to establish schools for
the Colored people in your district as practicable
There should be at least one good school in
each County and more if possible. To accomplish
this where ever the freedpeople can secure a piece
of land by gift or purchase and raise funds for
the purpose of building a School House the Bureau
will always assist them to the extent of Three
to Five Hundred Dollars less or more as they may
stand in need provided they can give satisfactory
pledge to support a Teacher when the building shall
have been completed and the school opened.
        I am Sir.
            Very respectfully
                Your obt. Servt
                F. W. Kendrick
        Capt. & Act. Sub-Asst C.

Fig. 3. Orders to encourage the establishment of schools among the freedchildren, issued to Haywood County Freedmen's Bureau Agent John L. Poston, 20 August 1867. Courtesy of the National Archives.

alphabet, twenty-nine were reading and spelling easy lessons, and only four were advanced readers. By May the following year, enrollment had increased to seventy students—thirty-five boys and an equal number of girls. Two were beginning the alphabet; thirty-eight were reading and spelling easy lessons; and thirty were advanced readers.

Scott's successor as bureau agent in Haywood County, John L. Poston, at the urging of his superiors, continued plans for a second school. Poston was a native of the area and one of the few white men of the county eligible for public office under the state laws passed in 1866.[14] Like many others in the county, Poston had opposed secession before the war started. Unlike others, Poston, his father, and his brothers did not change their views after secession. In 1863, Poston organized a group of sixty-three Haywood County men into Company E of the 13th Tennessee Cavalry of the Union Army. At war's end, with restrictions on voting by ex-Confederates, he was elected to the post of county clerk and joined other Republicans in political authority in the county.[15] Like many other officials at this level, Poston combined his position within the Freedmen's Bureau with the responsibilities of an elected office, serving as Haywood County clerk. In other societies dealing with the end of slavery, there were few members of the majority who, like Scott and Poston, cooperated with the freed slaves to promote the latter's advancement politically, economically, and educationally.[16] For their efforts, Poston and people like him earned the derision of some contemporaries, captured in the era's pejorative term "scalawag."

Other Poston family members also supported Reconstruction. John Poston's brother, William T. Poston, served in the legislature of 1867–69. That legislative session passed radical democratic measures of Reconstruction in Tennessee, including bills that enfranchised African-American men and provided for the education of the freedpeople. William Poston's son, William F. Poston, served in the legislature from 1878 until he was appointed U.S. district attorney for West Tennessee in 1883. The Poston family, roots and branches, were Republicans with an abolitionist sentiment that went back to family ties in North Carolina.[17]

Poston's initial correspondence from the bureau's district office in Memphis informed him that his reports on schools were "of greatest importance" and were to be forwarded to district offices on the twenty-sixth day of each month. Another letter that came early in his tenure urged continuity between Scott's effort and his own. The education officer in the Memphis district office told Poston that "the colored people of Brownsville have purchased a lot and wish help in opening a school." He instructed Poston to "urge the people to pay for their lot as soon as possible. Please see that the title is good." He asked Poston for an estimate of the cost of repairing the building on the lot in order to conduct school. In August, Poston received three hundred dollars "for the benefit of the Colored school" and a promise that

> wherever the freedpeople can secure a piece of land by gift or purchase and raise funds for the purpose of building a School House the Bureau will *al-ways* assist them to the extent of Three to Five Hundred Dollars less or more as they may stand in need provided they can give satisfactory pledge to sup-port a Teacher when the building shall have been completed and the school opened.[18]

Getting the bureau to deliver on its promise, however, sometimes took the intervention and prodding of others. For example, Nathaniel Leech, preacher of the Methodist Episcopal Church, Gallaway Circuit, wrote from Brownsville on 30 June 1868 to remind the bureau that it had not provided the assistance it promised:

> Dear Sir,
> the building was erected as per agreement by the co. people but they are not able to pay for lumber and sash and so on and they are yet expecting aid it will be a great disappointment to them if they do not get the promised help if it was obtained they would have a school soon I would say as a friend to justice and humanity if the promise can be fulfilled let it be done as it is a case of need if you can do any thing I would recommend that you send the money or communicate with Ms H. McMurry school director or with Just. Moore the member of the legislature for this county please write on this and let me know what will be done.[19]

Tennessee law, which provided public support for the education of all children, transformed the bureau's fledgling educational efforts in 1867. Bvt. Lt. Col. Charles E. Compton, superintendent of education for the Freedmen's Bureau in Tennessee, informed the bureau's Commissioner Howard that the law's "inestimable benefits . . . slowly extended so as to reach the colored people in the various parts of the State." From September 1868 to June 1869, the number of schools for the freedpeople nearly doubled, from 74 to 139. Similarly, the enrollments of the schools increased from 4,657 to 9,000, with slightly fewer female than male pupils. Attendance reached a peak of 9,477

Colored Public School. Brownsville, Tenn.

Fig. 4. Dunbar School, Brownsville, Tennessee, ca. 1910. This is thought to be a school built with Freedmen's Bureau Assistance. Courtesy of Dorothy Granberry and the Striving to Teach the Children Project.

students in February 1869. During this same period of time, the number of schools for the freedpeople, entirely supported by the Tennessee Board of Education, increased from 41 to 50.

Compton was optimistic. The work of the Freedmen's Bureau and several aid societies and church groups, like Leech's Methodist Episcopalian Church, had introduced the idea of establishing public, or "common," schools to educate both white and black children, and the idea had won public support:

> In general I am able to report a very satisfactory progress regarding the educational interest of Tennessee; public sentiment is improving and in many places where once open hostility was exhibited, when a colored school was ever talked of, the feeling has died away and now encouragement is given accompanied by good and cheering words and in a few instances substantial benefit conferred.[20]

"STEPS FORWARD IN THE WORK
OF COMMON INTEREST"

Little record of Poston's work on behalf of the freedpeople's schools remains. However, Compton's detailed reports on work in Tennessee to Maj. Gen. Howard at the Freedmen's Bureau in Washington provide the context for Poston's work and contain some specific references to West Tennessee and Haywood County. These reports explain that the newly freed people themselves supported the schools far more enthusiastically and generously than did the general public or the aid societies. By June 1869, of the 139 freedpeople's schools in the state, 22 were supported entirely by the freedpeople. Despite the heroic effort invested in these schools, Compton described them primarily in terms of their deficiencies:

> They are, of course, not of the highest order, lacking suitable buildings and in many instances, competent teachers, only the rudimentary branches are attempted but as they are steps forward in the work of common interest to all, they are worthy of encouragement, for in them are gathered many children, who without such opportunities would be wholly deprived of the meager advantages they offer.

On the other hand, Compton lavished praise on the schools supported by the Benevolent Associations of the Northern States. The number of the schools had increased, with public funding available, from five to fifty-nine.

> The operation of these schools has been a success beyond measure and an incalculable benefit to the colored people of Tennessee. . . . They have exploded the fallacy that the negro could not be carried beyond a certain point in education and the "insurmountable" obstacle always alleged to bar his progress at this point, was but a mythe [sic], which needed to be attempted, to prove that it did not exist.

Even in these supported schools, parents sacrificed so that the freed children could attend. Compton described for Howard "cases of extreme poverty, some of the scholars attended the schools without shoes during the winter, boys and girls were nearly naked until aided from contributions of clothing sent by the friends of the Freedmen from the North."

Despite the progress made, Compton reported difficulties in the work to extend educational opportunities. First, while state law funded schools, it did not provide for construction of schoolhouses. The freedpeople were stymied in constructing schools without state funds "owing to their scarcity of means, to provide suitable buildings." In cases where the freedpeople had the means to construct a school, Compton explained, "they have been unable to purchase the necessary suitable ground, on account of the prejudice in some of the white people to have a colored school in their midst." Compton attributed "the general apathy of the white people to render any substantial assistance in the erection of buildings for colored schools" to the fact that "white children were unprovided for in this respect."

A second obstacle that Compton reported was the perception that anything provided publicly was inferior, that "a 'Free School' is a Poor School."

> This idea, entertained by some of the wealthy and accepted as a truism by the most of the poor, had evidently become fastened upon the minds of too many people, from the fact that heretofore education was only for the favored few, who could afford to pay for it. . . . It will not be eradicated until the advantages of general education of the masses is made apparent through the medium of the common schools.

A third obstacle to the education of freedpeople, according to Compton, was the insufficient number of qualified teachers. One reason for the poor quality of instruction in some of the schools supported by the freedpeople was the poor preparation of the teacher, who often was a person who only recently had been a "scholar" in a similar school. Despite their efforts, neither the bureau nor the Benevolent Associations could recruit sufficient numbers of qualified teachers to staff the schools that freedpeople needed and were willing to initiate and support.[21]

"IT WAS THE INTENTION
THAT I SHOULD BE KILLED"

The bureau had difficulty retaining white teachers from the North, even if its agents were lucky enough to recruit them. Compton explained to Howard the dangers that drove teachers away:

> Many of the white teachers are compelled to board and live in colored families and are undergoing a proscription of society on account of the labor in behalf of the Freedmen which would certainly appall any one, who was expecting to be rewarded in this world for their efforts for the general good of this people. . . . I know many a strong man, who would rather face an enemy in battle than undergo it, and these teachers richly merit and are entitled to the highest praise for the courage, prudence and steadfastness exhibited in their duties.[22]

Most local whites shunned teachers of the African-American children, whether out of their own antipathy or fear of the antipathy of others. For example, one white landlord reneged on his offer to rent a white teacher a house after receiving the following threatening letter:

Humboldt Feb the 27 1868

Mr. G. H. Mitchell

> Sir, we are informed that you have rented a house to a white lady of bad repute who is teaching a negro day school and a night school besides we want you to eradicate this as soon as possible or mark the sequel. we did not suppose that you were a negro or a wellwisher of them; we give you timely notice so let you be as quick as possible and save your honor if you have any From those who will see to it[23]

Occasionally, a teacher in the new schools faced physical danger in addition to ostracism. In June 1868, for example, Isaac M. Newton left his teaching position after threats on his life. He had taught at the freedpeople's school in Somerville, Tennessee, in Fayette County, which adjoins Haywood. Newton's early experience led him to carry a pistol in his satchel along with his books and papers. His long account of his hasty and reluctant departure from his teaching duties conveys some of the terror that might come with the work as teacher in the schools of the freedpeople. Newton depicted for Compton how a trivial incident—teenage boys blocked his path on a sidewalk—escalated, given the tense times, into preparation for armed conflict between the races. Finally, Newton learned from his landlady,

> it was the intention that I Should be killed. That I would be killed if possible on the walk or at my School room, but that if they could not get any other chance they would attack me at her house. All my friends advised me to leave and believing that my life was in danger and that I could accomplish no further good without protection I left that night and come to this city [Memphis] having been taken in a wagon by Some colored people to Stantons Depot on the M. & O. R.R.
>
> I have been preparing my School for an examination which was to have taken place on or about the 20th of this month and if I can obtain the proper protection from the Bureau would like to return to Sommerville and close my present term as contemplated.[24]

The Memphis district officer explained to Nashville bureau staff that Newton's experience was neither trivial nor the result of a boyish prank:

> These boys are but doing the bidding of older, if not wiser heads, Mr. Newton during the past year met with violent opposition from that community. He has had pistols drawn upon him, missiles hurled at his head, and threats of violence and insulting remarks have repeatedly been made in his hearing. The opposition with which our colored schools are contending especially when the teachers are white, is greatly on the increase, and unless we take some prompt steps to stop such acts our schools will, in my opinion, be driven from the field.[25]

The superintendent of education for the Memphis subdistrict advised Compton of a strategy to reduce white people's opposition to the schools in West Tennessee: "The majority of the people are opposed to the education of the colored people if the schools are to be taught by white teachers—there is not however so much opposition where the teachers are colored."[26] Compton, like his predecessor, expressed to Howard the belief that preparing competent teachers from among the freedpeople "will work for the increased good of the race." He cited several colleges and normal schools in Tennessee that were instructing African-American men and women. These graduates would be able to teach in the schools of the freedpeople with less resistance, they suggested. These teachers would also serve as educated leaders of the freedpeople and respond to the desire voiced by the freedpeople for teachers of their own race.[27]

Early experience with college-trained African Americans dashed Compton's optimism that opposition to the freedpeople's schools would decline with the arrival of African-American teachers. In October 1869, two students from Fisk University in Nashville started a school with about fifty freed children in Weakley County. A month later, a mob of masked men took the two teachers at night from their boarding house. The mob marched them to the woods, whipped them, and threatened them with death if they did not leave their school and the county. This violence signaled the intolerance of some local residents for the work of competent teachers of any race among the freedpeople and the life-threatening danger of teaching.[28] One bureau officer in West Tennessee, who deployed troops to protect local schools, estimated that without the overt hostility and opposition of white citizens there would be at least four other schools in the county. Given the hostility of the present situation, however, he felt, "it will be impossible to sustain a col'd school without the immediate presence of US troops."[29]

SECURING RIGHTS UNDER THE LAW

Another of the subdistrict agents' responsibilities, according to the Freedmen's Bureau commission, was to protect freedpeople from reprisals and intimidation such as those visited upon the Fisk student-teachers. The agent was "to secure to the colored people their rights under the law":

> Listen to all their complaints and settle all disputes if possible without going to law, it is an expensive undertaking and should be avoided if possible, if

however, there is no other recourse for these people than to apply to the courts for protection and justice refer them to such honest attorneys and magistrates as will take an interest in their rights and that will deal justly with them. Whenever possible have the case brought before some magistrate at your station and appear for the complainant. Watch the officers of the law and see that each and every one do their whole duty in protecting these people.

It was the ordinary responsibility of bureau agents to report acts of violence and crime, "outrages" against the freedpeople. Scott and Poston did so faithfully in Haywood County. Assisting them was a detachment of Union soldiers stationed in the southern part of the county at Stanton. Scott asserted in an early report, dated 18 January 1866, "all cases of outrage arising between whites and blacks are promptly redressed":

This would not be the case, in my judgment, if all such difficulties came under the Jurisdiction of the civil Courts of the County, the officers of same being almost without exceptions antagonistic to the principles and workings of our Government. In every election questions pertaining to the present status of the freedmen are made the Act of suffrage; and where is the man seeking office and popular favors, who will sacrifice himself for the freedman, when in fact his whole feelings are against him?

. . . Should the Bureau system be abolished the condition of the freedman would be but little, if any, better than the slave. He is no friend to the government who desires and advocates a revolution in this respect, I care not what [h]is pretensions may be.[30]

When Poston assumed his post as subdistrict agent in Haywood County on 30 March 1867, he accepted responsibility to secure the rights of the freedpeople, including the conduct of schools. Poston reported initially that he found some white people who supported schools for the freedpeople, "but the opposition is strong enough to deter any person from engaging in it, they do not feel safe."[31] Poston's duty to protect the rights of freedpeople, despite the opposition of many whites, placed him, and the federal government, in a new role at the local level. This protective role immersed federal authorities such as Poston in local matters and in conflict.

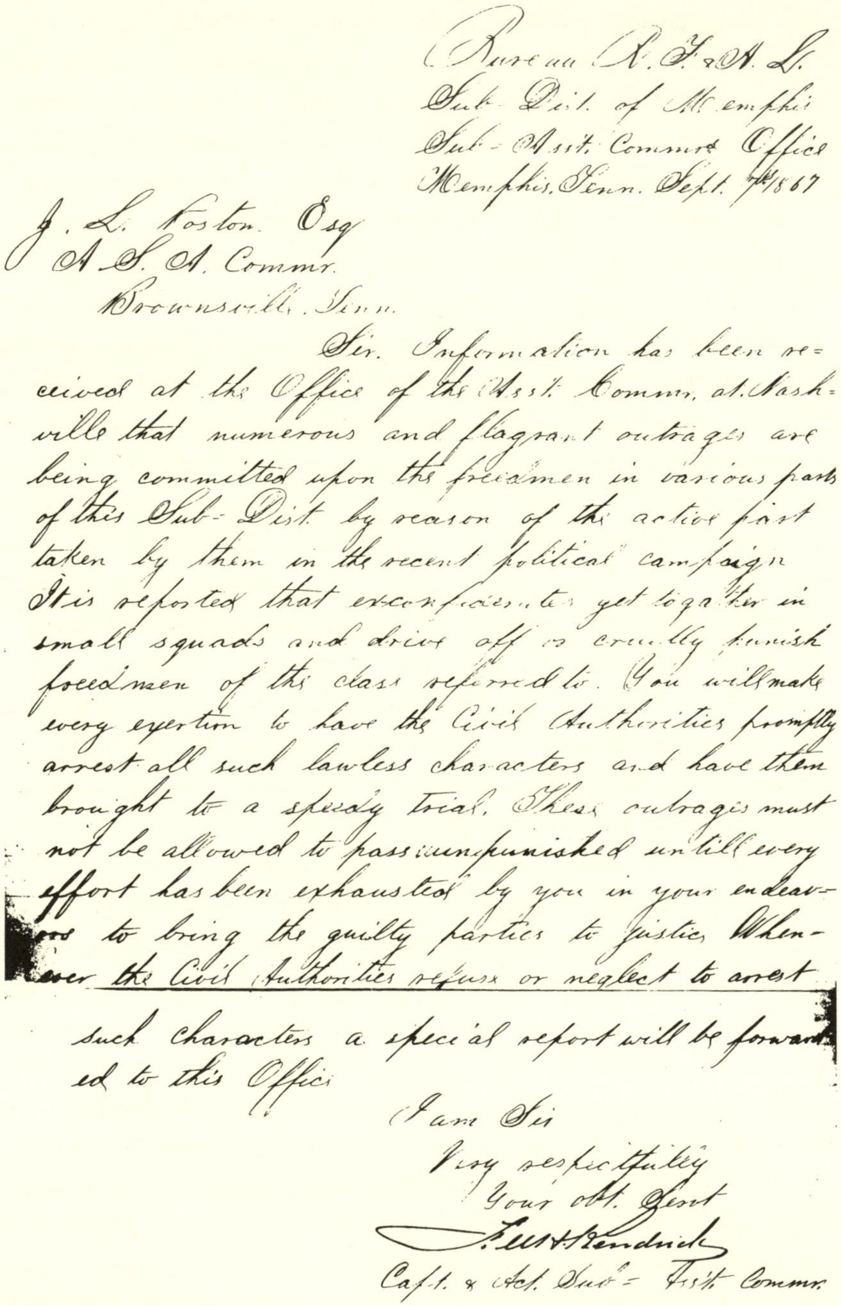

Fig. 5. The vote for freedpeople and the terror of the Ku Klux Klan came simultaneously. Freedmen's Bureau Agent Poston received orders on 7 September 1867 to protect freed-people from the nascent Klan and from retaliation for voting in the August primary. Courtesy of the National Archives.

The opposition to the schools was symptomatic of much broader conflict that would endanger not merely the schools of the freedpeople, but their civil rights and their very lives. In early April 1867, a "squad of guerrillas or outlaws" burned a school that had been started by a freedman in the northern part of the county, near Bells. This action marked the early emergence of organized political terror that eventually took the name Ku Klux Klan.

The violence that Poston and other bureau agents faced in the spring of 1867 coincided with new legislation that granted freedmen the right to vote. Governor Brownlow's reasons to champion suffrage for freedmen followed upon the requirements of the Fourteenth Amendment. It also followed a very practical calculation: "We have two reasons. . . . The first is a selfish one; it is necessary for sixty or seventy thousand votes to kick the beam, to weigh the balance against rebelism. The second is because it is proper and just."[32] With the votes of the freedmen, presumably loyal Republicans, Brownlow had a much better chance of staying in office and extending Republican victories down to the county level. Eventually, radical Republicans in Congress would pursue Brownlow's course for the same reasons.

The freedpeople organized groups called Loyal Leagues or Union Leagues to inform the new voters among them of the issues, candidates, and voting procedures. The leagues began in the North during the war and, at first, were most active in predominantly white, pro-Union sections of the Confederate states, such as East Tennessee. After the war, the leagues proliferated in places with concentrations of freedmen and new voters. As freedpeople's membership in the leagues increased, white membership declined.[33] Leagues held weekly meetings in election districts where they were active. Two representatives from each precinct formed the county council. Two representatives from each county council formed the state council. Northern abolitionist groups supplied the local chapters with pamphlets and other political materials endorsing the Republican Party. By 1867, in places like Haywood County, the leagues had effectively organized and informed large numbers of the new voters.

To many ex-Confederates, the leagues seemed but the local expression of a radical Republican conspiracy to deprive them of political rights. The organizations indoctrinated the newly enfranchised freedmen in Republicanism and mobilized them at election time. The leagues also forestalled formation of factions among the new voters. Freedmen with Democratic leanings were sanctioned, and radical Republicans, both white and black, fought moderates for control (and hence electoral support) of the party's machinery.[34] The leagues seemed intended to serve as a new, large bloc of support for the radical wing of the Republican party, which espoused the most restrictive legislation on the political reconstruction of ex–Confederates. Some white men in West Tennessee resented the leagues for an additional reason. Former slaves exercised new rights, while ex–Confederates lost rights they had had. Brownlow had disfranchised ex–Confederates by legislation in March 1866.

Some of the disfranchised expressed their resentment in unlawful and violent action to change the political system in Haywood County and in Tennessee. League meeting places, including schools and churches, were burned. The harassment of individual teachers supplied by benevolent associations increased if those teachers were also active league sponsors.

The Klan violence that began in Haywood County in the spring of 1867 targeted the league and its activity. For instance, on 13 May 1867, one month after Poston assumed his post, a Republican Party rally of several hundred people in Brownsville demonstrated the new level of freedpeople's political participation that the leagues fostered and Klan members opposed. The most prominent white and black Republican political figures from Memphis were in attendance—Ham Carter, W. H. Moore, and a former Union officer, Gen. William Jay Smith. These leaders made long speeches denouncing slave traders, former slave owners, and the oppression of slavery. They also talked about land redistribution for the freedpeople. This rhetoric, predictably, set off cheers for the Republicans in general and for Governor Brownlow in particular.

According to bureau reports, "a party of lawless men" jeered the participants for their support of Brownlow. One of the party finally fired several shots to disperse the rally. His gunfire evoked return fire, and a riot broke out, in which fifty to seventy-five shots were fired. Poston reported to his superiors in Memphis that Nelson Helm and one other freedman had been wounded in the riot. A Memphis newspaper explained the riot as "the legitimate result of the infamous teachings of Radical demagogues who for selfish motives are seeking to embitter the blacks against the whites." The reporter expressed shock that the first shots had frightened anyone since "it could be plainly seen . . . [they] were not toward the crowd."[35]

In contrast to this facile judgment, Lt. Col. Fred S. Palmer, sub-assistant commissioner for the bureau's Memphis District, directed Poston to consult with the U.S. attorney general of his district and to give him the names of all the witnesses to the riot in Brownsville. Poston's reports to Palmer helped the latter find and apprehend two of the white rioters who had gone to Memphis. Eventually six white men were placed under bond, and Palmer urged that they be indicted. He requested Poston to do everything to see that "no excuse can be offered by [the attorney general] or the jury if these parties are not held for trial."[36] Such unprecedented efforts by the bureau to protect the civil rights of the freedpeople now involved the federal government in matters that previously had lain within the jurisdiction of local authorities. Federal efforts to enforce state laws had flaws, however. Section 16 of the new state law, which enfranchised freedmen and which the bureau enforced, excluded freedmen from holding public office and from jury service. Thus, white men composed the entire grand jury in the trial of the rioters in Brownsville. The jury found true bills against the six white men for their parts in the riot. It also indicted eleven freedmen for their alleged parts in the riot.

Two months later, as the election of August 1867 approached, rumors increased that freedmen working for a share of crops would be removed from the plantations they worked if they did not vote as their white landlords directed them. Again the bureau intervened to secure the rights of the freedpeople. Palmer, Poston's superior in the Memphis office, authorized him "to instruct the freedmen in your agency to vote as they please whatever the immediate consequences may be." Palmer instructed Poston further to promise the freedmen compensation for any reprisals: "All freedmen who may be driven from their crops or turned out of employment in consequence of their political action will be provided for by the Bureau Agent until they can find employment for themselves."[37] Palmer explained to Poston that funds for this expense would be taken from funds appropriated by Congress.

After the election, Palmer requested Poston to take additional steps to guarantee the new civil rights of the freedpeople. Palmer wanted Poston to investigate "numerous and flagrant outrages . . . committed upon the freedmen . . . by reason of the active part taken by them in the recent political campaign" throughout the subdistrict, not just in Haywood County. Palmer described small squads of ex-Confederates who "drive off or cruelly punish freedmen" who had been active in the last election. Palmer directed Poston to "make every exertion" to have the civil authorities arrest these "lawless characters" and have them brought to a speedy trial. Palmer wanted the names of any civil authority who refused or neglected to perform his duty in this regard: "These outrages must not be allowed to pass unpunished until every effort has been exhausted by you in your endeavors to bring the guilty parties to justice."[38]

The election of 1867 demonstrated the commitment of the Freedmen's Bureau to the exercise of civil liberties by the freedmen in Haywood County. It also demonstrated the strength of the Republicans among the newly enfranchised freedmen. Democrats had hoped that a combination of carrot and stick, paternalistic kindness and threats of economic reprisal, would snare enough votes to put Brownlow and the Republicans out of office. They were disappointed by the election results. Brownlow gained 75 percent of the votes, Republican candidates were elected to Congress, and the General Assembly retained a Republican majority. Contributing to this Republican landslide, an estimated thirty-five thousand freedmen voted for the first time in 1867, about 75 percent of those eligible to vote. In Haywood County, 79 percent of the votes cast in the November 1867 election for governor were Republican. This pattern differed markedly from the antebellum party alignment that had divided white male voters evenly between Whigs and Democrats. The General Assembly, elected by freedmen voters, passed the 1867 public education bill, the first of its kind in the South. Its passage meant "inestimable benefits" that thrilled Compton, as he reported to Howard.

"SOUTHERN PEOPLE WERE VERY MUCH ALARMED"

Tennessee's 1867 election results foretold the Republican victories in store for other southern states. Military Reconstruction, which Tennessee had avoided by complying with earlier Reconstruction policies, was just getting under way in the other Confederate states. As in Tennessee, it would extend the vote to freedmen while disfranchising former Confederates. Republican governments would result, just as one had in Tennessee.

Political violence emerged as the means to overcome Republican dominance, as events in Tennessee demonstrated to other southern states. Violence had been employed widely in 1867 in West Tennessee. In several counties where African Americans formed majorities of the residents and voters, Democrats had won elections because violence deterred African Americans from voting. Political terror could upset Republican strategies. It could also end political careers. On 11 January 1867, for example, Almon Case, state senator from West Tennessee, was assassinated near his home. Case, like Poston, had both supported the Union during the Civil War and supported Brownlow in restructuring Tennessee's government.[39]

After the election of 1867, political violence became pervasive and organized in West Tennessee. The Ku Klux Klan became the military arm of the political movement to end Republican dominance in Tennessee. It claimed a political legitimacy that it would not confer on the elected officials of the state government. Leaders of the Klan, meeting at the Maxwell House in Nashville in the spring of 1867, had organized to purge the U. S. Constitution of the debilitating Fourteenth Amendment and to negate the "unconstitutional" laws that supported Reconstruction in the South.[40] By 1868, the Klan's agenda included the violent overthrow of Brownlow's state government. As the presidential election of 1868 approached, confrontations between the Klan and the Brownlow administration in West Tennessee escalated. The violence of the Klan towards the schools and teachers of the freedpeople became open, systematic, purposeful political terror. It was at this time, for example, that Newton had his trouble in Fayette County.

Brownlow treated the Klan's actions as a civil insurrection. The legislature authorized him to delegate local sheriffs to organize a citizens' militia to suppress uprisings. This was ineffective, since some white sheriffs were sympathetic to the Klan, and few sheriffs were likely to organize freedmen as militia to fight other county residents. In mid-1868, Brownlow acquired legislative authority to establish a state militia. At this point, Nathan Bedford Forrest, a former slave dealer, fabled Confederate cavalry officer, and reported head of the Ku Klux Klan, assured a newspaper reporter that if the militia were deployed, "There will be a war, and a bloodier one than we have witnessed." He expressed confidence that he could raise an army of forty thousand men in five days.

Forrest also protested that he did not want violence. He referred to events in Haywood County as proof that the Klan was under strict orders not to disturb or molest people. Three members of the Klan there had been court-martialed and shot for violating orders. Forrest described the Klan as an organization to defend ex-Confederates against the Radicals. He maintained that, because of armed response by the Klan, "the leagues have quit killing and murdering our people." In essence, he explained, the Klan, like the leagues, was a political organization that reached down to the precinct level. It differed from the leagues in supporting the Democratic, rather than the Republican, Party.[41]

Years later, in testimony before Congress, Forrest made clear that a central intent of the Klan was to counter the leagues. Almost always his replies to questions raised by the congressional committee members included complex qualifications. He invoked the Fifth Amendment that protected him from self-incrimination. His memory failed him several times in testimony about people and places connected with the Klan. He could only remember the names of two men who had given him any information about the Klan; one was dead, and the other, with some fellow Confederates, had settled in Brazil. In the main, Forrest's responses made such confusing testimony that committee staff members spent several pages reviewing his testimony to uncover two findings: the Klan had originated in 1866, and Forrest seemed to be a Klan leader.

In contrast, when it came to the Union Leagues, however, Forrest dropped his usual evasiveness and spoke at length, clearly and without lapses in memory:

> I think that organization [Ku Klux Klan] arose about the time the militia were called out, and Governor Brownlow issued his proclamation stating that troops would not be injured for what they should do to rebels; such a proclamation was issued. There was a great deal of insecurity felt by the southern people. There were a great many northern men coming down there, forming Leagues all over the country. The negroes were holding night meetings; were going about; were becoming very insolent; and the southern people all over the State were very much alarmed. I think many organizations did not have any name; parties organized themselves so as to be ready in case they were attacked. Ladies were ravished by some of these negroes, who were tried and put in the penitentiary, but were turned out in a few days afterward. There was a great deal of insecurity in the country, and I think this organization was got up to protect the weak, with no political intention at all.[42]

A REIGN OF TERROR

In contrast to Forrest's assurances that the Klan's intentions and practices were apolitical, other witnesses testified to the political intent of the Klan's violence towards the freedpeople. Gen. William Jay Smith, who had been a speaker at the Brownsville riot in 1867, headed the Military Committee of the Tennessee General Assembly—a committee that investigated Klan activity. Smith's committee heard from Jacob M. Davis, a fifty-three-year-old freedman and wheelwright. He recounted seeing a man come to Mason's Depot in Tipton County and distribute handbills about the Klan. He inquired about the Klan to a white man, Mr. McKenzie, with whom he was friends. McKenzie, Davis remembered, "made light of it." Two months later Davis discovered that McKenzie was a Klan member. He found women making Klan uniforms in a Tipton County home. When McKenzie learned what Davis had observed, this "friend" confronted Davis and warned him that the Klan would kill him if he told anyone what he saw.

> He said they were not going to hurt anybody who had not been in the Union army, or who had not meddled with them. Mr. McKenzie told me that if ever Gen. W. J. Smith came there to make a speech, they would kill him. This was the day after the Brownsville Convention, the 24th of July 1868. . . . I told them that I did not know much about politics, but from what I did know, I favored the Republican party. They wanted me to promise to vote for Seymour and Blair. I told them I never would do it; that I should vote the Republican ticket; that I believed the Republicans were my best friends. They then said if I stayed there, that I would be killed. I am not easily scared, and did not leave until my own friends advised me to do so to save my life.[43]

Davis had his run-in with the Klan about the same time that Newton was forced to flee his teaching position in Fayette County.

Reports like these led Smith's investigative committee to conclude that "a reign of terror exist[ed]" to restrict the civil rights of freedpeople in many counties of Middle and West Tennessee:

> The moving principle by which they [terrorists] are actuated would appear
> to be hostility to the State and national authorities; and in the minds of these
> men, to have voted for "Brownlow," or the "republican ticket," or to be a
> "radical," is the greatest of crimes. Your committee believe [sic] that during
> the past six months, the murders, to say nothing of other outrages, would
> average *one a day* or one for every twenty-four hours; that in the great ma-
> jority of these cases they have been perpetrated by the Ku-Klux above re-
> ferred to; and few, if any, have been brought to punishment.[44]

The Klan terror led to reenactments of Civil War hostilities. Poston, for
example, found himself fighting the forces of Nathan Bedford Forrest once
again. By summer 1868, Poston was no longer in the bureau. A reorganiza-
tion had eliminated the county substations, including the one in Brownsville.
Poston did, however, continue as county clerk until 1874 and was among the
Radicals whom the Klan intended to turn out of office. Poston had dealt with
Forrest and his followers during the war. The sixty-three men whom Poston
had organized into Company E of the Union's 13th Tennessee Cavalry
bivouacked at Fort Pillow as they moved to Memphis to join up with Union
forces. These men were among the six hundred Union troops attacked at Fort
Pillow by six thousand of Forrest's Confederate troops on 12 April 1864. No
battle could better illustrate the Civil War as a fight of neighbor against
neighbor. The largest part of the Confederate militia organized in Haywood
County served under Forrest's command.[45] Inside Fort Pillow, the Union
forces combined African-American troops from Alabama, Tennessee, and
Mississippi with white troops from West Tennessee, including Poston's
Company E. White Haywood County men attacked Fort Pillow, and white
and black Haywood County men defended it.

In a war noted for its carnage, the battle became infamous for the cruelty
of its aftermath. Two hundred and sixty-two of the troops in Fort Pillow were
African Americans. After the surrender of the fort, most of them were sys-
tematically executed. A soldier from Poston's company testified that, after the
surrender, he

> saw them make lots of niggers stand up, and then they shot them down like
> hogs. . . . The next morning I was lying [with the wounded] . . . The secesh

[secessionists] would be prying around there, and would come to a nigger and say, "You ain't dead, are you?". . . . Then they would make them get up on their knees, when they would shoot them down like hogs. . . .

There were hardly any [negroes] killed before the surrender. I reckon as many as 200 were killed after the surrender, out of about 300 that was there.[46]

An African-American soldier from West Tennessee testified:

I heard one of the officers say: "Kill all the niggers"; another one said: "No, Forrest says take them and carry them with him to wait upon him and cook for him, and put them in jail and send them to their masters." Still they kept on shooting. They shot at me after that, but did not hit me; a rebel officer shot me. He took aim at my side; at the crack of his pistol I fell. He went on and said: "There's another dead nigger."[47]

Poston and other soldiers, one hundred white and forty black men, were taken prisoner at the fort and, on the day after the battle, marched from Fort Pillow to Covington. From there they marched to Brownsville. The African-American prisoners were shot or hung along the march, so that by the time the detail arrived in Brownsville only the one hundred white troops were still alive. Five miles beyond Brownsville, on the road to Jackson at the Hatchie River bottom, the Confederate captors halted the column of prisoners at dusk. Maj. William F. Bradford, Poston's commander and the ranking officer surviving at Fort Pillow, was taken fifty yards from the column and shot by five of the guards. Witnesses testified that a week later his body had not been removed.[48] Poston, like Bradford, was regarded as a "home-grown Yankee," but the rules of war were applied to him. He was sent to Andersonville, the notorious prisoner-of-war death camp. He escaped from there and subsequently assumed command of Company A of the 14th Tennessee Cavalry Regiment around Nashville.

Now, in 1868, three years after Fort Pillow, the deep rifts that had led to the Fort Pillow battle and massacre expressed themselves anew. Poston's successor as bureau officer for Haywood County and four other counties was J. S. Porter. Porter reported to the Memphis office his fear of increased violence after the primary elections in August:

I think the freedmen will probably have a good deal of trouble with the Ku Klux during the present campaign, as the feelings of the ex–rebel soldiers are very bitter towards them notwithstanding the poor freedmen it seems have taken no part in politics in this part of the county as yet this year, but I suppose the fellows think they will and are trying to nip it in the bud. I think their intention is to scare, but if they fail to accomplish their object in that way I am certain that they will resort to very unfair or cruel means to carry out their designs. They doubtless intend to prevent the negro from voting in the Presidential election for *Grant*, and the negro are not at all inclined to vote any other man. Every law and order man in the county has serious fear as to what a few months will bring forth.[49]

Within a month, bureau officers reported widespread and increased intimidation of freedmen. In response, the Memphis office sent Lt. W. A. Miller to conduct an investigation of the numerous complaints about outrages in Haywood County. Miller reported a series of violent acts in a short period of time, amounting to a guerrilla war. Miller concluded that "freedmen living in the vicinity of Brownsville cannot get Justice, either in protection or person or property, at the bar; that it is the intention of the Disfranchised to force the freedmen to vote as they wish them to, or drive them from their homes and crops."[50]

Matters were just as bad in surrounding counties. In Bells Station, for example, Miller reported numerous incidents, none of which had resulted in legal action, because the perpetrators wore masks and so no definite proof of their identities was available. In many instances, freedpeople in such circumstances defended themselves. For example, on 25 August, five men, who robbed a number of freedmen and committed "other outrages," ran into a group of armed freedmen who killed one of them and captured his horse. The identity of the robbers was discovered through this horse, which one of them had rented for his marauding. After this event, freedmen organized "a Civil Guard and tendered their services to the Sheriff and other Civil officers" to assist in arresting the remaining members of the party.

Based on these events, which occurred over a three-week span, Miller reported the perception of local people that "whipping freedmen now was as common in Haywood County as it was before the war; that outrages were committed on the freedmen nightly; and they were afraid to report the same to the Civil Officers, or obtain warrants for the arrest of the parties. If they did so, they would have to leave the counties to save their lives."[51]

On the two nights immediately preceding the November election, Klan members were out in force and "roamed around the country visiting the Negro quarters and notifying the freedmen that if they went to the Polls and voted for *Grant* they would be visited again by them and punished for their temerity in so doing."[52] Porter reported that this intimidation and terror had "the desired effect. . . . Few votes were polled at Precincts in the rural districts in those counties where they were not encouraged and protected by the presence of U.S. Troops."[53]

"TENNESSEE IS PARALYZED"

One large land-owner of Haywood County, John A. Taylor, recorded his resentment of the franchise laws of the time. On election day in 1868, he wrote in his diary:

> This has been election day all over the United States. Grant and Colfax — opposed by Seymoore [sic] and Blair — I pray God some means may be devised by which the pressure under which the dead south has been groaning for several years may be relieved. I am debared [sic] the privilege of voting while every negro in the land enjoys it.

Several weeks later he reflected further, more angrily: "The meanest negro has the right to vote while the most enlightened of the prophetic race are debared the right."[54]

The means devised to end the plight of men like Taylor appeared in the 1868 election in Tennessee. The Republicans carried Tennessee for Grant, but their strength declined. All voters numbered 14,000 fewer than in the 1867 election. Grant received 18,000 fewer votes than Brownlow had received the year before, while the Democratic total was 4,000 higher. The combination of Klan political organization and political terror reversed the political tide in the state, especially in West Tennessee.

The effects of Klan terror extended beyond the obvious decline in votes and Republican strength. Local officials, encouraged by the election results, attacked the agents of the bureau. Immediately after the election, for example, Porter informed Palmer that he was about to be charged with "plotting to assassinate citizens" in Haywood County. Palmer assured Porter that the matter would be resolved satisfactorily but advised him to secure the services of a lawyer. Palmer had his own problems. He informed his superiors in Nashville that the local press had charged him with corruption and misuse of funds. The depiction of the agents of Reconstruction as repressive and corrupt was under way in Tennessee even as military Reconstruction was just beginning in other southern states.[55]

The political crisis after the 1868 election had to do with legitimacy and not merely Republican Party fortunes. The Klan's activity made clear that the elected government of Tennessee lacked the most fundamental element of political authority, a monopoly on force. Brownlow acted to regain that political authority. He treated the violence in West Tennessee as an armed insurrection. In February 1869, he declared martial law in nine West Tennessee counties, Haywood among them. Brownlow stood ready to deploy sixteen hundred troops, an action that Forrest had warned would bring on "a war . . . bloodier than the one we have witnessed." Tensions eased when Brownlow resigned later that month to become U.S. senator.

Brownlow's successor, Gov. DeWitt C. Senter, accommodated the Democrats, who in turn supported Senter in the election of 1869. His only opposition was another Republican who belonged to a less conciliatory faction. This candidate narrowly carried Haywood County, with 50.5 percent of the vote. In the state, Democratic support decided the election for Senter because the Tennessee State Supreme Court had declared the state legislation of 1866 that disfranchised ex-Confederates to be unconstitutional. Thus, many more ex-Confederates voted in 1869 than had voted in the previous two years. Victory for a Democratic candidate for governor was unlikely in 1869, so the newly restored Democratic voters supported the moderate Republican Senter, who won. In addition, Conservatives, the term for Democrats at the time, gained control of the state senate, 20 to 5, and in the House they established a 62-to-17 majority.

In four months, the new legislature repealed the laws of the previous legislature—the law to keep the peace and suppress the Klan; and legislation protecting the rights of freedpeople at work and freedpeople's access to public facilities and transportation. The two chambers voted not to ratify the Fif-

teenth Amendment because "it is class legislation of the most odious character. It singles out the colored race as its special wards and favorites, and upon
them confers its immunity, bestows its bounty, confers its affection, and seals
its love."[56] Foremost among its reactionary steps, the new General Assembly
made its very first item of business the repeal of the law for "the protection
and advancement of a system of free schools." The General Assembly also
passed laws prohibiting schools from accepting both white and black children. This legislature also planned the constitutional convention scheduled
for early 1870. Delegates were selected by universal male suffrage and were
overwhelming Conservative. The new constitution provided for African-
American suffrage but instituted a poll tax that would severely strap cash-poor
sharecroppers who intended to vote.[57]

In two years, from 1867 to 1869, Tennessee had completed a cycle,
moving through radical reform to radical reaction. In the aftermath of the
changes in Tennessee in 1869, Forrest urged the Klan to disband because it
"had, in large measure, accomplished the objects of its existence."[58] The state
government had established civil rights, new forms of economic activity, and
schools for the freedpeople and then retracted them in law and in practice.
This pattern would be repeated in other southern states, most of which in
1869 were just beginning the reform stage. As in Tennessee, reaction would
come after a period of deliberate political terror that deterred freedpeople
from political participation and severely tested the elected state government's
commitment to emancipatory reforms.[59]

At the end of 1870, bureau officers in Tennessee bleakly assessed matters
for Commissioner O. O. Howard. In June 1869, there had been 131 schools
in operation, with a total enrollment of 4,188. In June 1870, those numbers
had dropped precipitously, to 40 schools and 1,261 students. The report's text
expressed deep personal disappointment:

> Tennessee is paralyzed! The party in power in all its roots and branches is
> bitterly opposed to taxation for the education of the masses, and in regard to
> the freedmen prospect I can only repeat what has been said, and were this
> report a thousand pages, it would be but the ringing changes of the same
> idea. If the influence of the Central Government is withdrawn the cause will
> droop and its defenders will become discouraged.[60]

Not a single county moved forward to sustain schools in the six months after state support was removed from them. In addition, teachers and school supporters faced renewed hostility. Compton explained that overall violence had declined, given that legal means were now available to eliminate schools and since the benevolent associations would be unable to sustain schools without public support. The remaining violence was directed at the school-teachers. This new violence, unlike the old, was directed against both white and black teachers. Compton called the protection offered by local authorities for teachers faced with threats and reprisals "a farce."

Violence continued at election time and conveyed the impression, in Compton's estimation, "that the opponents of the colored race had regained a lost power . . . which placed a teacher of a colored school and the colored people beyond the protection of the law." Patterns of the violence suggested that the teachers of the freedpeople's schools were accepted best when they were least qualified to teach. Teachers prepared in normal schools or colleges in the North, whether white or black, were shunned, threatened, or "out-raged."

Compton's report made clear that the freedpeople were faring little better at work:

> In not a few instances, when the colored man has worked hard on the *share* system, . . . he has been subjected to a persecution. Before the time of the division of the crops he has been compelled through fear to abandon the lo-cality and lose the labor of the year. No civil action is taken to redress such wrongs for the reason that the party wronged is usually aroused in the night by several armed and disguised men (who thus escape detection) at his door, warning him to leave the neighborhood or suffer such consequences as their ideas of right and justice deem proper, and should these parties be known, he is afraid to prosecute before the courts on account of the malignant spirit, which would be produced in the community against him.[61]

THE INEFFACEABLE MARK OF THE LAW

Despite these serious setbacks, however, the work of the freedpeople, the bureau, and supporting groups had achieved a great deal in a short time. The roles played by freedpeople in these efforts are conveyed only at second hand, in reports of the bureau officials and others. For example, Isaac Newton describes how African Americans in Somerville provided him with an armed guard. Newspaper accounts make clear that freedpeople had large political rallies in Haywood County in 1867 and 1868. However scanty the reports of freedpeople's actions may be, they make clear that, in Haywood and surrounding counties, freedpeople had moved quickly from private to public efforts for emancipation. They led or supported initiatives for new schools. They voted and participated in political activities. They entered into new labor arrangements. And, when they could, they protested the inequities they found in them. These efforts expressed the new forms of emancipation engendered by changed laws and altered circumstances.

These same efforts fostered the creation of a set of institutions expressing the spirit of the new civil rights laws. Such institutions established the modest means to achieve a more complete emancipation. Among these institutions were, for example, normal schools to prepare teachers for the freedpeople's schools. When public funding of common schools was cut, the benevolent associations concentrated their support on institutions like Fisk University, Central Tennessee College, and the Normal Theological Baptist Institute, all in Nashville. In addition, Memphis and Chattanooga had schools with advanced grade levels.[62]

Efforts to obtain primary education for African-American children continued at the local level. Compton reported on the freedpeople's efforts to maintain their schools and the problems they encountered:

> In some localities upon the close of the schools under the law the teacher has opened a school upon the promises of the parents to pay a tuition fee for each scholar in attendance. I do not believe that this plan will be successful, for in the past, I have known a number of schools for the freedmen to be started on this plan, and a majority of cases the promises of the parents have lacked the fulfillment, and their assertions have been wanting in the proof, in one instance the colored people met together and to induce a teacher to come to them and open a school (Gibson County) promising a salary of Fifty (50) dollars per month. Nine (9) dollars were raised and paid at the end of the first month after that nothing. These promises are not made with any intentional wrong, but in many instances the extreme poverty of the race

renders them *unable* to fulfill an agreement, which is entered into, without a due consideration of the resources to meet it.[63]

Compton held out some hope that the reverses reported as the decade of the 1860s closed were only "the dark hour before the dawn":

> The benefit of the law . . . cannot have been enjoyed for two years, without leaving its ineffaceable mark. I am satisfied that organizations of free schools for the universal education of the people will be again successfully attempted, and the experience of the past will be but a sure guide in the avoidance of obstacles, mistakes and failures in the future.[64]

Compton was both right and wrong in his assessment. A dawn would come. It would emanate from these beginnings and its light would be intensified by the children and grandchildren of the freedpeople who engaged in the reforms of Reconstruction. But neither Compton nor his contemporaries could imagine how interminably long the night before emancipation's next dawn would be.

Freedom's Demise
1870 – 1900

2 For three decades after Reconstruction, reaction tarnished the bright promise of democratic equality for freedpeople in Haywood County, in the South, and in the nation. Few people personify the range of hope and dismay occasioned in this period as completely as Samuel Allen McElwee. Born a slave, he reached the pinnacle of educational opportunity open to African Americans at the time. After attending Fisk University, he entered law school and became a lawyer. He took political participation of African Americans directly into legislative chambers, serving from 1882 to 1888 as Haywood County's elected representative to the Tennessee General Assembly. In the mid-1880s, he and his parents became land-owners, thus achieving the highest form of economic security in the rural South at the time. McElwee's achievements made him one of the most prominent African Americans of the last part of the nineteenth century. He associated with those who played central roles in emancipatory efforts. After 1888, McElwee's career, like the promise of emancipation, became far less public, less visible. His life uniquely embodied a time that stretched from slavery, through the promises and policies of Reconstruction, through their violent suppression, to the beginning of the era of Jim Crow legislation that kept the black and white races separate and unequal.

GROWING UP FREE

After slavery ended, McElwee's parents, Robert and Georgianna McElwee, moved to Haywood County from neighboring Madison County in 1866.

Two years after the move, McElwee began his education in a county school supported, in part, under the new state law establishing public education. He continued classes in one of the Brownsville schools, probably the school for which Leech cajoled support from the Freedmen's Bureau. After exhausting local educational opportunities, McElwee, over a period of nine years, attended a series of colleges, all of which abolitionists and benevolent associations had founded. Inadequate funds prolonged and interrupted his education. He attended Oberlin College only one year. He then taught in Mississippi for several years and in Alabama and Tennessee briefly. Between school terms, when he taught, he sold Bibles and medicines in Tennessee. McElwee continued to study with a Vanderbilt student tutor who assisted McElwee in gaining admission to Fisk University. After a year of preparatory work, McElwee entered Fisk in 1878. He finished his studies in less time than the average student, which was seven and one-half years. When he graduated in 1883, he was slightly younger than the average age of Fisk graduates, twenty-six. McElwee almost immediately began to study law at Central Tennessee College, finishing that degree in 1886. He returned to Haywood County and won the first case he argued. About this time, he also entered the grocery and real estate business.[1]

For African Americans at this time, the opportunity to obtain a college education was rare and precious. By 1888, Fisk had graduated only 110 students in twenty-two years of operation. Only 43 of them had bachelor's degrees; others had diplomas for teaching. Of the Fisk alumni, three had become lawyers.[2] Between 1876 and 1909, all of Tennessee's African-American colleges and universities conferred, in total, only 525 degrees.[3] McElwee held two of them. Equally remarkable, he earned both degrees while serving in the Tennessee General Assembly, where only six African Americans had served before him. Several of those men, unlike McElwee, had been free before emancipation. In addition to his considerable educational achievement, McElwee was among the first men born in slavery to be elected to the Tennessee legislature and was the first African American elected to the House of Representatives from Haywood County.

Fig. 6. Samuel A. McElwee. Reproduced from William J. Simmons, *Men of Mark: Eminent, Progressive and Rising* (Cleveland: Geo. M. Rewell & Co., 1887).

DEMOCRATIC MAJORITIES
AND REPUBLICAN CHALLENGES

Political changes in Tennessee in the 1870s influenced the scope and efficacy of McElwee's political career and, more broadly, of African-American political participation in places like Haywood County. As we have seen, the 1869 election results assured a Democratic majority for the state constitutional convention of 1870. That convention revoked many of the Brownlow administration's measures and restricted others. The right to vote, for example, was restricted by a poll tax. The Democratic reaction against the emancipation measures went so far as to jeopardize the Democrats' political gains. Continuing violence led Gov. DeWitt Senter to request federal troops to restore order. The more radical Republicans in Tennessee sent a delegation of African Americans to Washington to testify before a congressional committee investigating Klan activity in the South. Congress briefly considered placing the state under military Reconstruction. This was a condition that Tennessee, alone among the Confederate states, had managed to avoid;[4] its imposition was Tennessee Democrats' worst fear.

Washington was tiring of the continued violence in the South, including Tennessee. Congress and the president declined to intervene. Instead, the message came that Tennessee Republicans would have to work matters out without federal assistance. Having seen the risk of federal intervention, moderates in the Democratic party reined in their fellows' reactionary extremes. Republican policies, ironically enough, had saved Tennessee from military Reconstruction; the moderates determined not to bring that form of Reconstruction on the state by excessive reaction to those policies.

For a decade, election victories in Tennessee swung back and forth between Democrats and Republicans. The Democrats won overwhelming victories in the election of 1870. But in 1872, the Democrats split into factions, and the Republicans won seven out of ten seats in the U.S. House of Representatives. The election also reduced the Democratic majorities in the Tennessee legislature. The Republican candidate for governor that year, Alfred A. Freeman, made a strong showing but lost. Freeman, a native of Haywood County, led the Republican party in seeking a political middle ground between Brownlow and the Democrats.[5] In 1872, as Republican candidate for governor, Freeman, hoping to put the party's radical past behind, urged moderates of both parties to form Republican majorities.

Events in Washington influenced the fluctuating fortunes of the Tennessee Republican party, including Freeman's strategy of finding a majority in the middle of the political spectrum. Charles Sumner, the architect of Reconstruction, was still in the Senate advocating legislation to expand the civil rights of the freedpeople and to enforce the terms of the Thirteenth, Fourteenth, and Fifteenth Amendments. The 1874 State Convention of Colored Men was particularly vociferous in support of federal civil rights legislation then working its way through Congress. The convention also protested existing state laws. For example, the convention endorsed racially mixed schools, arguing that segregation imparted "a spirit of caste and hate."[6] The support of the Republicans in Congress for civil rights legislation and the strength of the African-American vote created backlash support for the Democratic party among white voters in Tennessee. As civil rights legislation drew near to passage in Congress, those who opposed the Republicans reasserted terror's political role in Tennessee. The agitation over civil rights legislation in 1874 spawned a riot in Fayette County, during which three or four men were killed.

In Trenton, Tennessee, a massacre occurred. African-American men organized to defend the home of Joshua Webb from an attack they had heard was planned by the Ku Klux Klan. As the men marched, they were fired upon and engaged their attackers in a gunfight. Local law officials arrested sixteen of the African Americans for attempted murder and jailed them when they could not make bail. Three days after the shooting, a mob, at 2 A.M., took the men from the jail. Then, according to the federal district attorney, the mob "tied them together with ropes, marched them a few hundred yards distant to a bridge crossing a small river, and commenced shooting them indiscriminately, then and there, killing four and wounding others."[7] The mob continued another ten miles, where the remaining prisoners were shot to death.[8]

The massacre caused a sensation in Tennessee. Some white opinion leaders blamed Congress for the violence. In curious reasoning, they argued that the defeat of "civil rights candidates" in the August elections had disappointed some African-American voters to the point that they had threatened murder and arson. The lynchings at Trenton were reactions to those threats and indicated for some white Tennessee citizens that "a change of policy toward the Southern whites is demanded. Let Congress cease to confound social with civil rights, and the South will find peace, and in due time prosperity."[9] Another lesson, less publicized, was that terror formed a continuing part of the Democratic party's dominance in Tennessee and had not been merely an expedient used to gain power in the past.

The 1874 election sent to the Tennessee General Assembly a larger majority of Democrats who were determined to protect the state from federal legislative encroachments. And at the federal level, Sumner's death in 1875 marked the decline of advocacy for civil rights for African Americans in the national Republic party. The violence surrounding the 1874 election, and its outcome, seemed to some African Americans to offer conclusive evidence that the freedpeople's condition would not, and perhaps could not, be improved through the political process. Emancipation had brought a change in the legal status of African Americans but had not instilled in the white majority the political will to fulfill the promise of freedom. In the 1870s, 4,650 African Americans in Middle and West Tennessee, including Haywood County, left their homes in the hope of finding better conditions in Kansas. Several speakers at the Tennessee State Convention of Colored Men in 1875 endorsed the migration. In 1876, the National Convention of Colored Men met in Nashville and again took up the question of migration, generally discouraging it.

Benjamin "Pop" Singleton, a prominent leader of the movement for migration from Tennessee to Kansas, explained to members of a U.S. Senate committee investigating the migration that he was doing the work of God. He was withdrawing his people from the South until change occurred, at which time he would gladly lead a return migration to Tennessee.

My people, for the want of land—we needed land for our children—and their disadvantages . . . my race . . . that was coming down, instead of going up—that caused me to work for them. . . . We are going to leave the South. We are going to leave it if there ain't an alteration and signs of a change.

What do you mean by a change? Well, I am not going to stand bulldozing and half pay and all those things. . . . Allow me to say that confidence is perished and faded away; they [African Americans] have been lied to every year . . . My plan is for them to leave the country and learn the South a lesson . . . We don't want to leave the South, and just as soon as we have confidence in the South, I am going to be an instrument in the hands of God to persuade every man to go back, because that is the best country.[10]

In addition to spurring migration, the 1874 electoral gains for the Democratic party in Tennessee gave that party the chance to join other southern states and make major gains in the national election of 1876. Two-term Republican president Ulysses S. Grant was leaving office with a scandal-ridden administration. Military and congressional Reconstruction had run its course. As had happened in Tennessee a decade earlier, paramilitary terrorists in other southern states were working to suppress voting by African Americans. As in Tennessee, they were successful. The "solid South" emerged from the election of 1876. Henceforth, Democratic candidates for national office regularly won elections in Tennessee and the rest of the South.

Tennessee was so solidly Democratic that the party fell into factions. The state's debt dominated state politics and the Democratic party. Both parties had had a hand in creating it, with original legislation in 1856, subsequent legislation in Brownlow's administration, and refinancing under the Democrats in the 1870s. Democratic factions divided over the debt into the former Whigs and industrialists, who favored honoring the debts, and into groups of small and large farmers, agrarians and Bourbons, who favored varying forms of debt relief.[11]

Aided by bickering among these factions, in 1880 the Republican candidate for governor won with a plurality, including the bloc of African-American votes. Also elected to the House of Representatives in the Tennessee General Assembly were five African-American legislators. From predominantly African-American districts, they were the first to be elected since one African American had served a single term in 1872, another era of Democratic factionalism. African Americans had remained politically active throughout the 1870s, despite the lack of electoral victories. The State Convention of Colored Men annually expressed solid support for federal civil rights legislation and opposition to the repressive legislation appearing in Tennessee during the decade. By and large, African-American men voted as a bloc for Republican candidates. At the same time, some of them expressed dissatisfaction with their treatment within the Republican party. For example, they complained that they had not received a significant number of federal or state patronage appointments from Republicans.[12]

Even so, African Americans owed much of their continuing political participation and power to the Republicans. Republican officials at the county level thwarted efforts of state Democratic officials to disfranchise African-American voters, just as southern Democratic governors and legislators thwarted the efforts of Republican administrations in Washington to expand the civil rights of African Americans. Poston, for example, remained county clerk in Haywood County after serving in the Freedmen's Bureau. As county clerk, he had responsibility for voter registration until 1874. After that election, marred by violence and fraud, he was succeeded for a term by a man who had fought for the Confederacy. Poston's farm was in a section of the county that was organized into Crockett County in 1872. Whether he was defeated or simply withdrew from Haywood County politics because he now resided in another county is uncertain. In any event, he began a grain milling and lumber business in Crockett County. Republicans in Haywood County regained the county clerk's office in 1876, when John L. Sherman, the sheriff who had assisted Lieutenant Miller of the Freedmen's Bureau in his investigation of the Klan in the county eight years before, left the sheriff's office to win election as county clerk. From 1867, when the freedmen were enfranchised, to 1888, when new laws restricted the franchise of African-American men, Haywood County Republicans were able to deliver majorities to their candidates for governor. By expanding the electorate and protecting the political participation of African Americans, local Republicans became and remained the majority party in Haywood County.[13]

The example of Haywood County made the state Republican party keenly interested in continued political participation by the reliable bloc of African-American voters. These votes meant a margin of victory when the Democrats splintered, as in the 1880s. To maintain the loyalty of African-American voters, the Republicans gave African Americans more visible roles, including that of running for office. Five African Americans won election to the Tennessee General Assembly in 1880. That same year, Green Estes won election to the position of Trustee in Haywood County. Two years later, in 1882, Samuel A. McElwee was elected representative to the Tennessee General Assembly, unopposed. He succeeded W. F. Poston, nephew of John L. Poston, who resigned the post in 1882 to become U.S. district attorney for

West Tennessee.[14] McElwee entered the General Assembly with three other African-American legislators. Another African American, William Winfield, was elected registrar in Haywood County in 1883.

"THE DAWN OF A BETTER DAY
IN OUR SOUTHLAND"

McElwee spent his three terms in the General Assembly trying, largely unsuccessfully, to combat the Democratic tide of reaction that had eroded the state reforms of his Haywood County youth. He distinguished himself by his efforts to improve education for African Americans. As other African-American legislators had done in the previous session, McElwee pointed out the disproportionate shares of resources going to educate black and white children. The state's Constitution of 1870 forbade schools to accept students of both races. Subsequent allocations of resources developed a school system that had separate and unequal facilities for the races.[15]

McElwee explained to the legislature the specifics of this inequality. The legislature, up to 1881, had provided no appropriations for the education of African-American teachers. In that year, it provided $2,500 to be used for scholarships to help African Americans attend a "good colored normal school." In contrast, the legislature that year continued its appropriation of $10,000 to the state's all-white normal school, with the knowledge that the Peabody Education Fund would match that amount. Similarly, McElwee pointed out, the state had spent $300 on the education of African Americans out of the $390,000, not including interest, that it had received since 1862 under the Morrill Act's provisions for land-grant colleges. He asked that the legislature increase appropriations for the preparation of African-American teachers to $5,000.

He made three arguments for his position on this issue that he would repeat several times on other issues. The first, addressed to ex-Confederates and former slaveholders, asserted a personal debt that those who had served in the military during the Civil War owed to African Americans: "During the dark hours of war when your gallant [Governor] Bate with his devoted followers was far away on the bloody field, they [slaves] cared for the sick and dying at home; they tilled your lands and protected your property and your families." McElwee argued that African Americans had earned the right to an adequate education by their long years of "patient, unrequited toil, and industry."

In his second set of arguments, McElwee appealed to those legislators interested in the South's economic development and especially the growth of industry. He saw education as a necessary precondition for those changes. Investment in education would bring "the dawn of a better day in our Southland. Then with the dead issues of the past buried in the sea of oblivion and our homes, formerly devastated and laid waste by war, built up, with the mineral resources of our country developed, with the color line obliterated, and with our many manufacturing industries, the South will move on to a grand and noble future."

Reversing the argument used in the Tennessee legislature to reject the Fifteenth Amendment, McElwee argued that special legislation for whites was morally wrong; disproportionate distribution of funds was, too. All people of Tennessee, regardless of race, had an interest in an educated citizenry. Such a citizenry would safeguard the state's democratic institutions and attract people outside the state to migrate and increase the state's industrial workforce. His proposal, he said, benefited both races, but the concern that prompted his legislation came from "the loyalty to the race which I love and of which I am proud of the honor of identification, and by whose votes I occupy this seat."[16]

McElwee's third and final line of argument, addressed to the Democrats in the legislature, was dictated by the political factions and fusions of the time. His bill could not pass without the support of some Democratic legislators, as these formed the majority of the House of Representatives. Some African-American political leaders, disgruntled with the paucity of patronage and rewards won through their Republican allegiance, had shifted their support to the Democrats since 1880. Democratic support for his measure, McElwee argued, would be a clear signal that African-American voters did not have to look exclusively to the Republican party for benefits of government.

McElwee's speech was reported in the *Nashville American* and the *New York Globe*. It won the admiration of the legislators, who awarded him a gold watch for the oratory of his maiden speech. But the speech did not win sufficient support for the measure in the Tennessee General Assembly. His bill was tabled 55 to 38. A subsequent measure, increasing support for the normal school training of African Americans from $2,500 to $3,300, passed.

McElwee used this legislation to support the education of two young Haywood County men at Fisk University.

Several years later, in 1885, McElwee again defended education for African Americans. The University of Tennessee had provided scholarship money to Fisk University and Knoxville College for the education of African Americans in the state militia. The university, located in Knoxville, revoked its arrangement with Fisk and began supporting students only at Knoxville College. McElwee argued that Fisk was more conveniently located for the majority of African Americans in the state. He served on a committee to investigate the matter, and in 1887, the legislature instructed the University of Tennessee trustees to resume supporting students at Fisk, McElwee's alma mater.[17]

In addition to these initiatives, McElwee supported the educational initiatives other legislators proposed. For example, the African-American legislators proposed compulsory school attendance for all children between the ages of seven and sixteen. This provision for universal education would have benefited children of both races, of course. It had the solid support of the African-American legislators but failed to win a majority of other legislators.

Proposals on education widened the fissures within the Democratic party. In general, Bourbon Democrats, large land-owners, opposed compulsory education measures that increased the costs of education. Their children generally attended private schools. On the other hand, small land-owners, the agrarian Democrats, and wage earners favored educational measures that improved public education for their children. Some federal and state proposals for education forged an alliance among Republicans, former Whigs among the Democrats, and agrarian Democrats; but the alliance was not sufficient to pass McElwee's measure or other legislation.[18] Likewise, the efforts to institute the position of assistant superintendent of public instruction failed. African-American legislators had hoped to have a black man fill this position and assume primary responsibilities, and some advocacy, for schools for African Americans. The legislature defeated this measure in McElwee's second term. The measure proposing an administrative position for African-American schools acknowledged that separate school systems for the races were firmly established and that, to a degree, African-American legislators accepted that fact.

McElwee endorsed federal legislation for the improvement of education for African Americans as well. In particular, he urged the House of Representatives to support a resolution that called for the Tennessee congressional delegation to support an education bill originated by James G. Blair, a Republican from Maine. The legislation recognized the separate educational systems; it sought only to require that federal aid be applied to African-American children and teachers in proportion to their numbers in a state with segregated schools. McElwee's measure was tabled by a vote of 51 to 41.[19] Similar legislation lost in the U.S. Congress as well. McElwee's measure divided Tennessee Democrats along Bourbon, Whig, and agrarian lines. In addition, his measure elicited the states' rights position of the agrarian Democrats. These legislators were interested in securing benefits for Tennessee children with federal funds. They did not want federal stipulations on the use of those funds, however.[20]

"A COMFORTABLE SEAT
FOR A SHORT RIDE"

McElwee's election to the Tennessee General Assembly signaled the extension of emancipatory efforts by African Americans to state government. For the first time, a significant number of African Americans dealt directly with state legislation. Unfortunately, they failed to succeed in reversing the discriminatory legislation of the 1870s.

Fearful of pending federal civil rights legislation in 1875, the Tennessee legislature passed state laws to subvert them. The federal statutes intended to make it unlawful to discriminate or to hinder African Americans from full and equal enjoyment of theaters, public transportation, hotels, and places of amusement. Indicative of the declining commitment of the Republican party to civil rights by this time, the measure had no provision for enforcement. Nevertheless, the Democrats in Tennessee, bolstered by the election of 1874 and by a backlash to federal civil rights efforts, passed legislation to negate any semblance of expanded freedoms for African Americans. Tennessee laws, passed in 1875, permitted proprietors of public facilities to segregate African Americans within, or to exclude them from, public places. It afforded proprietors of public services control over their use "as perfect and complete as that of any private person over his private house, carriage, or private theater, or place of amusement for his family."[21]

By the time McElwee entered the General Assembly, efforts to repeal the 1875 state law were losing momentum. In 1881, one measure to repeal the law outright lost in a narrow vote of 31 to 29. Another measure to repeal the provisions of the state law, as they applied to railroads, never came up for a vote; instead, the legislators worked out a compromise. Railroad companies would neither have to open all cars to African-American passengers, nor would they be permitted to relegate African-American passengers to second-rate accommodations. The legislative compromise required railroads to provide separate but equal facilities for African-American passengers. In these sections, "all colored passengers who pay first-class passenger rates of fare, may have the privilege to enter and occupy." The bill passed in the Senate, where no African Americans served, 18 to 1. In the House, where four African Americans served, the bill passed without any of their votes, 50 to 2. Two of the African-American representatives voted against the measure, one was absent, and one abstained.[22] This would not be the last time that African Americans voted against "improvement" measures that actually represented a substantial loss for their race. In theory, African Americans had gained equal facilities, but the law required that they be segregated. Such measures clashed with the hopes of people like McElwee, who championed assimilation of the races within one set of American institutions and services. In practice, railroads did not change their policies and ignored the law. Their actions provided the grounds for Ida B. Wells' famous, albeit unsuccessful, lawsuit that protested Jim Crow laws at the outset of their hegemony.

Ida B. Wells, who would be among the first to protest the lynchings of African Americans in the South and also would be a founding member of the National Association for the Advancement of Colored People, began her overt political protest concerning the conditions of African Americans on a train in Tennessee on 4 May 1884. African Americans steadily had protested the separate facilities provided for them in railway travel. Their seats were in the second-class car. These might be in a smoking car, which was not segregated. Sometimes the cars for African Americans also served as the baggage car. At best, McElwee and others had to suffer inconvenience as a result of these arrangements, and, at those times when drinking led to abusive language and behavior in cars from which African-American passengers could not move, they suffered real hardship. The arrangement was a clear indication that even African Americans with education, income, and position were not to be allowed accommodations equivalent to those provided for comparable white people. To add insult to the injury of these arrangements, African Americans paid first-class fares for accommodations inferior to those of whites traveling first class.

On the ten-mile trip from Memphis to her school in northern Shelby County, Ida Wells refused to move from a coach reserved for white ladies and their attendants. The car she was told to ride in was open to all people, regardless of color or gender. The Tennessee law thus had both created equality for the races and preserved the best facilities for whites only. The twenty-two-year-old Wells protested that the coach that was "equal" for African Americans was a smoking coach which smelled of tobacco and liquor. She refused to be relegated to that car and insisted that her payment of first-class fare entitled her to a seat in the obviously preferable coach where she was. The conductor tried to drag her from her seat, but, as she recalled, "the moment he caught hold of my arm I fastened my teeth in the back of his hand."

> I had braced my feet against the seat in front and was holding to the back, and as he [the conductor] had already been badly bitten he didn't try it again by himself. He went forward and got the baggageman and another man to help him and of course they succeeded in dragging me out. They were en- couraged to do this by the attitude of the white ladies and gentlemen in the car; some of them even stood on the seats so that they could get a good view and continued applauding the conductor for his brave stand.[23]

Wells left the train at the first stop rather than go to the other car, but she began a journey through the courts that tested the intent of the law to protect her civil rights. Wells won a civil suit in the state circuit court against the railroad company and was awarded five hundred dollars in damages. The railroad company appealed to the state supreme court, which overturned the lower court's verdict. The court found: "It is evident that the purpose of the defendant in error was to harass with a view to this suit, and that her persis- tence was not in good faith to obtain a comfortable seat for a short ride."[24]

In addition to demonstrating her individual bravery, Wells's 1884 suit tested the national climate for civil rights. It was the first suit of its kind since the federal courts had turned civil rights over to the states. Thus, it tested the consequence of that action.

In 1883, the U.S. Supreme Court had found the Civil Rights Act of 1875 to be unconstitutional and had left it to the states to remedy discrimination. One of the cases which resulted in the 1883 Supreme Court decision had originated in Crockett County in 1876. In August, which was election time, four African-American prisoners were beaten by a mob of twenty men. One of the prisoners died. In a result unusual for such cases, the white mob members were arrested and later indicted by a federal grand jury. The Poston family, prominent in the county and the courts, may have had a hand in this rare prosecution. The indictment alleged that the mob members not only had deprived the African-American prisoners of their civil rights but also had prevented state and local officials from protecting the civil rights of their prisoners.

The U.S. Supreme Court found that the law prosecuting the white men for denying the African-American prisoners due protection under the law was unconstitutional. The court went further and demarcated attacks on state and local officials and those on African-American victims. Eight justices reasoned that the Fourteenth Amendment prohibited the states, not individuals, from violating the civil rights of persons. The amendment did not supersede the states' authority to prosecute the actions of individuals such as the attackers. The law, according to the court majority, exceeded the provisions of the amendment and so could not be used to justify prosecution of individuals for hindering the state from guaranteeing some people their constitutional rights. If the state was prevented from securing a person's civil rights, that person and the state and local authorities had recourse to state, but not federal, lawsuits.[25] The language of the Court's decision echoed the Tennessee legislature's rejection of the Fifteenth Amendment a decade earlier. It disavowed any status as "wards" for African Americans and emphasized their citizenship within states. Wells concluded, "The supreme court of the nation had told us to go to the state courts for redress of grievances; when I did so I was given the brand of justice Charles Sumner knew Negroes would get when he fathered the Civil Rights Bill during the Reconstruction era."[26]

One week after she made this statement, Wells found new strength. She attended a meeting of the Negro's Mutual Protective Association, whose ideas on self-help and self-reliance she considered "the best thing out." She found that "the negro is beginning to think for himself and find out that strength for his people and consequently for him is to be found only in unity." In addition, she saw Edward Shaw in attendance. Shaw had participated in electoral politics since Reconstruction and had been at the 1867 rally in Brownsville. Now his "dignified, patriarchal, and stern demeanor and bearing" meant, for Wells, "that the men of the race who do think are endeavoring to put their thoughts in action for those and to inspire those who do not think."[27]

DELAYING THE ARRIVAL
OF JIM CROW

The 1883 action of the United States Supreme Court gave greater importance to the state legislation that dealt with discrimination. It thus indirectly provided federal support to the restrictive Tennessee legislation of 1875 and tested the ability of legislators, such as McElwee, to change it. After McElwee entered the General Assembly, he joined efforts to repeal the 1875 legislation and the 1881 railroad provision compromise. These efforts were unsuccessful. African-American legislators served in a body that continued to legislate and sanction the separation of the races. This separation at first was not complete. It became complete as white legislators reconciled the theory of equality with the practice of discrimination. For example, they argued that the compromise legislation on railroad facilities protected the rights of African Americans to separate and preferred accommodations for first-class fares. They ignored the fact that those accommodations were seldom provided and that, when provided, they were little better than the lower-class accommodations for white travelers. During the 1880s, Tennessee and the nation moved from laws that permitted African Americans access to public services, to laws that in practice restricted their access, as separate and equal facilities became unavailable despite their having been required by law.

In addition to these issues, McElwee, together with the other African-American legislators, addressed several practices that dramatically affected African-American laborers. In the 1860s, Tennessee had avoided the restrictive Black Codes enacted in the other southern states.[28] Republican control of the governor's office and the legislature and the contracts and participation of the Freedmen's Bureau had prevented enactment of labor laws that reintroduced slavelike terms of labor. But in the legislative term of 1874–75, Tennessee's turn came to adopt this restrictive legislation. It became unlawful, after 1875, for a person to entice the employees of another person away from their employment. The same legislation increased the lien that a landholder had on the crop of tenants or sharecroppers. These laws tied African-American workers to their landlords and creditors. Their labor was tied to their crop, the crop being owned by the landlord, who could bring criminal charges against anyone who attempted to hire a dissatisfied worker. The fine for enticing someone else's worker away from an employer and a debt was one thousand dollars.[29] Should workers leave the employment of a landlord, the provisions of this law made it unlikely that nearby landlords would hire them.

Without employment, a worker, especially an African American, was subject to arrest under another 1875 law. The vagrancy law made it a misdemeanor "to neglect to engage in an honest calling" or "to tramp or stroll" without visible means of support. Once arrested, a person entered a penal system that was a central element of the subordination of African Americans, featuring as it did a system of labor worse than slavery. From 1865 to 1880, the prison population in Tennessee increased sixfold. The number of African-American inmates increased thirteenfold, from 66 to over 821. Between 500 to 600 convicts were leased as laborers to coal mines, railroads, and large farmers, including Nathan Bedford Forrest. The revenue paid for their labor provided Tennessee "a handsome profit," according to the superintendent of prisons, and an incentive to imprison the most able-bodied black males.[30] The leased convict laborers paid for the system with their lives. During McElwee's second term of office, 163 African Americans died while in custody of the state and under lease for their labor.[31]

The 1880s provided an opportunity to change these labor laws, including the leasing of convict labor, which Tennessee officials touted as a model program.[32] But if some individual legislators were willing, the entire legislative body was not. In 1887, the legislature rejected a proposal to abolish convict labor leasing. Earlier efforts to ease the strictures on agricultural workers, enforced by the prison system, also failed.[33]

McElwee was moderately successful in pressing for legislation to end or modify minor discriminatory laws. In his third term, the legislature conferred legal marital status on former slaves who had lived together as man and wife in other states and who moved to Tennessee. Major discrimination laws survived McElwee's challenge. Thus, after his third term, it was still unlawful for men and women of different races to marry. His effort to end racial discrimination in the selection of juries also failed.[34]

McElwee's major success was in introducing special programs for African Americans, separate from those of whites, and winning support for programs of benefit to both races. In addition to gaining more support for the education of African-American teachers, he served as president of the West Tennessee Colored Fair Association and the Memphis Fair Association. He won legislative appropriations for fairs for African Americans, including a fairground in Haywood County. His greatest single legislative success was the creation of an asylum in West Tennessee for the mentally ill, including $85,000 for its support.

"MY MOST SOLEMN PROTEST AGAINST MOB VIOLENCE"

By 1887, McElwee was one of only three African-American legislators left in the Tennessee General Assembly. In February 1887, he introduced anti-lynching legislation in the House of Representatives. His speech illustrated the skill with language that had won him national notice. He recounted to the General Assembly details of a rash of lynchings in West Tennessee. He dwelt upon the lynching of Eliza Wood the preceding August, a lynching that had appalled Ida B. Wells as well.[35]

News of the lynching had reached Wells in California, where she was visiting an aunt. On the way, she had stopped in Topeka, Kansas, to visit with friends among the Exodusters. By this time, Wells had started writing for African-American newspapers and other publications. Upon hearing of the lynching, she wrote what she considered a "dynamatic article to the G. C. P. [Gate City Press, Kansas City, Missouri] almost advising murder!" Wells saw Wood's lynching as an expression of contempt for Wood's legal rights and personal dignity and for those of all African Americans:

My only plea is the pitch of indignation to which I was carried by reading an article . . . concerning a great outrage . . . A colored woman accused of poisoning a white one was taken from the county jail and stripped naked and hung up in the courthouse yard and her body riddled with bullets and left exposed to view! O my God! can such things be and no justice for it? . . . It may be unwise to express myself so strongly but I cannot help it and I know not if capital may not be made of it against me but I trust in God.[36]

Lynchings were increasing at this time, when the legal protection of African Americans were declining. By the time of the Voting Rights Act in 1965, 3,445 lynchings had been reported; many more went unreported. Whether reported or not, lynchings impressed on black people the contempt of some white people for their rights and dignity and the acquiescence of almost all white people in the expression of that contempt.

McElwee spoke to his legislative colleagues as the bloody chapter of racial lynchings was beginning in America. He related to them the pattern of lynching emerging throughout the South: "It is remarkable to note the sameness with which these reports read. It seems as if some man in this country had the patent by which these reports are written. Statistics do not show the number of Negroes who have in the past few years been sentenced in Judge Lynch's court, but judging from the number coming under our observation we are convinced that the number is most astounding." He condemned the lynch mob members and those who did not protest the lynchings. His speech took the legislators to Jackson on the night of Wood's lynching:

Look at that poor woman . . . as she is taken from the jail and followed by that motley crowd to the courtyard.

The bell is rung, they enter the jail and strip her of every garment, and order her to march — buffeting, kicking, and spearing her with sharp sticks on the march . . . She is swung up, her body riddled with bullets and orders issued not to interfere with her until 9 o'clock the next morning, in order that she might be seen.

McElwee's rhetoric then ushered his fellow legislators to heaven to hear an angelic chorus of innocent victims of mob actions in the South:

> Hundreds of Negroes, yes thousands, from all parts of this Southland, are to-day numbered with the silent majority, gone to eternity without a tomb to mark their last resting place, as the result of mob violence for crimes which they never committed. As we to-day legislate on this question, the spirits of these Negroes made perfect in the paradisiacal region of God, in convention assembled, with united voices, are asking the question, "Great God, when will this Nation treat the Negro as an American citizen?"

As he had done in his maiden speech four years previously, McElwee spoke as a representative of African Americans about measures of benefit to both races:

> I am not here, Mr. Speaker, asking any special legislation in the interest of the Negroes, but in behalf of a race of outraged human beings. I stand here to-day and enter my most solemn protest against mob violence in Tennessee.
>   . . . The interest of the white man is the interest of the black man, that which hurts one will hurt the other; therefore, as a humble representative of the Negro race, and as a member of this body, I stand here to-day and wave the flag of truce between the races and demand a reformation in Southern society by passage of this bill.[37]

McElwee's anti-lynching measure failed, but narrowly. The General Assembly tabled it by a vote of 41 to 36. In fact, neither Tennessee nor the federal government ever passed anti-lynching legislation. The federal government preferred to treat lynchings as murder and to leave them to the jurisdiction of the states. The states abided by local practice, which included subordination of African Americans by occasional violence.

A reformation of southern society did come shortly after McElwee's speech, but it was not the reformation that McElwee had asked for. It restricted rather than expanded the political rights of African Americans. It was not a truce in the conflict between the races but a new assault in the battle on the rights and freedoms of African Americans. In fact, within a year,

McElwee, now thirty years of age, himself became a victim of renewed political repression.

"AMONG THE ABLEST OF COLORED MEN"

McElwee's eloquence and ability drew much attention to the issues of black people and to himself. In 1885, the Republican party nominated him for speaker of the house. His nominator, a former slaveholder, introduced McElwee as "the peer of any member on this floor." He also suggested that this nomination indicated the Republican party's support for African-American officeholders and stood as "another evidence of where the race must look for recognition."[38] McElwee lost the election in the Democrat-controlled chamber. Republicans honored him further, however, when he was elected temporary chairman of the 1886 state Republican convention. McElwee also became an ambassador for Tennessce. In 1885, he served as commissioner in the Colored Department of the New Orleans Exposition. His speaking engagements throughout the country brought him to the attention of reporters in New York and other areas.

By 1884, McElwee clearly was one of the most visible African-American leaders in Tennessee. In that year, he was prominent in a convention of African Americans intended to revive the annual State Convention of Colored Men. The convention had a sweeping platform, for which McElwee was the prime spokesman. The platform called for national aid to education; for the "industrial and material interests" of African Americans; and for increased security within African-American households. In direct response to the U.S. Supreme Court's decisions of the previous year weakening the civil rights measures of the 1860s and 1870s, the convention discussed "Equal Privileges in the Jury Box of the State Courts and Our Civil and Political Rights, the State and Federal Government, in Proportion to Our Strength."

In an hour-long speech on the second day of the convention, McElwee addressed the questions before the assembled men and women. He spoke specifically to the Supreme Court decision, handed down six months before, that rescinded much of the Civil Rights Act of 1875: "There was a good law enacted in our behalf by the nation, and today it stands a dead letter by the action of the United States Supreme Court." Few people so clearly demonstrated the benefits of Reconstruction and the civil rights laws. At age twenty-five and after education in the schools of the Freedmen's Bureau and of the freedmen's societies, McElwee was a forceful spokesman for African Americans. At the convention, his delegation of forty-eight members was third largest in size, exceeded only by those of Shelby and Davidson counties, where Memphis and Nashville were located. He was not only younger than most other delegates but also he was one of the few who had been born a slave. Lacking both biracial parents and antebellum freedom, he addressed other leaders who had had one or both benefits. He spoke of the changes that were possible through legislative action:

> We have been called here from the different sections of the State to consider questions of very great moment to the colored race and to the entire country. Coming as we do from the different sections of the State, it is hoped we represent the feelings and needs of those we represent.
>
> May our actions indicate clearly and unmistakably that the injustice done the race in any part of the country meets with our unqualified disapproval. May the people of this great nation see and take cognizance of the fact that beyond this and similar conventions, there is a deep, underlying current that furnishes thoughts and feelings which here find expression. . . .
>
> We say to the white men of this country, the white men of the South, that the colored men have rights which must be respected. [Applause.]
>
> Congress cannot make laws that do not apply to every man; so it is not legislation that we need. The laws are good enough, if they were only enforced. Give us no more laws, but enforce those we already have.
>
> We demand equal rights in the jury box, and we demand civil and political rights. . . . There was a good law enacted in our behalf by the nation, and to-day it stands a dead letter by the action of the United States Supreme Court. We respectfully demand at the hands of the American people better treatment, more just treatment at their hands. Our race made a glorious record during the late war. When the Union was about to be cast asunder the negro stood to the post and received the bayonet that was aimed at the heart of the nation. Everyone present knew how faithful and devoted the colored people were to the old flag, the stars and stripes. The colored people recognized the

need of government aid in education, and respectfully ask for that aid. The status of the negro was not what it ought to be, but we have done well under the circumstances. Another thing, the white men must be made to understand that when our women are insulted and outraged that we will protect them, even with the shot-gun if need be. The machine shops of the country were closed against the colored men, and the trade unions rejected them, and they were left only to take up politics or preaching, and in either place he is about as much out of place as a bull in a china shop. We stand upon the threshold of a great political contest. We are glad there is to be an issue. We hope the Democrats will give us a square fight on the tariff. Our party is a unit on all national questions. We are stronger than ever before, and our prospects are brighter than ever before. We hope to drive Democracy [Democrats] to the wall and will drive it there.[39]

McElwee's speech won wide approval and was noticed as far away as New York. It was not, however, adopted as the convention's sentiment, because its closing partisan Republican rhetoric upset some older political operatives. These men saw wisdom in stating positions but not in offending one political party while working toward the implementation of those positions. They resented a party that, in effect, told African Americans, "You can run for magistrate or letter carrier, but we white Republicans must have all the big offices and control the schools."

In 1884, McElwee carried his partisan Republican views and his growing reputation to the national convention of the Republican party, where he was a delegate. According to Fisk publications, he "won quite a mark" there. "He was often the center of attention in knots of distinguished delegates, where indomitable cheek, self-confidence, and push always enabled him to acquit himself creditably. He was strongly recommended as a suitable man to second the nomination of Blaine. He delivered a speech in the caucus prior to the convention and received marked attention." A report in the *New York Times* alleged that McElwee offered his vote for sale, but he "ably refuted the charge and showed pretty conclusively that the malignity against him emanated from political enemies in his own State."[40] Fisk was particularly proud of this young alumnus.[41]

McElwee's and Fisk's admiration was mutual. In December after his graduation, McElwee dropped by Fisk with two prospective students, T. J.

Austin and J. A. Lester. Both men were eligible for educational support at Fisk, thanks to the legislation that McElwee had supported in 1883. Austin graduated in 1885 and returned to Brownsville to teach. He left Brownsville before the end of the year to become the first principal of Lane College, the new college for African Americans in Jackson, Tennessee. The fact that African Americans occupied leadership positions at Lane distinguished it from other African-American schools of the time. Only one of McElwee's faculty at Fisk, for example, had been an African American. Fisk University installed its first African-American president only after World War II. By 1884, Fisk publications referred to McElwee as "our esteemed friend" and took great pride in his achievements. For example, the school paper reported that his thesis, "Injunctions," written upon completion of his legal studies in 1886, "was highly spoken of by many who were present" at McElwee's graduation. He was valedictorian of his law school class of four. His graduating class at Fisk had numbered only ten.[42]

McElwee's association with Fisk brought him into contact with several people who would profoundly affect American race relations. In spring 1886, as a widower, McElwee resided at Fisk while studying law. His first wife had died the previous year. Upon her death, McElwee had taken his five-year-old son and three-year-old daughter to West Tennessee, where he left them in the care of his and his wife's parents, respectively. He returned to Nashville and took up residence at Fisk. There he undoubtedly came into contact with a newly enrolled Fisk student from Massachusetts, W. E. B. Du Bois. Of the effect of having so many talented African Americans together at Fisk, Du Bois wrote: "Some mornings as I look about upon the two or three hundred of my companions assembled for morning prayers I can hardly realize they are all my people; that this great assembly of youth and intelligence are the representatives of a race which twenty years ago was in bondage. . . . It is a bracing thought to know that I stand among those who do not despise me for my color."[43]

In 1887, McElwee won the confidence of another African American who exerted a profound influence on American race relations. Only four years after his own graduation, McElwee, then 28, was invited by Booker T. Washington to serve as the main speaker at the sixth commencement of Tuskegee in Alabama. Another five years elapsed before Frederick Douglass received the same honor. Washington, in announcing McElwee's selection as speaker, explained, "Mr. McElwee is among the ablest of colored men, and as an orator he has few equals."[44] William Jenkins, a Fisk University faculty member, cautioned Washington, "You must not expect too much of him as he is much younger than anyone that you have heretofore had." But Jenkins added reassuringly, "And yet, I have no doubt that he will make you a good speech. He represents the young men of today. And has had much experience for one of his age."[45]

It was probably inevitable that McElwee would also meet Ida B. Wells at this time. Both had commented strongly on the lynching of Eliza Wood as a measure of the depravity of lynching. Wells and McElwee shared an interest in Fisk, and mention of both appeared regularly in the *Fisk Herald*.[46] Both had publicly protested the Jim Crow laws.[47] In June 1887, just two months after the court decision in her train case, Wells wrote to McElwee. When both attended a press association conference in Louisville later that summer, their meeting had a spark of romance. Wells confided to her diary that she had exchanged pictures with him "almost against my will. I hardly know him well enough." They spent a morning visiting sights around the city.[48] Wells's fame lay ahead; after that summer, McElwee's political fame would soon be over.

Before the end came, however, the summer of 1888 provided McElwee another prominent role as a delegate to his second Republican National Convention. At the convention, McElwee entered the name of a fellow Tennessean, William R. Moore of Memphis, in nomination as the vice presidential candidate of the Republican party. Moore had been a speaker at the Brownsville political rally twenty years earlier. McElwee's brief speech from the floor apologized for the lack of electoral votes from the South since 1876. He affirmed the strength of southern Republicans with all the over-statement and bluff expected of a national party conventioneer:

Oppressed by Southern Democrats, and forsaken by the Republicans of the North, we have stood firm and remained true and loyal to the cause of the party we regard as the grandest that ever existed on the American continent.

Tennessee is ready to-day to lead in the break of the solid South, and thereby assist in wresting this government from the hands of the Democratic party; and if this convention, in its wisdom, shall nominate the gentleman whose name I propose, Tennessee with the grandeur and glory of her past history and her hopes of the future, will be forever redeemed from the hands of the Democratic party, and placed on the roll of the Republican States of the Union.[49]

What was surely high drama for McElwee soon turned into burlesque. A delegate from North Carolina arose, but instead of seconding the nomination, he went into a long story about a Scotsman from his district. The story of a drinker and the apparent inebriation of the storyteller brought the convention to laughter and disorder several times. The delegate interrupted his remarks to explain "soberly" that "this is the proudest hour of my life." Seemingly incredulous, he asked a question that had a sober barb beneath its drunken expression, "Am I talking to a thousand Republicans, and white ones at that?"[50]

The seriousness of McElwee's action was recaptured by a delegate from Mississippi, who rose to second Moore's nomination. He explained that a southern candidate on the ticket would help Republicans cultivate "much ground in the South." Tennessee was a prime example of the potential in the South: "Thousands of old Whigs are true to their first love, and where Democrats are satisfied that they can never develop their resources except under Republican auspices." As further evidence of Tennessee's potential, the speaker pointed to the election of a Republican governor and "more tolerance of opinion, more law and order and cleaner elections than anywhere in the South."[51]

McElwee's role in the national party indicated a continuing influence of African Americans, one that prompted the party's presidential nominee, Benjamin Harrison, to pay attention to civil rights during the campaign. Harrison was the first president to propose an anti-lynching law. Altogether, though, the 1888 party platform had fewer planks on civil rights than the 1884 platform. Just as the prominence of civil rights dwindled, so did both the influence of African Americans in the Republican party and the political career of McElwee.[52]

FIVE MINUTES TO SPEAK,
FIVE MINUTES TO ESCAPE

National and state political changes contributed to McElwee's political fall, which was even faster than his rise had been. The tide of the agrarian movement was rising and with it the power of rural, white, small land-owners increased in the Democratic party and in state government.[53] White leaders of the Tennessee Republican party attempted to ride this tide and, in a "lily-white movement," purged African-American leaders, including McElwee, from their ranks. They reasoned that the African-American vote was assured for Republicans, even without African-American leaders in the party. African-American voters, they predicted, would not bolt to the far more racist Democratic party in Tennessee. If African Americans formed a third party, these lily-white Republicans calculated, it would not hurt them; a gain of new white voters would give Republicans the edge on Democrats. The Republicans' primary purpose was to woo and win moderate Democratic voters. Their strategy repeated Freeman's 1872 effort to revive the moderate Whig faction of the Republican party and to win the support of moderate Democrats. These tasks would be easier if African Americans had a smaller role in the party or left it entirely. Holding African Americans in the party while trying to win new, white adherents from the Democratic ranks was proving too difficult a political task. For example, after a disappointing political rally in Brownsville in 1884, one pundit suggested that the ordinary Tennessee Republican message had "too much Whig . . . for the nigger and too much nigger for the Whig."[54] The new Republican strategy disavowed the radically democratic element of its own party. By 1888, the visible African-American Republicans made up the largest remnant of the party loyal to radical democratic policies. They voiced the loudest protest against the most inhumane aspects of labor, prison, education, and race policies of the 1880s.

In addition to a decline in Republican party support, McElwee faced new, violent opposition from Democrats in West Tennessee. The agrarian movement increased in strength within the Democratic party.[55] The party's new leaders resolved to end the political equation that had coupled Democratic party factionalism with Republican party discipline, added a bloc of African-American votes, and equaled Republican electoral victories, including those of McElwee. In August 1888, shortly after he returned from the national convention and began his campaign for reelection, armed white men saw to it that candidates of the all-white "citizens ticket" won the primary elections. They roved Haywood County in bands intimidating African-American voters, just as the Ku Klux Klan had done twenty years before.

The Klan had disbanded as a paramilitary extension of the Democratic party in West Tennessee after the 1869 election. Armed white men reappeared at various times, however, reviving the Klan's tactics to guarantee election outcomes, as they had in Trenton in 1874. Thus, on election day in November 1888, men with rifles again roamed Haywood County, stood by polling places, and "guarded" the ballot boxes and the places where ballots were counted. McElwee's efforts to rally support and voter turnout on election day ended after threats against him by a group of armed white men. Newspapers reported the arrival of more white men on election night "armed with shotguns, Winchesters, carbines to squelch any inclinations among the defeated Republicans to rise."[56]

The Republican State Committee claimed, "We were defrauded out of electoral votes of Tennessee, as well as one if not two members of Congress." Specifically, the committee estimated that Republicans had carried Shelby County (Memphis) by 2,000 votes, but the Democrats claimed a 4,245 majority. Similarly, the committee reported that Republicans had won in Fayette and Haywood counties by 1,100 and 1,500 votes respectively. The official results, however, reported Democratic victories by margins of 2,833 and 238 in the presidential election.[57]

Federal election supervisors reported unmistakable fraud in one district in Haywood County, but with shifts in the state's Republican party and the preponderance of Democratic control, the election results were not contested.[58] Tennessee Republicans found little support for their complaints. National party leaders had reasons of their own not to demand scrutiny of these election results. Harrison, the Republican candidate for president, had won the election in the electoral college only. He had fewer votes than the incumbent Grover Cleveland in the popular election. Protesting elections in Tennessee, or any other state, would only invite protests and scrutiny of the presidential election.

Unlike the election twenty years previously, McElwee had no Freedmen's Bureau or federal presence to protect the franchise of African-American men and to recompense them for any losses they incurred for voting. Three times successful in consecutive, preceding elections, McElwee received just 732 votes, some 1,500 less than his previous totals, in November and lost his first campaign for public office. Haywood County and West Tennessee lost his leadership shortly after that. According to stories handed down to McElwee's grandchildren, the armed partisans of the newly elected officials gave McElwee ten minutes to leave from Allen Station. McElwee used five minutes to speak, and then, with an armed guard of twelve men, he used his remaining five minutes to escape.

LOST RIGHTS

The election results of 1888 began a dramatic reversal of political patterns in the county and the state. From 1867 to 1888, only two gubernatorial elections in Haywood County had been close.[59] In every other election in that time, Republican candidates for governor regularly carried Haywood County with 60 percent of the vote. However, in 1888, the Democratic candidate won by a two-to-one margin, the same margin by which the Democratic candidate had lost in the previous election. The election of 1888 finally delivered the county from Republican control—or "redeemed" it, in the term of the day. Democrats controlled local offices in Haywood County for the second time since freedmen were allowed to vote and for the first time since 1876. This time the reversal in Republican and Democratic strength went beyond an election result. The state election results permitted the Democrats sufficient political control to change laws defining the electorate and assured a new alignment of party strength. Henceforth, Democrats would be in the majority in Haywood County.

The 1889 Tennessee General Assembly met without McElwee and encountered few impediments to the systematic disfranchisement of African-American voters in the state. This disfranchisement consolidated Democratic power. The legislature passed four laws that gave local registrars discretion in applying voter registration regulations, impeded poor men from registering, and confused the election process so as to disqualify illiterate voters. Together, these laws virtually eliminated the African–American vote in some places in Tennessee. Without supportive registrars, such as Poston had been, Haywood County African–American residents had little influence at the polls.[60]

The results of these laws appeared immediately. The total number of voters dropped, with Republican voters dwindling in larger proportions than Democratic ones. In Haywood County this meant that the majority of eligible voters, African–American men, were removed from the list of registered voters and impeded from placing their names on the list again. By 1890, just two years later, the voter turnout had been cut to 1,504, about 40 percent of the average for elections in the 1880s. The county electorate was now 66 percent Democratic, about the same percent it had been Republican in the past. As Haywood County had been solidly Republican since 1867, it would now be solidly Democratic until 1964. As the Republicans had expanded the electorate and become the county's majority party, the Democrats now contracted the electorate and regained majority status.[61]

As the number of registered African–American voters declined in places like Haywood County, Jim Crow rose as the unelected monarch of race relations. White political officials, insulated from electoral reactions by African–American voters, enforced the restrictive laws against African Americans and reinforced the informal repression and contempt that inspired those laws. A key aspect of that repression and contempt was lynching that reached its peak in the 1890s. In 1888, 69 African–American men and women and an almost equal number of whites were lynched. In 1892, the number of African–American men and women lynched increased to 161, and it averaged 154 annually during the decade of the 1890s. Of the 120 lynch victims in Tennessee from 1889 to 1899, 89 were African American. Twenty-three of them were lynched in West Tennessee and 10 in Memphis.[62]

GAINING AND ALMOST LOSING THE LAND

With the removal of African Americans from politics, other efforts began to separate the most successful of them from their economic achievements. By 1880, the number of African–American land-owners in Haywood County had reached 123, about 5 percent of all farmers there and less than one in one hundred of the county's African Americans.[63] Among those acquiring land

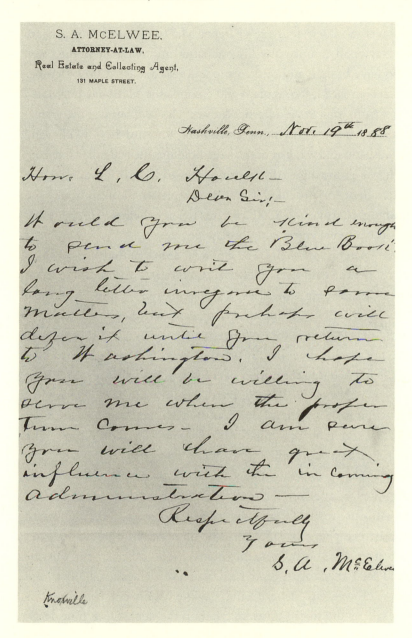

Fig. 7. Letter from Samuel A. McElwee to U.S. Representative Leonidas C.
Houk, 19 November 1888, sent immediately after McElwee's electoral defeat
and flight from Haywood County. Courtesy of Lawson McGee Library,
Knoxville, Tennessee. Calvin M. McClung Historical Collection, L. C. Houk
Papers.

in the 1880s were Samuel McElwee's parents. McElwee entered the grocery business in Haywood County after his graduation and while he studied law. He may also have bought and sold cotton and real estate.[64] On 7 October 1887, in exchange for $1,485, Robert and Georgianna McElwee purchased 165 3/4 acres from John R. and Bessie Walker. Mrs. Walker was the grand-daughter of Haywood County's first slaveholder, Richard Taylor. The land she and her husband sold was part of the large holdings she had inherited from her father. It was unusual for African Americans to have this much cash. It is possible that their son provided it, but he had placed all of his books and office furnishings in trust for a $200 loan just the year before. He spent that year, 1886, in Nashville completing his law degree.

McElwee's parents told their great-grandchildren that they had obtained the money to buy the land during slavery. Recounting stories told to them by their great-grandparents, McElwee's grandchildren—Ethel Black, Julia Ford, and Robert McElwee, living in Los Angeles and in their seventies when interviewed—recalled being told: "Grandma Georgianna's daddy showed her a whole pot of money and said, 'When slavery ends you come and get this money.' They hid it in the corner of the hen house." Robert McElwee believed, "Her father stole the money. That's the only way he could have had it. He stole it and gave it to her. I don't know what he had in his head but I reckon he was trying to fix things for his daughter. He didn't know if he was going to live a slave or not."

Robert and Georgianna might have been land-owners, but they still had to borrow money to raise crops on their land. The debts they incurred could ensnare an African-American land-owner just as surely as they ensnared tenants and sharecroppers. In January 1889, three months after their son's electoral defeat and banishment from the county, Joe Sternberger, Brownsville attorney and land speculator, recovered a judgment against Robert and Georgianna McElwee for a debt of $152.20. The McElwees' land was con-demned for sale by the sheriff to make good on the debt. On 8 June 1889, Sternberger bought the land at auction for $178.60, one-eighth the price the McElwees had paid eighteen months earlier.

That ordinarily would have ended the landholding experience of the McElwees, as similar episodes did that of most other African Americans. This couple, however, had a son who was a lawyer. In October, after Sternberger's purchase, the McElwees sold the land to Georgianna Shelton for "a certain lot of ground on Maple St. in Nashville." Shelton was a widow and ran a boardinghouse where McElwee lived. Shelton was mulatto and born in New York, most likely free, in 1849. On 6 June 1888, McElwee married Shelton's daughter, Georgia M. Shelton, who was ten years younger than he was. Somehow, McElwee and Shelton managed to confuse title to the land and prevented Sternberger from disposing of it. In May 1890, Sternberger relinquished claim to the land in exchange for payment of the debt he held against the McElwees. The McElwees and Georgianna Shelton then sold one hundred acres of the land to James Riley for $200.00 plus $559.90 to cover debts of Samuel McElwee from his grocery business and debts of his parents. Later, it was determined that the original lot of land purchased contained 195, not 165 3/4, acres. The McElwees paid James Walker one dollar for title to the additional acreage. At the end of the century, after several years of legal maneuvering, Robert and Georgianna McElwee, former slaves, owned ninety-five acres of land and were among the small number of land-owning African-American farmers in Haywood County.

While the McElwees acquired land, other African-American farmers in surrounding counties again tried to acquire political influence as a means of improving their economic condition. The Colored Farmers Alliance, started in 1886, claimed 1.2 million members in the South by 1890. This alliance worked parallel to its white counterpart in advocating federal policies similar to those initiated during Reconstruction—loans for mortgages and land purchase, and improved schooling for African-American children. Four counties in West Tennessee (not including Haywood) organized chapters that sent representatives to a state convention in 1889. Several factors contributed to the demise of the alliance by 1892. Prominent among them were reprisals occasioned by the threat that an African-American farmers organization might provide support to the Republican party. It was in precisely this period that lynching became predominantly a white-on-black act of violence in the South.

LESS CHANCE FOR IMPORTANCE AT HOME

After 1888, Samuel McElwee did not return to Haywood County, other than to visit, for the rest of his life. At the same time that he worked to preserve his family's land in Haywood County, he sought a new niche in politics. In Haywood County the removal of African Americans from political life was complete and, in Tennessee, nearly complete. Consequently, McElwee looked to the Republican party for a position in the newly elected Republican administration of Benjamin Harrison.

Soon after moving to Nashville, McElwee wrote to U.S. Congressman Leonidas C. Houk, the most powerful Tennessee Republican in the federal government and arguably the most powerful southern Republican in Congress. McElwee and Houk had participated in the 1884 and 1888 national conventions and other party functions and knew each other well. McElwee wrote to Houk to request the "Blue Book" of federal positions that would be available within the administration of the new president. He expressed the hope that Houk would "be willing to serve me when the proper time comes."[65]

Three days letter, McElwee wrote in firmer tones to Houk. He had decided "to ask to be sent as Minister to Hayti." Emancipation had come to Haiti through a revolution that created the second independent nation in the Western Hemisphere.[66] An independent black nation provided a Republican administration the opportunity to appoint an African American to federal service. McElwee no longer hoped for Houk's support, he expected it: "I would be very glad to know that I shall have your endorsement & influence for the position. I am sure that you will have great influence with the administration. Let me hear from you."[67]

A week letter, McElwee wrote a long letter and carefully explained his request. He expressed the dilemma of African-American politicians who had lost their place in local and state politics and now looked to the federal government and the national party for continued opportunities for political careers. His firm yet cooperative style conveyed ambition combined with resignation:

> I shall ask for this position [of Minister to Haiti] not because I think I shall prefer going abroad to accepting a good position at home, but in my opinion I think I would stand a better chance for that than I would for anything of as much importance at home. As to the positions in our state of importance I supposed they would be given to White republicans, terefore [sic], I would not ask for anything in the state, as I do not care to do any thing that would invite antagonism.[68]

Houk was deluged with requests for patronage appointments, given the Republican defeat in Tennessee and the party's national victory. None of the requests was better organized and orchestrated than McElwee's. In February 1889, Houk received several lengthy letters from prominent Tennessee Republicans endorsing McElwee for the appointment as Minister of Haiti. Remarkably, none of them mentioned McElwee's race as a factor for consideration in his appointment. Edward B. Stahlman, publisher of the Nashville Republican newspaper, the *Banner*, wrote to Houk "at the insistence of Hon. S. A. McElwee." Stahlman thought his recommendation hardly necessary, since Houk knew McElwee "so well, that I do not see how a letter from me can be of much service to him." Stahlman did believe that McElwee's "services entitle him to recognition at the hands of the Administration" and referred to some work for the Republican party that McElwee had done in New York after his electoral defeat.[69]

McElwee secured several other notable endorsements. J. C. Graham, writing on the stationery of the county clerk of Lauderdale County, notified Houk that "I have seen and consulted with a large number of the Republicans of Lauderdale County, and find them almost unanimous in the wish that he be appointed." Graham thought it unnecessary "to say that he is well qualified by natural endowments and education attainments for the position." Graham did not go into great detail in explaining that McElwee "now, for political reasons" lived in Nashville.[70]

The "Republicans of Gibson County, Tennessee assembled" also petitioned Houk to use his influence to secure the position for McElwee. They expected McElwee's nomination would "meet the hearty endorsement of the Republicans throughout the state." Their petition made reference "to the merits of Mr. McElwee, . . . [and] the struggles which he had gone through for the Republican party" but offered no details about them, "for with these, we are satisfied you are already knowledgeable."[71] Similarly, the "assembled students" of Fisk University, "representing the progressive and energetic colored citizens," asked Houk to assist McElwee in securing the minister's post to Haiti.[72]

Finally, a group of forty Republicans in Madison County, which adjoins Haywood and was McElwee's birthplace, sent the strongest letter to Houk endorsing McElwee. It expounded on McElwee's political contribution:

Mr. McElwee possesses in the fullest measure the confidence and esteem of the Republicans in this vicinity and no-one contributed more largely than he to the magnificent showing made by the party in this county at the recent elections. His name has a rallying force and magnetism in this county possessed by no other, and like a celebrated Scottish chieftain of old — "one blast upon his bugle horn is worth a thousand men." Every Republican of Madison would consider it a personal honor to have Mr. McElwee recognized in a substantive way by the incoming administration.[73]

The Harrison administration did appoint an African American to the position of minister to Haiti. It was Frederick Douglass, not Samuel McElwee. Formerly prominent Republican African Americans, now like McElwee turned out of office, far exceeded the number of appointments that the Republicans were willing to make to African Americans.[74] There is no indication that, after losing out for the most prominent appointment of an African American in the Harrison administration, McElwee received any position. He may have received an offer he refused. Another former African-American Tennessee legislator, Thomas Sykes, could do no better with the new administration than to secure the position of elevator operator in the federal customs house.[75]

African-American Republicans were in competition with white Republicans, too, for patronage. Many whites had been displaced and in some cases exiled, as McElwee had been. For example, the former white county clerk of Haywood County, Poston's successor, wrote to Houk asking for assistance.[76] Ike K. Revelle wrote to Houk in 1889 from the Northwest Territory. Revelle had impeccable Republican credentials. His father had served with Poston in the Union army volunteers and had been killed at Fort Pillow. Revelle married Poston's daughter Eugenia, cementing a bond between the families of two brothers in arms, both staunch Republicans. He had served in the legislature with McElwee. Prominent white Republicans with antisecessionist pasts came under close scrutiny and suffered reprisals at this time of Democratic triumph; many competed with African Americans for patronage appointments.[77]

McElwee's fortunes within the Republican party declined at this time also because the party now disavowed its own record on behalf of freedmen and its African-American former leaders. Some Republican leaders in West Tennessee and Congressman Houk in Knoxville did not participate in this

Fig. 8. The Negro Building, Tennessee Centennial Exposition, 1897. From *Official History of the Tennessee Centennial Exposition*, edited by Herman Justi (Nashville: Brandon Printing Co., 1898).

"lily-white movement." Nevertheless, with the disfranchisement of African-American men in the wake of 1889 legislation, Republican leaders had less reason to fight for the continued prominence of African Americans in their party.[78]

In resolving tensions between white and black Republicans, with their differences over race issues, the national Republican party had been guided by the two reasons that Brownlow had put forward in 1867 for giving the franchise to freedmen: first, to gain a margin of victory over Democrats; and, second, to do what was right. With disfranchisement, the margin of victory disappeared. Republicans had a choice. They could protest the disfranchisement of African-American men and attempt to restore the ballot to this minority, who could no longer deliver the southern states in national elections. Or they could seek a new margin of victory in a restricted electorate among white voters in the moderate portions of the Democratic party.

The latter strategy reduced tensions within the Republican party. With a diminished political role for African Americans within the party, Republicans had less reason to fight over race issues. From 1867 to 1888, African Americans were elected to office and held power to the extent that they held absolute superiority in numbers or a balance of power in a place. Without superior numbers or a balance of power, African-American voters could be ignored by Republicans and Democrats alike. Republicans could contest Democrats on other issues to garner white votes. Their ranks would be solid, because fewer African Americans would be allowed into them, and those allowed would be more moderate. African-American protests against this strategy strengthened such arguments by white Republican leaders.

This strategy, implicit for some Republicans and explicit for others, gave the party leaders less incentive to seek the election of African Americans in districts where they were the overwhelming majority. It also gave them less incentive to promote any African American to a visible leadership role within the party. The party's reasons to defend African Americans lessened as the antisecessionist generation, especially those in West Tennessee (such as Poston and those who supported McElwee's bid for the position in Haiti) grew old and lost influence in the party. For example, John Poston died in 1884, and his brother died in 1890. McElwee's considerable past accomplishments failed to translate into bright future political prospects because of changed conditions within the Republican party, both in Tennessee and in the nation, and in the electorate in the South.[79]

McElwee gradually moved from a public to a private career, from public spaces to private ones. He developed a substantial law practice in Nashville and formed part of the African-American professional elite there. His previous public notoriety kept him in the limelight among African Americans, especially at Fisk, his alma mater. In the first half of 1890, McElwee spoke at Fisk four times. His reputation as an orator stimulated high expectations among his audiences, and McElwee delivered. His speech "Twenty-Five Years in the South" emphasized the paramount importance of the race problem and protested whites' demeaning characterizations of African Americans, such as calling the latter "gregarious." In 1890, McElwee began a short stint as editor of a newspaper that he and a friend started.

Over the decade, McElwee faded from public view. The publications of Fisk continued to mention his accomplishments in the 1880s,[80] but his appearances at Fisk grew fewer and less prominent. In 1896, he spoke at Fisk's thirtieth anniversary. In February 1898, McElwee joined prominent African Americans at memorial services for John M. Langston, father-in-law of James C. Napier, Nashville's most prominent African American at the time.

McElwee did not speak at the event. Nor had he spoken on 14 June 1897 at Fisk University Day at the Tennessee Centennial Exposition. Instead, Napier spoke "in behalf of the colored citizens of Nashville."

"WE ARE NOW ON TRIAL"

McElwee's absence at the Tennessee Centennial Exposition program reflected significant changes in the place of African Americans in national politics. In the last decade of the nineteenth century, several expositions demonstrated the status of African Americans, including the role of covert and overt protest against that status. For a time McElwee served on the executive committee of the Negro Department of the Tennessee Centennial Exposition. He thus had a hand in organizing a grand symbol of the politics of reduced freedom and racial repression so prominent in the last decade of the nineteenth century.[81]

In 1896, as the U.S. Supreme Court deliberated on the case *Plessy* v. *Ferguson* , the Negro Department of the Tennessee Centennial Exposition eloquently expressed the new spirit of race relations. The Spanish Renaissance architecture of the Negro Building proclaimed the contemporary absorption with Spain and its empire. Within a year of the exposition's opening, America was at war with Spain; in six months our nation had wrested the mantle of empire from that faded power. In so doing, the United States accepted southern views on the necessity and appropriateness of recognizing differences among races. These views included the beliefs that the white race was superior to all others and that white people must wait patiently as people of other races acquired the education and prosperity needed before they could govern themselves. The U.S. Supreme Court, in *Plessy* v. *Ferguson*, provided the constitutional authority to maintain "separate but equal" facilities, including schools. This decision formally inaugurated the Jim Crow era and repudiated the Reconstruction experiment with democratic equality. The colonizing experience of the United States thus began with the simultaneous subjugation of nonwhite races both at home in the South and abroad. In the 1890s, America exported its views on racial subordination across the oceans to Cuba, the Philippines, and Puerto Rico. After circumnavigating the globe, that subjugation returned to America as a renewed commitment to racial inequality.[82] As John W. Burgess, whose views would dominate American historiography for half a century, observed at the time:

> The Republican party, in its work of imposing the sovereignty of the United States upon eight millions of Asiatics, has changed its views in regard to the political relations of races, and has at last virtually accepted the ideas of the South upon that subject. The white men of the South need now have no further fear that the Republican party, or Republican administrations, will ever again give themselves over to the vain imagination of the political equality of man.[83]

The Negro Building of the Tennessee Centennial Exposition attested to the reconciliation of the North and the South on racial matters. According to the official history of the exposition, "The South has been misunderstood and grossly misrepresented, and it therefore hopes that investigation will do what argument has failed to accomplish." The Negro Building offered whites from the North the opportunity to investigate how "the white race in the South has shown its friendliness by affording the negro race a splendid opportunity to show what they can do, and they will rejoice to find that the opportunity has been wisely and magnificently improved." The exhibits also affirmed the southern contention that "the natural home of the negro is in the South; its climate is best suited to his physical nature, and its people, though once his master, are his natural friends. None other understand him so well or so readily win his affection and respect."[84]

The accomplishments of African Americans displayed in the three hundred different exhibits in the Negro Building demonstrated "that the white and black people of the South understand each other perfectly and do, if left to themselves, get along as pleasantly and peaceably as any two races that ever dwelt together in any other country or in any other age."[85] McElwee served on the executive committee of the Negro Department for a while but apparently stopped participating before the building opened. His reasons may have been political. On the other hand, he and his wife were beset with personal tragedies at this time. Four of their six infant children died between 1890 and 1899.[86]

While McElwee's reasons for dropping from the committee are not clear, other prominent African-American leaders discouraged participation in expositions of this type for political reasons. Ida B. Wells, for example, had opposed African-American participation in the Columbian Exposition in Chicago in 1893. By this time she had achieved national recognition as a columnist, writing in several newspapers under the pen name "Iola." Wells began a crusade against lynching and measured racial matters by the occurrence of and lack of punishment for lynching.[87] She placed the arrangements for African Americans at the Columbian Exposition in the context of racial repression.[88]

Wells collaborated with Frederick Douglass on a pamphlet to protest the neglect of African Americans in the planning and conduct of the fair. President Harrison had named a large commission to plan the exposition, without an African-American member. Wells and Douglass set themselves up in the Haitian exposition. Douglass had completed his ministry in Haiti in 1891. He retained sufficient influence and respect in that country to serve as Haiti's commissioner to the exposition.[89] Foreign visitors to the Haitian exposition received copies of the pamphlet prepared by Wells and Douglass.

Wells broke ranks with Douglass over the conduct of Negro Day at the exposition. Wells criticized fair organizers for promoting the day with two thousand free watermelons and lamented the consequences she anticipated: "The spectacle of the class of our people who will come on that excursion roaming around the grounds munching watermelon will do more to lower the race in the estimation of the world than anything else." Douglass saw the day as a platform. He gave a speech that day that articulated the alienation of the African American. It was not his prepared speech but a spontaneous reaction to jeers from some white men in the audience. He struck the themes of the Tennessee State Convention of Colored Citizens three decades earlier: "There is no Negro problem. The problem is whether the American people have loyalty enough, honor enough, patriotism enough, to live up to their own Constitution. . . . We Negroes love our country. We fought for it. We ask only that we be treated as well as those who fought against it." Douglass protested the fact that reconciliation of northern and southern whites entailed excluding African Americans from American life in general and the Colombian Fair in particular. Wells boycotted Negro Day, but newspaper accounts convinced her that Douglass had made a magnificent achievement out of two potential disasters, Negro Day itself and the initial heckling at his speech.[90]

Despite Douglass' achievement, the fact remained that the Columbian

Exposition offered African Americans much to protest. The Tennessee Centennial Exposition too had flaws, but there protest took the subtler and sometimes contradictory form of efforts to disprove racist assumptions. In Nashville, the Negro Bureau, without McElwee, accepted the opportunity, as Wells had put it, "to pace before the world." Richard Hill, chairman of the executive committee of the Negro Department of the Centennial Exposition, explained at the cornerstone ceremony:

> We are now on trial—the most severe test as to what we have done, and are now doing, since our emancipation. The American people have spent no small amount of money and energy for our intellectual and moral training. Many are now asking, What has it all amounted to?
>
> Now is the time to prove all this. The managers of the Tennessee Centennial have given us, at a cost of nearly $13,000, the most beautiful building on the grounds (250 x 100, three stories), and have placed it on the prettiest site. The Southern railroads have generously offered to bring our exhibits and return them free of charge. *They have also granted us equal railroad accommodations.* In fact, everything that could be done for us has been done, except to make the exhibits.
>
> Our duty, then, is plain. If we fail to do it, it will be to our everlasting shame.[91] [Emphasis added.]

The Negro Building of the Tennessee Centennial Exposition was separate and had the appearance of being equal. Speaker after speaker extolled the building as an example of what white and black southerners could do, separately. The exhibitions in the building demonstrated the achievements of African Americans and constituted a measure of change when compared with such exhibits at preceding expositions—New Orleans, 1885, and Atlanta, 1895. The white organizers of the centennial reduced fares on Negro Day to twenty-five cents for adults and ten cents for children. This permitted record crowds of African Americans to attend.

In the ceremonies of the Negro Building, history was rewritten to explain the Jim Crow era of which the building was a part. Past divisions were seen as those between master and slave, white and black. The pro-Union, antisecessionist, radical Republican past was removed from the history of the white race. The organized political efforts of African-American voters, the

Union Leagues and the Conventions of Colored Men, and the sophisticated efforts to form coalitions with parties and factions earned no mention. In the South, war monuments, such as the one in the courthouse square in Brownsville, commemorated the county's dead but only those of the Confederate side. Among those not commemorated by the monument were the Haywood County men killed in Union army uniforms at Fort Pillow.

If memories remained of this complicated political past, people were encouraged to purge them. Speaker after speaker, at programs in the Negro Building, portrayed as mistakes past efforts to secure the political participation of African Americans. This new blend of voice and loyalty disguised the dwindling opportunities for African Americans to exit their condition and accommodated to white power. In place of politics, African Americans were being given the opportunity to prove themselves both worthy of Anglo-Saxon esteem and qualified for the benefits of that esteem. The official history of the exposition explained the disfranchisement of African Americans as a positive step toward reducing the confusion of the black race and helping its members to concentrate on hard work as the surest means of improvement:

> Thirty-odd years ago a race was emancipated and, in a sense, left to battle for itself. Its struggle for a livelihood was complicated by political obligations for which it was not prepared by previous experience. Suffrage and office-holding were novelties, and to exercise the one and obtain the other seemed to occupy its entire time and obscure every other object in life. . . . The negro race is not alone in its shortsighted policy of exaggerating the importance of the political problem and their part in its solution. Great nations have risen, flourished, and extended their empire without consulting the masses—without popular elections. . . . The problem of self-help . . . is more important, more interesting and more fruitful of good results than the pursuit of politics or of office-holding. There is work for all; there are offices for only a very few.[92]

Booker T. Washington came to Nashville and to the Negro Building on Emancipation Day. He repeated themes that became the unofficial terms of reconciliation between the races in the South. These would be repeated regularly as a conservative credo by some African Americans.[93] First, the problem was a "Negro problem," not one of both races or a "Caucasian problem," and the political remedies of the past were inappropriate.[94] Second, the appropriate remedies would come from economic development and recognition that the African American was starting at the bottom. Third, civil rights would flow from economic achievement. Fourth, the adversity of the slave past actually prepared people for solving current problems. As Justi, writing the *Official History of the Tennessee Centennial Exposition* (1898), commented: "These results come to the negro as to all races, by beginning at the bottom and working gradually up toward the highest civilization and accomplishments. . . . In all history can you find a race that possessed property, industry, intelligence, and character, that has long been denied its rights? . . . Every large plantation in the South during slavery was, in a measure, an industrial school."[95]

The tenets of the Tuskegee Creed announced at the Tennessee Centennial appealed to white people in Nashville, the South, and Washington, D.C. Past political efforts had been mistaken, so their repudiation was justified. Slavery had had positive features that could contribute to solving the problems of the day. Finally, the economic progress of African Americans awaited their own effort, and their civil rights awaited their economic progress.

Washington told his Nashville audience that blacks and whites had mutual interests that they ignored at their own peril:

> My white friends, we are bound together by a tie which we cannot tear asunder if we would. There is no escape; you must help us raise the character of our civilization or yours will be lowered.
>
> My friends of the white race, we are one in this country. The question of the highest citizenship and the complete education of all concerns eight million of my people and sixty million of yours. We rise as you rise; when we fall you fall; when we are strong you are strong; when we are weak you are weak; there is no power that can separate our destiny. No member of your race can harm the weakest or meanest of my race without the proudest and bluest blood in your civilization being degraded. The negro can afford to be wronged; the white man cannot afford to wrong him. Unjust laws or customs injure the white man and inconvenience the negro.

Finally, Washington's major appeal, especially to African Americans, was to turn the deprivation and past repression of African Americans into a moral advantage. Pride and dignity were within the reach of African Americans, if they looked inward for their capacity to suffer the wrongdoing of others towards them:

> I propose that the negro take his place upon the high ground of usefulness, forgiveness, and generosity, and that he invite the white man everywhere to step up and occupy this position with him, and if the white man cannot accept the invitation we will then prove that this is a white man's problem rather than a negro problem.
>
> . . . No race can wrong another race simply because it has the power, without being narrowed and dragged down in its moral status. We are a patient, humble race. There is plenty in this country for us to do. Away up in the atmosphere of goodness, forbearance, patience, and forgiveness, the workers are not many or overcrowded. If others would be little, we can be great; if others would be mean, we can be good; if others would push us down, we can push them up. Character, not circumstances, makes the man.[96]

As the nineteenth century closed, the condition of African Americans had not changed much since the beginning of Reconstruction. Previous reforms had been revoked and discredited. The most notable change of the 1890s was the diminution of hope for civil rights and the muffling of protest over the economic conditions of African Americans. The loudest voice of the time, that of Booker T. Washington, urged loyalty to the contemporary political and economic system and to the people who ruled it. His position precluded political remedies to the problems of African Americans, neglected college and professional training in its emphasis on industrial and trade training, and, in its sermonlike emphasis on starting life at the bottom and in providing no time frame for achieving any higher starting point, seemed to advocate perpetual subservience.

There were African Americans who dissented from Washington's views and resented his prominence. One such dissenter was John Hope, a faculty member at Roger Williams College in Nashville, who later became president of Morehouse University in Atlanta. On Washington's Birthday, 1896, at a time midway between the Atlanta exposition and the Tennessee Centennial Exposition, Hope addressed the Negro Debating Society of Nashville, expressing views sharply at odds with Washington's:

If we are not striving for equality, in heaven's name for what are we living? I regard it cowardly and dishonest for any of our colored men to tell white people or colored people that we are not struggling for equality. . . . Let us not fool ourselves nor be fooled by others. If we cannot do what other free-men do, then we are not free. Yes, my friends, I want equality. Nothing less. I want all that my God-given powers will enable me to get, then why not equality? Now, catch your breath, for I am going to use an adjective: I am going to say that we demand *social* equality. In this republic we shall be less than freemen, if we have a whit less than that which thrift, education, and honor afford other freemen. If equality, political, economic, and social, is the boon of other men in this great country of ours, of *ours*, then equality, politi-cal, economic, and social, is what we demand. Why build a wall to keep me out? I am no wild beast, nor am I an unclean thing.[97]

Speakers like Hope with dissenting views stood far from the general public, occupying only those segregated public spaces remaining among African Americans. McElwee's eloquence was no longer heard in public places. Forced from the forum of the legislature, he steadily yielded platforms within the African-American community as well.

McElwee's history exemplified the opportunity available in the late nine-teenth century for an African American to make incredible advances within one lifetime. His career and personal fortune far exceeded what had been available to him or his family in slavery. The pitfalls he encountered exem-plified the fate awaited those who attempted to advance African Americans as a group. Like the political reforms of the 1860s, which had made his rise possible and which by the 1890s had been revoked, McElwee's meteoric political career ended in an apolitical place set aside for him. It was as if the advice implied in the state supreme court's opinion in Wells's railroad case had become national practice. African Americans were expected to ask only for "a comfortable seat for a short ride." In 1901, McElwee moved to Chi-cago, where the voice of hope for emancipation could still be heard, albeit in places primarily located within the African-American community.

The Interregnum of Emancipation
1901–1954

Freedom's Surrogate
1901–1940

3 Samuel McElwee arrived in Chicago the day after Independence Day, 1901. Chicago offered him, and the tens of thousands of African Americans it attracted in the next two decades, greater opportunities and different race relations. Back in Haywood County, social and economic relations between the races had solidified in a social order with African Americans at the bottom, with few rights. Chicago and Haywood County exemplified very different stages of race relations coexisting within the nation in the first two decades of the twentieth century. On a personal level, McElwee's two families lived in very different worlds. McElwee's grandchildren, who remained in Haywood County, and his daughters, who grew up in Chicago, embodied polarities among African Americans.

CHICAGO AND THE CREATIVE YEARS, 1900–1914

McElwee's arrival in Chicago preceded the mass migration of African Americans that was to begin in 1914. The time from 1900 to 1914 was one of great change in the city. During this period, from her base in Chicago, Hull House, Jane Addams led several movements for social change in the United States. These years, which largely coincided with McElwee's time in Chicago, were the "creative years" of Hull House.[1]

One of fourteen thousand African Americans to move to Chicago between 1900 and 1910, McElwee became one of the city's forty-six African-American attorneys. In his new home he found a social and economic system very different from that of the South, where an increasingly rigid caste system separated white and black races. This caste system prevented African Ameri-

Greatest Circulation in THE MIDDLE WEST. also A Time.

A Sacred Memory of 200 Lynched Heroes of the United States During the Past Year.

The Chicago Defender.

If You See It In The DEFENDER, It's So.

PRICE 5 CENTS

VOLUME V— NUMBER 53. CHICAGO, ILLINOIS, SATURDAY, DECEMBER 31, 1910.

MRS. J. E. WRIGHT APPEAL

THE WOMAN'S COTERIE CLUB

Applauds Their President After She Finished Her Paper and Defender Representatives Published Same For a Program

THE INQUIRY

5,000 ATTEND BALL

Knights of Pythias Makes Sweep—Greatest Gathering of Any in Years.

LITTLE EGYPT ABSENT.

DR. E. R. ROBINSON LOSES ONLY SON BY DEATH.

End Came To Young Man In Michigan, Was At One Time a Flat University Student. The Doctor Will Bring Youth At Mt. Glenwood For Family.

NICKEL SAVINGS BANK GOES UNDER.

Could Not Stand Pressure—New Officials Did Not Take Charge—Depositors Will Lose All—May Reopen.

PLEA OF THE EDITOR.

WHEN IN THE LAST DAYS OF DEPARTING YEAR WE LOOK BACKWARD AND SEE THE BODIES OF 200 HEROES LYNCHED AND 900 INNOCENTS PUNISHED BY TWO-THIRDOOD BY OUR SOUTHERN WHITE FRIENDS, WE MOURN AND SEND A REQUEST TO THE GOVERNMENT. THE GREATEST WE WORLD HAS EVER SEEN WHICH WOULD EMPLOY OUR CRIMES TO BE INSTITUTED IN HER DOMAIN. BLOOD WE SHARE OUR INTERESTS WILL SHARE WITH YOU IN RAISING A DESERTING VOICE, AND WE LOOK FORWARD TO A MORE HAPPY NEW YEAR FOR THE MOB OF OUR AMERICAN MINISTERS, WHO DURING A LYNCHING HAVE THEY TRIED TO STOP THE MOB OR OFFER A PRAYER FOR THE LYNCHED WHILE OTHERS OF THE WEALTHY WHO REST IN THEIR POSITION. THE WE HUMBLY BEG GODS MERCY ON THE AMERICAN GOVERNMENT AND ITS CITIZENS.

THE EDITOR.

Fig. 9. The front page of one of the few "voices" of African-American protest in 1910, the *Chicago Defender* (31 December).

cans, despite wealth, education, or accomplishments, from achieving a status equal to that of the lowest class of white people. African Americans, as a caste, rested on the bottom of a pyramid-shaped society. Among them, a blunted class structure emerged from the base of society like the stump of a tree cut down after the reforms of Reconstruction. McElwee had belonged to an educated, affluent African-American professional elite in Nashville. No matter how high African Americans like McElwee might rise, however, they remained rooted in the bottom of society, never seen as the equals of white men and women of comparable or less education and professional experience.[2]

In Chicago, McElwee found a more open society; here he had the chance to excel in his profession. He traveled to Chicago to conduct a three million dollar lawsuit involving a railway company—an opportunity unavailable to him in Tennessee.[3] One of the Chicago papers, *The Broad Ax*, took note of McElwee's arrival in Chicago. Monthly, an article appeared relating the development of his law practice and other activities. For example, the paper reported that on 1 September 1901, McElwee spoke before the South End Sunday Club on "The Needs and Possibilities of the Negro in the Twentieth Century." McElwee opened an office on South Clark Street in downtown Chicago, where, *The Broad Ax* assured its readers, "Mr. McElwee is amply prepared for all kinds of law business."[4] He lived with his wife and three children on Forest Avenue, in an affluent African-American section of Chicago. They attended Quinn Chapel, a prestigious church for African Americans. *The Chicago Defender* claimed that there were two kinds of Colored Methodist churches in Chicago, those that applauded and those that didn't. The congregation of Quinn Chapel was the kind that did not applaud.[5]

Chicago in this decade became a biracial society. The thousand African-American professionals of Chicago developed a class structure rising like a sapling from the truncated reforms of Reconstruction, as talented and accomplished African Americans now migrated to Chicago from the South. Affluent African Americans in Chicago were affluent Chicagoans; their society existed parallel to white society and touched it at all levels.[6] Within this class structure, African-American aspirations and protests found voice. Ida B. Wells, who had first come to Chicago to protest the Columbian Exposition, remained in Chicago, becoming increasingly active and increasingly prominent. At this same time, McElwee completed his withdrawal from public life and his disengagement from political issues. In the years both lived in Chicago, there is no indication that McElwee and Wells associated with each other or moved in the same circles. Wells remained a very political person, of whom we know much. In Chicago, McElwee became a very private person who left little record of his later years. *The Broad Ax* continued to report on McElwee's travels and activities, though less frequently, until 1905. After that, the paper noted, "if he continues to forge to the front in the next two or three years, he will be compelled to occupy a much larger suite of offices."[7] In fact, he later moved his office to Twelfth and Halsted, a predominantly white area not far from Hull House. His clients at this location were primarily Jewish.

Distance, caste, and class loosened McElwee's ties with the children of his first marriage, whom, as we have seen, McElwee left in the care of their grandparents when his first wife died in 1885. Georgia Shelton McElwee, McElwee's second wife, was biracial and had very light skin. McElwee's grandchildren in Haywood County even mistook her for white, from the pictures they saw of her. Sam's father had been biracial, too, and the children of Sam's second marriage were light in color. The prospect that his three daughters might assimilate into white society in Chicago distanced his Haywood County family more than mere geography necessitated.[8]

Occasionally, events from McElwee's rural southern past intersected with his life in Chicago. Wells, for example, led a vociferous protest among African Americans in Chicago over an incident dramatizing the violence endemic in sharecropping. In 1909, in December—still "settling up time" for landlords and sharecroppers—Steve Green, an African-American farmer in Jericho, Arkansas, who was originally from West Tennessee, informed his landlord that he intended to leave at the end of his contract for the current crop to take a better offer from another landlord. His landlord warned him that if he left, the county would not be big enough for both of them. Green left anyway, and his landlord, with three other men, came to Green's cabin to make good on the threat. The gang shot Green four times before he got his rifle from his cabin and began shooting back. One of his shots killed his former landlord.

Green then fled. He took refuge in a friend's cabin, but the mobs searching for him made it dangerous for anyone to shelter him. Green took precautions against the mobs and their hounds, filling his shoes with pepper and even at one time wallowing with hogs in mud to keep the hounds off his trail. He escaped and eventually reached Illinois and Chicago.

An acquaintance in Chicago disclosed his presence there, and Arkansas authorities sought his return. While awaiting extradition in a Chicago jail, Green attempted suicide by eating ground glass. Wells learned of Green's plight through a newspaper account of his suicide attempt. She understood that his extradition to Arkansas meant his lynching. She intervened to prevent this, asking an attorney to take some action to protect Green. He obtained a petition for a writ of habeas corpus and a stay of extradition. Local police disregarded the stay and, without notifying the attorney or the courts, released Green to the custody of Arkansas authorities. Other Illinois authorities, responding to Wells's demand, literally raced to retrieve Green before the train on which he and the Arkansas law officers traveled crossed the Ohio River and left Illinois jurisdiction. Green recounted that his guard assured him that he was the most important "nigger in the United States since there was a reception committee of a thousand waiting for him in Arkansas with a lighted fire." At the last moment, before the train crossed the river at Cairo, the county sheriff arrived and removed Green for return to Chicago.

In Chicago Green found a system of justice different from the one he had known in Arkansas. First, the courts held the police accountable for their actions towards an African American. The Chicago police who had released Green faced charges of contempt for disregarding the court's orders. Second, a judge agreed with the arguments of Green's three lawyers, presented in a hearing that lasted six and a half hours, about the danger that awaited Green in Arkansas. The judge denied extradition and ordered Green released from the custody of the Chicago police. Chicago African-American newspapers reported the story in terms "thrilling and vital enough to remind one of the many miraculous escapes of our forefathers in slavery days."[9] Moreover, the trial set a precedent. It involved Chicago's African-American community in the defense of a fugitive from the new slavery of sharecropping. Green's attorneys were African American, not white men. They were able to establish important legal points that implied the inability or unwillingness of a southern state to protect African Americans from lynchings. These momentous outcomes were attributed to Ida B. Wells, "that watchdog of human life and liberty."[10] A few days after the trial, Green spoke at a public rally at Quinn Chapel. Although McElwee was an active member of Quinn Chapel, there is no mention of his presence at the meeting nor of his participation in any of the events surrounding the Green case.[11]

Chicago established another precedent without McElwee just a few months later. In November 1910, African Americans in Chicago joined the Democratic tide in the national election. Old alliances between them and the Republican party were broken. The reasons offered echoed those given by the few African Americans in Tennessee in the 1870s who broke with the Republicans there. The party had not offered African Americans positions in the party or in government in proportion to their support. *The Chicago Defender* captured the significance of this shift in its headline: "Boys of 1870 [African-American men of the Reconstruction era] Have Sworn to Vote Democratic if Jim Crow Cars, Lynchings, White Men Living With Black Wenches Are Not Made to Marry, and the Former Entirely Abolished."[12]

McElwee, one of the "boys of 1870," withstood these changes and remained a staunch Republican. A man who had been caught up in events of the 1880s and had made his mark on them, he died in 1914 with "the wish of the family that quietness shall prevail." Having been associated with many who provided important leadership in the pursuit of racial justice, McElwee died outside their circles. The *Fisk Herald* eulogized that his death "deprives us of one of the most learned members of the bar in our race." The Chicago African-American newspapers printed lengthy obituaries noting his prominence as a Chicago attorney and describing his political activity in Tennessee.[13] Back in that state, white newspapers noted McElwee's death and recalled his distinguished career as a "reasonable" spokesman for African-American interests. This veneer of admiration seemed thin, in light of the white majority's unwillingness to support the modest proposals of this "reasonable" legislator. The admiration also ignored McElwee's losing battle in the 1880s to forestall regressive changes in race relations.

The *Nashville Banner*, the Republican newspaper, eulogized McElwee in genteel, racist terms. Its obituary extolled McElwee for staying in his place: "He was never a partisan, but labored hard and conscientiously for the betterment of his state and his race. On no question did he ever make himself offensive, and in no instance was he ever known to intrude himself into any presence where on account of his race he would be unwelcome." The notice went on to diminish the luster of McElwee's achievements. It made no mention of his law degree; cited two legislative terms, not three; and timed his law practice in Nashville at one or two years, not twelve. The obituary did offer the highest praise possible for an African American within the racial caste system: "He was a real Negro with no foreign blood in his veins, and in point of intelligence was the equal of any member of his race that has ever risen to prominence in the nation."[14]

When McElwee was nominated for speaker of the Tennessee General Assembly in 1885, a supporter described him as "the peer of any member" of the legislature. Thirty years later, no African American, whatever his accomplishments, could be viewed as comparable to white people.

"ANOTHER LONG STEP
OF COOPERATION"

The distance that geography, time, class, and caste had created between Samuel McElwee and his Haywood County family delayed their receipt of the news of his death. Word came to the McElwees in Haywood County from a family member in Memphis. Robert, his grandson remembered:

> Aunt Minnie, she lived in Memphis, she told papa that his daddy was dead. He came home and told my mother. He said, "Papa dead." She said, "Uh, uh, uh. And Sam was just here too." She said she would pack papa's grip for him to go. And he said there was no need for her to wash and press his shirt. Mama said, "Aren't you going to your daddy's funeral?!" in that very way. He said, "Papa's been dead a week."

The gulf within the McElwee family suggests the distance separating some African Americans from others at the time. In Chicago race relations might have changed, but in Haywood County economic subordination and political repression remained their hallmarks. By the time of McElwee's death, these twins of oppression constituted an ironclad system of class and caste.

On the evening of 23 November 1909, a train arrived in Brownsville bearing Booker T. Washington and his advocacy of limited freedom for African Americans. For the previous five days, Washington had conducted an "educational pilgrimage" through Tennessee and parts of Kentucky. Brownsville was one of the last stops on this pilgrimage. To avoid both the embarrassment of assigning Washington second-class facilities and the legal and extralegal repercussions of providing him first-class accommodations, railroad companies circumvented Jim Crow laws by providing a separate train for his exclusive use on this trip. During the week, Washington spoke in twenty-two cities to audiences totaling fifty thousand people; a third as many more had to be turned away at the doors of halls filled to capacity. Some twenty thousand white people joined his audiences.

The correspondent for the *New York Evening Post* reported the tour "promises to be long remembered as an event of immeasurable benefit, not only to the Negroes of this state, but throughout the whole South."

> Certain it is that this state-wide tour will leave its impress on the white people of Tennessee, as well as on the black. They have flocked to hear Dr. Washington by the thousand, and nine out of every ten white men who have heard him have gone away convinced that his solution of the problem is the true one. It is not too much to say that these men will take the earliest opportunity to put into practice, or to assist the Negroes in putting into practice, the gospel that this leader of his race is preaching.[15]

The gospel that Washington preached on this pilgrimage was essentially the same message he had delivered at the Atlanta and Tennessee expositions. The political content of his remarks drew special attention. He urged cooperation between the races, including in the political matters from which African Americans were now excluded:

> The Negro acts with his white neighbor in every walk of life but when election day comes along he goes in the opposite direction. When he learns that the white man whose lead he follows, whose advice he seeks every day in the year except one, may be just as good a leader or adviser on that day as any other, another long step toward the co-operation of the races will be taken.[16]

In contrast to African Americans in Chicago, who sought political voice by moving from the Republicans to the Democrats, Washington urged African Americans in Haywood County to remain loyal to the whites in politics.

Washington's message found adherents among the white people of his audience. Many expressed admiration for Washington. Some spoke of improved racial cooperation. The most complete statement, the one most frequently referred to during Washington's tour, was given by John R. Bond, circuit court judge in Brownsville. Bond expounded on a theme that McElwee had used twenty-five years earlier. At that time, McElwee had argued for specific public programs for African Americans to compensate them for the loyalty they showed while their masters fought in the Civil War. Now Bond suggested that white people repay that debt with personal kindness, not beneficial policies or laws, towards African Americans. He explained that as a southern white man he owed "a debt to the Negro that I can never repay":

> During the War, the Southern white man left his home, his wife and his children to be taken care of by the Negroes, and I have yet to hear of a single instance where that trust was betrayed or where they proved unfaithful, and ever since that time I have sworn by the Most Divine that I shall ever be grateful to the colored people as long as I shall live, and that I shall never be unfair to that race. I have always since thought that a white man is not a man who does not admit that he owes a duty in the sight of God to the colored people of this country. . . . If there was ever a people in this country who owed a debt to any people, it is the Southern white man to the Southern colored man.

Bond made no reference to the image of rapacious, insolent "negroes" that Forrest had invoked to explain the Klan's efforts to defend themselves and that D. W. Griffith would soon revive in his film *The Birth of a Nation*. Nor did Bond refer to the thousands of exslaves who took up arms to defend their freedom in places such as Fort Pillow. Twenty years after the systematic, legal disfranchisement of African Americans began in Tennessee, Bond regaled his audience with stories of loyal and devoted African Americans who apparently had been content in slavery. The pendulum of white people's depictions of African Americans, swinging between Sambo and savage, was back in the Sambo portion of its arc. The savage had been tamed and the democratic genie returned to its bottle. Without the threat of the African-American savage to justify overt economic subordination and political repression, southern whites now reverted to arguing that African Americans were content with these conditions.[17]

The personification of this devotion and contentment was the "mammy." Bond illustrated his debt to African Americans with a story of his own mammy. Bond's mother had died when he was an infant, he said, and an "old black mammy," whom he never mentioned by name, "took me in her arms and nursed me and cared for me and loved me until I grew strong and to manhood." Later, when Bond was a father, the "old black mammy" continued her steadfast loyalty to his family, even risking her own life. The youngest of Bond's children, he recounted, had smallpox, and another was thought to be contracting it. The second child had to be quarantined alone, since it was not safe for Bond or his wife to attend to her:

> But just about that time the old black mammy, this same black mammy who nursed and cared for me, appeared. Black mammy was heard from. "Smallpox or no smallpox, that child cannot stay in that room by herself tonight or no other night, even if she takes the smallpox and dies tomorrow"; and she did go into that room and stayed in that room until morning, and was willing to stay there as long as it was necessary. God bless her old soul!

Bond then summarized the hopeful message that whites had sent in response to Washington's tour. It combined admiration of Washington, dedication to improvement of the condition of African Americans, and condescension.

> I am glad to see Mr. Washington here and to have him speak to us. He is a credit to his race, and would be a credit to any race. I wish we had more men like him all over this country.
>
> Mr. Washington, I pray to God that the Spirit may ever guide you in your purpose to lift up your people and that you may inspire all Southern white men as well as Southern colored men to lift up and elevate your race.

Bond assumed that African Americans were at the bottom of society, from whence they could be lifted. In Chicago, at the time of Bond's comments, African Americans were urging the abolition of restrictions that prevented African Americans from rising on their own. And in Arkansas, Steve Green was about to become a fugitive as a result of his efforts to better his position in society.

In terms of race relations, reporters from national newspapers treated the South as a land apart. They marveled at Bond's speech, reported it widely, and noted the optimism it inspired. They overlooked the image of African Americans as powerless, as well as the violence that image had required. Emancipation efforts were ignored and, in their place, Bond and the reporters depicted loving interracial relationships of fidelity and service. Reporters used Bond's speech to distinguish relations between black and white people in the North and those in the South:

> The paradox of Southern life, from the point of view of a Northerner who does not understand the local conditions, is that while Southern people frequently seem opposed to Negroes in the mass, the personal relations between the races are on the whole kindly. These friendly personal relations between individual colored men and individual white men, Mr. Washington insists, must be made the basis for the final reconstruction of the Southern States.[18]

GRANDPA SAM—HERO OF THE WORLD
AND A MISSING GENERATION

In Washington's talk in Brownsville, he stressed rural life. He urged his audience to stay in the country, acquire land, and raise their children in an environment which he viewed as better than that of urban areas. He acknowledged that the inadequacy of schools, which had stimulated his trip, impeded satisfactory life in rural areas. Washington placed the burden of improving rural education on white citizens. His message gained enthusiastic support from both white and black people in his audience.

The McElwee family personified this Tuskegee Creed. When Washington's train came to Haywood County, Samuel McElwee's father and mother were still there, farming the land they had bought and held onto. They had raised Samuel McElwee's son, Robert, as their own son. In 1908, Robert and Georgianna McElwee, Sam's parents, deeded over to Sam's son, Robert, the fifty-six acres they still owned.[19] The land was an important guarantee that

Robert would not someday have to defend himself from a white landlord, as Steve Green had done in nearby Arkansas. Robert McElwee, Sam's son, not only was a land-owner but was educated as well. He taught school, as his father had done, and preached in a local church. By Haywood County standards for African Americans, the McElwee family was educated and prosperous. They personified the individual economic achievement that Washington extolled for African Americans in rural areas. The family was highly regarded by whites and blacks within the county's caste system and occupied the second highest rank in the class system of the county's African Americans. Professionals, ministers, and merchants in the towns of the county occupied the highest rank in that class order.

Robert McElwee, Jr., Samuel McElwee's grandson, was born the year that Washington's train came to Haywood County. He was one of the twelve children of Robert McElwee, the son of Samuel McElwee and his first wife. Robert, Jr., remembered a visit by his grandfather to Haywood County in fall 1914, when he was five years old. His recollections indicated that the McElwee family was a space in which values were imparted and upheld. Among these values were intergenerational authority. Here the children also learned how skin color dictated caste and class differences among African Americans, even in their own family:

> My father would mind him (Grandpa Sam) just like he wasn't married himself. I was just a little boy and it looked funny to me. Grandpa Sam would come in and tell my daddy what to do and he would mind him. Grandpa Sam took the darkness from his mother. She was African. His father, Grandpa Bob, was lighter. He was part Irishman.
>
> It seems like to me he had something on his mind last time I saw him. He looked like he was studying about something. It looked funny to me. He would hitch up the buggy before day and he would go to the place that he was going and stay all day until it was night. Then, when night come, he would come back in the night. And that's when I figured he was scared. They drove when it was dark. They were bound to be dodging. It was dark when they leave and when they come back. They had some friends in Brownsville. They would go down and see them, hide the horse and buggy.

Skin color was a factor in the Haywood County McElwees' relations with their Grandpa Sam. Robert remembered that Ruth, McElwee's daughter of his Chicago family, had a camera and that she offered to take pictures for a penny. He also remembered that his Grandpa Sam was anxious that the pictures not be shown in Chicago. Evidently he wanted his light family in Chicago kept separate, as much as possible, from his dark family in Haywood County.

Important class differences distinguished the McElwees of Chicago and those of Haywood County. Robert remembered Ruth as a "little lady" with manners unlike those of any other twelve-year-old girl he had met. Likewise, Robert remembered the novelty for Ruth of taking a bath in a tin tub, which was the only manner in which he and his brothers and sisters bathed. Eventually, skin color ended his grandfather's visit unexpectedly and frighteningly:

> My cousin was seventeen and she carried Ruth to church one evening. It frightened the neighbors. Ruth was so white they were afraid that the white folks wouldn't like it. They were afraid that the white people would think a white person was in our house. They would come and burn it up. Black neighbors came and said, "You had better hide her and tell Sam to get her out of here." They thought they would hang everybody.
>
> The next morning, before day, Grandpa Sam got up ready to leave. He left before day. I knew that he slipped out. I think he was scared. He went back to Chicago and we never heard from him since. That was the last time I saw him. A couple of weeks from then, he was dead.

Over the years, Robert and his brothers and sisters learned guarded respect for their Grandpa Sam. Robert guesses that his Grandpa Sam was missing from stories within the family because "when white people told Grandpa Sam to stay away, daddy was scared to say too much about him." Robert McElwee and his brothers and sisters did learn enough to understand that Grandpa Sam was part of a distant and different political past in the county. Robert McElwee remembered:

> Now, they tell me back in Haywood County it was good before it got terrible. Back when Grandpa Sam was pleading law, he was making it good for the black folks. Then I heard, there was a white woman in trouble and

she wanted him to plead her case. She told them that she didn't want no-body to plead for her but Sam McElwee. And they would do anything the white lady said, the white man would. They told Grandpa Sam he could plead the case if he came in the back door and don't let nobody see him. So he went down and pleaded the case.

Look like to me, that's what started it all. He won the case and I believe they got worried about that and they sent him away. From then on, it seemed like to me they ran him out of town. They gave him ten minutes to leave town. He took five of them and spoke. And he used the other five to leave town. He had men protecting him, white and black. When those guys got it in their head to get their Winchesters and guarded him until he got on the train, they were going to shoot those guns. You see it wasn't like it's come to be.

The way people told it, they blamed Grandpa Sam for leaving there. The way I see it, he had to leave there. The way I see it, he was probably running for his life.

Ethel McElwee Black, Robert's sister and another of Sam McElwee's grandchildren, also learned to be proud of her grandfather. She maintained her family name in marriage. Her Grandpa Sam was "a hero of the world" in those days: "He was a great person. We learned that he had started the institution at Bolivar [the mental hospital]. He started the fairgrounds for black people too."

In most respects, however, it was as if the family had missed a generation. Sam McElwee's father and mother were Grandpa and Grandma to his grand-children, his son's children. It was a tightly-knit family that wove four gen-erations into three. According to Robert McElwee:

Grandpa Bob was more of my grandpa than Grandpa Sam was. If I wasn't riding his neck, I was pulling his hair. If I wasn't pulling his hair, I was doing something. He would take me by the hand all the time when we was walk-ing. He was a good man.

Grandpa Bob was crazy about kids. He would hitch up the wagon and put all the kids on it and then ride down the river bank with one wheel down the slope of the river bank and all of the kids spilling out of the wagon. He would be scattering us out all over the road. All over the bank.

I remember time when a car would come, he would take his handker-
chief out of his pocket and he would flag a man down that was coming towards him in a car and tell him to stop it because his mules were scared of it.
And he used "By the way" all the time. He would say, "By the way, son," and
so and so and so and so. He used "By the way" all the time.

He would buy all the kids books and pencils and tablets and things. He
was crazy about us kids.

He couldn't read and he would count on us kids reading the newspaper
for him. Then, he would get out there on the creek and tell everybody what
happened.

There are some things I can remember so well. I can remember my
mother. I remember one day she was going to work and she said we were
going to have chicken for dinner. I was two or three years old. And she left. I
went into the yard and there was a hen carrying sixteen little chicks. I killed all
of them and put them under that tub. When my mother came back I met
her and I said, "Mama, I killed your chickens for you. All you got to do is
cook them." She cooked me too.

Robert McElwee and his sisters, all in their sixties and seventies at the
time they were interviewed, recalled with childlike glee how they would drag
the chair in which their great-grandmother Georgianna sat through the
kitchen and into their bedroom and encourage her to tell them stories. They
were particularly fond of stories of the times when she and their grandpa had
been slaves. One story explained how Georgianna used her father's money
to win her husband and escape field work. Ethel McElwee Black recounted:

My Grandma Georgianna was from Africa. She and my grandpa got acquainted with one another working in the fields. They worked as slaves together.

My mother would tell me that Georgianna was kind of stubborn. Grandpa
Bob said that he would have to carry his row and her row too. He said he
had to keep his eyes open with two sticks so that he could keep both rows
done. They would give the ladies fifty licks and the mens a hundred if they
didn't do their work.

Grandma Georgianna told Grandpa Bob, if he helped her out, they
weren't married then, they were in slavery, if he helped her out, when they

Fig. 10. Robert and Estella
McElwee, 1990. Photograph
by the author.

got out she could show him where a pot of money was. Grandpa Bob didn't
like doing his row and her row, so he went to old master, and he told him
that she just couldn't do it. And that he wished that he would take her in the
kitchen and let her work in the house. And then she went to work in the
house.

And when slave time broke, they went and got this pot of money. She
told him to help her and she fell in love with him. Grandpa married her and
got the money. I used to hear Grandpa Bob say, "Georgianna, I didn't marry
you for love, I married you for your money."

"OUR PARENTS TAUGHT US
WHAT TO SAY AND DO"

Memories like these prompted Ethel McElwee Black to say, "You would
have had a ball as a kid growing up then. It was good when we were coming
up." But other experiences prompted her to declare adamantly, "I never want

Fig. 11. Standing, left to right, Estella McElwee, Robert McElwee, Julia C. McElwee Ford, 1990. Seated, Ethel McElwee Black. Photograph by the author.

to go back. I wish I had left twenty years before I did." Those other experiences conveyed the simple, central truth of African-American life in Haywood County after 1888. According to Robert McElwee:

> Every white man was the law. I don't care if he was elected or not, he was the law, at that time, for the colored. If you were working for shares, the man you were working for, that was your law. They tell other white men, "Don't bother them [his tenants]," they don't bother them. They tell them, "Do bother them," they do.

Ethel McElwee Black recalled the many ways in which the children learned, within the family, that their place was subordinate to that of white people:

> My older sister was sick and Ms. Mamie sent for her to come help her. My sister was sick and couldn't go. The landlord came up and told her she had better come when Ms. Mamie said come. They all had to go up there and work because he said work. That's the way it was. You know that's the truth.

Our parents taught us what to say and what to do. Mind your own business and you got along.

I'll say this much. If you said, "Yes sir" and "No sir" and you didn't bother the white folks or didn't bother the white women, you could live. They would call you nice. If a black man got a new car, he did not pass the white man. He did not dust him.

I remember one little thing. Whenever you got to about fourteen, my parents would let you go shop for yourself. My daddy gave me enough money one day for me to go shopping. I went to the store and this tall, nice-looking, blond man showed me something, and then he said, "Oh, this is a pretty dress." And I said, "Uh-huh." Then he said, "What did you say!?" I said, "Oh, yes sir." I knew what to say. I knew he would break my neck. No, I did not like Brownsville. It was more like slavery than anyplace. It was sweet coming up because I didn't know any better. You could mind your own business and stay out of trouble, but there was no business to mind but what they said to do.

My dad taught us to respect everybody, to say "Ms. So and So" because he didn't want no harm to come. He knew what would happen if we got out of line. He always taught us to say, "Yes sir" and "No sir"; respect Mr. So and So and respect Mrs. So and So. He wanted no harm to come to us, because he knew what would happen if we got out of line. And he taught us to act right. They really put him up on the highest podium there because he was one of the most respectful black men there was.

Avoiding harm and winning respect within a system of economic subordination and political repression entailed complying with an elaborate code of conduct. Violating the code could embroil a person in a life-threatening situation. The McElwees well remembered the tenets of the code of behavior because, for most of their lives, their very survival, individually and as a family, depended on its rigorous observance. For example, Robert McElwee recalled the lengths to which his father went to prevent conflict with his white neighbors and the respect he earned for that:

One white neighbor plowed three feet onto my dad's land. Another had done the same thing. A third had done the same thing. They had just taken his land like that. I know I used to say, "Papa, I wouldn't let them do me

like that." And he said, "When I sell this place, I'll sell every acre that belongs to me." He said, "That don't hurt us."

Those white people around there, they were crazy about my daddy.
They were white lawyers and a white doctor. My dad stayed with the white
doctor when he was a boy, when he went to school in Brownsville. My father
taught school. He was a preacher and a teacher. The kids did the farming.

Winning respect entailed more than acquiescence and accommodation,
the outward signs of loyalty. It also required taking advantage of the limited
opportunities that local officials provided African-American sharecroppers—
for example, schools. Robert McElwee, Samuel's son, attended school in
Brownsville, probably the same school his father went to. He lived with a
white physician, Dr. Edwards, during that time and did chores in exchange
for his room and board. The school he attended continued the educational
tradition of Reconstruction. As late as 1914, the Dunbar School, started with
Freedmen's Bureau assistance, offered four years of instruction in Latin. The
school benefited from the excellent leadership of John R. Gloster and Dora
Morris Gloster from 1887 to 1915. Their son, Dr. Hugh Gloster, later became
president of Morehouse College in Atlanta. By 1914, however, leadership
such as the Glosters' was being criticized. Booker T. Washington's call for
industrial arts education drowned out most talk of other approaches. There
was resistance to implementing an industrial arts curriculum, but the pressures
of philanthropists overcame it. It was about this time that the Dunbar School
changed its name to the Haywood County Training School.[20]

Despite the extraordinary local African-American educational leadership, the schools for African-American children had improved little since
Reconstruction. Samuel McElwee's grandchildren recalled their unsatisfactory education:

> You see the way they used to teach school, they didn't go any higher
> than the eighth grade. You could teach school if you finished the eighth grade.
> When you finished the eighth grade, you could go out and teach school or
> do anything you wanted. I went to fifth grade.
>
> We didn't have much of school, three or four months. By the time you
> got to learning your lessons, it was time to quit. We just had three months. I
> reckon we had about thirty children in our school; one teacher, one room,

all grades. August or September we were in school. We would let out for
the crop and after Christmas we would go back. Then you would go until
about March. You would stop school then. You wouldn't go no more a while.
Then you start up again in August.

Severe inequalities between the schools for black and for white children
in Haywood County remained after fifty years. In fact, even funds allocated
for black children went to improve the education of white children, widen-
ing existing disparities. State officials allocated school funds to a county in
accord with the size of its school-age population. In Haywood County,
officials garnered funds for African-American children whom they did not
enroll in school or for whom they spent as little as possible. Only slightly more
than half of school-age African-American children might enroll in school.
The average African-American teacher had forty-six students in a class,
twenty-nine more pupils than white teachers instructed on average. Money
drawn for African-American children not enrolled and money saved on the
operating costs of the African-American schools went to the white schools
of the county. This pattern permitted Haywood County officials to operate
white schools for longer terms than those in schools of far wealthier counties
of the state. This advantageous funding formula prompted Haywood County
officials to oppose school reforms such as compulsory school attendance.
Such a measure would have required expenditures on the African-American
children for whom they were intended, instead of on white children.[21]

Even amid these limitations, some individuals continued to forge some
limited progress. For example, Hester Currie Boyd developed a new school
in the Pilgrim Rest area of the county in the 1920s. Her method was exactly
the same as that employed by her predecessors in the 1860s. She led fundraising
efforts in the community to purchase land with a clear title. She then secured
a commitment from the county school board to finish a building for a school
if local people provided and erected the framing for the building.[22]

Despite all the burdens attendant upon the era's race relations, Robert
McElwee felt lucky to be part of a land-owning family: "I thought my life
easy, coming up. I think I had a good life but it could be because I stayed on
my dad's farm." Even after leaving his dad's farm, he had it better than most
other African-American farmers. He arranged terms for his labor that were
about as good as a young African-American man could expect, and far better

than those the Freedmen's Bureau had arranged for Henry Knox in 1865.
Robert McElwee had his own tools and equipment. Consequently, he was
able to put more into a crop and borrow less to make it. He was on the far
end of the prosperous side of sharecropping. He provided his landlord one-
third of the value of the crop and kept the rest. He took great pride in his
economic status:

> I wasn't no sharecropper and I didn't work no halves. I worked on the thirds,
> after I went out from my dad's home and we were just out there working. I
> worked on a third after I left my dad. The lady I worked for, she gave me ev-
> erything except the cotton. I got corn, soybeans, syrup, beans, corn, okra, peas,
> everything. I got everything I raised except the cotton. I gave a third of that.

Despite his relative prosperity, McElwee recognized the injustice of his
condition. Winning the respect of white people was not so important that he
ignored every form of injustice. McElwee preserved his dignity and integrity,
and won further respect from white people, by protesting personal affronts
in perilous, barely sanctioned ways:

> It was unjust. It was unjust there. But I got along. It might be the reason
> the way I talked. I talked to them in a way they reckoned I was crazy. And I
> acted crazy. I did.
>
> I could have got hurt doing this but I was independent. I was married
> and I thought myself a man. I wanted to be a man.
>
> I went out where I did my business at for supplies. You didn't have to
> buy nothing but flour, sugar, and coffee. And if you didn't drink coffee, you
> didn't have to buy that. Sometimes, when you ran out of sugar, you could
> use syrup [sorghum]. I told him I wanted a stand of lard, a barrel of flour,
> and 100 lbs. of sugar. That would have lasted us all that year. It was just me
> and my wife. It was just about $13. It would have lasted the whole year;
> everything was so cheap.
>
> I asked for 100 lbs. of sugar, he throwed me 10 lbs. I asked him for a
> barrel of flour, he throwed me a 40 lb. sack. I walked out. I thought anytime
> a man asks for something, if he can pay for it, he should get what he asked
> for.
>
> I reckon he came out to the porch to see where I was gone. He called,

"Hey, Bob. Bob. Wait a minute. Why didn't you want those groceries?" I said, "That ain't what I asked for." He said, "Get your wagon and bring it in back and get what you want. Don't you tell nobody about it."

Another time, after our first child was born, we needed a little extra cash and I went out and asked for a $15 loan. He said he wouldn't give me any money but he wrote out a ticket for $200. He said my wife and I could go to his store in Brownsville and get anything I wanted. We went and looked around and found a pair of little shoes and I paid $1 for them of my own money.

I saddled my horse on Monday and went out back to him. I pitched the ticket at him. He looked at it and he looked at me. He said, "I thought you wanted $15 worth. I told Ms. Lucille to let you all have anything in the world you would want. She wouldn't let you have it?" I said, "I got what I wanted. I'm here to pay you back."

He said, "Come on into the back of the store." I went back there. He said, "You can get a little money from me. When you ask for it, don't ask me in front of nobody."

There were fewer opportunities to express self-worth and dignity with employers. However, McElwee availed himself of the small, sometimes furtive ways that came along. Generally, these conflicts came down to contests between him and an employer over minor matters of great psychological importance.

My boss did me all kinds of ways. I went up to the house once, and he was having breakfast. And he said, "Preacher, have you had breakfast?" And I said, "No, I haven't had breakfast yet." And he got up, and he went out of the room, and he left his whole jar of peanut butter. He came back, and that peanut butter was still there. I didn't touch a bit of it. He tried to get the ups on me. He said, "You know what, preacher, I could lock you into the house and fill that house up to your chin with money. When I came back the next morning there wouldn't be a dollar missing." There wouldn't. There wouldn't be anything missing. I wouldn't steal nothing. I did those things out of devilment.

These contests with white people had their dangers. McElwee did not challenge "peckerwoods."

A peckerwood is a real poor white man who ain't got nothing. A peckerwood would get a black man killed. If you just walk by and touched a woman
and she squealed, he would come back and tell lies about what you had done. If
there was one thing not to do, it was don't fool with a peckerwood. He would
come around and talk his head off and turn around and try to make trouble
for you.

The best protection against this form of danger was an employer. When
confronted with another farmer who insisted that McElwee leave his employer and come farm with him, McElwee did not deal with him directly.
Instead, he went to the woman for whom he farmed and asked her to tell the
other landlord to leave him alone. She did not deal with the landlord directly
but provided McElwee authority to tell him that "Ms. Patty said that I had
better not go to work for you."

If you tended to your own business, minded your landlord and obeyed
them, you could have no trouble with them. But if you didn't do what they
told you to do, they didn't care nothing about you. They would turn you
loose.

They would mind one another. If you told them to let me alone, they
would let me alone. They could be fixing to hang me, you could walk out
there and say, "What are you fixing to do with that boy?" They would say,
"We are going to kill him." And if you said, "Turn him loose. I don't want
to hear of you after him no more," or something like that, they would turn
me loose. You were the law. That's the way they figured, and they wouldn't
harm you.

What distinguished the McElwee family was that they earned the respect
and protection of other white people in addition to their landlords. White
people in authority permitted them to defend themselves against some other
whites and offered to protect them if they did.

The sheriff, Tip Hunter, took up for my dad when my dad got in a little
trouble. A man wanted to hit my dad, and Tip Hunter told my dad, "Put
your shotgun in the car and if he tries anything, shoot him." Tip Hunter
told him that if the man bothered him, shoot him.

Tip Hunter loved the McElwee family. I had rode in the car with him. He talked like there was no-one like Uncle Bob. "There's nobody like Uncle Bob."

My older brother John bumped a white lady on the street, and she accused him of pushing her. The white man came and grabbed him, but another man came and asked what they were doing. And they said how the woman said John had pushed her. And the man said, "Why, that's Bob McElwee's son."

That was an adequate defense of John's assertion that he had bumped her accidentally.

The McElwee family met the challenge issued by Booker T. Washington. They owned land. They farmed conscientiously and successfully. They attended school and took advantage of every educational and self-improvement opportunity afforded them. Their father was both teacher and preacher, the two most prestigious positions in the African-American community of Haywood County. These achievements won the family the respect of the white community. In political terms, the McElwee family had risen in the caste structure as high as a rural African-American family could rise. They were on a level with "peckerwoods," and their disputes with the latter could be adjudicated by white sponsors, informally.

THE SOCIAL CHANGE
OF EMANCIPATION

Caste and class imposed restrictions on the McElwee family; but within these systems, McElwee family members, and many other African Americans, found a surrogate for emancipation. Legal emancipation, the state and national laws of the 1860s, had removed the racial demarcation of slave and free. Prior to legal emancipation, only a small portion of African Americans became free. Although some African-American free people lived in Tennessee before slavery ended, they were generally absent from rural areas. Haywood County had only forty-one free African Americans in 1860.

The social structure of slavery, however, had two enduring characteristics that continued under legal emancipation, which the McElwee family incarnated.[23] First, there continued to be immense differences between the positions of white people and black, and between groups of black people. Slavery clearly set most members of one race apart from most members of the other. True, there were some free African Americans, who had the highest status among African Americans. The status of even a free African American, however, was lower than the lowest status of white people. Likewise, while house slaves had greater standing, on average, than fieldhands, they still ranked lower than the lowest class of whites.

For the freedpeople, legal emancipation meant improved access to education and the right to own property. These measures changed the class structure within the local African-American community in a manner unimaginable under slavery. In twenty years, Samuel McElwee moved from slave to teacher, merchant, attorney, legislator, and land-owner.

However, McElwee's meteoric rise was remarkable precisely because it was unusual. Few African Americans had the opportunities for education and land-ownership that buttressed McElwee's early career. His career suggested how fast an individual might ascend in education, wealth, and achievement. It did not suggest how many African Americans might ascend to the same level. Nor did it suggest an end to the conditions under which most African Americans lived at the time, including poverty and threats of physical violence. McElwee's son also became a teacher and land-owner. The next generation—Robert, Jr., and his brothers and sisters—attained neither as much land nor as much education as their father and grandfather had, because educational and economic opportunities for African Americans in Haywood County had declined.

During the period of legal emancipation, a division based on economic self-sufficiency replaced the distinctions of slavery among African Americans. In places like Haywood County, African Americans who left slavery with nothing but freedom had the scantiest means of economic self-sufficiency; most such people remained at the bottom of the county's social structure, locked into sharecropping within the agricultural economy.

A second enduring characteristic of slavery's social structure which survived into the era of legal emancipation was the way white values and power dictated the class structure within each race and also governed comparisons between races. Differences among African Americans increased precisely because some of them acquired the education and the manners of white society. Distinctions between McElwee's two separate families, urban and rural, northern and southern, illustrated the substantial class differences that arose among African Americans during this period of legal emancipation. Such a simple matter as taking a bath demonstrated class differences. Ruth McElwee, daughter of the Chicago family, found a bath in a tin tub a novelty, while such a bath was the only kind McElwee's grandchildren in Haywood County knew.

Biracial parentage was another factor influenced by white norms that affected the African-American class structure of legal emancipation. African Americans with biracial parentage were likely to have more advantages, just as they had had in slavery.[24] Slaves with a white parent had had more opportunities for training and work in the house. Robert and Georgianna McElwee, Sam's parents, reversed the usual order of race and place. He had a white father but worked in the fields. She was African and worked in the house. Samuel McElwee's marriages restored slavery's genetic class code. Both his wives were light-skinned, as his father had been. His second wife, Georgia, was especially light, as were their children. His Haywood County grandchildren think the difference in skin color separated his two families more than wealth or education.

Changes in the African-American class structure altered relations between members of the two races. White people with little or no opportunity to become self-sufficient remained at the bottom of white society's scale, but now they appeared comparable, in economic terms, to many of their African-American neighbors. Similarly, white people who before legal emancipation had had no counterparts in the African-American community now encountered African-American merchants, attorneys, teachers, and clergymen. With the development of this professional class, a set of separate institutions under African-American control, including stores, schools, and churches, arose. Many whites found such changes threatening.

Notwithstanding the gains that some few African Americans had made, the violent repression of legal emancipation restored aspects of slavery's racial divisions. A caste structure removed the ambiguities of class and race that legal emancipation fostered. The class structure among African Americans became truncated at the top and controlled by white officials. A major effect of the racial caste system was to diminish the status of the most prominent African Americans. No matter how high one might ascend in the class structure within the African-American community, that position was inferior, in at least some aspects, to the comparable position in the white community. The most ordinary white person could vote, for example, but far better qualified African Americans could not. Similarly, Ida B. Wells's first-class train ticket failed to give her access to the best accommodations available. These were reserved for white women and their gentlemen companions.

Repression included restricting the institutions that supported legal emancipation. African-American professionals, such as attorneys, were not allowed to practice in Haywood County. Similarly, the status of African-American men as voters in practice was denied. African-American teachers taught in clearly inferior schools under the direction of white officials. Churches remained the only institutions under African-American control. The question of how high African Americans might rise within their community now had a simpler answer. They might become land-owners, they might reach the top rung of the tenant farm system, they might preach, and they might teach. The very upper reaches of the African-American class structure were occupied by those who provided professional services for other African Americans and lived in towns. But the position of any African American was now inherently inferior to that of a white in a similar position.

Newspaper coverage of Samuel McElwee's death clearly reflects the caste and class structures of legal emancipation. The Fisk and Chicago newspaper coverage attested to McElwee's prominence in his profession and his race. Obituaries in the white Tennessee papers noted his prominence in his race but treated his race as a caste that could not be compared to whites. He was, in the words on one obituary, "the equal of any member of his race."

The freedom that Samuel McElwee and his parents had enjoyed during Reconstruction was replaced in this era of legal emancipation by the stature accorded the McElwee family within the caste and class structure of Haywood County. That stature, however, could not win the family the right to vote. In fact, because he was employed by a white school board, Samuel McElwee's son was reluctant to attempt to register. Such an action might have disrupted his efforts to "get along with white people." Ethel, his daughter, remembered, "My daddy would want to vote so bad but he couldn't vote. He would talk about that it would come that you could vote, but he never did get to vote. My daddy would talk, 'Things are going to be right so we could vote.' And he would talk about how one day things were going to be brighter for me than it was for him." The McElwee family, despite their considerable success within a system of subordination and repression, waited for the actions of others to return to them the right to vote.

Freedom's Pursuit
1940

4 In 1939, a small group of African Americans in Haywood County began a modest effort to regain the civil rights lost after 1888. They started a chapter of the National Association for the Advancement of Colored People (NAACP). A year later, delegates from the chapter inquired about procedures to register to vote. Members of this group differed from the McElwee family. As professionals, small business operators, and teachers in and around Brownsville, these town residents enjoyed higher status and prestige, among both whites and blacks, than even the most successful African-American farmers. After their inquiry concerning voting, however, the NAACP chapter members discovered that the violence and terror that enforced sharecropping controlled their own conditions as well. Their modest "movement" was violently repressed.

TENNESSEE TIES TO THE NAACP

The NAACP came to Haywood County via a circuitous route that led through Chicago and involved two people, Ida B. Wells and W. E. B. Du Bois, who had lived and worked on emancipation in Tennessee. In mid-July 1901, shortly after Samuel McElwee had moved to Chicago, Fisk-educated Du Bois published an article critical of Booker T. Washington. Du Bois attributed Washington's ranking as leader of both whites and blacks on race relations to the fact that his program—relinquishing African Americans' rights to the ballot, to other civil rights, and to higher education—appealed to whites. In Du Bois's estimation, Washington rallied the support of southern whites because white conservatives saw his Atlanta Compromise as capitulation. White moderates accepted Washington's plan as a temporary measure allowing improvement of race relations, much as the Freedmen's Bureau agents had accepted sharecropping. Du Bois concluded that Washington's emphasis on industry, saving, and self-improvement appealed to northern whites and southern white politicians for different reasons.[1]

Du Bois expanded this essay for a book published in 1903, *The Souls of Black Folk*. In the book, he outlined views of the caste and class condition of African Americans that he said were also held by many educated African-American men and women:

> They know that the low social level of the mass of the race is responsible for much discrimination against it, but they also know, and the nation knows, that relentless color-prejudice is more often a cause than a result of the Negro's degradation. . . .
>
> So far as Mr. Washington apologizes for injustice, North or South, he does not rightly value the privilege and duty of voting, belittles the emasculating effects of caste distinctions, and opposes the higher training and ambition of our brighter minds,—so far as he, the South, or the Nation, does this,—we must unceasingly and firmly oppose them.[2]

Ida B. Wells had known Du Bois since his college days at Fisk. She had opposed Washington's views earlier than Du Bois, but his essay brought fresh insight to her and her husband, Ferdinand L. Barnett. Barnett also had a Tennessee connection, having served as secretary to the 1879 Colored Men's Convention in Nashville. Immediately after the Du Bois book's publication, Wells and Barnett participated in a parlor debate over the book. They and their Chicago friends divided over Du Bois's criticism of Washington:

> Most of those present, including four of the six colored persons, united in condemning Mr. Du Bois' views. The Barnetts stood almost alone in approving them and proceeded to show why. We saw, as perhaps never before, that Mr. Washington's views on industrial education had become an obsession with the white people of this country. We thought it was up to us to show them the sophistry of the reasoning that any one system of education could fit the needs of an entire race; that to sneer at and discourage higher education would mean to rob the race of leaders which it so badly needed; and

that all the industrial education in the world could not take the place of manhood. We had a warm session but came away feeling that we had given them
an entirely new view of the situation.[3]

Wells wrote to Du Bois praising the book but also chiding him for not
taking time to confer with Jane Addams, who had attempted to meet him in
Atlanta. Wells would not have made such a mistake; she was an organizer who
worked closely with nationally prominent people across the country on
matters concerning racial equality. Her crusade against lynching had been an
early and lonely protest, but her effective intervention in the case of Steve
Green had involved the cooperation of many other people. Her letter to Du
Bois was written on the stationery of the Anti-Lynching League, which she
chaired.[4]

Du Bois combined organizing with scholarship. He was much better at
scholarship and later found an appropriate combination as columnist and
essayist. Now, however, in 1903, shortly after publication of *The Souls of Black
Folk*, Du Bois turned his hand to establishing a national organization. He did
not have the success that Wells had had. In July 1905, Du Bois called together
African Americans whom he and a few colleagues considered to be the best
and the brightest of the race, its "talented tenth," to establish a national
organization to press for greater equality for African Americans. The platform
of this group, the Niagara Movement, demanded voting and higher education for African Americans, and abolition of the caste system based on race
and color. It also called for leadership ready to organize protests to achieve
the platform goals. The Niagara Movement supported legislation to reduce
the congressional representation of states that limited the suffrage of African-
American men. John Hope, who in 1895 had been one of those in Nashville
who had criticized Washington, served, in 1906, as president of Morehouse
University and chairman of the Niagara Movement's education committee.
Du Bois's effort failed. In a few years, the Niagara Movement dissipated. The
elite composition of its membership seemed inconsistent with the group's
radically democratic positions. Washington's opposition also contributed to
its demise.[5]

The organizing efforts of Du Bois and Wells merged in 1909. An ad hoc
committee circulated a national petition in favor of using observation of the
centennial anniversary of Lincoln's birth to focus the nation's attention on the

unfinished work of emancipation. Wells signed that petition and, with Jane Addams, worked on a Chicago committee to organize an evening program celebrating the birth of Lincoln and protesting the condition of African Americans. Du Bois was the main speaker for the event.

Several months later, on 31 May and 1 June 1909, Wells and Du Bois met again at the National Negro Conference, an outgrowth of the organizing that had occurred to secure the petition in January. The upshot of this spring meeting was the establishment of a committee of forty charged to spend a year in deliberation and to make a report the following year. Du Bois, without anyone's knowledge, substituted a member of his Niagara Movement for Wells on the committee. He explained to her, in apology, that he had reasoned that her organization, the Douglass Center, would be represented by another woman, who was white, on the committee of forty. This reasoning added insult to injury, since he identified her with the initiative of another person and took little cognizance of her own protest and organizing efforts during the past two decades. He offered to retract his action; she refused the offer. Others intervened. The committee was expanded to fifty members, and Wells received a place on it. In 1910, Wells and Du Bois served on the committee that founded the NAACP; both brought their Tennessee backgrounds to that organization's work.[6]

Wells and Du Bois belonged to what Du Bois called the "self-regarding camp," those educated upper-class African Americans who experienced most personally the limitations imposed by a caste system. The NAACP urged the removal of caste barriers that limited the professional as well as the basic opportunities of African Americans. Washington, in Du Bois's analysis, represented the "self-sufficing camp." This was the group at the bottom of African-American society, its members kept there by a caste system that restricted institutions of social and political change. Du Bois depicted Washington as advocating that African Americans acquire the basic skills needed to provide for their own needs. Doing the latter Washington saw as a prerequisite for high self-regard. Du Bois wrote eloquently of the need to go beyond these measures and beyond exit—that is, beyond ameliorating the condition of a few self-regarding African Americans. In reaching for racial equality, Du Bois envisioned transforming American democracy:

The advocates of protest and higher training among colored people see that the Negro cannot gain anything more than a material and partial victory by becoming more and more self-sufficing. Two camps of self-sufficing and self-regarding peoples will never constitute a democracy. Every white advance in the conception of social justice must be shared with the Negro. . . . The Negroes must not meet . . . exclusion with a self-sufficient "Well, I shall achieve in some other way." They must insist on achieving in that particular [where they are excluded] . . .

To achieve the proper solution of this problem, in short, simply means that whites as well as Negroes shall be guided by ideals as well as by opportunism, shall have the courage of their lip service to spiritual realities, shall either admit that they do not believe in democracy at all but only in the struggle for existence, or else pursue their achievement of democracy in the only way possible, by frank recognition of and action upon the spiritual implications of democracy and self-consciousness.[7]

Washington and Du Bois challenged each other in productive ways. Du Bois challenged Washington and his followers to show how self-sufficient farmers could acquire the vote or end lynching. Washington challenged his critics to demonstrate the utility of poetry to a plowboy. Du Bois challenged Washington and his followers to demonstrate how African Americans would receive essential services and defend their civil rights without increased opportunities for African Americans to become attorneys, legislators, and public officials. Washington challenged Du Bois and others to demonstrate how America could deny the political rights of an economically strong group. Complete economic emancipation, according to Washington, would remove barriers to opportunities for African Americans and raise the status of those African Americans who were self-sufficient.[8]

Du Bois's self-regarding position included political participation. Washington's position emphasized it far less. Each position encompassed contradictions. Washington himself was not apolitical; in fact, he was a power broker. Criticism of him by Wells and Du Bois centered on his dominance in the discourse concerning race relations and the power of his "Tuskegee machine" to gather and allocate resources.[9] On the other hand, Du Bois's politics could be elitist and his political judgment poor, as in the Wells incident.

As the NAACP began, Washington died without an heir. It is doubtful that anyone could have maintained the control he exercised in racial matters. Changes in the southern agricultural economy diminished the need for poorly paid, unskilled labor. This need had been the economic foundation for Washington's views and for his popularity. As the significance of the southern economic changes gradually became apparent, the NAACP challenged the reconciliation of North and South based on acceptance of southern views on race. The NAACP worked at the national level, but its energy came from local chapters which it encouraged to work for civil rights.

These chapters attracted successful professional African Americans in many places. They also provided a stream of dues to the national organization to support its litigation, its lobbying efforts, and the research and publications of Du Bois, who had joined the organization's national staff at its creation. In 1939, the national office of the NAACP received a charter from a brand-new chapter in Brownsville, Tennessee.

THE DAVIS FAMILY

Three charter members of the Brownsville NAACP chapter were Elisha, Casher, and Thomas Davis. It was not unusual for them to be prominent in an effort of this kind. These sons of Ike Davis viewed themselves as the agents of progress and change within the African-American community and, indeed, the entire county. They were well beyond self-sufficiency economically and well placed in the self-regarding camp.

Ike Davis was a model African American of the type praised by Washington in his 1909 Brownsville speech. Davis was about the age of Sam McElwee's son Robert and, like him, was among the very few African-Americans in Haywood County—and in the South, for that matter—who owned land. The Davis family had a better life than most other African-American families in Haywood County and occupied a standing in the community comparable to that of the McElwee family. Ike Davis worked as a rough carpenter, a trade that brought the family a 'cash income. Land-ownership and wage work gave the Davis family an economic security rare among African-Americans at the time. Most other African-American farming fami-

Fig. 12. Ike Davis, father of Elisha
and Casher Davis, ca. 1920. Courtesy
of Debra Davis.

lies seldom escaped debt and earned very little cash income—certainly not
enough to accumulate the wealth needed to purchase land.

Casher Davis, Elisha's younger brother, recalled that his father "worked
so hard":

> I can remember him leaving in the morning when it was still dark; walking
> with arthritis; he would walk five miles. In those days, we thought he was a
> big deal. He was a carpenter. But now, since I learned a little about carpen-
> try, he was a rough carpenter. But there was demands for his service. And he
> was kind of well-to-do in the area.

Even having cash did not guarantee an African-American farmer the
opportunity to buy land. He had to find someone, most often a white person,
who would sell him land, and another person who was willing to extend him
credit for the purchase of the land. Land and loans were difficult to obtain.

In Haywood County in 1925, African Americans made up almost 70 percent of the population but only 8 percent of the land-owning farmers. Census figures report 359 such African Americans in a total African-American population of more than 17,000. Moreover, at this time the number of African-American land-owners was declining rapidly.

Ike Davis had something that gave him an advantage in acquiring credit and land—a white father. This paternity was not widely acknowledged, and Ike's children were not sure which white man was their grandfather. That sort of parentage children were not supposed to know much about, and, even as adults, Ike's children remained reluctant to discuss it. But Ike Davis's father was someone of sufficient influence in the white community to insure that his unacknowledged son would be able to borrow money for purchasing land. On 20 October 1900, shortly before Elisha Davis's birth, Ike Davis paid $350 for forty-four acres of land. Davis paid $100 at the time and promised to pay $50 every year on 15 November, his son Elisha's birthday, for five years. He purchased property called "the Marcum land," adjacent to the poorhouse farm, from J. E. Stewart and his wife. The importance of owning land was not lost on the sons of Ike Davis. It gave the family a degree of economic security and, most important, reduced the family's dependence on white landlords and employers. Their mother told her children that Ike Davis's last words to them were, "I got the land. You keep it."

Even with these advantages however, times were difficult, and family income seldom exceeded expenses. Some of the sons combined farming with wage work, as their father had done. But even this arrangement could not provide for all the children. Elisha was the fifth child among seven boys and five girls. There was not enough land to permit each of the Davis sons to enter farming on the family land. So, rather than revert to tenant farming as the McElwees had done, Elisha did what some four million rural southerners would do in the four decades between 1920 and 1960—he migrated north. He and his new bride Nann went to Chicago in 1928. People like Elisha flowed in streams from the counties of the rural South, following a family member, a friend, or someone else who could provide support, introductions, and employment prospects in a new place.

Elisha and Nann Davis stayed in Chicago just that summer. Nann was pregnant, and Elisha's brother, who lived in South Bend, Indiana, was adamant that they must move. He judged Chicago no place for a child and

Fig. 13. Nann Davis with infant
Evelyn, ca. 1930. Courtesy of
Debra Davis.

suggested that they relocate to nearby Niles, Michigan. They did. Not unlike
other migrants, Elisha returned to Haywood County after a few years. His
father had died, and he and his family returned home to help his mother. They
returned to the Davis farm, where they lived until 1938. In that year, his
family moved to Brownsville, where he operated his own automobile service
station.

Ike Davis was distinct among African-American men in Haywood
County in another way—he voted. By 1900, when Elisha Davis was born,
only a handful of African-American men had navigated the shoals of disfranchisement and remained registered to vote. Ike Davis was among them.
Casher Davis recalled his father's account of an exchange he had with a
neighboring white man:

> We had the little Dezern school on the back of our farm, that's where
> they used to vote. My dad was telling me one day, that election day, he walked
> the fence line going back there to vote. Mr. Jim Osburn said, "Ike, where
> you going?" He said, "Well, I just thought maybe I'd better go over there

and vote." He said, "Oh well, there ain't no use your goin', Ike, because it ain't goin' to count no way." Apparently, my father voted.

We don't know if he was a Democrat or Republican but down there if you weren't a Democrat you didn't know nothing about politics, no way, especially black people. It was a long time down there, we didn't get newspapers. We had no radio or TV. You just went out there and listened to what someone else said.

Ike Davis had no African-American candidates for whom to vote. The time of African Americans' active participation in politics in Haywood County was only a boyhood memory. Ike had been a teenager when Samuel McElwee represented the county in the state legislature. The voting practices of a few African-American men such as Ike maintained a fragile strand of continuity between past African-American political participation and the present.

By 1939, the sons of Ike Davis had assimilated into their own self-concepts their father's example and his legacy of land-ownership, modest savings, and political participation. Like their father, they owned land, participated in the wage economy of the county, and figured among the "successful" African-American citizens of the county. Thomas was a porter in Brownsville's Capitol Theater. Casher Davis farmed and worked for the Coca-Cola bottling plant in Brownsville. Elisha Davis operated a service station in Brownsville. Casher Davis recalled:

> We thought, you know, if there was anyone in the neighborhood, especially among the black people that was kind of doing pretty good, it was us. Only one black family within five miles of us had land. None of the others had it. They were sharecroppers. The "man" would not let them make big money. It was just about two or three colored people in that area that owned their own property. We were one of them and we kind of thought we were doing something.

The calendar on the wall of Elisha Davis's service station in 1940 quietly proclaimed his continuing commitment to change. The snapshot depicted Elisha lifting a large blindfold from the faces of his two sons. The short, handwritten caption read: "Poem: Lifting the veil from the faces of the coming generations of Haywood." The words captured in brief the instruction and the resolve that his father Ike had bequeathed.

THE NAACP BEGINS

The Davis brothers had the help of many others, but especially of Milmon Mitchell, in starting the Brownsville NAACP chapter. Mitchell was a representative of the Atlanta Insurance Company and had his office in Jackson, Tennessee. He traveled from there throughout the counties of West Tennessee selling insurance and encouraging his clients to begin chapters of the NAACP. He was familiar with Haywood County because his grandfather still lived there.

> Elisha and I were very good friends. I knew him before the NAACP thing ever came up. I knew Nann, his wife; Casher, his brother; Evelyn, his little daughter. We were very good friends.
>
> The white people thought a lot of Elisha. He had a lot of white friends around there. I know he used to talk a lot about the white fella he bought his gas from. How nice he got along with him. There were a lot of nice people in Brownsville, white people, Christians.
>
> When Elisha found out that we had an NAACP branch in Jackson, he and Buster Walker said, "We should have one in Brownsville." Buster Walker, Elisha Davis, and Elbert Williams came over to my office in Jackson. Voting, that was the sole purpose of organizing the branch in Brownsville. In Jackson, 26 miles from Brownsville, we voted.

Mitchell was raised in Memphis, a segregated city but one in which African Americans voted, as part of Boss Crump's Democratic political machine.

> I was born and raised in a segregated society but I was never able to accept it. I was born and raised with this idea, when you see the white folks coming, you are supposed to wait until they get on. I always resented it. I never did approve of it in my mind that it was the right thing to do.

Mitchell's company supervisors encouraged his work with the NAACP. The company insured African Americans, and it was good public relations for the company to be involved in a civic venture of this kind. It gave Mitchell visibility and brought him into personal contact with prominent African-American residents who were the most likely clients for his insurance company. Mitchell had established several branch offices of Atlanta Insurance Company in his region of West Tennessee. He conceived of organizing NAACP chapters parallel to his insurance company. Each branch office would initiate and sponsor one or several NAACP chapters. Each branch manager would have dual responsibilities for the insurance business and the NAACP. Mitchell unknowingly was creating an organizational structure similar to that of the Freedmen's Bureau. Mitchell's organization had a different base, obviously, and a far more limited purpose—that is, the political organization of African Americans to regain the right to vote—but it took the form of coordinated, decentralized efforts on behalf of African Americans.

The Haywood County NAACP chapter's charter listed prominent African Americans of the county, all well qualified to vote and also likely customers for insurance. Fourteen of the charter members taught school, and, of the fifty-three original members, only seven were farmers. The list also featured day workers, a mortician, and a physician. Twenty-three of the original members were women who reported working as housewife, nurse, or beautician. No tenant farmers, such as the McElwees, were on the charter list. Their constant debt, low incomes, and dependence on white landlords made sharecroppers unlikely insurance clients or NAACP members. The vast majority of the members listed Brownsville addresses.[10]

Irma Newbern served as secretary to the chapter. She and her husband ran a dry cleaning establishment in Brownsville that served the African-American community. Grounded in that separate economic base, the Newberns owned their own home and business and, as she remembered, "didn't deal with whites." She and her husband met with other chapter members in each other's homes. Generally, the location of the meetings was given only to members and kept secret from others. The monthly meetings drew about twenty to twenty-five members who reviewed grievances, primarily, and discussed steps to redress them.

By October, the chapter had several farmers from outside Brownsville as members. Among them, or representing them, were Tom and L. V. Sanderlin, who had just joined the Farm Security Administration's Haywood County Farm Project in the Stanton area of the county. That federal project had bought the Douglas plantation, terraced it, and improved it. The government then divided it into thirty-nine plots ranging in size from 90 to 110 acres, on each of which the FSA built a house, a barn, and a smokehouse. The former tenant farmers on the plantation and others from the surrounding counties could apply to rent these plots, with an option to buy. This project was one of thirteen in the South set aside exclusively for African-American tenant farmers. Tom Sanderlin jumped at the chance to become a land-owner, as did others like him in the area. The unusual opportunity for African-American men and women to obtain land transformed them into political participants as well. The project provided an economic base different from that of the Newberns, but Sanderlin's income was also protected from local white control. By October, three other families from the project had joined the Sanderlins as NAACP chapter members.[11]

Whatever the reasons for his initial involvement, Milmon Mitchell's NAACP work soon became far more than a public relations gimmick for his company. Mitchell devoted substantial effort to the substance of racial prejudice and discrimination. During 1940, he had a controversy with the management of the local Montgomery Ward store about a sign over the water fountain reading "For White Only." After a number of African Americans in Jackson unsuccessfully complained about this discriminatory practice, Mitchell took up the complaint. The manager of the store removed the sign rather than installing a separate and equal fountain for African-American customers. The NAACP Jackson chapter's members were successful middle-class African Americans of the city and adjoining area. Lane College, the school founded in 1887 with a Fisk graduate and protégé of Samuel McElwee as its first principal, attracted well-educated professional African Americans to Jackson. This stratum of people found the petty segregation practices, such as separate water fountains, particularly offensive. Ministers, teachers, professors, and two doctors were listed among members of the 1940 board of directors of the Jackson NAACP chapter.[12]

Mitchell, like Samuel McElwee half a century earlier, dealt with instances of violence toward African-American people. At this time the problem was not mob violence but police brutality. Mitchell wrote in his annual report for 1940, "Negroes are still manhandled and unnecessarily beaten, and in some cases murdered by the city and county policeman."

Mitchell also led Jackson's African-American residents in a boycott of the

Fig. 14. Milmon Mitchell, 1989. Courtesy
of Milmon Mitchell.

Piggly Wiggly and Kroger grocery stores. The boycott protested a management action against young African-American teenagers who assisted customers with their grocery bags in the stores' parking lots. The teenagers were not
employees of the stores and assisted only those people who requested help.
They made reasonable wages from tips given by people they assisted. The
managers, responding to a few complaints, prohibited black teens from doing
this work but permitted white teens to continue. Six ministers who were
NAACP members preached against the stores' new policy and urged the
members of their congregations not to shop in the stores. The boycott succeeded. Both stores removed their racial restrictions and agreed to try to get
additional stores to permit African-American teens to do such work, too.

Most of Mitchell's work in the last half of 1940, however, was taken up
with events in Haywood County. The problems that he dealt with had their
roots in the political subordination of all African Americans and the economic
exploitation of most of them. African-American tenant farmers and sharecroppers were, in the estimation of Mitchell, "virtually in slavery."[13] African-
American families seldom escaped debt that bound them to white landlords
and kept them in grinding poverty. The problem that Mitchell dealt with in
1940 was the violent suppression of a modest challenge to these political and
economic forms of subordination.

INQUIRIES AND INQUISITIONS

The problems that occupied Mitchell for more than a year began on 6 May 1940, when five men—Rev. Buster Walker; John Lester, a farmer; John Gaines, a farmer; Taylor Newbern of the Brownsville dry cleaning plant; and Elisha Davis—went to the county registrar's office. The group inquired about procedures to register to vote in time for the presidential election that year.

The group soon found itself in a maze of conflicting advice. The county registrar referred the group to the city judge, who demanded to know, "What committee is this?" Davis and the others informed the judge that they were not a committee and simply sought advice and assistance in registering to vote in time for the presidential election. The judge referred them to the chairman of the elections committee, a cotton buyer, who was out of the city that day. The group had been told somewhere along the way that registration would not be open until August, three months away. The five NAACP members decided to drop the matter for a while.

Other men, who were white, took the matter up and warned the group members to stop their inquiry. The next day, for example, the deputy sheriff visited the Reverend Mr. Walker and told him that he should not encourage Negroes to vote "or there would be trouble." This was intended as a friendly warning, and the deputy asked Walker not to tell anyone that he had spoken to him. Two weeks later, Elisha Davis had a visit at his service station from a white man who also delivered a friendly warning. As Davis recalled, this man explained that he had heard that Davis was "a member of some organization getting Negroes to vote. Let the thing drop or Negroes will get into some serious trouble. The people down at the courthouse say they will run you and Walker out of town if you try to vote."[14]

A week later, on 27 May, an African-American attorney from Jackson, J. Emmett Ballard, who was chairman of the Legal Redress and Legislation Committee of the Jackson NAACP chapter, heightened the tension in Brownsville and the entire county. He had come to Brownsville to represent Solomon Bailey, an African American on trial on charges of shooting a white man. Bailey's trial had drawn much attention because it followed by only five months the death of a white constable, shot by another African-American man. Haywood County had not seen an African-American attorney since McElwee. Ballard had been warned by white officials not to appear as the attorney in the case. When the case was called, a mob of white men in the courtroom threatened Ballard, promising that they would not permit a "nigger" to practice law in the courts of Haywood County. According to Mitchell's account, "The mob's spirit was so tense, that it was necessary for the sheriff to rush Ballard out of town, leaving his car behind." The next day, the judge in the case called Ballard and informed him that another attorney, a white man, had been appointed in the case and that his client had been tried, found guilty, and sentenced.[15]

Reprisals continued and broadened. By the first part of June, NAACP members found that they were no longer being granted credit by merchants and bankers of the county with whom they had done business for years. Teachers among the NAACP members were threatened with termination for their participation in the local chapter. Reports circulated in the African-American community that whites were opening the mail of persons identified with the NAACP, in an effort to obtain information about the organization and the activities of its members. On 13 June, Mitchell wrote to Walter White, secretary of the NAACP, summing up the crisis atmosphere in Haywood County:

> For two years a faithful few of us have made every effort to convey the principles of the NAACP in this section. The time is here for the National Office to render some valuable service in this section. The Colored Citizens in Brownsville are now crying like children in the wilderness and they are now waiting to see if this organization will come to their aid. This entire trouble grew out of an effort made by the NAACP to qualify Negroes to vote in Brownsville.[16]

Walker and others visited J. D. Bomer, mayor of Brownsville, to get advice. Bomer assured the group that they had the right to vote—"as much right as I have," Walker recalled Bomer telling them. Bomer did not "blame" them for their aspiration but lamented "trash among my group," some of whom had already come to him complaining about "colored people wanting to vote." As Walker recalled, Bomer told him and the others with him,

"These rednecks, there is no telling what they will do. It's just a proposition that I cannot handle. I don't know what will be the outcome." Bomer later verified these events and expressed shock at what had transpired in the interim.[17]

The suspicions of white Brownsville residents about the NAACP prompted some to seek additional information on the chapter. Casher Davis's boss, for example, asked Casher to inform on the members and activities of the NAACP. He offered to forgive Casher's debt for two pairs of work overalls "if you would just get out there and see if you can't stop that NAACP."

Casher's boss's curiosity was piqued by events on the night before he made his request, 14 June. A prominent African-American businessman in Brownsville attempted to enter the NAACP meeting on that evening. The members of the local chapter refused him admission, ostensibly on the grounds that he was not an NAACP member. Less ostensibly, those at the meeting suspected that he would report on the meeting to white leaders in the city. The chapter's refusal to admit him ratcheted the tension up another notch, and violence began. Some white men decided to deal with this "problem" in their own way.

"DON'T KILL HIM, BUT GET HIM OUT OF TOWN"

Led by Tip Hunter, night sheriff in Brownsville, several carloads of men began an inquisition on the night of 15 June. These men traveled to Buster Walker's store that evening but did not find him there. John Outlaw, a teacher and NAACP member, had hustled Walker out of Brownsville to Stanton, where he spent the night before slipping out of the county completely. Having missed Walker, the mob began a search for other NAACP members. They picked up a young African-American man, Jack Adams, who was walking in Brownsville with his girlfriend and forced him to lead them to Elisha Davis's home.

Nann Davis, Elisha's widow, remembered what happened then. She had little knowledge of the NAACP or of Davis's involvement with it, although she had been a charter member. She remembered Eli as a protective person who didn't want to bother her with problems he might be facing. That evening had been an ordinary one, except for an unusual question. When Eli came home, he inquired, "Has anyone been here?" Nann responded, "No." She recalls an evening spent getting the seven kids ready for bed, an evening entirely ordinary except for that question.

After midnight, pounding on the front door startled her and Elisha from their sleep. Their bedroom was in the front room of the house, so their unknown visitors were only a door away. Her husband handed her two pistols and told her to put them under the pillows, to sit on the bed, and not to move. She asked, "Why?" But he answered only, "Don't move. Stay right there."

When Elisha opened the door, he saw a mob of fifty to sixty men in his yard and eight or more men on his porch. He recognized several of them. Two worked for Dan Shaw, president of the Brownsville Bank; one was a WPA worker; the county's highway commissioner was standing on his porch, as well as a grocer and two truck drivers whom Eli knew. Three of the men entered. One was Albert Mann, farm foreman for Dan Shaw; the other two were policemen—Tip Hunter, who was running for sheriff at the time, and Charles Reed.

The two police officers ordered Elisha to dress and forced him to do so. Years later, Nann Davis remembered those tense, nightmarish moments in her bedroom:

> So these guys stood at the door with these big long poles, you know the kind you drive cattle with. I said, "What do you want?" They just came on in and said to Eli, "Put your pants on and come and go with us." He knew all of the men. Some of them he was raised up with. I kept asking, "What are you gonna do with him?" But Eli just kept telling me to shut up. I said, "What are you gonna do with him?" They wouldn't answer me. All they would say to Eli was "Come on." All he did was put on his pants, he grabbed his shoes, and they said, "You can put those on in the car."

They moved from the front room of the house out onto the porch, into the crowd there, and then merged into the mob in the yard. Nann followed them to the door.

> When they moved out, I went to the door and I had already grabbed one of the guns. But when I looked up and saw all of them, I said to myself, "Don't

do that." I saw four cars, and I had a houseful of kids, so I didn't explode. I looked out, and I said to them, "Where are you taking him?"

Finally, one of the mob gave her the first indication of the mob's intent: "You will never see this black son-of-a-bitch again. We are going to kill him." It would be almost two months before Nann Davis would see her husband again.

Elisha Davis, in a sworn affidavit, recounted the events of that evening after the mob took him from his house. Hunter led him through the mob in the Davis's yard to a car parked in front. He got in the car with Hunter and the other police officer, Reed. They drove six miles to the Forked Deer River Bottom. Jack Adams, whom the mob had swept up before Davis, was still in the car. At the river bottom, the mob crowded around Davis and Adams. Davis interceded for Adams, who had no connection to the matters that fueled the mob's angry energy.

Looking around at the mob and his interrogators, Davis recognized several of the men. He recalled Albert Mann threatening him, "We brought you here to kill you. But I ain't gonna let them do it. They all want to know about that organization named the National Association for the Advancement of Colored People and who the members are of the organization and what you Negroes intend to do." Davis explained about the NAACP, including its purpose to encourage African Americans to vote. Others pressed him for the names of NAACP members, promising that they would kill him if he didn't give the names. Davis gave the names of some other members of the Brownsville branch. He not only told them of the plans to encourage African Americans to vote, but also that several white officials in Brownsville had attended the organizational meetings of the NAACP and had encouraged them in their intent.

Some of the mob began to intervene on Davis's behalf, shouting down others in the mob. Tom Freeman, a wealthy white man in the county, evidently had heard what was going on and had sent word to the mob, "Don't put your hands on him. Don't hurt him." Davis had worked for Freeman as a boy, and Freeman interceded for Davis, from afar but successfully.

Others knew of the events on the river bottom that night as well, including Dan Shaw, the Haywood County banker. Eli recounted later to his brother that he had heard one of the policemen say, "No. Uncle Dan told me not to take no part in this and for you folks not to hurt him." Casher Davis is sure that Dan Shaw, "Uncle Dan," knew Elisha's white grandfather and interceded on Elisha's behalf, possibly for this reason. From the grave, the furtive white grandfather of an African-American man could still extend a protective hand. The third police officer in the mob protested again, "Uncle Dan said, 'Don't hurt him but get him out of town.' Uncle Dan told me not to have nothin' to do with it."

The mob released Davis but promised that if he ever came back to the county he would be killed. Davis asked to return to his home to gather some clothing, but the mob denied that request. Davis ran from the mob and its unspent anger into the bush and up the river bank. Gunfire rang out as some mob members fired after Davis to punctuate their intent.[18] Nann Davis remembered that the mob then turned on Jack Adams and "beat the snot out of him."

TAKING REFUGE

Davis walked eight or nine miles to the highway that runs to Jackson. Two African-American men whom he did not know picked him up and gave him a ride to Alamo, Tennessee, where he went to the residence of Dr. L. D. Thomas, also a charter member of the Brownsville NAACP. Thomas called Mitchell in Jackson. Mitchell drove out immediately.

> I had in mind that something like this had happened. It was all over town that they had threatened him and that he had better leave town and all that. He wouldn't tell me what had happened but I knew it was something like that. I drove out there and he was a little frightened. I had my gun with me. I was a little frightened that they would try to stop me on the way out. But Alamo isn't too far from Jackson, fifteen or twenty miles. When I drove up, I didn't see him. Finally, he came out from between the houses. He was waiting outside, between the houses, at the side of the house. As I drove up, he appeared. I brought him back to my house. On the way back, he was telling me what happened. He seemed frightened.

In the meantime, unaware of the whereabouts of her husband and concerned for his safety, Nann woke her oldest son, Isaac, as soon as the mob left her home Isaac was nine years old. "Isaac, get up, they got your daddy," she whispered. As he shook off sleep, he responded, "Momma, where did they take him?" She answered, "I don't know." She recounted the unimaginable events that had just taken place in the adjacent room. Isaac asked, "Well, Momma, why didn't you call me and I would've gotten rid of all of them?" She turned their conversation from the past events to things that needed to be done and told him, "When it gets daylight, I want you to go to your Uncle Casher." He offered to go at that time, but she insisted, "No, I don't want you to go until it gets daylight."

They sat on his bed in the children's room in the dark with the other six sleeping Davis children, the youngest of whom was eight months old, and talked. Almost fifty years later, she recalled that night clearly:

> It was quiet. You couldn't even hear a dog bark. I just sat. We just sat there on the bed and talked. I woke Isaac for company. I didn't dare go back to sleep. We would just talk about little different things. He would want to know: "Why did they take my daddy?" "What are they going to do with him." And things like that. Now what could I tell him. I didn't know. And he would say, "What is it all about?" And I would say, "Votin'." But what did he know about voting, you know. So we would just kind of rattle off something and maybe we would feel good for a little while. The guns were still on my bed under my pillow.

Finally, the night passed. With the first gray light of Sunday, Isaac announced to his mother, "Momma, I'm ready to go." She said, "Well go, and tell your uncle they got your daddy." It was about a mile for him to go, and Nann recalled the sight of his leaving in his distinctively bowlegged run.

As news of the incident spread that morning, people came to Nann to express their concern. There was little to tell them. Some wondered why Nann hadn't come by that night for help, but Nann doubted that people would have responded to cries of alarm at night. She was not sure what could have been done at that time, anyway. Just as she feared that her use of one of the guns would have started a battle, so she thought now that her raising a general alarm might have started a war. As news of Elisha Davis's abduction spread, so did the consternation of the African-American community. Some churches canceled services that Sunday.

One of Nann's visitors that morning brought news of Elisha's whereabouts. The cousin of Dr. Thomas, to whose home Elisha had gone, came by and told Nann that Elisha had reached Thomas's house that morning and was alive. Thomas had called this cousin in Brownsville and instructed her to convey that message in person. Telephones were no longer to be trusted, because the mob might have ears.

When Isaac returned from his uncle's house, Nann took the seven children to the home of Elisha's mother and sister in Brownsville. "We just walked out of the house with just the clothes we had on. We left the food in the house." So began three months of hiding.

Casher was stunned by the news of his brother's disappearance; only slowly did he begin to piece things together and to connect them with the NAACP activity. He recalled his conversation with his boss, Mr. Lee, the day before, when Lee had inquired about the NAACP meeting on Friday night. "What was going on?" "Why were some people kept out of the meeting?" Isaac's message frightened Casher; he too was a charter member of the NAACP. He could very well be the mob's next victim. He looked around his home. The grass in his yard appeared trampled. He feared that the mob might have been there or might come. He left his home and walked three miles into the country, where he took refuge for several days upstairs in a sharecropper's house. Other neighbors brought him food there.

CASTE AND PLACE

In hiding, Casher Davis reflected on his fugitive status and on the essence of race relations, especially the "place" of an African-American man in the class and caste system of the time.

> It wasn't like nothing would happen to you if you were good. If you went too far, you'd know it quick. Their phrases were: "Negroes don't do that." "We don't stand for that." And "You can't do that." We knew how far to go, and if you went too far, we knew good and well they'd clash you with a bullet.

Oh, hell, yeah. They'd beat you up. I remember when this [black] man beat up our [white] neighbor there who ran the country store. This colored fella beat up Mr. Willard Musgrave because he called him a black so, so, so. He ran off because he knew he could be killed for that if they caught him, and they never caught him.

They had this little, young fella down there that was kind of nosy. He had been bothering Mr. Joe Morris and all of this came together when this Goodman boy hollered at Mr. Joe Morris. Well one day, Goodman was in the barn and Mr. Joe Morris came in the back and Mr. Guy Harold, his son-in-law, came in the front, pulled that boy out of the barn there and took a stick, didn't hit him on the head, but they sure beat him up. They told him, "Black so and so, don't you never talk to me or my daddy-in-law no more. I'm going to kill you."

I watched them beat him up there. And after they beat him up, they put the stick over there in the corner. Mr. Guy Harold went on, left.

Guy Harold had a particularly notorious reputation in the county. He ran the work farm where African-American men, when arrested, could be sent to serve their sentences. The work farm was on the land of the county poor farm set aside by Poston and others during Reconstruction. As with other measures of that time, the purpose of poorhouse land changed. That land now provided a facility for enforcing the vagrancy laws of 1875. Harold was a bit player in the continuing drama of subordination of African-American labor. The combination of frequent arrests of African-American men on minor charges and the cruelty of the work farm found its way into the lyrics of a blues song by Sleepy John Estes. Estes warned:

If you hobo through Brownsville,
Don't be peeking out.
Billy Whitten [police officer] will get you
Mr. Guy Harold will wear you out.

Ordinarily, African Americans of the status and reputation of the Davis family did not have to worry about harsh treatment of the kind that Casher Davis knew could be meted out. In fact, the position of the Davis family permitted its members to chide some white people, gently, about violence:

A little later in the week, Mr. Joe Morris, a good man, came and said, "Cash, we kind of hated to do it but that boy has been insulting me and insulting me and insulting me." I told him, "Mr. Morris, my Dad would turn over in his grave if he knew you would do something like that." He said, "Cash, I didn't want to but I just had to do something to stop him because he was getting too hard to manage."

Out of this mix of violence, repression, and respect, the Davis brothers, like the McElwees, fashioned some semblance of order and principles of conduct. Now, while in hiding, Casher reflected on those principles and the miscalculation that he and his brothers had made about them:

What I am talking about is here, I was raised with white kids, slept with them and ate at their table, they ate at my table. But later on, these same young boys I grew up with, Mr. Guy and Mr. James, after they got eighteen, I had to start calling them "Mister."

So when you go through those things, you expect anything. You don't take no chances. You know your place. You stay in your place. You don't insult those persons.

Now NAACP, we thought wasn't all that bad. At that time, we didn't think it was beyond our place. Joining an organization that can't hurt you and if it helped me, it would sure help the whole community. Our good white friend told Eli, "Hang in there Eli. Hell, we'll help you."

We kind of thought that we were leading Negroes and that if anything was to be done that was what we ought to do. We thought we were working with the white community to do something.

We were always doing something up at Willow Grove School, where we were born, five miles out of Brownsville towards Jackson. We kind of thought we just sort of started something there.

I was always working hard and it seemed like they were helping us trying to make a living. I just thought we were what we supposed to be. I got me a job which was nice. And I did what I was supposed to do, I thought. Elisha had a business, his service station. We just thought we were doing all right.

What I thought was, we had one real rich colored fella, that businessman we didn't let into our meeting. The NAACP wasn't approved by him and his supporters. They really didn't want the NAACP. I guess they sent him to spy on that meeting. When he came, he wasn't allowed in because he was not a member. And when he left, he probably reported this to those white men who really objected. And then they got hard.

Whatever they said was the law. If they wanted to hang somebody, they would go tell them that he tried to rape the white lady. While he's locked up in jail, they don't see him no more. Things of that nature would happen.

But with Elisha it was strictly a matter of his business: "You got no business running a station. That's a money's people's job with colored people working for them." You know. For a colored fellow to have a service station, that was something. So far as they're concerned, Eli and I, we went beyond our place. We thought it was leadership, a black man with a service station. The moneyed people knew what we were about. But we went too fast. It wasn't time.

Eli and Casher went beyond their caste if not their place. They were successful and had risen among the African-American residents of Haywood County. But no matter how high they went, they could not cross a line that marked the most ordinary white person as better than the most extraordinary African American. That line prescribed separate castes, not merely races. No matter how high one rose within the lower caste, one's position never reached much further than the lowest position of the higher caste in some matters, including voting. Conversely, no matter how low one sank in the white caste, one could always claim superiority to the highest members of the African-American caste. In Haywood County, this claim of white superiority included civil rights.

"Good white friends" might encourage some black persons to consider themselves the equals of some white people. But generally these friends fell silent when the "trash" or "rednecks"—the "peckerwoods," as Robert McElwee called them—enforced caste distinctions with the harshest measures, humiliating or repressing African Americans regardless of their status and achievements. The numbing silence of the "better" white citizens attested to the fact that white mob terrorists had more defenders among whites than their victims had. The majority's tacit support expressed the same caste prejudices as the mob's actions. Even with all their experience of racial subordination, wise and perceptive people such as Casher Davis sometimes forgot the pervasive, subtle fact of caste and were stunned upon rediscovering

Fig. 15. The charter members of the Brownsville chapter of the NAACP, 1939. Elbert
Williams, lynching victim, is the first person on left, second row. Elisha Davis is the third
person from the left, second row. Casher Davis and Rev. Buster Walker are on the right,
second row. Courtesy of Cynthia Rawls Bond.

it: "Now people encouraged you and people, on the other hand, condemn
you for trying to do good. We didn't quite understand it. And when it
happened, it was a blow. We just couldn't believe it."

THE MOB TAKES A LIFE

Casher Davis traveled surreptitiously within the county for several days. He
walked at night by routes hidden from the road. While he was visiting his
sister and mother in Brownsville, a policeman came to the house. He had
received a report that something was happening to Mrs. Davis, Casher's
mother, and expressed concern for her safety. He asked Casher where Dora
Davis was. Casher responded, "Back there."

It was a remarkable scene, typifying the distorted social relations that Jim
Crow had established. The white sheriff expressed concern for the welfare of
a black woman, mother of a man that a police-led mob had taken from his
home, threatened, and banished a short time before. In the house was her
youngest son, fully prepared to shoot the sheriff if he was detected.

Those police came runnin' in there and I'm sitting right there by the door with that old .32 pistol layin' there with my hat on top of it. They walked in the door and asked, "Where's Dora Davis?" I said, "Back there."

"Ms. Davis, they said somethin' was happening to you. What's happenin'? What's wrong?"

Momma just said, "Ain't nothin' happenin' to me, child. No, ain't nothin' happenin' to me."

Well, I don't know why they got that funny call. They walked right by me and I went right on out.

That brush with discovery was close enough for Casher Davis:

As soon as the sun went down and it got dark, I snuck out and went into the weeds and walked back out into the country another four miles. I spent another night. Someone called me and said they would be going to Memphis and be ready, get out of there. Get out of there as quick as I could. There would be a car ready in a few minutes to take me to Memphis and to go to a certain address and someone would take care of me that night.

Casher made it to Memphis that night and the next day took a bus to Henning. There he spent the night with his sister. The next day he continued on to Newbern, where he took refuge in his sister Clara's residence.

Five days after the abduction of Elisha Davis, the mob formed again and took two more victims, Thomas Davis, Elisha's brother, and Elbert Williams. On Thursday night, 20 June, at approximately 9:30 P.M., Tip Hunter; Ed Lee, Casher's employer; and Milton Osburn came to the home of Thomas Davis and began inquiring about NAACP activities. The three men took Davis with them in their car and drove to the home of Elbert Williams. According to the affidavit of Annie Williams, Elbert's wife and another charter member of the NAACP, the couple had just listened to the world championship heavyweight bout between Joe Louis and Arturo Godoy, which Louis won by a knockout in the eighth round.

Tip Hunter came to our home sometime between 10 and 11 P.M. at 210 Bradford in Brownsville and asked me if Elbert Williams lived there. I told him that he lived there and was getting ready to go to bed. He asked to see him. My husband, Elbert Williams, came into the room with his pajama pants and a vest on. Officer Hunter asked Elbert to come with him and took him to an automobile parked in front of the house.[19]

Williams, in his pajama pants and shoeless, joined Thomas Davis in the car. They were taken to the police station, locked up, and questioned further by the same three men who had gone to Davis's home. About 1:30 A.M., Hunter released Davis. By that time a mob of approximately forty or fifty white men were outside the jail. Davis passed through the mob, went home, and immediately left for Jackson. By 6 o'clock the next morning he had joined his brother Elisha in Jackson as a fugitive from a mob in Brownsville.[20]

Annie Williams went to the police station later that night to inquire about her husband. She was told that no-one was there. She returned home. On Friday morning, she went to the jail again and asked the officer in charge about her husband. She recalled that he replied, "They aren't going to hurt him. They may just ask him a few questions, but they'll let him loose. If he doesn't come home in a day or two, come back and let me know." She left the jail and went to Jackson, Tennessee, to Mitchell's insurance office and talked to Thomas Davis about the events of the previous night. Davis assured her that, at the time he was released, Elbert had been in the jail.

Mrs. Williams did not hear from her husband all day Friday, and on Saturday she did what African-American people so often had to do when in trouble, she sought assistance from an influential white man. She went to the man who employed her and her husband to ask his assistance in finding Elbert. They both worked for the Sunshine Laundry, Elbert as a fireman and she as a checker. Her employer assured her that he and his father would do what they could and regretted some "hard-headed people, a bunch we can't do anything with."

At 7:30 on Sunday morning, Mrs. Williams finally heard about her husband. The African-American undertaker, Al Rawls, sent word that she should come to the Hatchee River. A fisherman had found a body in the river. She went and found her husband's body. The coroner at first refused to take the body from the water, but Annie Williams insisted that he do so. Once the body was on the river bank, the signs of torture and death on it were unmistakable. Williams's head was twice its normal size from beatings. Holes in his chest indicated either stab or bullet wounds. Williams's hands and arms were still tied, and a rope tied to a heavy branch remained around his neck. The group on the river bank put Williams's corpse into a box and took it away for immediate burial. Friends advised Williams's wife to return home but not to stay at home that night. She immediately left Brownsville for Memphis. There she sold the car that she and Elbert owned and left for safety among friends in Farmingdale, New York.[21]

Freedom's Delay
1940–1954

5 The lynching of Elbert Williams touched off a series of protests that tested the legal protections available to African Americans in 1940. These protests also changed local struggles into a national effort. Davis, Mitchell, and others came to call by their first names people who before had inhabited a world of politics far distant from them. The NAACP mounted a national effort to redress the wrongs committed in Haywood County. The U.S. Department of Justice launched a brief, internally subverted investigation. These unsuccessful actions together demonstrated that, at this time and in some places, white people could still hurt, kill, and rob African Americans without punishment or even arrest. This stark evidence of their vulnerability terrified most of Haywood County's African Americans.

MOBS AND MOTIVES

People in Haywood County reacted to Elbert Williams's lynching with fear. Robert McElwee remembered the night of Williams's abduction and the ensuing search for him. In a startling irony, McElwee, the grandson of the last man to express the voting power of African Americans in the county, dug the grave, literally, for Elbert Williams, a man killed for attempting to regain a portion of that power. McElwee lived on the road from Brownsville to Jackson—the same road along which, in 1864, the Confederate soldiers had marched their Union army prisoners from Fort Pillow and on which a small detail had executed the Union force's commanding officer. McElwee had been sleeping on the porch, for the cooler air, on the night of Williams's abduction:

So many cars passed my house that night. I said to my wife, "Look at those cars come by here." I was lying on the porch and saw about twenty carloads of them. When I saw those cars go down the road, it scared me. It scared me pretty bad. They were carrying him [Williams] on down the road to kill him. I didn't know he was with them then, but I knew that later, and when he didn't show up in two days we knew something had happened to him. We didn't know if he was dead or living, but we knew something had happened to him.

I knew Dick Williams well. We'd play games together. He was an empty talking boy. But he didn't mean no harm by it. He put power behind his words. He wasn't bad. It's just that when he was talking he would put power behind his words. Like, "Oh no, man!!" "I ain't so and so!" I went to school with him.

I helped dig his grave. The undertaker called out to my home and told me and my brother to open the grave for Dick Williams and that's all he would tell us. There was no question. He was buried in Taylor Chapel graveyard. The only people there at the cemetery were us that opened the grave. It was pretty sad. They cut his tongue out, cut his privates off, and stuck them in his mouth. I just thought it was mean of those people. You couldn't open the casket. Al Rawls brought him.

Ethel McElwee, a young girl at the time, recalled her fear following Williams's lynching: "Oh, I was scared to death. I was very small but I was so feared I couldn't sleep. I even put the covers over my head in the summertime. It was hot. Scared to death."

Other people, whether in hiding or not in hiding but in fear, began speculating on Williams's lynching. Robert McElwee interpreted Williams's death as a consequence of his violation of the cardinal principle of survival: obey your boss. Williams's employer might have intervened to save Williams, according to McElwee, but he didn't because Williams had disobeyed him.

Dick's boss had a daughter and she would borrow Dick's car and go to Jackson. And they told him to quit letting her have it. He was working for her daddy. They saw her going to Jackson, and they had told him don't let them see him lend her his car anymore. They told him, "Don't let me catch you lending that car anymore to my daughter." And Dick let her have the car again. They told him what to do, and he didn't do it.

You see, Dick had in his head that, with what he was doing, he could outdo them. I think the thing was, they had this NAACP, an organization the colored people could control their rights. You see, that's where his little mind was. They broke it up.

I was not a member of the NAACP. I was glad I wasn't. They were picking you up. I knew lots of people who were members. I knew Buster Walker and the others. They slipped out. Many of them, just leave and leave and leave and leave. It got to the point I thought everyone was going to leave. So many people left there.

I was scared until Al Rawls told me what he [Williams] did, then I wasn't frightened so much. Because if you did what they told you to do, you weren't in no danger. You see, if he hadn't lent that car again, he would not have got killed. He worked for the man that got him out of the house. He wouldn't have got killed if his boss man stood up with him.

McElwee learned that the mob's membership was widespread. The knowledge surprised him, just as it had surprised the freedpeople of the area when the Klan began seventy years earlier. This knowledge McElwee kept to himself. "The people in that mob, you'd be surprised, they were people you would talk with everyday. They were people you'd run into and talk with everyday. And you'd think they were something else. But they were people, you'd really know. The very richest white man back there knew about what was going on."

Others interpreted Williams's lynching in terms of his challenge to the old politics of subordination. Williams had a temper, and people considered him outspoken, too much so sometimes. Perhaps he talked back to the mob and thus sealed his execution. Williams was Nann Davis's cousin, and she too had a tendency to be outspoken. She recalls, "Elbert was one of those people who just didn't back up, you know. You see, there is a time to speak and a time to be quiet. We just figured he lost his temper. Like I had to be quiet that night the mob came for Eli. Eli could be quiet." An important lesson on survival in the African-American community was how to bend with the storm.

Casher remembered that Williams sometimes lacked caution:

Williams had a little temper. If you didn't approach him the right way, he would holler, and that's all they wanted him to do. I feel he probably got smart with one of the mob.

It was probably coming a long time. I worked next to him for seven years, and I would beg him don't talk so loud and he would say, "I don't care. I don't care if they hear me."

I just know that one of those men who heard that talk was really mad with him, and I just know that they really wanted the opportunity. I know because I'm right there with him five and one-half days a week. He would come out and see me sweeping or something, and he would say, "What are you doing, old man?" "I'm working." "Well, stay there, I got something to tell you." I would say, "Well, I'll see you later on." And he would answer, "You scared? You ain't got time to talk?" I kind of believe he might have brought some of it on himself, but only because place meant that you did not speak openly about some things.

A much more mercenary motive may have contributed to Williams's lynching. During the week, Williams had traveled to Jackson and spoken to Elisha Davis about his service station. Williams agreed to return to Brownsville and see if he could lease Davis's station and continue operating it for the benefit of Davis and his family. Williams had made inquiries about such an arrangement. As Hunter led Williams to the car from his home that night, Thomas Davis called from the car for him to tell them about the arrangements he was making. Obviously, the four men in the car had been discussing plans for Elisha's garage and equipment.

While Williams was making his plans, the sheriff had seized Elisha Davis's equipment. The sheriff allegedly had done this to satisfy a loan that a white man had made to Davis for the equipment. But Davis swore that he had bought and paid for the equipment himself and owed no money on it. Within a month, two white men designated by the sheriff began operating the garage, using Davis's equipment without any compensation to Davis or his family.

It was not uncommon for a lynching to cover up the theft of a black person's property. Certainly someone enjoyed a modest windfall, as the Davis family members fled the county, leaving homes, livestock, equipment, and land behind. Nann recalls that her furniture and livestock were left behind and that, to this day, she has no idea what happened to them. Likewise, Casher

Davis and his wife left household furnishings and livestock behind, including a mule he had ridden when he courted his future wife. The Davis family's property had provided them security and status. Now, they lost most of their property without a trace and lacked the ability even to inquire about its disposition. Elisha's mother and sister eventually sold their home in Brownsville for what they could get. The family farm in the country was simply lost. Theft and envy were part of the lynching tradition and undoubtedly played a role in Williams's death and the banishment of the Davis family.[1]

AVOIDING THE GRASP
OF THE MOB

Whatever the mob's motives, the death of Elbert Williams was certain, and African Americans in Brownsville feared more reprisals. After two weeks in Brownsville with her in-laws, Nann Davis and her children left town and took refuge in Newbern, at the home of Elisha and Casher's aunt, Willie. Nann's oldest daughter, Evelyn, who was ten at the time, recalled the time in Brownsville and Newbern as one of great fear.

> People were contacted to come and get us. They would come to pick us up in a truck. They would cover us up like we were fruit. We always took back roads. The only time we took a highway was when we were going to Jackson. I remember being on a highway going to Jackson. We did not know if we were safe or not. You're riding on the road and you don't know what's coming up behind you. And we were all down on the bed of that truck. Covered up just like fruit. We lived in absolute terror.
>
> Because we did not know where our dad was, that instilled a lot of fear in us.
>
> Everything was so hush-hush and very secretive. You did not dare talk too much. I don't think they let us do anything outside. They kind of kept us in and fed us. Just my mother and us kids.
>
> I am sure our friends were armed, and they were watching the house where we lived. The children stayed indoors all of the time. In the evening, no lamps in the house were lit. The family lived in complete fear, uncertain of how far the arm of the mob might reach.

Nann remembered it also as a sleepless time: "My kids may have slept, but I sat up. I would take a nap during the day, but sleep at night, no. No. We would keep watch. One would watch and the other one would sleep, then the other one would sleep and the other would watch."

Casher Davis had preceded Nann and the Davis children to Newbern. For the next year, he worked in his sister's restaurant and did odd jobs. He remained cautious and wary. He watched every car, suspicious of all cars with Haywood County license plates and concerned that someone driving a car with another county's license plate might have been hired to injure him. He recalled, "It was tough. We were dodging."

THE NAACP
"GETS DOWN TO BUSINESS"

As the Davis family members retreated to secret places, events in Haywood County garnered national attention. Mitchell telegraphed J. L. LeFlore, chairman of the regional conference of southern branches of the NAACP, with news of Thomas Davis and Elbert Williams's abduction. Mitchell sent this wire on Friday morning, as soon as he had learned of the events. LeFlore was in Philadelphia attending the annual meeting of the NAACP. He read Mitchell's telegram to the entire conference:

> MOB CONTINUES TO TERRORIZE MEMBERS OF THE BROWNSVILLE
> BRANCH, THOMAS DAVIS, ELBERT WILLIAMS ATTACKED LAST NIGHT.
> WILLIAMS STILL MISSING, MOB DETERMINED TO RUN ALL MEMBERS OUT
> OF TOWN, SOMETHING MUST BE DONE IMMEDIATELY. CITIZENS IN THIS
> SECTION MUCH ALARMED OVER SITUATION.[2]

The conference members were already aware of the reprisals against the county's chapter. Conference planners had invited Rev. Buster Walker, one of the charter NAACP members who had eluded the mob the night they took Elisha Davis, to make a presentation to the entire conference on the mob action and other reprisals before the abduction of Davis and Williams. Walker spoke on 21 June. He knew only that Williams was missing but not that he had been lynched. Walker wrote to Mitchell immediately after his talk. He described men and women weeping as he recounted events that had befallen himself and others in the county. Tears then turned to action. "The NAACP got down to business," Walker wrote enthusiastically. The conference members wired the United States president and others in Washington. Walker naively wrote that he would soon have an appointment with President Roosevelt and urged Mitchell and others to hold on for a few days: "Tell everybody to hold on just a few days longer and we will show the country a trick . . . Now I just wanted you to hear from me I know it will give you some ease so you just look to the Lord he will make things all right. By your friend and Bro. as ever."[3]

LeFlore also wrote to Mitchell immediately after the conference, on 25 June. He reported the indignation of everyone who learned of the "reign of terror . . . to deny colored citizens lawful rights guaranteed by the Constitution." LeFlore assured Mitchell and Davis that they offered "a testimony to the courage of the race" and that they were "rendering heroic service to the Nation." He also requested pictures of Davis, Williams, and scenes in Haywood County to use in publicity campaigns.[4]

Walter White, secretary of the NAACP, mounted a national campaign that measured the ability of the NAACP to mobilize federal authorities on civil rights issues. White requested that William H. Hastie, NAACP counsel and chairman of the NAACP's National Legal Committee, arrange meetings for Walker and Hastie to inform federal officials about Haywood County. Hastie, Walker, and another NAACP Washington staff member met with O. John Rogge, U.S. assistant attorney general, and secured from him a promise that the FBI would immediately investigate the events in Haywood County.[5]

White met on Friday with the U.S. district attorney at Memphis, William McClanahan, while White was in Memphis to give a speech. White also met with Mitchell and Elisha Davis later that same day. Thomas Davis had fled to Nashville, leaving Elisha as the only mob victim left in the area. On Tuesday, 1 July, White wrote to McClanahan summarizing the facts of "the trouble at Brownsville" and expressing his belief that ample evidence showed a violation of federal law, particularly of Title 51 of Section 18 of the Federal Criminal Code.[6]

This law was a remnant of Congress's attempts during Reconstruction to protect the civil rights of newly freed people of the South. These measures, passed by Congress between 1865 and 1875, had stirred violent reprisals in

Tennessee elections. The specific law that White referred to formed part of statutes passed in 1870 and 1871; it had been aimed at the Ku Klux Klan. Much of the protective legislation had been struck down by the Supreme Court in its 1883 decisions on civil rights, at the start of the Jim Crow era. Those decisions had delegated responsibility for protecting the civil rights of African Americans to the states. Samuel McElwee, of course, had tried unsuccessfully to get Tennessee to expand the protections that the federal government had reduced. By 1890, few state protections remained, and the broad federal legislation of the 1860s and 1870s had been narrowed considerably. The NAACP now urged the Justice Department to build its case on the portion of that legislation that continued in effect. The law that White cited prescribed punishment for interfering with the civil rights of others. The law did not concern lynching, although lynching Williams because of his part in a voter registration drive would fall under the law, just as the mob's action towards Elisha and Thomas Davis did.

White understood the difficulty of securing enforcement of these laws. He had worked since 1918 to get lynchers punished for murder, to deliver innocent African-American people from mob justice, and to secure enforcement of the remaining laws protecting the civil rights of African Americans. Now, in yet another case, he was urging prosecution not for lynching but for the charge that fell under federal law, criminally interfering with another person's civil rights. He wrote to District Attorney McClanahan:

> There would seem to be little question that a federal law has been violated and the violators of that law are known. . . .
>
> We therefore, vigorously urge speedy and uncompromising action by the Department of Justice in the apprehension and punishment of those who are guilty of violating the law and in the protection of innocent persons who have thus been mistreated for no other reason than that of wishing to exercise their Federal right to vote.[7]

THE NAACP'S STAKE IN THE CASE

The NAACP had a very substantial interest in the events in Haywood County. The event recapitulated the violence against African Americans that had led to the NAACP's creation. The group had taken as its basic goals ending violence against African Americans and securing equal protection of the laws for them. Often—precisely, 191 times between 1882 and 1940—anti-lynching legislation had marched up Capitol Hill in Washington without success. In 1940, the NAACP had progressed very far toward passing anti-lynching legislation. The House had passed a bill in January, and in March the Senate Judiciary Committee had reported the bill favorably, recommending passage by the Senate. During the summer months of 1940, the NAACP at last was close to securing passage of federal legislation on lynching, one of the organization's key goals since its founding in 1909.[8]

Williams's lynching and the mobs's actions against the Davis brothers illustrated the continuing need for the legislation that the NAACP was prodding the Senate to approve. The number of reported lynchings had declined in the 1930s, with 130 reported in that decade. In May 1940, one group which documented and surveyed lynchings and related incidents declared that the nation had concluded a twelve-month period without a reported lynching.[9] White was determined that the public not think that lynching had ceased. Such a public perception obviously could impede the NAACP's efforts to gain anti-lynching legislation. At best, White argued, the nature of the lynchings had changed. There were far fewer public lynchings such as the murder of Claude Neal in 1934. Press and radio had known of that lynching and advertised it beforehand. The lynching lasted all night, and a crowd of four thousand took part, beating, stabbing, shooting and finally hanging Neal. The police did not interfere, nor did officials prosecute mob members later.[10] The Williams case was a "quiet," not a public, lynching, in which the police may have participated. Williams's lynching proved the continuing need to protect African Americans from lynch mobs, and in its legislative effort the NAACP needed such proof.

Previous legislation had failed on Capitol Hill, due to the opposition of southern senators and the silent complicity of an administration that looked the other way so as not to threaten Democratic party unity. The events in Haywood County might be the catalyst to garner both Democratic and Republican support and prevent southern Democrats in the Senate from scuttling yet another bill by filibuster. White had the support of northern urban Democrats and labor leaders, two important elements of the Democratic coalition. He needed to stifle his white southern opponents, who formed part of the broad New Deal coalition. The Haywood County case could help. The NAACP's annual report cited Williams's lynching as "the outstanding case in 1940 and evidence that lynching continued underground."

The stakes in the ensuing contest over Williams's lynching and the suppression of the Brownsville chapter were very high for the NAACP locally as well as nationally. Mitchell explained to national officers that the credibility of the NAACP was at stake. Local people had organized chapters and made initiatives to register to vote, in the belief that the NAACP had the strength to protect them and to guarantee them their rights. Mitchell wanted the NAACP to validate their belief. On 1 July, just a few days after White had met with McClanahan, Mitchell warned White that the U.S. district attorney in Memphis was a "dyed in wool" prejudiced southerner from West Tennessee and that he would not act on the case "without pressure from [the national] office." Mitchell suggested that this was "an opportune time for us to let members of the race in Tennessee know the strength of our organization."[11]

Mitchell asked other NAACP branches for assistance. He wrote to Rev. S. L. McDowell, head of the Nashville NAACP chapter, to suggest that the Reverend Mr. McDowell and other chapter members contact the governor to request the protection of the national guard for the NAACP leaders, including Elisha and Thomas, who wanted to return home. The FBI was in the county on 1 July investigating the lynching and mob action, but "Lord only knows what will happen after the federal men leave the town." Elisha Davis traveled to Nashville, where he spoke to the NAACP chapter there about events in Haywood County and requested its support.[12]

ORDINARY AND
EXTRAORDINARY CONCERNS

Mitchell worked feverishly the weekend after his meeting with White. He sent off a flurry of letters, including one that urged Buster Walker to come back from Washington and Philadelphia to lead a march in Haywood County to demonstrate a lack of fear. It was a remarkable expression of courage, coming as it did one week after Williams's death: "We can't give up the fight now, the people are depending upon us to carry the fight to the limit. There is no danger in being in Brownsville since the Federal men have been making their investigation but we want some sort of protection for the people after the Federal men have gone."

Mitchell combined his courage with his continued confidence in the "better class of whites" who had supported the initial NAACP chapter's inquiries about voting. Mitchell thought these whites represented "our best chance to push the fight":

> This is the opportune time for us to fight for our rights as citizens, if we don't the whole country will be terribly disappointed.
>
> I don't know what suggestion you will offer upon your arrival, but I am thinking that we should demand some protection from the State and lead our people to the polls and vote them.[13]

While the NAACP and its officers, locally and nationally, played for high stakes, others had other much more personal and immediate concerns. Elisha Davis's sister and mother had left Brownsville, shortly after Nann took the children to Newbern. They sold their home for what they could get and moved to Jackson. When the Davis women reached Jackson, they rented half of a duplex home. Elisha continued to live with Mitchell in Jackson and talked with Nann occasionally on the phone. They talked clandestinely, Nann recalls: "You didn't call no names. The phone rang. You just said, 'Hello, and so and so and what not.' You didn't call no names. You knew who you were talking to, and we just assumed they were listening in on our phone calls."

Elisha began worrying about work, income, and support for his family almost from the time he escaped the mob. He was concerned to regain his equipment or to gain compensation for its loss. Working in Jackson was a major problem. Elisha feared being seen in the streets and was afraid that mob members would come and seek him out. Davis wrote to White the day after seeing him in Memphis to inform him of the extraordinary difficulties he faced in meeting his ordinary responsibilities:

> I gambled everything, my home, my business, my life, my family (wife and children) in order to prove to those people in Brownsville, Tennessee,

that the NAACP was alright. I felt that whatever happened that I would be safe under the wings of the National Association for the Advancement of Colored People.

At present I am separated from my family. I'm not making any money. I feel not secure in the least. After having told all in the case my life here in this town is a constant threat. I am willing to remain here a while and help all that I can both you and Mr. Mitchell. But I want to get you to do this favor for me. Help me locate a secure job away out of this state so that I may protect and support my wife and seven children when these matters are over. I need work, Mr. White, and I believe that you with your many contacts will be able to help me secure just such a job when these matters are straightened out.[14]

Even Mitchell, in the midst of this, occasionally turned to ordinary matters that now seemed trivial in comparison to the events of June. Mitchell expressed modest concern about Walker's insurance policy. Mitchell continued to carry Walker even though by late July Walker owed $3.60 in insurance premiums.[15]

Roy Wilkins, assistant secretary of the NAACP, sent Davis twenty-five dollars on 17 July for support of his family and issued a national appeal for further assistance. As part of that appeal, Wilkins asked Mitchell to locate Walker. Wilkins felt that Walker would be an effective speaker for a national campaign "by telling the dramatic story of Brownsville, firsthand." Walker returned briefly to the Memphis area in early August, only to flee again after a short while when he learned that men were inquiring of his whereabouts.[16]

"NO EVIDENCE HAS BEEN BROUGHT OUT"

In the meantime, a veil of fear shrouded Haywood County. I. L. Newbern, secretary of the Brownsville NAACP chapter, requested that Walter White send no mail pertaining to the NAACP to her because of this "terrible uproar we're undergoing." She reported her suspicion that the mail was being opened and the common fear of bodily harm. She was "on the spot and afraid to stay at my home at night." She expressed hope that her name would not be revealed as an NAACP member because of whites' apparent intent to run all

NAACP members out of Brownsville: "Really, I'm almost scared to death. Being threatened and watched is a terrible predicament to be in. My husband and I are on the verge of moving also."[17] They moved to Clarksville, Tennessee, later that summer, leaving their cleaning business behind.

The NAACP pressure resulted in an FBI investigation. White, like Mitchell, believed that the U.S. district attorney in Memphis "would not do anything unless real pressure was brought on him." Indeed, McClanahan's first opinion was that no federal statutes, only state laws, had been broken. He informed his Washington superiors of his judgment that the lynching of Elbert Williams was a murder that fell under state law and therefore was within the jurisdiction of local police. At least since the time of Samuel McElwee, African Americans in West Tennessee had seen all such murders, with very few exceptions, go unsolved and the death officially listed as resulting "from unknown causes at the hands of parties unknown." The NAACP argued persistently and successfully, through Hastie, that the mob actions had violated the federally protected rights of Williams, Davis, Walker, and others. Hastie persuaded the Justice Department to order an FBI investigation.

The investigation was ineffective. FBI investigators did not do as well as the NAACP had done in its own investigation. Proceeding as the Freedmen's Bureau had in 1868, the NAACP in a short time had gathered affidavits from several county residents about the mob action and the identity of the mob members. The FBI reported finding no witnesses. Thurgood Marshall, who had only recently become special counsel to the NAACP, took over the case from White and specified the source of the FBI's investigatory failure. When the agents arrived in Brownsville, Marshall alleged, they checked in with local police, including Tip Hunter. According to Marshall, the FBI agents then traveled with Hunter during the course of their investigation. Hunter was present as the agents questioned people in Haywood County. The FBI's standard procedure of respecting the jurisdiction of the local authorities limited the investigation's effectiveness. Marshall crossed swords with J. Edgar Hoover and the FBI, and would continue to do so.[18]

The FBI's investigation was ineffective by intent, too. Concern over Williams's lynching took a back seat to the FBI's concern with Communist influence in the NAACP. The FBI's director, J. Edgar Hoover, emphasized the Haywood County case's "terrible effect on morale . . . laying the groundwork for Nazi, Communist, and Fascist agitators, and how important it is that

proper attention be given to the economic situation involving Negroes."
Hoover informed White of the importance "that reputable Negro organizations be diligently alert to keep Nazism, Communism, and Fascism from
attaching themselves to Negro movements." He assured White that the field
offices of the FBI would be vigilant to detect infiltration into the NAACP.[19]

Over the next two years, agents interviewed people in the Memphis and
West Tennessee area about Communist influence in the NAACP. The agents
concluded in mid-1941 that the NAACP in their area was "not considered
a Communist front organization." Another year of investigation "failed to
develop any information tending to show un-American activities on the part
of the NAACP or its members." The special agent in charge closed the case
in August 1942.[20]

The FBI's overriding concern about Communism was not apparent to
Elisha Davis on 25 July, when two agents visited him in Jackson. Davis wrote
to White immediately after the visit, exhibiting hope and pride in the investigation:

> Two FBI men came to see me to-day and I gave them the names of all known
> members of the mob that took me away from my home in Brownsville. I also
> gave them the information as to how and why the whites ran us out of town.
>
> Although I am isolated from my home and family I sincerely believe that
> God is with us in our fight for justice. I again want to thank the NAACP for
> the great fight it is making for me and my people at Brownsville.
>
> I am hoping that the members of the mob will be punished to the fullest
> and I stand ready to identify them to anyone who is interested in improving
> our condition at Brownsville.[21]

The FBI had visited Mitchell before their visit with Davis. Mitchell, unlike
Davis, lost confidence in the investigation as a result of the visit:

> I was on the second floor and these gentlemen came up to my office. I
> couldn't hear them. They were two big, white fellas that knocked on the
> door and came in. They pulled out their identification and showed me they
> were FBI. They said, "We want to talk with you about the Brownsville situ-
> ation." They asked me some questions about what happened to Elisha. I

said, "All I know is what he told me. That they took him and told him if he didn't leave town, they would kill him."

They asked me how long had I been affiliated with the NAACP? What other organizations I was with? He was looking at his paper as if he was reading something that was authentic, "You're Communist too, aren't you?"

I said, "I'm a what?" "Communist." I said, "No, I'm not a Communist. I was brought up Methodist. In fact, I really don't know what a Communist is."

They said, "There are several Communist organizations around here carrying on un-American activities."

I said, "I am not a part of them." Other than Democratic, Republican, I don't know anything about any political organization."

They asked me so many questions that finally I said, "The report I sent in was pertaining to what they did to Elisha. I didn't do anything to him. I just made out the report and notarized it."

They started getting hostile towards me and that made me kind of wonder if I should be hopeful. They wanted to know how long I had been a member of this organization and what was the purpose of it. Now everybody knew what the purpose of the NAACP is. So they talked a while and said they would be getting back to me. After they first came, I thought, "This was a bona fide investigation." But when they left, I felt it wasn't.

Despite his own disappointment and the general atmosphere of fear, Mitchell worked with the NAACP to regroup and begin new efforts for voter registration in Haywood County. He continued to visit Haywood County in the conduct of his insurance business. His presence testified to the commitment of the NAACP to the African Americans of Haywood County, but Mitchell was determined to prove to the white community, too, the commitment of the NAACP. Mitchell wrote to the NAACP office in early August to express his appreciation for its support and his own determination to continue to fight in Haywood County:

> Victory for us in Brownsville will mean a great lesson to all of the whites in this section, the whites in Brownsville have already realised [sic] that the N.A.A.C.P. is no top water organization.
>
> Will be glad to render any service possible in furthering our fight at Brownsville.[22]

Mitchell actually grew bolder. On one occasion, a car followed him for ten miles in Haywood County. He suspected that he was a target for mob action, and he was right. A service station attendant, a white man, explained to Mitchell later that a carload of men following Mitchell had stopped at the station where he worked. He told them that they should just wait. Mitchell stayed with a friend on Bradford Street, he explained, and they could go there at night and take him, as they had Elbert Williams.

Mitchell was determined not to go like Williams. He carried a gun and intended to use it if necessary:

> Lynchings was so common then, they started keeping scores. At the end of the year, "We only had fifteen lynchings last year." "We only had six this past year." Just like it was a game or something. But still, there were people involved in doing the lynchings but no-one was ever charged. I resented that. And being a young man, I was willing to give my life. I was going to make history. I was going to take one of them with me. I said, "If they mess with me, someone's going to heaven or hell with me."

Mitchell had decided that the courage of the Klan and the mob rested on their numbers: "I found out they're bear when they're twenty-five or thirty, but they're cowards other times."

The process of justice also fueled Mitchell's determined indignation. On 13 August, the Haywood County grand jury heard evidence on Williams's murder and reported that it had made "a careful and earnest investigation, examining people from all works of life, and no evidence has been brought out that might place suspicion on anyone as having a part in the case." To Mitchell, the finding was a joke. Elisha Davis stood ready to identify the men in the mob that abducted him. Mitchell was also ready to provide sworn affidavits naming mob members who had abducted Thomas Davis and Elbert Williams. Such affidavits would not be conclusive evidence sufficient to convict anyone of actually murdering Williams, but they certainly would have cast suspicion on some men as having had a part in the murder. The grand jury did not have this evidence, and local police, obviously, were not about to produce any evidence that would identify their own members as participants in or leaders of the mob that had abducted Williams and the others.[23]

Jackson,
Tennessee.
June 29, 1940

Hon Walter White
69 Fifth Ave
New York
City.

10299
JUL 1 - 1940

Dear Mr White,

I was more than pleased to have the pleasure of seeing you and talking to you in regards to my present Condition. I gambled everything, my Home my business, my life, my family (wife & children) in order to prove to those people in Brownsville Tennessee that the N.a.a.Cp was alright I felt that whatever happened that I would Be safe under the wings of the National Association for the Advancement of Colored people.

At present I am seperated from my family. I am not making any money. I feel not secure in the least after having lost all in the case my life here in this town is a constant threat I am willing to remain here a while & help all that I Can both you & my Mitchell But I want to get you to do this favor for me. Help me locate a secure Job away out of this state so that I may protect & support my wife + seven children when these matters are over.

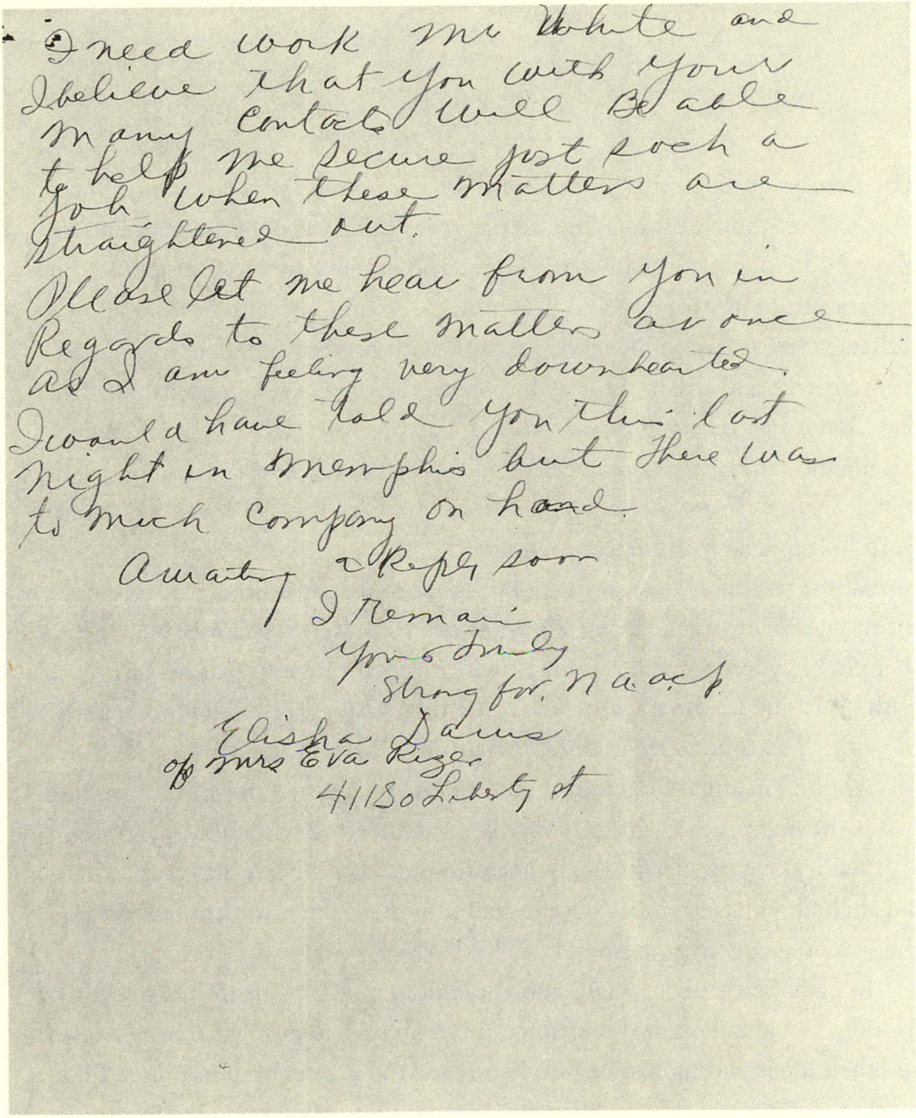

I need work mr White and
I believe that you with your
many contacts will be able
to help me secure just such a
job when these matters are
straightened out.
Please let me hear from you in
Regards to these matters at once
as I am feeling very downhearted.
I would have told you this last
night in Memphis but there was
to much company on hand.
Awaiting a Reply soon
I Remain
yours truly
Strong for N.a.a.c.p.
Elisha Davis
of mrs Eva Riger
4115 o Liberty st

Fig. 16. Letter from Elisha Davis to Walter White, 20 June 1940.
Courtesy of the Library of Congress.

THE DAVIS FAMILY REUNITES

The verdict of the grand jury suggested that the tide of repression, which Mitchell had thought was falling, actually was rising to cover the incidents in Haywood County. Elisha Davis's hope eroded. He had had no income for two months. His property was gone. His tools and equipment were gone. Others were operating his service station with his tools. He had lived apart from his wife and children for eight weeks; their lives were permeated with fear. Davis had received twenty-five dollars from the NAACP, about the amount he had been making weekly before the vortex of reprisal had dragged him away from Brownsville. He was caught up in national events but severed from his home and all that was familiar.[24]

White responded to another of Davis's requests for assistance. Davis used the money White sent to bring Nann and their children to Jackson. He visited them in Newbern to make arrangements for their move. It was his first visit with his family in two months. Evelyn, Elisha's daughter, then ten, recalled the visit: "He came to see us but it was just for a brief period. It was like they brought him in and whisked him out. It was long enough for him to see us. It was the night they went to Nashville for a meeting with Walter White."

Nann Davis recalled her feelings at this reunion with her husband: "I was like a child with a new toy." Nann had important news for her husband—she was pregnant with their eighth child.

In early September, Nann and the children moved from Newbern to Jackson. It had been ten weeks since the mob had taken Elisha from home and their life in hiding had begun. Nann and the seven children joined Eli's mother and sister in the duplex they were renting. They remained cautious and out of sight. The children slept in the one bedroom, and the adults slept on a half-porch that was partially enclosed with latticework. The adults did not sleep at the same time. Nann instituted the same system of night watches that she had conducted all summer: "One person slept four hours, the other kept watch. Then the one watched and the other slept." Eli continued to live with Mitchell at his home.[25]

Thelma Shell Price's mother rented one half of her duplex to the Davis family and ran a boardinghouse in the other half. Here she provided lodging to black chauffeurs and nannies who accompanied white businessmen or families but could not stay with them in the Southern Hotel, one block away. Price's mother was aware of the danger involved in renting to the Davises, but she was determined not to be threatened. Price, who at the time of this study still lived in Jackson, recalled, "They more or less kept them inside, indoors. I asked one of the little girls, one of the daughters, if they could come out and play and she said, 'No, they can't.' . . . It was very small in that apartment, especially with all of them. There was a living room and a kitchen and a bedroom and another little room where you could make a bed. Not a full bedroom but a place where you could make a bed and lay down."

THE NAACP CHALLENGES AMERICA'S HONESTY

Walter White came to Tennessee and appeared with Davis at a rally in Nashville on 29 August. He derided the grand jury verdict:

> The grand jury report that no evidence could be found as to the perpetrators of that outrage is ridiculous. I am no expert investigator but in a very few days I was able to gather concrete evidence establishing the participation of thirteen persons in the kidnapping and murder of Williams and the driving out of seven other Negroes from Brownsville. All this evidence and the names of witnesses willing and eager to testify have been placed in the hands of the United States Attorney at Memphis and the Department of Justice at Washington.

In a speech reported in newspapers across the country, White placed the events in the context of American democracy, as McElwee had done with Eliza Wood's lynching fifty-three years earlier. White also played on the themes given him by J. Edgar Hoover and invoked the rise of totalitarian states, such as Hitler's Germany, as a reason to deal with this and other lynchings:

> The white people of Brownsville, Tennessee, who last June lynched Elbert Williams and drove seven other Negroes from their homes because

the Negroes of Brownsville wanted to exercise their constitutional rights to vote in the coming presidential election, thereby helped Hitler and deserve a letter of thanks from the Nazi leader.

Dark and perilous days lie ahead of America. The tides of totalitarianism sweep ominously down upon the shores of what some orators call "the last remaining democracy." We ask America if she wants the twelve million Negroes of this country to believe in their country's honesty when it opposes race hatred and bigotry dictatorship. If so, then America must wipe out the kind of Hitlerite and bigotry for which the Brownsville tragedy stands.

White also took the occasion to drive home the need for federal anti-lynching legislation. The death of Williams and the actions against other NAACP leaders in the county obviously contradicted the assurances of southern political leaders that the states could enforce existing laws to deal with these matters. White pointedly attacked one Tennessee Democratic senator and the old southern tradition of opposing federal action on local violations of rights:

In 1938 your Senator Kenneth McKellar . . . put into the Congressional Record of January 17, 1938, telegrams from the governors of fifteen Southern states, one of them being the then governor of Tennessee, which stated that no federal legislation against lynching was necessary as the states could and would act vigorously, promptly, and honestly to prevent lynchings and punish lynchers. The Brownsville lynching clearly shows how much faith can be placed in those pledges. As far as the public record shows, the State of Tennessee has done absolutely nothing to punish Williams' lynchers whose identities are known, and obviously does not propose to do anything. It is therefore imperative that the fight for federal antilynching legislation must be renewed and doubled in intensity, since once more the impotence of the state has been demonstrated.[26]

NEW EFFORTS AND NEW THREATS

While together in Nashville, White, Mitchell, and Davis planned a registration effort on 4 and 5 September in Haywood County. White telegraphed the FBI in Memphis and Assistant Attorney General Rogge about their plans and requested protection for the African Americans who would make this effort.[27] White wired Davis as well, to tell him of his requests.[28]

The registration effort fizzled. Assessments of that failed effort demonstrate how wide was the gulf between the Justice Department's view of the situation and that of the NAACP leaders. Rogge wired McClanahan to provide FBI agents as White had requested. He later heard back from McClanahan that "all Negroes who attempted to register were allowed to do so in a lawful manner . . . there were no violations." Rogge relayed this information to the NAACP.

Davis and Mitchell had very different information about this voter registration effort. As they heard it, only one person went, and no one registered. R. B. Bond, Davis's landlord, who was an NAACP member and was still living and teaching in Haywood County, conveyed this information to Davis and added, "Elisha, the people are scared to go up there. They say they would go if it was agreeable with the white people. You don't have no idea how dangerous it is to go up there. A white man told my cousin, before this thing was settled, the river would be full of Negroes."[29]

The letter reached Davis in Niles, Michigan. He had left Jackson for Niles in early September to find work and a new life for his family. Davis believed that contacts he had there from his earlier move would be important in starting over. Niles was also suitable because it was out of the migratory stream of African Americans from Haywood County. Only the Davis family had migrated there. Thus, there was less chance that news of the family's whereabouts might be reported to officials in Haywood County, as Steve Green's location had been reported to Arkansas authorities. Davis forwarded Bond's letter to Walter White and described his own situation:

> I have not heard from my family and neither have I the money to go and get them, so if there is any possible way you could suggest, so I could go get them here, I can get relief. Kindly answer me as soon as you can, for I am almost crazy, walking around in circles.
>
> I am closing, hoping for the best.[30]

White forwarded the information about the fizzled registration effort to Rogge, contradicting or at least amplifying McClanahan's report. White

Agents attempted to contact
in Brownsville.
                                                  To date he has not contacted
this office.

Agents also attempted to locate   and were advised

6

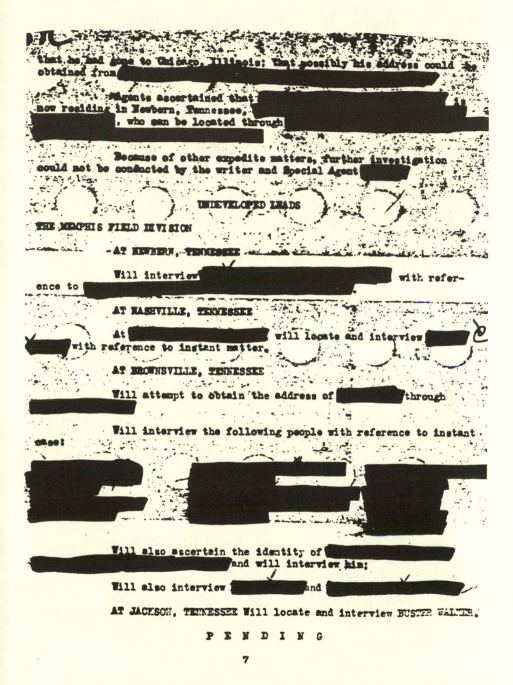

Fig. 17. Two of more than a thousand pages in the Justice Department's file on the lynching of Elbert Williams. Access to this file was obtained through the Freedom of Information Act. More than fifty years after the case, large segments of the file remain hidden from public view.

explained his own problem with credibility, because of the Justice Department's handling of the case. He had defended the Justice Department against rumors of ineptitude and indifference, but the Justice Department's actions had done nothing to refute the rumors or validate his defense.[31]

For White, Mitchell elaborated on the fear that had stymied registration efforts in Haywood County, relating this fear directly to the Justice Department's lack of action. The Justice Department had made no effort to prosecute Hunter and other officials in Haywood County. This fact gave African-American residents no reason to believe that the department would protect them on 4 and 5 September in an effort to register to vote. The Justice Department had evaded responsibility in the case of Williams's lynching and the other deprivations of civil rights in Haywood County, by arguing that these were state matters that fell under the jurisdiction of police whom the aspiring voters had every reason to fear. "Members of the mob that lynched Elbert Williams can be seen in Brownsville each day going about their work as if they had killed only a rabbit."[32] In fact, the status of some of the mob members had been enhanced in the time since Williams's lynching. Tip Hunter had won the Democratic party's nomination for sheriff and was assured of election in November, given the party's predominance in the county. Mitchell concluded his 9 October letter to White with a statement combining anger and courage: "If the FBI men are offering an alibi that they are unable to locate the members of the mob, I am willing to personally lead them to each man named in the affidavits executed by Elisha and Thomas Davis."[33]

By December, Mitchell was convinced that the Justice Department was stalling on the case and would continue to do so. Still, he and others continued to write to the U.S. attorney general, whose administrative assistant again replied that there seemed to be no violation of federal law. He suggested that Mitchell "present in detail all the facts" of this case to the U.S. attorney in Memphis, the very man Mitchell was trying to circumvent or pressure.[34] Nevertheless, on 31 March 1941, Wendell Berge, assistant attorney general for civil rights, ordered further investigation into the case.

Behind the facade of ineptitude, some federal authorities covertly sabotaged the investigation. The Freedmen's Bureau had promptly investigated and prosecuted the outrages against freedpeople of Haywood County in 1867 and 1868. Now, in 1940, another federal agency that had been created to protect the civil rights of freedpeople delayed investigations and derailed possible prosecutions. In Memphis, U.S. Attorney McClanahan initially hesitated to conduct an investigation into Williams's lynching. Later, he delayed and limited the investigation of charges against Sheriff Tip Hunter by Davis and others. McClanahan put off reporting to superiors in Washington, citing the "serious phases of this case, which require the most careful consideration."[35] Several times McClanahan explained to the people in Washington the need for more investigation. At the same time, however, he told local FBI agents that he saw no need for additional investigation and instructed them to limit their interviews regarding the cases.[36]

McClanahan's delaying tactics extended beyond procrastination to real resistance to investigating Williams's lynching. From the beginning, McClanahan had professed his commitment to enforcing federal law but also explained to the Washington office that

> those of us on the ground fully appreciate the fact that the racial situation in counties like Haywood is such as to require extremely careful handling. . . . The negroes in that county outnumber the white people two to one. Notwithstanding this situation, the friction between the negroes and the whites in that county has been at a minimum for a period of many years, and my observation is that there has been no serious mistreatment of the negroes by the whites in that county.

McClanahan continued with an exposition of state jurisdiction over some of the matters that the case involved. He attributed the demand for a federal investigation and the problems in Haywood County to "agitation which originated with outside sources." Apparently referring to the NAACP and attorney Ballard's appearance in court, McClanahan explained the resentment of white citizens over "officious and mischief-making activity on the part of people who do not live in that section at all and who are not acquainted with the problems of the colored people." The white officials of the county, McClanahan assured his superiors, preside over state courts where "a Negro can, in our judgment, get just as fair a deal in controversies . . . as a white person." McClanahan urged that any FBI involvement be "very quiet and discreet." He had confidence that the grand jury "will get at the real facts" and worried that "ridiculous publicity could touch off black on white violence." He pointed out that a white man had been killed and another seriously wounded. On the other hand, Williams was the only Negro killed, "if he was killed," McClanahan qualified.[37]

Twice his Washington bosses asked McClanahan to take the case to a federal grand jury, but he never did. Wendell Berge, U.S. assistant attorney general, wrote to McClanahan on 31 March and 2 October 1941, asserting his view that the case warranted presentation to a federal grand jury. Both times McClanahan requested delays to permit more investigation. At the same time, he restricted interviews and investigation by local FBI agents.

McClanahan's delays carried the day, and his doubts eventually infiltrated the FBI's last report on the case. This document expressed McClanahan's skepticism about the charges. The agents reported that they could not substantiate that Williams had been killed by a white mob. They suggested another possible explanation of Williams's death: "The Negro element has been having trouble amongst themselves for some time, which was a result of friction between members of the National Association for the Advancement of Colored People and the non-members." Hoover's last report on the case repeated his agents' report about trouble in "the Negro element."[38]

Milmon Mitchell believed that the African-American community indeed had splintered, though certainly not to the point of violence. The violence and terror it faced had widened any existing divisions within the community. By August, Mitchell complained, he had become the "target of many criticisms from certain Uncle Toms in this section who are supposed to stand well with white folks." Prominent African Americans, including some former NAACP members, not only disavowed the registration effort but also blamed Mitchell for starting the trouble:

> There were blacks there who considered themselves leaders, who considered if blacks started voting and what not, they would be pushed out of their position of authority. Their position of authority was limited to the extent of going back and telling the white folks all the things that the "niggers" were doing. I had them to call me and say, "If I were you, I wouldn't come back over here anymore." I went to go in a little restaurant over there in Brownsville and a lady closed the door in my face, a black woman. I had been going over there to get a little coffee and what not for a long time, she closed the door in my face.

That was somewhat typical in those days in small towns. There were certain blacks who labeled themselves as the mouthpiece of the rest of the blacks. This "whippersnapper" comes in from Jackson to set up the NAACP. The NAACP in those days, well, the whites resented it. They started talking, "Y'all better leave that NAACP alone. That Mitchell is going to get you all in trouble." So we had problems within our group.

I'd tell them, anyone who expects to have freedom, who expects to enjoy their rights, has to be willing to pay the price. I don't mean lynching. I mean the loss of prestige, the loss of influence. You stay in good with these white folks, but you should be willing to forego that so that this little black man here could vote.

In December 1941, the NAACP was still pursuing the case. The Japanese bombed Pearl Harbor, the United States declared war, and Thurgood Marshall traveled to Haywood County with Mitchell. They stopped at the courthouse "for a look at Tip Hunter." Mitchell recalled that moment well:

We walked into the courthouse and Tip Hunter was sitting in his office. I pointed him out to Thurgood and said, "That's the one that asked Elbert to come with him. He had a couple of questions." Hunter looked up and saw Marshall, he's a great big man, and looked down again real quick, acted like he didn't see us. He didn't have much courage without twenty or thirty men with him. Acted like he didn't see us.

Mitchell and Marshall traveled in the county and interviewed people regarding the case. They found and interviewed John Outlaw, who had driven Buster Walker to safety on 14 June. Marshall also traced Jack Adams, the unfortunate bystander swept up by the mob in its search for Elisha Davis, to Chicago. During their travel Marshall and Mitchell heard a rumor that, two months previously, Hunter had released an African-American man from jail at 2 A.M. who was found beaten to death the next day.[39]

While Marshall made this effort, the gears of legal justice ground slowly to a halt. The chief of the civil rights section of the Justice Department reasoned that the charges of those threatened would be contradicted by those accused. The latter were all prominent citizens who denied the charges. The whites began to close ranks around the story of factional fighting among

African Americans. Even Hunter now admitted taking Williams and Thomas Davis to the police station; however, he had done so, according to his testimony, to investigate "rumors of a factional strife among the negroes."[40] The Justice Department decided to close the files on the case involving Tip Hunter in January 1942. Marshall wrote to Assistant Attorney General Wendell Berge requesting that the Justice Department reconsider that decision. He recounted for Berge the deleterious action of FBI agents sent to Haywood County to investigate the charges against Tip Hunter. Marshall agreed that "this is not a clear cut case with a dozen eyewitnesses, but it is a case with two witnesses as to a part of the act and an eyewitness to the entire transaction who was also the victim (Davis). There have been convictions on circumstantial evidence alone, without any eyewitnesses."

Marshall also underscored the importance of the case: "All of the Negroes in Brownsville know that Hunter killed one man and ran several other Negroes out of town who had attempted to register. If no action is taken against him by the department, the intimidation of the Negroes who want to register and vote will be complete."[41]

Mitchell wrote to Francis M. Biddle, U.S. attorney general. Mitchell reviewed for Biddle the old charge of rape used against African-American men to justify intimidating or lynching them. But, Mitchell pointed out, Elisha Davis had not been accused of rape, only of expressing his interest in voting:

> In the name of justice, I am appealing to you as head of the Department of Justice to re-open the case involving Tip Hunter of Brownsville, Tennessee. The faith of 13,000,000 black American citizens and the fairness of your department will be shaken if the perpetrators of this dastardly deed are not subjected to due process of law. Certainly, now our country should foster the faith and loyalty of its minority groups and your democratic principles.[42]

Despite the letter, Berge responded to Mitchell that the department was closing the case due to insufficient evidence. Mitchell wrote to Marshall, "Brother Thurgood," reflecting on the decision of the Justice Department:

> I was shocked to learn that the case was closed due to lack of sufficient evidence. I suppose we will have to dig up Elbert Williams to prove that he is dead.

I don't think we shall ever have a case any more clearcut than this one. We shall never have a case with eight or ten eyewitnesses to lynching. What Negro would have followed the mob that took Elbert Williams from his home? The mere fact that he was taken away without a legal cause should warrant prosecution in my opinion.[43]

Mitchell was taken off the case by a call to defend democratic principles in another way. He was drafted, despite his age, 36, and having a dependent, his wife. The draft board's decision removed him and his leadership from West Tennessee. To add insult to injury, Mitchell's induction took place in a center named for Nathan Bedford Forrest, the Confederate cavalry officer, commander at the massacre of Fort Pillow, and the first grand wizard of the Ku Klux Klan.

"HERE YOU COULD VOTE WITH NO QUESTIONS"

In October 1940, the Davis family left West Tennessee, with its ongoing investigation, for Niles, Michigan, and a new set of race relations. The family joined the stream of millions of African-American southerners migrating to the North and other places.[44] Nann Davis remembered the family's trip from Jackson to Niles with some humor:

Eli borrowed a friend's car, Grandpa Finley, and he used his car and come got us. That was done at night and under cover too. There were seven kids and me and him. I was carrying Walter. We carried everything we had. I had this bottle of wine, that I made, in this pillow I was supposed to be sleeping on and I held that pillow like it was a baby.

We had zero when we left. Eli came ahead and got a house. People brought us food and clothes. When I got to Niles, I had a home.

Elisha wrote to Walter White from Niles to thank him for the support of the NAACP and to inform him of his plans to start an NAACP chapter in Niles, which he eventually did. He also registered to vote and saw to it that Nann and all his family members registered to vote as well. Nann remem-

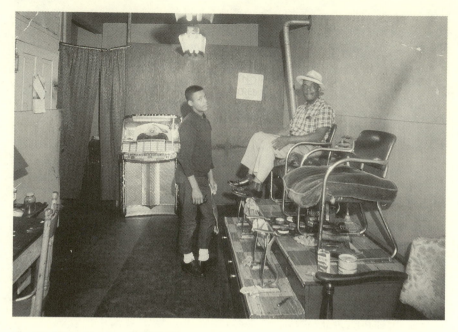

Fig. 18. Elisha Davis and son Paul in shoeshine parlor operated by Davis in Niles, Michigan, 1962. Courtesy of Debra Davis.

bered registration as a simple matter: "All I had to do was to go to City Hall and put my name down." Casher joined his brother in Niles in August 1941 and ended fourteen months of hiding:

> I came in August 13, 1941 and registered then. Eli pressured me when I got here. We came through damnation for wanting to vote and couldn't, which led up to all that down there.
>
> Now when we got here, according to him, we better register. That was one of his greater ambitions. We got out of that mess down there and here you could vote with no questions. After three or four months, I had no fear of registering.

In addition to his political goals, Elisha Davis had the immediate goal to re-establish financial security. He found work in the service department of an auto dealership. With some savings he accumulated, he later opened a secondhand furniture store. He wrote to Mitchell, late in 1940, assuring him

Fig. 19. Nann Davis with her sons and daughters, in Niles, Michigan, October 1989.
Photograph by the author.

that he would repay him for his kindness and costs as soon as he could. The
family's needs increased in November, when their new baby, Walter Wendell
Davis, arrived. The new boy's name was derived from Walter White, reflecting the family's new association with the NAACP; and from Wendell Willkie,
reflecting the family's old association with the Republican party. Willkie was
the Republican candidate for president in the 1940 election, in which Davis
had intended to vote. The infant's birth was complicated, and Nann was very
ill for a while. The following year, Nann Davis bore another son, Milmon
Mitchell Davis. This infant son died within a year.

Casher Davis remembered the problems he had in adjusting to his new
life in the North when he joined his brother in Niles:

It looked dark. But I was young. I always did work and would work. I
didn't cry too much. I just said, "Well listen, life is a battle and I'm going to
win it."

But I wouldn't trust nobody. The first two years I worked, I wouldn't

Fig. 20. Casher Davis, October 1989. Photograph by the author.

trust nobody. I cut me a two-and-a-half-inch pipe, a hole in each end. I blocked one end and stuffed money in there until I couldn't get anymore in it. I wouldn't trust anybody.

When you go through what we went through, it was awful. When you get so that you can't trust nobody, you think you can't trust nobody, it's bad. Oh yes, I kept money two or three years because I wouldn't trust the bank. The bank in Brownsville, they were white people. I came to Niles and I looked at the banks here. I saw the managers and they were white people. I looked at them and I said, "I'm going to stick some more money in the pipe." It was awful.

Trust returned to Casher Davis's mind and heart, but only with time and other changes.

In the meantime, Milmon Mitchell also had adjustments to make—to army life. He was devastated by the death of the Davis's infant son, Milmon Mitchell Davis, but he found energy and reason to protest new forms of racial discrimination. He developed a peptic ulcer from the diet at Fort Benning and was hospitalized. Upon his release, he looked for a ride back to his barrack.

The driver of the jeep that provided soldiers transportation would not take him. The driver explained that he could not take an African-American passenger. Separate accommodations on public transport, which Ida B. Wells had protested sixty years previously in Tennessee, now had a new opponent. Mitchell wrote letters complaining of his treatment. He credited those letters with his early release from the army.

Shortly after his return to civilian life, Mitchell found himself haunted by his involvement in the 1940 protests in Haywood County. After his service, Mitchell returned to Jackson but shortly left for Detroit. Another district manager for Atlanta Insurance Company had gone to Detroit, and he filled Mitchell's mind with tales of the earnings to be made there. Mitchell went to Detroit but soon decided to seek more secure employment with the postal service. His application asked questions about membership in subversive organizations, to which he replied, "No." His application was denied, and he was told that his membership in a Communist organization made him ineligible for postal employment. He called an attorney, the head of Detroit's NAACP, and, after a hearing, he was approved for employment:

> I thought these guys who had me in my office nine years before had something to do with that. I wondered how these two guys could interview me; didn't have any concrete evidence that I had done anything wrong; how could they get that put on a record against me?
>
> That just goes on to tell you the situation that we blacks were in. Any person who was white and had any kind of authority could make just about any charge against you.

"ABOLISH ALL LEGAL DISTINCTIONS BY RACE OR COLOR"

Unlike the Davis family, most African Americans left their farms and sharecropping because mechanization of agriculture made their labor redundant and so made it impossible for them to make a living or even continue in the poverty they had known. Between 1940 and 1970, the number of agricultural laborers in Haywood County declined by almost five-sixths. The African-American population of the county was cut in half. Like African Americans from other counties, black laborers left Haywood County in streams, following friends and relatives to New York, Indiana, and Illinois, drawn initially by wartime industry and later by friends and family members who had preceded them.

Few of the migrants left for explicitly political reasons, as the Davis family had, but their movement soon was to have profound political impact. African-American migrants from the South, about 1.6 million of them by 1940, found fewer obstacles to registering and voting in the North. The support of African-American voters for Democratic presidential candidates, such as Harry Truman, greatly influenced changes in the Democratic party. These votes made up the margins of victories for Roosevelt in 1944 and Truman in 1948. Truman, under pressure from the third-party campaign of Henry Wallace and the Progressive party, embraced the cause of civil rights and established a Presidential Commission on Civil Rights.

The commission gave the NAACP and others a new voice in government. It investigated Thurgood Marshall's charge that the FBI had bungled its investigation of the Williams's lynching. Marshall later intensified his criticism of the FBI and its director, J. Edgar Hoover, earning Hoover's enmity. In a delayed response to Marshall's charges, Hoover investigated the FBI's conduct in the case with far more alacrity and decisiveness than the FBI had shown in the case itself. He ordered his three top assistants to re-examine the case and the FBI's conduct. He chastised two assistants for taking too much time to reply to the charges of White and Marshall concerning the FBI's ineptitude. Eventually, all agents in the case denied being accompanied by Hunter during their investigations. Nonetheless, Clyde Tolson, the FBI's associate director, concluded, "This case received poor supervision both in the field [from McClanahan] and from the seat of government." Having made that judgment, the bureau discussed strategies for "damage control" if criticism of the case's handling continued.[45]

In 1948, Truman proposed a comprehensive civil rights bill—the first since the Grant administration—that contained anti-lynching legislation. Truman's positions on civil rights undid the knot that held southern Democrats in a national coalition with labor, ethnic groups, and urban and industrial areas. Southern Democrats nominated Strom Thurmond, governor of South Carolina at the time, for president of the United States.

Truman gained new allies in that 1948 election, even as he lost old ones. About 40 percent of African-American southerners who had migrated by 1945 had gone to California, Illinois, or Ohio. Truman carried these three decisive states by a total margin of fifty-two thousand votes. The new African-American voters in these states clearly had made a difference in the presidential election.[46]

Elisha Davis was not among the new African-American Democrats who created Truman's majority. Davis maintained his allegiance to the Republican party of abolition and emancipation. The Republican party had been the party of the freedman during Reconstruction in Haywood County. Samuel McElwee, of course, had been a Republican. The electoral victory of a Republican president in 1952 buoyed Davis's spirits. With hope and confidence, Davis wrote to Thurgood Marshall early in 1953 to explain that he was continuing his efforts to have Hunter and others prosecuted with the attorney general recently appointed by newly-elected President Dwight D. Eisenhower. Davis asked Marshall to send his records to Washington. He expressed his continuing hope that justice might be done.[47]

Late in 1952, on 9 December, Davis telegraphed Marshall, "I am urging the Court to abolish all legal distinctions by race or color."[48] Marshall on that day entered the third and final day of arguments before the U.S. Supreme Court in *Brown* v. *Board of Education*. The decision in that case would usher in a new day in race relations in the United States. Three-quarters of a century after the first large migration from West Tennessee and other parts of the South, the children of migrants, those children's children, and their children's children's children were challenging the separate-but-equal educational system of Topeka, Kansas. Marshall convinced the Court that the segregation of black and white children in different schools was unconstitutional.

That decision overturned *Plessy* v. *Ferguson* and other laws mandating segregation, which in Tennessee law dated back to 1870. Tennessee African-American legislators in the 1880s had skirted the issue, attempting to gain more resources for African-American children within the segregated school system. Local authorities in places like Haywood County had used the meager resources available for all children to widen the gap between the educational opportunities available to white and black children. The decision in *Brown* v. *Board of Education* placed federal authorities in conflict with local and state authorities over social policies, as they had not been since Reconstruction. For more than forty years, the NAACP had worked to expose the hypocrisy of the "separate but equal" doctrine and to reverse the insidious racism that had inspired it. Now the federal government was compelled to acknowledge that same hypocrisy. When the Court ruled school segregation unconstitutional, it removed major supports from the throne of Jim Crow. The civil rights movement would remove more and end the interregnum of emancipation.

SECTION III

Emancipation from Within

1955–1990

Freedom's Renewal
1955–1965

6 After 1954, the struggles for emancipation changed. The Supreme Court, in *Brown* v. *Board of Education*, ruled that separate but equal schools were unconstitutional. Pressure to eliminate segregation in other facilities followed; then came pressure to restore the vote to African Americans in the South. The federal government gradually began to support the sort of emancipation efforts that had been undertaken locally, covertly, or unsuccessfully for one hundred years. Now the repression of local emancipation efforts sometimes attracted federal attention, as it had in the 1860s. With increasing federal action, local protests against economic subordination and political repression moved from private to public spaces. In those public spaces, those who continued the struggle for emancipation in Haywood County—people like the McElwees and the Davises—expressed themselves in different manners.

"WE HAD CROSSED THE MASON-DIXON LINE"

The mid-1950s brought changes for the McElwee family. Relations between the races were improving in Haywood County then, according to Robert McElwee: "I'll tell you things were getting better when I left there. My white neighbor told me to call his three-year-old daughter 'Miss.' To say, 'Yes, Miss,' and 'No, Miss.' I told him I could not do that."

The objection of this man in his mid-forties to this request for deference to a three-year-old child brought no harsh rebuke or reprisal. McElwee understood this as a sign that relations between the races were changing.

The economic structure of the county was changing as well. McElwee marveled at finding okra a cash crop: "I made fifteen cents for a half-bushel basket. I had so many, I made five hundred dollars on that okra." McElwee's entrance into a cash economy coincided with a general decline in tenant farming, the core means by which African Americans earned a living in the county. As a result, family economics took a downward turn. The McElwee family, like many other African Americans, lost their land.

In 1951, the son of Samuel McElwee, an attorney, died without leaving a will. Unwittingly, he jeopardized his children's continued ownership of land. Thousands of other African-American land-owners did the same in the following decades.[1] A local banker paid one of the McElwee heirs $250 for his share of the land in April 1952. The banker then insisted that the land be sold to determine its real value and divided equally between him and the other heirs. Robert McElwee recalled:

> That banker wanted that farm real bad. He had been wanting that farm for years and years. He bought my brother out. And we went to pay him off and he wouldn't take the money. He said we had to sell it. We sold it to him. That's the way he come to have it. He wasn't exactly honest, but he gave us more for the farm than anyone else would.
>
> You know that farm didn't do him no good. He didn't live two years after he bought it. It didn't do him no good.

Soon after the sale of the farm, in November 1952, Robert McElwee left Haywood County for California. He was tired of farming, and the sale of the farm offered him a chance to move and start over in another place. He and his family joined his Aunt Minnie, the daughter of Samuel McElwee, in Los Angeles.[2] On that trip, McElwee and his family crossed the state line and left behind Tennessee's restrictive legislation concerning segregation in public transportation that his grandfather and Ida B. Wells had protested seventy years before:

> We came out here by train. Back home, I wondered all the time, how come they put the black in the front of the train; put the colored up in front of the train and wouldn't put the white up there. When a white got on the bus, we got up and got back. And you kept doing that until you got to the back of the bus. But on a train it was different; blacks were in the front. I was told that the reason they put the colored up there at the front because of the boiler busting and scalding them first.

When we got to Missouri, the porter announced that we had crossed
the Mason-Dixon Line, and people could get up and sit where they wanted.
Everybody could do that. Everybody was on their own. That is the law. The
law protects you here. You can sit anywhere you want.

The family stayed in the seats in which they had begun the trip. They did not
move but were aware of their freedom to do so, if they wanted. McElwee
enjoyed his new freedom without exercising it.

With the move to Los Angeles, McElwee left farming for wage labor.
This shift exposed him to a new set of race relations on the job. His boss at
the warehouse where he worked asked that McElwee not use "Yes, sir." and
"No, Sir." That sounded too servile. McElwee obliged and began calling him
"McClusky" as some other workers did. But, for a new employee at McElwee's
level, that form of address showed insufficient respect. Finally, they hit on the
right combination, and McElwee learned to call his boss "Mr. McClusky."
McElwee recalled, "I thought they were some of the best people I ever
worked for. Every Christmas, they gave me a $100 bill and then made Santa
Claus come round to the children with toys. I made more than $70 a week,
and back home I made $70 a year."

"GET DOWN TO THE HALL
AND PUT YOUR NAME DOWN"

In Niles, Michigan, Elisha Davis and his family enjoyed a freedom unattain-
able in Haywood County. He clung so tenaciously to his Republican loyalties
that he became known as "Mr. Republican." Casher sometimes got angry at
his brother's politics:

> They called him "Mr. Republican" down at the Senior Citizen's Cen-
> ter. He was "Mr. Republican." We had Russ Webster, he was "Mr. Demo-
> crat." You only got three hundred colored votes, and we divided them. I
> saw many elections where with twenty-five votes we could have won.
>
> I used to fight with him about some officials and say let's get them out
> of there and put someone in who will take care of poor people. But because

that official was a Republican, he would say, "No. Maybe you're right, but let her stay in there."

Every election he would have all these signs up out his yard saying vote Republican, you know. He just would not compromise.

Elisha Davis's children also remembered that, when they turned twenty-one years of age, they went to register to vote. "The way he [Elisha Davis] was, he would come home and say, 'You're twenty-one, get down to the hall and put your name down.'" Once registered, Evelyn, Davis's oldest daughter, remembered, "You had to vote. Otherwise, he dragged you down there. Not literally, but the car was sitting out there, the door was open, you went."

By and large, the children of Nann and Elisha Davis grew up without knowledge of segregation until they left Niles. Both Isaac and his brother Joseph met segregation while in the military. Isaac served in Korea, in a black U.S. Army regiment that survived despite a presidential order to disband such units. Isaac died in 1963 from an illness he contracted in Korea. Joseph, Isaac's younger brother, also encountered segregation in the mid-1950s while traveling in Kentucky to his army base:

> I got to Louisville and saw these signs, neon lights, "White Folks Only."
> I went into the station, and this guy says, "Nigger, your place is around there."
> Now I wanted to drop him. Maybe it was my daddy in the back of my head
> saying, "Go around him." I went to the other side. It was this little spot no
> bigger than my mother's front room. I could sit anywhere I wanted on the
> bus from Detroit, but in Kentucky it was the first time I had to sit in the back of
> the bus.

In addition to the lessons about voting regularly and dealing with prejudice, Davis conveyed to his children the anger and disappointment that his experiences in the South had imparted.

> Sometimes he would use the term *peckerwood*. He would call me aside and
> say, "That peckerwood, son, has caused you many a problem." When he
> would use the term *peckerwood*, he was angry. The peckerwood could be
> black or white. It was the person, low-down, who had done somebody
> wrong. It didn't have anything to do with a person's skin color. It came

from all that heartache that he went through. Horror, heartache, that's when that *peckerwood* would come out.

Migration meant change in emancipation status for the Davis and McElwee families in the 1940s and 1950s. For African Americans in Haywood County, however, change would come later, with the movement for civil rights. When the movement came, it followed a trail of events leading back to an earlier time of frequent, overt repression.

THE PAST REVISITS HAYWOOD COUNTY

As much as anyone, C. P. Boyd embodied the history of emancipatory efforts in the county. His maternal grandfather, Murph Currie, had served as a Haywood County magistrate before the reversals of the election of 1888. In the repression that followed, his mother exemplified the leadership role that remained available to African Americans. She not only taught school, but also organized local residents in one section of the county to begin a school for their children. Three-quarters of a century after the time of Freedmen's Bureau, Boyd's mother, Hester Currie Boyd, continued the tradition of school development for African-American children at Pilgrim Rest. As we have seen, she raised funds locally and convinced local authorities to finish a school building framed by local residents.[3] Boyd viewed his mother's work, teaching and organizing schools, as her politics. Occasionally Boyd saw his father's politics flare despite the sense of vulnerability inculcated in years of reprisals:

> My father had a temper, and he could be very strong. I remember a deputy came out to collect the poll tax. Now my father didn't vote, but you had to pay the poll tax or work on the roads one and a half days anyway. So the deputy came to the house about that. Dad refused to pay and told him he wasn't and to get off his land. That scared me. That was not the language you spoke to white people, never mind a deputy.
> Another time, a white man stole the battery for my father's car. We were one of the few black families in the county with a car. I'm not sure how, but my father got the battery back somehow. The white man came to our house

with a pistol. He made sure we could see it, the handle was sticking out of his pocket. My father told him he wasn't giving the battery back: "That's my battery. You're lying." That's what my father said. I was scared. You just didn't speak to a white man like that. My father was ready to shoot it out.

In addition to these lessons in resistance, Boyd's father gave him some of the political history of the county. His father passed on a remnant of Samuel McElwee's lingering reputation—he had "sold the Negroes" out. Over time, Boyd had tempered his father's judgment with his own view. His father, Boyd reasoned, had not made any serious inquiry into McElwee's career and simply expressed the general disappointment of African Americans that one of their leaders had not been able to forestall the decline of their political rights. McElwee's reputation had suffered as a result. Boyd's boyhood memories also included the story of his father's father having voted in Dancyville in 1888 and having been assured by the polling officials with sarcastic confidence, "You won't have to worry about voting much longer."

Boyd took steps to regain the franchise that his grandfather had exercised. After teaching in a neighboring county for eight years and voting there, Boyd returned to Haywood County in 1958. Soon after his return, he went to the courthouse to register to vote.

When I came back to Haywood, I went down to change my registration. I just had to change my registration from Decatur to Haywood; then I could start to vote. That was my position.

I went down, looking innocent, wearing a pair of jeans, a tee-shirt, and ball cap. I went into the registrar and told her I had moved back and I wanted to change my registration. The lady looked all bothered. She said, "You ask the sheriff or talk to Mr. Moore, the county court clerk." He's a great guy. I knew him very well. I went to him and said, "Mr. Moore, the lady told me to bring this to you." I showed him the form and explained to him that I had moved back and I wanted to change my registration. He looked at the form and looked at me and said, "You'll have to take this to Decatur County. We are not allowed to register them here." He meant Negroes.

Boyd took his solitary crusade another step and visited with the chair of the voter registration commission, Dr. W. D. Poston. Poston was the scion of the family of Republicans, Union supporters, and of John L. Poston, Freedmen's Bureau agent in Brownsville in 1867. The conversation between the two men was a remarkable scene. Each of them was removed from Reconstruction by two generations, and each stood at the threshold of a second Reconstruction in the county. Like their grandfathers, they had been brought together by conflict over the civil rights of African Americans. Neither man was aware of the other's family history in this regard.

Poston's stance differed more from his ancestors' position than Boyd's did. Poston was on the three-person voter registration commission because the law required it to include a member of the minority party, and he chaired the commission because it was his turn to do so. He had no particular commitment to the civil rights of African Americans, and he did not support Boyd's effort to register to vote. Boyd remembered him as "the run-of-the-mill average Haywood County Caucasian who out of fear did not want blacks to vote. He and they were afraid we'd take over everything." Boyd recalled his own fear at their meeting. He talked a friend into accompanying him to Poston's cattle farm, where he intended to gain Poston's permission to register to vote. Boyd knew better than to address Poston directly with his reason for visiting:

> I used a little psychology. He was fearsome looking. He had on shades so I couldn't see his eyes or their expression. He was real suspicious of my being out there. So I talked to him about his cattle. He had show cows and bulls that he showed all over the South. I commented on his fine cows and told him how my dad would like to have a part of his prize bulls. I loosened him up. He warmed up. Just before I left, I said, "Oh, there's one other thing. I'd like to register to vote." He said real quiet, "The books are closed now. Next year, they'll be open. It would be all right then." He did not volunteer anything, and he put me off a whole year.

Boyd's private, individual crusade to regain his right to vote became a public, group crusade for the rights of all Haywood County African Americans in the aftermath of Burton Dodson's trial and with the formation of the Haywood County Civic and Welfare League. Boyd was a distant cousin of Burton Dodson, who lived nearby in Fayette County. In 1941, following an argument between Dodson and a white man over an African-American woman with whom both men were sexually involved, Dodson had engaged in a gunfight with a deputized mob. Several men had come to Dodson's home at night, and in the melee, one of the "deputies" had been killed. Dodson had escaped during the confusion of the gunfight. He became a fugitive from Fayette County "justice." In 1959, eighteen years later, word got back to Fayette County that Dodson was to be found in East St. Louis, Illinois. Authorities brought him back to Fayette County to stand trial. This trial exemplified some of the changes that had occurred in the years since his flight.

An African-American attorney from Memphis, James F. Estes, defended Dodson. Estes's appearance was a "first" for Fayette County, just as the 1940 appearance of J. Emmett Ballard had been for Brownsville. Estes, unlike Ballard, was not expelled, and he achieved three remarkable outcomes in Dodson's trial. First, he established a new role for an African-American man in the Fayette County courthouse. Estes was neither a janitor nor a defendant but entered the courthouse on official business. Second, Estes was able to secure a complete trial for Dodson. The lynching that would have been inevitable in 1941 did not occur. Dodson, in his seventies at the time of his trial, was sentenced to twenty years in prison, later reduced to ten. The third result of the trial, though incidental to the trial itself, produced the most profound consequences in the region. Estes challenged the absence of African Americans among prospective jurors, who were selected from the voter registration lists. Among the 16,927 registered voters of the county, there were only 17 African Americans, and they never served as jurors. Estes asked the white prospective jurors if they believed that African Americans should vote. To the amazement of the African Americans, who packed the courtroom to observe the trial, the white men of the jury pool responded that African Americans should have the right to register and to vote.

Genuine or not, these answers shattered generations of silence on this mechanism of subordination. Shortly after the trial, in early 1959, with help from Estes, the Haywood County Civic and Welfare League was established by C. P. Boyd, Odell Sanders, Tom Sanderlin, Bettye Douglass, and many others. A comparable group was formed simultaneously in Fayette County. The Haywood County group had a charter, just as the 1940 NAACP chapter had had. A league member went to the courthouse to pick up the charter. As he left, a white man hit him over the head with his cane. His blood fell on the charter, a fact that league members found very significant. It reminded them of blood shed in the past as whites moved to keep their parents and grandparents from exercising their civil rights, and recalled the possibility that their own blood might be shed, too. The white attacker denied any political motive for an action he described as spontaneous: "Didn't no charter or nothing like that have anything to do with it. It just flew all over me because he stepped on my foot as he was coming out of the courthouse."

The league member, Omar Carney of Stanton, declined to press charges: "I don't want to cause no disturbance." Estes, the league's attorney, charged that the incident had been deliberate. "They don't want Negroes to come in the courthouse." The county judge dismissed Estes's remark as ridiculous.[4] The attack reminded the league members of their vulnerability before county law officials, and they resolved never to go alone to the courthouse. The incident demonstrated that singularly trivial encounters, like those between teachers of the freedpeople's schools and local white residents of a century before, still could provoke profound hostility if they formed part of a political action.

THE HAYWOOD COUNTY
CIVIC AND WELFARE LEAGUE

Just as changes had occurred between Dodson's flight and his trial, so there had been changes since the last modest African-American effort at voter registration in Haywood County. The league's charter members were people quite different from the NAACP members of 1940. The 1959 group came predominantly from the rural areas of Haywood County, while the NAACP members of 1940 had been primarily from Brownsville. The 1959 group represented ordinary African-American folk, farmers, unlike the group in 1940, who were teachers, professionals, and wage laborers of the African-American community.

One important segment of the 1959 group consisted of land-owning African-American farmers from the Douglas community of Haywood County. These families had become land-owners through the New Deal's Farm Security Administration program and its Haywood County Farm Project. Tom Sanderlin and some others from the Douglas community were among the handful of African-American residents who had joined the NAACP in 1939 and now joined the Haywood County and Civic Welfare League in 1959.

This group of African-American land-owners demonstrated, as the Davis family had, the crucial correlation of economic security, land-ownership, and political participation. Unlike Ike Davis, however, this group had come to own land through participation in a federal program, rather than through the beneficence of white patrons or an accident of birth.[5]

The movement in 1959 had more in common with the county's Union Leagues of the 1860s than with the NAACP chapter of 1940. The Haywood County Civic and Welfare League even replicated the structure of the Union Leagues. The leagues of both eras organized down to the precinct level, and each local chapter sent two delegates to the county league. The leagues also were similar in their broad membership base, their functions, and their outside support. The Rural Advancement Fund contributed financial support to the 1959 movement locally. This fund had its roots in the Southern Tenant Farmers Union, which had been active in eastern Arkansas in the 1930s and during the 1940 purge in Haywood County. Citizenship Schools, begun on the Sea Islands of South Carolina, instructed students from Lane College in Jackson in literacy training, so that they could help rural Haywood County African Americans meet the literacy requirements for voter registration.[6]

The NAACP remained active nationally and in the South, through the efforts of outstanding people such as Medgar Evers in Mississippi. But in the coming movement for civil rights, the NAACP no longer had the exclusive or even the dominant leadership role. The Congress on Racial Equality (CORE) played an important part in the movement for civil rights in Haywood County. The Student Nonviolent Coordinating Committee (SNCC) and the Southern Christian Leadership Conference (SCLC) drew inspiration from events in Haywood County.

The new movement, both nationally and locally in places like Haywood County, was sustained by African-American migrants who had left the South but still closely followed events in the counties they had left behind. They contributed funds to relieve victims of reprisals and to support organizing and legal efforts to achieve change. California and Chicago CORE chapters, for example, were prime supporters of the Haywood County drive in the 1960s. The Chicago CORE chapter sponsored "Operation Freedom" in Haywood and Fayette counties. By 1961, in the estimation of local organizers, much of the work on voter registration had been accomplished. The major tasks remaining included securing land for African Americans to cultivate; amassing capital for crops, seeds, and fertilizer; and diversifying the economy to create new employment opportunities.[7]

The differences between the efforts in Haywood County in 1940 and in 1960 reflected an essential characteristic of the new movement for emancipation. In 1960, the movement, both in Haywood County and around the nation, protested not only the chasm of caste between the two races but the fissures of class among African Americans as well. As such, this was the most radically democratic movement aimed at race relations since Reconstruction.

As Boyd remembered it, his worst experience with prejudice and discrimination came not in interaction with whites, but through humiliation at the hands of African-American students and teachers at the segregated county high school he attended:

> I ran up on a social problem when I went to the city. It was like a racial problem. This was an all-black high school in Brownsville, but the city kids had the same prejudice against us country kids that you would find between blacks and whites. We couldn't get into the plays. We couldn't get into the cliques. We were on the outside looking in. Teachers thought we were loafers, but we weren't. I came to school late one day, and I didn't know some things. I tried to explain to the teacher that my father's car broke down, but she kept saying, "Shut up. Shut up."
>
> I never will forget that day.

Boyd was in school with teachers and with the children of some of the men and women who formed the 1940 NAACP chapter. Their efforts at change had not encompassed all African Americans in the county. The right to vote would have enhanced the positions of most of them within the African-American community. The NAACP chapter members had asked to vote partly because it was their right, but partly also because they felt they merited this dispensation from disfranchisement by white people. In their estimation, they had met the standards of conduct established by the white community and so had proved themselves different from, and better than, the poor, rural African-American farmers of the county. When the NAACP members saw how their demands angered the white community, they relented. But their subordinate caste position did not alter the class distinctions by means of which they separated themselves from African Americans like

Boyd, who lived outside of Brownsville. Such class distinctions made the subordination of caste a bit easier for these elite African Americans to endure.

In his effort to regain voting rights for African Americans, however, Boyd dealt primarily with issues of caste. The violence that enforced the rules of caste for both blacks and whites took precedence over the humiliations that enforced class among African Americans. Boyd remembered the pervasive aura of fear that the Williams lynching cast, even twenty years later, over his own and the league's efforts to regain the vote:

> Everybody remembered Elbert Williams's lynching. Those who weren't big enough to remember, they heard about it enough from the other folk to know about it. That was one of the best known facts. Plus that the mob was allegedly led by the sheriff and a lot of the leading businessmen came out.
>
> When the FBI came to me during the movement, I told them, "If any group of white folks comes to my house, if the sheriff or anyone else wants to arrest me, they better come between nine and five in the daytime. If they come at night, I've got some good guns, I don't smoke, I don't drink coffee, I'm not nervous, I can hit a squirrel's left eye at fifty yards." I said, "I am going to shoot to kill. I'm not going to waste any warning shots. I'm letting you know now. I'm going to shoot to kill." I asked, "What am I supposed to do if I am attacked by a mob?" They said, "You can call the sheriff." I said, "The sheriff might be leading the mob. I might call you after I've slain every one of them I can. If anyone sets a cross on my yard, I intend to light it with this M-1 carbine."

In 1960, because of the growing movement for civil rights in the South, determination overcame fear in Haywood County. In 1960, the African Americans of the movement did not inquire of white officials how to gain their rights, as the group of five had done in 1940. Nor did they attempt to win white officials' approval for the exercise of their rights, an effort that had led Boyd to meet with Poston. The African Americans of the 1960s firmly demanded the rights they were entitled to as Americans and as human beings.

African Americans in the movement harbored some resentment toward those relatively affluent African Americans who would not participate in efforts to help those who had less than they needed. White-made black leaders—especially the teachers and school administrators, and some African-

American businessmen—took their cues from white officials and not their African-American "brothers and sisters." Some of these people had been charter members of the 1939 NAACP chapter, but in 1960 they were unwilling to risk their positions of authority by leading efforts to lift the weights of repression.

The movement in Haywood County, like the movement elsewhere, could not eliminate differences among individuals of the same race or of different races. It could not prevent people from thinking themselves better than others of the same race or of a different race. The movement could work, however, to see, first, that the prejudices of whites did not determine the standard by which blacks would be judged, and, second, that white prejudices no longer led some African Americans to limit the aspirations and achievements of other African Americans.

NEW EFFORTS AND OLD REPRISALS

One event that propelled registration in 1959 demonstrated that whites and blacks had common vulnerabilities. This event had bizarre ties to the events of 1940. Sheriff Jack Hunter, the brother of Tip Hunter, was shot and killed by a African-American man, Willie Jones. Jack Hunter had entered the police force in 1940, during the summer of Williams's lynching. Jack eventually succeeded his brother as sheriff. On 24 July 1959, he went out to serve a routine summons in a child-support case. Though the summons was for Willie T. Jones, Hunter mistakenly went to the home of Willie M. Jones. When Hunter arrived, Jones, an older man without young children, knew there had been some sort of mistake. Hunter insisted that Jones get in the car and go with him. This was a dangerous thing for an African-American man to do, as Jones understood. He went into his house to escape the sheriff. Hunter circled behind the house and attempted to enter the back door, ripping off a screen. When Hunter poked his revolver in the door, Jones shot him in the face with a twelve-gauge shotgun. Hunter died immediately. Police took Jones into custody, an act that for years, under such circumstances, had briefly preceded a lynching. This time, however, Jones was furtively transported out of the Brownsville jail—the same place where Elbert Williams had been held—to reduce the likelihood of a lynching. The coroner took Jones from the jail in a coffin within his hearse. He drove through a crowd of men that had assembled around the jail. Like the crowd through which Thomas Davis had walked twenty years earlier, this mob, with liquor and hate mongering, might have transformed itself into a lynch mob.

When Jones was not lynched on the night of his arrest for the shooting, African Americans in Haywood County knew that something had changed. Jack Hunter had been feared, as other police, including his brother Tip, had been before him. It had been rumored, and widely believed, that Jack Hunter had vowed, "The first nigger to show his face in the courthouse to register to vote, I'll blow his head off." But two months into the voter registration drive, Hunter had not killed anyone and himself had been killed by a shotgun blast in the face. Historically, such an offense had been punished by "Judge Lynch." Now, instead of being lynched, Jones had been taken secretly to a jail in a neighboring county. In two separate trials, two all-white, all-male juries found Jones guilty of first-degree murder with mitigating circumstances. The judge levied a sentence of twenty years and one day. On appeal, the Tennessee Supreme Court reduced the charge to voluntary manslaughter and imposed a sentence of two years, to include the time Jones had already spent in jail awaiting trial and during appeals.[8]

As Jones's trials and appeals went forward, white opposition to African-American voter registration remained obdurate. Haywood County officials continued steadfast in their refusal to recognize changed laws and changing times. Officials there even conducted the nation's last white-only primary in 1959. The NAACP had challenged the constitutionality of all-white primaries in other parts of the country. The federal courts had invalidated them, based on what was by then well-established evidence that they were discriminatory in intent and unconstitutional in practice. Jack Hunter won the Democratic nomination for sheriff, posthumously. His brother, Tip Hunter, again became sheriff.

It was an entire year later, in May 1960, before a newly constituted county election commission conducted registration for new voters. It was the first registration since the Civic and Welfare League had signaled its members' determination to register to vote. In a six-day period, 141 African Americans registered. Delaying tactics caused long lines in the hot summer sun. African-American registrants were not allowed to sit or stand on the grass of the courthouse lawn or to leave the hot sidewalk. When some registrants reached the courthouse steps and sat down, they found that battery acid had been left on the steps to eat through their clothes and damage their skin. Others remembered courthouse employees shaking pepper from the windows down on the people below. The NAACP filed a complaint with the U.S. Civil Rights Commission over "slowdown" tactics and the intimidation that faced those who attempted to register to vote. They cited events of 19 May as an example of the slowdown tactics. Although ten African Americans were registered that day, at least eight times as many were turned away after waiting in line all day.[9]

The happenings in Haywood County brought a federal response. The FBI came in, of course, but its investigations uncovered little that had not been reported in the newspapers. Just as in 1940, events in Haywood County demonstrated the FBI's unwillingness or inability to investigate charges that the civil rights of African Americans had been violated. In 1940, the Memphis U.S. attorney had circumvented the intent of the Justice Department and subverted the investigation by local FBI agents.[10] In 1960, however, federal agencies besides the FBI also responded .

Two representatives of the U.S. Commission on Civil Rights arrived in Brownsville in mid-June and began inquiring into procedures for the registration of African Americans. Their presence heightened the existing tension. The day after the representatives' arrival, Sen. Estes Kefauver came to Brownsville on campaign business. During the usual handshaking, he faced an unusual accusation. A deputy sheriff, George ("Buddy") Sullivan, charged that Kefauver had ordered the U.S. Commission on Civil Rights investigation in the county. Kefauver denied this. He walked with the deputy from the jail to the courthouse, past a line of African Americans waiting to register, to meet one of the commission representatives and discuss the charge. The representative, Ward E. Bonnell, denied telling Sullivan that Kefauver had ordered the commission investigation and called Sullivan a liar. Sullivan punched Bonnell on the side of his face. Bonnell recovered and was approaching Sullivan, when Kefauver, a U.S. senator campaigning for reelection in a southern state, stepped between them. His action prevented the spectacle of federal and local authorities expressing their conflict in a common fist fight.[11]

Local authorities took to enforcing laws in peculiar and repressive ways. A week after his fight with Bonnell, for example, Sullivan arrested Rev. Hiram Newbern for disorderly conduct. Sullivan accused the African-American minister of interfering with voter registration efforts at the time by blocking a street. Newbern was fined fifty dollars.

Despite such intimidation, the list of African-American voters grew, reaching 203.[12] As it lengthened, so did reprisals. Those who registered found their landlords evicting them. African Americans actively involved in politics, in 1960 as in 1940 and 1868, found their credit threatened or revoked by local merchants. Merchants circulated lists of registered African-American voters with checks next to the names of leaders; the lists were used to determine who merchants would trade with and who they would not. Many African Americans were denied services by store owners, doctors, and even suppliers of bottled gas, who supplied fuel for heating and cooking. White bankers refused farm loans to African-American registered voters, and white gin operators refused to accept their cotton crops.

Bettye Douglass, a member of the Farm Security Administration Project in the Douglas community and a prominent leader of the 1960 voter registration drive, recalled most vividly the reaction of her white doctor to her political involvement:

> Doctors got to where they didn't want to wait on you. They would tell you, "Go to your black doctors because I don't want nothin' to do with you."
>
> It was so funny. My baby was five or six when she had her first operation. And it wasn't more than six months when she had the other one. The doctor teased her all the time, "Girl, I'm going to have to put a zipper in there. You come back here one more time, instead of sewin' you up, I'm going to put a zipper in there." He just kidded and carried on with so much foolishness. And then to change like that, he wouldn't see her because my name was on the charter of the League.
>
> I didn't get angry with the doctor but when you lose the confidence you have in a person, especially someone who operated on your baby, you lose everything.

Likewise, Tom Sanderlin recalled drastic changes in his dealings with white people in the county. Like Elisha Davis, he was surprised and deeply hurt by the changes: "I thought that some of my white friends I had were my best friends in the world, but when I got my name on that charter, I'd speak to them, and they'd ask me what could they do *to* me, not what could they do *for* me."

July 1960 marked the beginning of federal intervention, for the first time in almost a century, to stop the evictions and other forms of retaliation for the political action of African Americans. John Doar, a newly appointed attorney in the Justice Department's civil rights division, decided to circumvent the FBI and came to Haywood County to do his own investigation of charges that had reached his office. Boyd had traveled to Washington earlier in 1960 with other voter registration leaders from Haywood and Fayette counties. They testified before the U.S. Civil Rights Commission about their plight. The commission later described theirs as the most important case to address the economic dependence of African Americans or to arise under the 1957 civil rights legislation.[13] Boyd later visited the Justice Department and spoke to Doar, inviting—or challenging—the lawyer to come to Haywood County to deal with matters there.

Doar eventually did arrive, and Boyd took him to a furtive meeting in a rural church. By dealing directly with African-American farmers in Haywood County about their federal rights, Doar was resuming the role played by Freedmen's Bureau agents such as John Poston. Doar inquired if any of the people assembled had received eviction notices. Almost everyone there said yes. Doar left shocked. What he had seen and heard convinced him that the efforts to prevent African Americans from registering to vote in Haywood County were inconceivably pervasive and harsh. From those sharecroppers he collected fifty affidavits, along with copies of their eviction notices, as evidence of retaliation against them for registering to vote. Doar's visit to Haywood County had changed his estimation of the problem and would change procedures in the Justice Department as well. Doar's subsequent efforts in Haywood and Fayette counties were to be termed "the most imaginative use" of the 1957 civil rights legislation.[14]

ELECTIONS, EVICTIONS, AND INJUNCTIONS

The November 1960 election saw a larger number of African-American voters and more Republican votes than was usual in Haywood County. Nixon garnered 1,188 votes but still lost to Kennedy, who received 1,871.

Orville Faubus, the former Arkansas governor who had defied court-ordered desegregation in Little Rock, received 257 votes. Only once since 1888 had a Democrat received less than Kennedy's 56 percent of the county's vote. That was in 1948, when county Democrats had split among Thurmond, Truman, and Wallace. Many factors, including Kennedy's religion, contributed to his poor showing in the county. But the newly registered African Americans included a large number of Republican voters. By tradition, African Americans in Haywood County were Republican. The efforts of the Eisenhower administration, the U.S. Civil Rights Commission, and the Justice Department gave the new voters further reason to support Republicans.

The election results increased the number of eviction notices. Local authorities and landlords were far less concerned with the county's vote in a presidential election than with the change a new bloc of votes could make in local elections. Some landlords gave the families until 1 January to move. More than four hundred families were evicted, mainly in Fayette County. Many took up residence with family and friends. Others moved into tents. Two settlements of families living in tents sprang up in December 1960 in Fayette County. A much smaller tent city, of about thirty families, went up in Haywood County at the same time.

One important difference between the climate in 1940 and in 1960 was the role of the federal government. Earlier, the NAACP nationally and locally had spent much effort cajoling the federal government to act, without success. Now, league members could depend on the Justice Department or, more specifically, on John Doar, as they had depended on the agents of the Freedmen's Bureau. Doar initiated legal action against the economic sanctions and refusals of services in Haywood County. He increased his efforts after the flood of evictions following the elections. On 18 November 1960, the Justice Department amended a lawsuit it had brought in September to include thirty-six additional land-owners who had evicted their tenants, along with the original defendants, who included the mayor of Brownsville, the county sheriff, the superintendent of schools, and local merchants and bankers. On 14 December, the Justice Department brought a similar suit against eighty-two defendants in Fayette County. When the federal judge in Memphis denied the injunction, Doar went to the Sixth Circuit Court of Appeals, which granted it.

The Justice Department preferred to secure injunctions rather than taking the cases to court. Ironically, injunctions had been the subject of Samuel McElwee's thesis in law school. Initially, local African-American leaders were upset about the Justice Department's decision not to prosecute. They wanted to see people accused of wrongdoing brought to trial, just as they had been and would be. Doar convinced them of the wisdom of relying on injunctions and not going to trial. He asked Boyd who would make up a jury in a court trial. Boyd answered, "White people." Doar asked, "How are the white jurors likely to find the defendants?" Boyd, recalling the long history of trials of white people for crimes against black people, answered, "Not guilty." With that verdict, the defendants would be off the hook, and a signal would have been sent to those who opposed African-American political participation that repression could continue without punishment. Doar pointed out that the federal courts and the Justice Department, because of their responsibility to enforce the injunctions, would be active participants in future voter registration drives in the counties.

White residents in the counties probably would have returned a verdict of not guilty, as Doar and Boyd reasoned. The local newspaper attributed the evictions to mechanization of agriculture, not politics. It asked rhetorically, "Can the United States Government require land-owners to renew loans for 1961 against their will?"[15] Other whites interpreted the evictions as a normal result of the annual year-end "settling time."

With an alacrity not seen during almost a century, the federal government pursued the enforcement of civil rights. The hearings, decisions, and appeals conducted between 23 and 30 December resulted in a temporary restraining order enjoining land-owners from carrying out the evictions scheduled for 1 January 1961. The Civil Rights Act of 1957 was being enforced, and people from the league were testifying in federal court on behalf of themselves and their neighbors and friends. The Justice Department, in contrast to its stance twenty years earlier, encouraged such testimony. Bettye Douglass testified in federal court about the actions taken against her and her family: "John Doar and I went to Memphis, and we testified. I was nervous. Being with Mr. Doar, he really lifted me up. He told me not to be afraid of nothing, and I wasn't. He told me just to tell the truth. And when you tell the truth, that's all that counts. I could just go through those matters like nobody's business."

The injunction prohibited economic reprisals, including eviction or changing terms of tenancy, for the purpose of interfering with voting rights.

Other groups from around the country supported the effort in Haywood County. CORE's "Operation Freedom" coordinated the work of church groups and college students. Some of the members of these groups ran into problems in the county. For example, Rev. Maurice F. McCrackin was arrested for loitering. His associate, David Henry, was arrested for speeding. Both men refused to pay their fines and entered jail, where they began a hunger strike they called a "fast for justice."[16] In February 1961, five white students from the University of Michigan came to the county to deliver food and clothing they had collected in a campus drive to support the registration effort in the county. One of them, Andrew Hawley, was arrested for running a stop sign, and his companion, David Giltrow, was charged with resisting arrest. Charges against both of them were dropped in exchange for their agreement, under protest, to leave the county immediately. Sheriff Tip Hunter explained that they were permitted to leave food and clothing but that he ordered them to leave the county because "they were in the Negro section of town and I didn't think that was a good place for them to be."[17] These incidents presaged the treatment of other civil rights workers later. Of course, they also echoed the treatment of teachers in the schools of the freedpeople a century before.

"THE DEPARTMENT HAS OBTAINED RELIEF"

Doar was acting in a lame-duck Republican administration, as newly elected President John Kennedy and his brother Robert, who was to be U.S. attorney general, made plans for the new administration. But events in West Tennessee, in which Doar played a role, overtook the Kennedy's plans. The sixth question asked of the new president in his first press conference dealt with civil rights in West Tennessee: "Does your Administration plan to take any steps to solve the problem at Fayette County, Tennessee, where tenant farmers have been evicted from their homes because they voted last November and must now live in tents?"

The President's vague answer renewed the hopes of African Americans in West Tennessee and elsewhere:

The Congress, of course, enacted legislation which placed very clear responsibility on the Executive Branch to protect the right of voting. . . . I supported that legislation—I am extremely interested in making sure that every American is given the right to cast his vote without prejudice to his right as a citizen. And therefore I can state that this Administration will pursue the problem of providing that protection with all vigor.[18]

The Kennedy administration then acted to support the voter registration effort in West Tennessee. Leaders of the movement met with the attorney general in Washington and had regular access to members of his civil rights staff. Boyd and Odell Sanders, especially, would call collect to talk with Doar, who had given instructions to accept their calls. In June, Kennedy authorized the secretary of agriculture to send surplus food for the evicted families in Fayette and Haywood counties. That action set off a furor. State officials hindered implementation of the program, criticizing it as unneeded. Local planters complained that the program was especially unnecessary at this particular time. Six months before, evictions had been justified with the argument that the available labor supply exceeded demand, but evidently the surplus now had vanished and labor shortages rendered federal support unnecessary: "Cotton chopping will begin shortly and not only will we use all of the surplus labor here, but we will have to import field hands. . . . There is plenty of work available for anyone who wants to work."[19]

The administration learned a great deal from its efforts in West Tennessee. Robert Kennedy saw that voting rights constituted the administration's strongest political and moral avenue of approach to civil rights. He also learned the value of people like Doar, a Republican, who remained in the Kennedy Justice Department.[20] As in 1940, the nation noticed events in Haywood County. The cases were decided by July 1961, and the repressive measures were enjoined.

At the end of 1961, Robert Kennedy sent his brother a report summarizing the Department of Justice's civil rights activities that year. The department had intervened in Macon County, Alabama, home of Tuskegee University. Even at the place of Booker T. Washington's fame, the accommodationist era had ended. Since the department's intervention, 675 African Americans had registered to vote in Tuskegee. The department had filed fourteen new cases of discrimination in the registration process and had carried out investigations in sixty-one other counties. The department under Eisenhower had intervened in only three cases in all. The Kennedy Justice Department, for the first time since the election of 1867, offered federal protection to any African American "for intimidation or reprisal for the exercise of their right to register and vote. The legal rights possessed by the Government to protect its citizens in this respect have been clarified and expanded by court decisions." Illustrating this protection and expanded power, the attorney general explained, "The Department also has successfully obtained relief from the Court of Appeals for the 6th Circuit to protect Negroes registering to vote in Haywood and Fayette Counties, Tennessee, from economic reprisals through evictions and otherwise."[21]

Other events overshadowed those in Haywood County from 1959 to 1961. The largest portion of Kennedy's memo explained how the department had become involved in desegregation of interstate travel, when "freedom riders" set out to violate Jim Crow segregation on the buses and in the bus terminals of the South. That desegregation effort had coincided with the first successful voter registration drive for African Americans in Haywood County. Both events, in different ways, propelled the civil rights movement forward and past the position of the Kennedy administration. Among the freedom riders were two members of SNCC, a newly founded organization. SNCC would come to lead the civil rights movement by organizing groups like the Haywood County Civic and Welfare League in other parts of the rural South.

THE NAACP RETURNS
TO CONTINUE THE FIGHT

The NAACP nationally battled for a place among other groups and individuals in the new effort for civil rights. Locally, the organization attempted to relate its past efforts to the new ones in Haywood County. By 1960 standards, however, the NAACP seemed as accommodationist as Booker T. Washington had to an earlier generation of African Americans. Moreover, the NAACP seemed elitist.

In Haywood County, efforts to reestablish the NAACP chapter centered on Cynthia Rawls, daughter of Al Rawls and a member of the most prominent African-American family in the county. Charles Allen ("Al") Rawls, the family patriarch, was a mortician who had established several funeral homes in West Tennessee and an insurance company, Golden Circle, in Brownsville.[22] In December 1960, as Doar was in court seeking injunctions, members of the NAACP national office decided that "the time is ripe for another branch" in West Tennessee and that Miss Rawls was the best person to organize it. In January, the NAACP sent a representative to investigate conditions. He was arrested and convicted for disturbing the peace. In addition to opposition by white law officials, the NAACP delegate found dissension in the ranks of the local movement leaders. In particular, leaders of CORE advised local leaders not to cooperate with groups such as the NAACP.

This advice was in part a function of class differences and in part on a difference in strategies. The NAACP continued to emphasize a top-down strategy that attempted to break caste lines in order to secure greater freedom and opportunity for exceptionally qualified African Americans. Such an approach contrasted boldly with the strategies of other organizations. SNCC, for example, developed local leaders in an effort to break racial barriers for all people denied basic rights, such as voting. Both strategies called for political change, but the NAACP's voice was related more to exit for individuals than to change for a whole group of people.

Local leaders in Fayette County were less inclined to cooperate with the NAACP, but in Haywood County, the Civic and Welfare League remained inclusive in its tactics. The Memphis NAACP chapter contributed supplies to the relief effort in Haywood County. Officers of that chapter also wrote to President Kennedy to follow up on his January press conference comments.

By April, Cynthia Rawls and others had organized an NAACP chapter and conducted a formal dedication on 7 May 1961. Mildred Bond, a staff member in the national office, presided over the dedication service. She was the daughter of Ollie S. Bond, the Brownsville mortician who had been president of the Brownsville NAACP chapter in 1940. The NAACP press release wove past events with the ceremony that day: "A young woman who fled this southern town with her parents 22 years ago, returned here today to continue the work they started and for which they suffered the burning of their home and exile."

The release described Haywood County as "one of the nation's major civil rights storm centers," noting that current events there had their roots in a time when "the body of Elbert Williams, NAACP leader, was fished from the river." The release embellished the already sufficiently violent events of 1940. Dramatically, it reported that Ollie Bond had learned of the registration effort in the county in June 1960 and had died of a heart attack a few hours later.[23]

In general, the approach of the NAACP was accommodationist. Its members raised broad questions concerning the social and economic condition of local African Americans and their civil rights, in terms of the self-interests of the white community. The twenty-one-member chapter sent a letter to merchants in the county that listed "just a few of the many injustices and grievances that have been voiced by our people":

> As citizens who helped to make the town what it is today, we are continually abused when we attempt to register. We are denied free access to the registrar's office and the presence of a law enforcement officer ushering us into the registrar's office tends to intimidate us.
>
> Those in your employ are afraid to attempt to register because they are afraid that they will be fired.
>
> You have seen us arrested and fined unreasonably, and often times beaten. We are constantly humiliated by the abusive language used by those you have placed in office.
>
> We often are made to wait in the stores until a white customer is waited upon who entered after we did.
>
> Large signs, especially in the courthouse, "For White Only," are humiliating.
>
> We do not receive the proper respect from law enforcement officers.

The chapter members protested this treatment. African Americans represented the largest group of consumers in the county. But we have not been given the privileges that we so justly deserve, economically and politically. . . .

Please use your influence to see that these injustices are eliminated.

If you condone these acts we will know by the fact that they continue to occur.

As consumers, we need you. As distributors and producers, you need the consumer.[24]

The chapter also wrote a letter to Sheriff Tip Hunter that expressed both the genuine appreciation of some for Hunter's record and the intimidation that almost all African Americans experienced:

Your record through the years has been one which we have observed and we feel that you will continue to deal in a fair and impartial manner. However, we were deeply hurt by your statement . . . when you announced that you did not solicit the Negro vote.

We ask that you deal with us according to our deeds and always in the framework of the law. We realize that we must be law abiding citizens and must pay for our misdeeds according to the law. Our only hope is that you deal with us as you would any American citizens . . . with mercy and justice.

We always want to work within the law. If we are at error thinking that we as Negroes should be allowed to walk freely to the registrar's office as do our white brothers, please let us know.

Please give these matters your prayerful consideration and let us hear from you within the next several days.[25]

Discussion between white and black leaders did occur but much later. On 22 March 1962, the chairman of the county board, the president of the First State Bank, and a local attorney met with leaders of the Civic and Welfare League and the NAACP. The white participants began the session by pointing out that they were meeting over strong objections from the white community. They went ahead, however, to determine "just what the Negro community desires." Minutes of the meeting indicate that the African-American participants at the meeting outlined the following desires: (1) "Integration of the public schools and libraries"; (2) "Representation on the Mayor's Commission"; and (3) "General improvement of the status of the

Negro citizens." The meeting had no resolution, but the desires of the African–American community were on record.[26]

Boyd remembered participating in another similar meeting and recalled the effort of the league to work with "the better class of whites." As with Milmon Mitchell's efforts in 1940, he discovered that this group of whites was not yet ready to protest openly the rigid segregation that others enforced.

> We had some biracial meetings with some level-headed white men. I remember the judge told us, "Before I would let my children go to school with negro children, I would move out of the county." Now Odell Sanders and I took that and played with him. "Now Judge, we're surprised to hear that. We might expect that from farmers in the county but you are an educated man." You know, we expressed our surprise!
>
> I also spoke up about the water fountain. They had two fountains. One on the east side for whites and one, far less attractive, on the north side, for "Colored." They also had a cooler in the courthouse. I took a drink from it and a few days later a sign went up, "Whites Only." I told one of the white men at our meeting, "I have lived all my life without white water and I think I can continue to get along without it. But why do we have water in a public place that I support and I can't drink from it." He said, "Well, you know, Mr. Tip [Hunter] is in charge of the courthouse and you know how he is." Well, sometime later they removed the cooler from the courthouse and tore down the fountain outside.

THE McELWEES
AND THE MOVEMENT

Robert McElwee witnessed a portion of the movement in Haywood County at first hand. His mother died in 1960, and he and his brothers and sisters traveled back to the county for her funeral. There he learned of the tent city. In addition, he learned that the man with whom he traded and to whom he had, on occasion, "talked crazy," was among those the government was prosecuting. The latter action confused and frightened him. It contradicted what he had come to expect of American government:

I remember that time. We were out there. People made people move off the farm; wouldn't let them make no crop. Took the land; wouldn't let them make no crop. They had a tent stretched out somewhere. People would go and live there. I don't know what happened but the government or some-body made them stop moving people off the farm. Made these people work on the farm.

They put a lot of white people in court. The man I used to trade with, thought the world of, they put him in court. They did! They put him in court. When they put a man like that in court, that scared me to death. They [local authorities] could do anything then. That is, the government that did that. Black folks had a hard time trying to understand what the government was trying to do. It was miserable in a way, putting a white man in court. They didn't treat white people that way.

Despite the fear that she shared with her brother, Homer Zell McElwee Hess, sister of Robert McElwee and the granddaughter of Samuel McElwee, was among those African-American men and women who registered to vote in small but steady numbers in 1960. She and her husband stood in line to register that summer:

I registered to vote 'cause my daddy said that's why granddaddy was sent away; mostly for trying to fix it so people could vote. It was really my par-ents who taught me who my grandfather was.

It was tough. It was tough. I was scared, yessir. Who wouldn't have been? I didn't know who was going to start to rioting or what was going to hap-pen there. My husband wasn't afraid 'cause he wasn't afraid of nothing. I went with him.[27]

Several years later, Robert McElwee was again frightened by changes in the relations of the races. When the movement left the rural South and moved to urban areas of other parts of the country, it more often expressed itself in violent rage. In Los Angeles, in 1965, for example, Watts exploded in riots. "Watts was scary. There was burning. They were turning cars over and they were setting fires. It was scary. I worked all night that night. I didn't even go home. I don't know why they were burning those houses, they were only hurting themselves."

His sister Ethel and her husband spent several days alone in their home and left only because groceries ran out. Even after that time, they found that "everything was closed."

ELISHA DAVIS RETURNS
TO WEST TENNESSEE

The early actions of the Kennedy administration to safeguard the civil rights of African Americans inspired hope in Elisha Davis for the redress of the 1940 actions against him. He wrote to officials of the Kennedy administration, as he had written to every administration since 1940. In early November 1962, Davis heard from Burke Marshall, chief of the civil rights division of the Justice Department. Marshall's letter offered no hope for prosecution. He explained that the statute of limitations prevented prosecution of the violation of Davis's civil rights.

In the following year, 1963, Davis's Aunt Willie, with whom Nann and the children had hidden in 1940, died. This event brought Davis, Nann, and several of their children back to West Tennessee for the first time since his expulsion. Davis took his children to the area of his family farm and they visited the Willow Grove Church, but he pointedly avoided any travel to Brownsville. For some of his children, it was their first trip "south" and a learning experience for them.

John was nineteen, and his father nervously explained the difference between the world of Niles, Michigan, and the world in which he now traveled. "It was my first time in the South. We had people come to the house all the time, 'from the South,' but the younger six of us had never been there. My dad was concerned with my heavy foot when I drove. He said, 'Son, you can't get us arrested.'"

Davis did not explain fully his desire to avert any police attention while in Tennessee, but he responded quickly when John asked directions from a white man and began his request with a shout, "Hey!" "He pulled me aside and told me it was different here. That I was to say, 'Yes, Sir' and 'No, Sir.'" Similarly, John's cousins in Newbern instructed him in the use of side doors and front doors and other aspects of the etiquette of race that indicated African Americans understood their subordinate place. John had not learned any of this etiquette away from the rural South. In the North, African-American youth such as the younger Davis children grew up with far less sense of subordination.[28]

THE MOVEMENT IN HAYWOOD COUNTY

In 1965, the civil rights movement was in full swing in the rural South. In August, President Lyndon Johnson signed the Voting Rights Act, which spurred new efforts to register African-American voters in Haywood County. The act was partially a response to a drastic change in the southern electorate, including in Haywood County. In the 1964 election, for the first time since 1884, the county saw a majority of votes go to the Republican candidate for president. The shift in the county had begun in 1960, with support for the third-party presidential bid of Orville Faubus. The erosion of white Democratic support continued in 1964, with a narrow Goldwater majority in what had been a solidly Democratic county. After an informal reconnaissance of the South, presidential aide Lawrence O'Brien reported to President Johnson that white Democratic voters throughout the South, like those in Haywood County, were voting Republican. The best hope of maintaining a Democratic margin of victory in the South, O'Brien suggested, was to create a new bloc of loyal Democratic voters. In part, the Voting Rights Act of 1965 recalled the Republican strategy of a century before to capture a loyal bloc of votes among African Americans, sufficient to insure electoral majorities.[29] Election results after 1965 were disappointing. The county, like much of the rest of the South, delivered a majority of votes to only two Democratic candidates for president between 1964 and the time this book went to press. In 1976, Jimmy Carter carried the county with 65 percent of the votes. In 1992, Bill Clinton won with 59 percent.

In other ways, however, through registration efforts and the consequent election of African Americans to local political offices, the Voting Rights Act changed the county and the nation substantially. The significance of that change has been obscured by the party realignment of white Democratic voters which was discernible in the South despite the Republicans' overwhelming defeat in 1964.

The intensified efforts to register African-American voters in 1965 stimulated new violence. Nightriders threw dynamite at the home of league leader Odell Sanders on 16 May and destroyed one side of his house. In defense, African Americans organized themselves to watch and guard their homes, just as African Americans had done in 1867 and as Nann Davis had done in the wake of the violence surrounding her first political participation.[30] As expected, the exalted Cyclops of the Haywood County Klavern of the Ku Klux Klan denied that the Klan had had anything to do with the bombing. The bombing followed several tense nights for northern white civil rights workers then living in the county. They had called both the police and the FBI to report five or six cars traveling up and down the same road in front of their residence every ten to fifteen minutes for two hours. They also reported shots fired from the cars and several cross burnings in the area that evening. Reports of such intimidation of white civil rights workers gained broader press coverage than intimidation of the African Americans with whom they worked.[31]

As in times past, these white civil rights advocates from outside the county took refuge with the African Americans they were trying to help. Tom Sanderlin, a member of both the 1940 NAACP chapter and the 1960 Civic and Welfare League, afforded some young civil right workers protection:

> There were some white girls here. They come back one night and said, "Mr. Tom, someone's after us." I said, "Y'all carry y'all's car behind the house." She drove the car behind the house. I told my wife to open the door and put all the lights on. When they passed here, don't know why but they passed here several times, but the door was wide open and they didn't see no car out there and we had the light on. They didn't come in.

Two months later, a white family reported another act of violence, as a 22-caliber bullet struck the side of the house. Neighbors reported a light green car, which belonged to a local African-American family, on the road just before the shooting. Deputy Sheriff George Sullivan, notable for his altercation with the civil rights commissioner five years before, called the FBI for assistance in his investigation. The FBI declined to assist, citing no evidence that federal law was involved. Sullivan complained of a double standard: "They came over in May when a civil rights worker had called them that a Negro house had been shot into. I thought they would help on this also, as it was the same kind of thing. The only difference was that Negroes had supposedly shot into a white man's house this time, and in May, white people were reported to have shot into a Negro family's house."[32]

Other white residents underscored the political significance and the civil rights implications of the event. The shooting occurred in a district where African-American voters outnumbered white voters 400 to 85. The primary was only one month away, and the likelihood that two African-American candidates would win was very high. The shooting was interpreted as an attempt to intimidate white voters in the district. The primary election did result in the first election of African Americans in the county in the twentieth century. Dan Nixon and A. D. Powell were elected county commissioners from the overwhelmingly African-American District 9.

With the election completed, new registration efforts began and more threats of violence were heard, even as Watts exploded in riots. The same federal judge who in 1959 had denied John Doar's request for injunctions against local merchants, farmers, and officials now denied civil rights workers' request that local officials be enjoined from "violence, threatening, and molesting." Members of the Haywood County Student Union and the West Tennessee Voters Project had asked for protection of white and black civil rights workers and marchers participating in a demonstration on 7 August. Two hundred people demonstrated in a steady downpour that Saturday afternoon. They presented four demands to Julian K. Welch, the mayor of Brownsville:

> Equal powers and pay for Negro police and protection in the form of impartial law enforcement and arrests.
> Better school facilities such as books, hot lunches, more school buses and better roads.
> Immediate desegregation of all cafes, theaters and recreation facilities, including reopening of the county swimming pool on an integrated basis.
> Fair employment in all factories and governmental jobs.

Police overpowered a white man, a guard at the prison built at the Fort Pillow site, with a loaded rifle near the demonstration just after marchers left. It was the only visible threat of violence. Forty state police and FBI agents were on duty during the demonstration.[33]

The following Saturday, the civil rights groups demonstrated again, but this time they focused on county officials and policies. They particularly objected to segregation in the courthouse. This surprised Tip Hunter, who told a reporter, "Everything is open to Negroes here. We have never tried to discriminate against them." The Ku Klux Klan rallied at the courthouse that evening.[34]

Reports of the demonstrations that summer resembled those of political rallies in Haywood County one hundred years previously. They suggested that county politics indeed had changed. The interregnum of emancipation had ended, and in Haywood County, political participation by African Americans seemed, in some ways, to be taking up where it had left off so long ago.

Freedom's Expression
1965–1990

7 Being permitted to vote did not automatically insure African-American men and women an entree into public life or public office in the 1960s any more than it had in the 1860s. After they secured access to the ballot, further protest was necessary to make voter registration effective and to enhance opportunities for African Americans to participate in public life. Political participation also presented African Americans with some old dilemmas in new forms. For the most part, however, new types of participation have meant greater involvement with public services such as school breakfast programs and paved roads. The availability of these services measures, in individual lives and on a day-to-day basis, the concrete significance of dramatic social and political movements, including civil rights.

ELECTORAL HISTORY IN HAYWOOD COUNTY

The 1867 Tennessee law enfranchising African-American men left major gaps in the political participation of African Americans. The law, for example, specifically excluded them from public office and jury duty. Although that law was later changed, in Haywood, a county where most residents and voters were African American, African Americans were elected to public office only much later in the 1880s. Similarly, when African Americans regained the vote in 1960, at first their ballots did not insure electoral success or access to other public positions for African-American candidates.

Odell Sanders broke the color line for political candidates when he ran for alderman in Brownsville in 1964. Along with C. P. Boyd, Sanders had founded the Haywood County Civic and Welfare League. His electoral effort marked the first time an African American had run for public office in

Haywood County since McElwee's electoral defeat in 1888. Sanders lost by a six-to-one margin. The successful candidate, incumbent Fred T. Jones, had status in the African-American community. He was the coroner who had intervened to save the life of Willie Jones in 1960 by taking him from the Brownsville jail.

Sanders's defeat illustrated, more than the popularity of his opponent, a fundamental problem in the local electoral system. The district Sanders sought to represent was predominantly African American. The election for the district, however, was citywide. A predominantly white electorate determined the representative of this predominantly black district. Sanders's defeat indicated the difficulty facing an African-American candidate in an at-large election. To put it another way, African-American candidates had a better chance of being elected in districts with predominantly African-American electorates, but only if voters in each district elected their own representative. When the electorate was biracial, even with a slight majority of African Americans, the cohesion of white voters increased. Cohesion among African-American voters, however, declined as their proportion of an electorate increased. They split into factions supporting numerous African-American candidates, and some continued to support white incumbents, further dividing their votes. Single-member district elections, in a district with an electorate that was overwhelmingly African American, offered an African-American candidate the best prospect for success.[1] Under these conditions, two African-American candidates for county commissioner won electoral victories in 1965. They were the first African Americans elected to public office in the county since Samuel McElwee and after the 1965 voter registration drive.

For African Americans to attain public positions and public responsibilities, then, entailed a shift from at-large elections to single-member elections. Without such a change, access to public positions was limited largely to appointments. Appointed positions were doled out slowly and selectively by the whites in power to a few carefully chosen members of the powerless majority. For example, the African-American custodian of the city hall was selected to serve on the county grand jury in May 1961.[2] As in the voter registration slowdown of 1960, African Americans were permitted into the arena of public decision making one at a time and with considerable delay. Between 1960 and 1969, the exclusively white Haywood County Commission did not appoint one African American to any public position, board, or commission.[3] Federal law prohibited restricting voter registration, but restriction of access to elected and appointed offices had yet to be challenged.

In 1968, Sanders and others entered the courts to test whether federal law would support new forms of African-American political participation. A federal judge upheld Sanders's complaint that African Americans were underrepresented on Haywood County jury lists. Thenceforth, county officials were required to obtain names for jury lists from tax records, telephone directories, electric utilities, "and other available and reliable sources of names," in addition to voter registration lists. Sanders's suit also had sought relief from underrepresentation of women on the jury lists, but this was denied by the judge.[4]

Another federal lawsuit placed pressure on state and county governments to desegregate the county school system. A freedom-of-choice plan, which allowed students to choose a school to attend, had brought a small number of African-American children, about 1 percent, into the previously all-white schools, but no white children into the all-black schools. The federal court decided that, under this plan, progress in desegregation was too slow. The judge ordered county officials to conduct the ninth and tenth grades for all high school students of both races in the previously all-black Carver High School, and to conduct the eleventh and twelfth grades for all high school students of both races in the previously all-white Haywood High School. This desegregation plan was to be implemented in September 1969. The court agreed to postpone its desegregation plan for one year if construction of a new building for an integrated high school was authorized by 1 August 1969 and ready for use a year later. A wave of arson, some of it affecting African-American plaintiffs in the desegregation case, greeted the court decision.

The all-white county school board and a host of prominent white community leaders campaigned for the construction of a new integrated high school. The school board emphasized the need for new facilities. An accrediting association had classified the existing Haywood High School as substandard and unsafe. The all-black Carver High School had never met minimum standards. White leaders were now free and eager to acknowledge that the county's separate facilities had been unequal and, even at best, inadequate for white students. The choice, as the board explained it, was simple: "The County must either spend substantial amounts renovating Haywood High and Carver and enlarging Haywood High, at a cost of several hundred thousand dollars, which would be a temporary solution at best; or build a new high school."

The new high school would cost more than the renovation, but, for the school board and others, it was the more attractive option. The state, for example, agreed to provide one-fifth of the $2.5 million estimated cost. The new construction would include using "the best portion of Carver" for trade and vocational classes. Supporters of the new construction pointed out the advantage of vocational training "for those students whose academic records indicate that for their betterment a trade be sought for them." Finally, the county officials approved a half-cent sales tax to pay for bonds to finance the school construction. This tax would diminish the property tax increase needed to finance any new construction. The county commission, however, in approving the sales tax for a referendum, specified that it could be used only for the construction of the new school. Advocates of the sales tax estimated that property taxes would have to be increased more to renovate the two existing buildings than to build the new facility.[5]

The sales tax increase required approval of the voters of the county. The referendum confronted African-American voters with a dilemma. On the one hand, approval would result in a new, integrated school. On the other hand, the school board's integration plan entailed losses and risks. First, there was the loss of Carver High School. Under the court's plan, black and white students would attend a renovated Carver High. The facilities that had housed the separate systems would be attended sequentially by children of both races. Resources would be allocated to bring the Carver school building, teachers, and students up to standards applied equally within all schools in the system. The African-American community would see its own Carver High School enhanced and made equal to the schools of white students, even if Carver would never be as fine as the proposed new school. Carver High, named after a famous black man, was an institution shared by every member of the African-American community whose education extended to high school. Community cohesion would be weakened by the school's demise. Second, the new building posed a risk to African-American professionals in the community. A new integrated school would eliminate the African-American school administrators and perhaps teachers who had operated the separate schools for African-American children.[6] The court-ordered desegregation

HAYWOOD COUNTY PRECINCT VOTES

1968 Presidential Election and 1969 Sales Tax Referendum

| | **Presidential Election** | | **Sales Tax Referendum** | |
| | | | | |
Precinct	Presidential Votes	Total Wallace (%)	For Sales Tax (%)	For Total Votes
District 1				
Hillville	100	67	17	42
Eurekaton	68	79	40	35
District 2				
Dancyville★★	280	33	18	125
Shepp★	39	85	91	22
District 3				
Stanton★★	350	37	48	126
District 4				
Union★	274	46	61	106
District 5				
Allen★	120	63	60	68
Holly Grove	248	63	50	80
District 6				
Mulligan	292	49	41	129
District 7				
South★	905	48	56	439
Northeast★	759	51	76	376
Northwest★	621	44	63	200
Rural★	412	52	78	358

Table (continued)

	Presidential Election		Sales Tax Referendum	
Precinct	Presidential Votes	Total Wallace (%)	For Sales Tax (%)	For Total Votes
District 8				
Rudolph	245	72	36	87
District 9				
Brummett★★	311	17	31	136
District 10				
Forked Deer★★	187	23	20	97
Woodville	65	80	15	34
District 11				
Nut Bush★	151	47	53	55
Tibbs	94	63	37	43
District 12				
Clark★	97	74	93	29
Total	5,618	48	55	2,587

★ Precinct with Wallace majority or plurality and majority for sales tax. Predominantly white voters.

★★ Precinct without Wallace plurality and majority against sales tax. Predominantly black voters.

p=.025

plan would have kept those administrators and teachers in place. Third, the integration plan entailed the risk that making Carver a vocational school would justify resegregation of African-American children. It was likely that African-American children would be those deemed better suited to a trade than to an academic high school education. After all, early in the twentieth century, Booker T. Washington's advocacy of such a plan had been almost universally endorsed by white leaders.

The sales tax referendum really gave voters three choices. Those voting for the sales tax were voting for a new and integrated high school building. Those voting against it could either be protesting integration altogether, or expressing a preference for the alternative court plan of integration that would take effect if the new building was not approved. Most African Americans voted against the sales tax. They voted for school desegregation, with continued use of both schools (with renovations) and their existing faculty and administrators. Just like the African-American state legislators of 1881, these African-American voters feared that a measure ostensibly aimed at integration could take away more than it gave, and they voted against it. Most white residents voted for the referendum, which carried by a narrow margin, 1,428 to 1,159.

Voting on the new sales tax correlated unexpectedly with the previous year's presidential election (see table). George Wallace, governor of Alabama, had run for president in 1968 as an independent candidate opposing federal racial desegregation measures. Among the three presidential candidates, he won a plurality of 48 percent in Haywood County. Of the county's twenty precincts, thirteen had similar results in the 1968 presidential election and the 1969 sales tax referendum. That is, people voted for a segregationist and a school integration plan, or they voted for the Democrats, with their strong civil rights stand, and against a school integration plan. In nine of these thirteen precincts, where voters were predominantly white, there were majorities or pluralities for Wallace and a majority for the sales tax. The remaining four precincts, which had predominantly African-American voters, delivered majorities against Wallace and against the sales tax.[7] The new school building proceeded. Several years later, in 1990, C. P. Boyd and others renovated the former Carver High School building. It now serves as a community center.

The federal court intervened in school matters again when it required the county commission to reorganize the school board. Previously, the county commission had selected members of the board on an at-large basis. Now, under orders from the federal court in West Tennessee, the commission elected seven members—five representing specific districts and two chosen at large. The African-American candidate for the predominantly African-American District 3 seat was a veteran of the voter registration effort. The county commission passed him by and selected a white man to represent District 3. All the other candidates for the four remaining districts were white. Odell Sanders and eight other African Americans nominated themselves for the two at-large positions. Two white men were also on the slate of at-large candidates. On the day of the election, both white candidates withdrew. The county commission thus had only African-American candidates for two vacant at-large positions. It selected Odell Sanders, who had received all but one of the commission votes, to the first position. The county judge then declared W. D. Rawls, who had received no votes in the balloting, the winner of the second position. After lawsuits and travail, two more African-American men reentered public positions in the county. One was a product of the latest movement for civil rights, while the other, a member of the county's most prominent African-American family, had been selected by white officials.[8]

"THEY HAD DESTROYED
A WONDERFUL PERSON"

For Elisha Davis, the changes of the 1960s in Haywood County did not erase the memories of 1940. He visited Haywood County in 1977 for the second time since he had been banished. He traveled with his oldest granddaughter and her husband and showed them, furtively, some of the men who had run him out of the county. They were still living. He was very circumspect in informing people that he was in the area. He went to Brownsville only to visit and stayed in a motel outside of the city. He showed a degree of fear that surprised his granddaughter: "I knew his fear was real. And when he was afraid, I was afraid too. He never showed me fear. I never had reason to fear, like my grandfather."

The younger Davis children remembered their father's efforts to communicate some of the family's experiences in Haywood County and the lessons to be drawn from them. These children reached adulthood when the civil rights movement was in full swing. John recalled, "Sometimes he would say things about the South when we had people from the South, family from the South. But to sit down and say, 'Daddy had to run from here. Mother had done this.' I can't remember ever that we actually sat down and did this."

Florence Davis, another of the seven younger children, remembered that each child had some partial information: "He would call us out to the garage sometime or another to talk about something. It would eventually revert to the time that they were run out of Tennessee. But he would just make the statement or something. Then he would start pulling out his papers and say read this or look at that."

Nancy, another Davis daughter, had her talk with her father at the time she was engaged:

> There are interracial marriages in our family. He kind of warned me about that. "Now if you're going to do this, this is going to happen. They did this to me and this can happen to you and that sort of thing."
>
> And I think that this was probably the first time that he was letting me know, "Hey Sis, this is what you are to be in store for. Because this happened to me." I was twenty-three years old, and this is the first time I knew what he had gone through. And it was the time I had the greatest respect for him. He said, "You want this, you go for it." He wasn't telling me don't because the man I was marrying was white. He was talking about what I would have to go through. That's when I realized what he had been through. I think that when he thought I was grown, he pulled me aside and gave me that speech.[9]

The greatest pain occasioned by those memories of 1940, as Elisha Davis conveyed his heartache to his family, came from the realization that he had known the men in the mob that night. They had known him. Until that night, he had thought he was on friendly terms with them. Then he learned not to judge race relations by appearances, and he tried to teach his children the same lesson.

In 1969, the police killing of Walter Ward, a twenty-five-year-old African American in Niles, Michigan, confronted the Davis family and their community with an ugly remnant of the racism about which Davis had warned his children. Ward was John Davis's age and a friend of many of the other Davis children. He competed in high school sports, served two tours of duty as a paratrooper in Vietnam, and left the service with the rank of sergeant. He returned to Niles after the war and worked in the summer youth program of his home town's police department, which recruited him to be a police officer. Davis's son John speaks of Walter as "an idol" and a role model for young people of both races: "There was a lot of intense anger because they had destroyed a wonderful person. Walter could do anything. Walter was six foot six and weighed 250 pounds."

Ward was killed when he attempted to intervene in a melee involving white and black teenagers at the Burger Chef in Niles. The police account alleged that a crowd of 150 to 200 teenagers was out of control and threatening the police on the scene. According to police testimony, Ward interfered with the police, including firing two shots at one of the police officers. The officer shot Ward three times, killing him.

Eyewitness accounts differed from the police testimony. Six of the eyewitnesses claimed that Ward had attempted to break up the fight before the backup police were called in. Ward asked the dog-handling officers to hold off using the dogs, promising that he would get the situation under control. The police disregarded his request and set one dog upon African-American youths in the restaurant. This made matters worse. As exits from the restaurant were blocked, it was difficult for patrons to escape the bedlam of dogs and scared teens. As police were arresting an African-American teenager outside, Ward apparently told the boy to submit to the police. At this time, all witnesses agreed, one of the officers with a dog came up to within the dog's striking distance of Ward. Ward told the officer, "Don't put that dog on me, or I'll kill him." The team then attacked Ward, who ran to his nearby car and returned with a gun. These witnesses claimed that Ward shot, once or twice, directly in front of the dog. Ward's height, six and a half feet, and his proximity to the dog, eight feet, made it evident where Ward shot. As Ward shot, the officer drew his revolver and shot Ward. According to the witnesses, the officer shot Ward at intervals. His first shot sent Ward to his knees. His second and third shots hit the kneeling, slumping Ward. One witness recalled, "I couldn't believe how slow and deliberate it was." Another witness, the wife of a Niles businessman, lamented, "The worst part about it is that this was one of the fellows that tried to keep the younger kids from getting in trouble."

The Davis family was, and remains, certain that Ward was a victim of police violence that night. Davis's daughter Mary recalled that Walter had stopped by her house that evening. Later,

> two hundred people must have come to my house that night to tell me that Walter was dead. My daughter was there. There were all these thirteen- and fourteen-year-old children. And Walter said, "Do not turn that dog on those children." Here it is, all of these little children and here they come with these dogs and they turn the dog loose in this restaurant and this dog is chasing all these children. And that's why Walter told them not to turn that dog on the kids. That's all they were, nothing but kids.
>
> They told Walter, "You shot at my dog, you might as well shoot at me."

The death of Ward divided Niles. Old grievances and new racial divisions surfaced. There were no references to Haywood County, but the criticisms of Niles were familiar to Elisha Davis and applicable to the Haywood County he remembered. The first and only African-American member of the Niles school board lambasted the mayor at a public hearing: "Your Safety Board is one of the biggest jokes in the black community. It has no black members—like most Niles boards—and it is run by a man who has no conception of how to deal with highly charged racial situations."[10]

The past president of the NAACP chapter, which Davis had started in Niles, spoke on race relations to the Rotary Club, which had no African-American members.[11]

A crowd of 750, most of them African Americans, demonstrated in the center of Niles. More than 100 blocked major thoroughfares in the town to protest the killing, which the police department ruled justifiable homicide. A group of 300 white high school students conducted a pro-police demonstration. Violence occurred as well; a shotgun blast shattered the window of the mayor's restaurant, and a poorly made Molotov cocktail failed to ignite when thrown on a lawn.

Davis participated in public meetings and worked behind the scenes to calm the situation. He and John traveled to Lansing and met with their state legislator. This meeting brought the lieutenant governor to Niles in an effort to restore order. The public hearing into Ward's death raised new problems and heightened distrust. The all-white panel decided that the shooting death of Ward had been justified. For Elisha, Nann, and Casher Davis, Ward's death was a painful lesson in how little race relations had changed in thirty years. On the other hand, Davis's and the African-American community's ability to gain a hearing and to voice protest measured how much had changed since 1940.

One local columnist drew lessons from Ward's death that applied to race relations in Niles that May and during the hundred years preceding it:

In the past four days who has not learned that Niles, like the rest of our country, is split into two societies—one black and one white; who has not heard or made such statements as:

—We can't let them take over our city.

—They have no respect for law and order.

—They think the law has no meaning.

—They don't control themselves.

—We can't let them get away with that.

They against we. We against they. This is not the language of society. It is the rhetoric of war. . . .

But if the lines of battle are drawn, can they be erased? What can be done? Who will do it?

It is the white community that must answer this question. Whites are the majority and the majority does rule, both legally and by sheer force of number. As long as a white "we" excludes blacks, it is merely a question of time before even more serious confrontations between the races occur.

The whites that are willing to abandon the racially defined "we" for the sake of dousing the embers of white-black warfare in our community must also be willing to bear the label of traitor. They must be willing to honestly try to find out why conditions in Niles are seen as unjust by many black citizens.

Most important, they must be willing to try to change those things that actually are unjust. . . .

It will take courage to talk to a person with a different colored complexion about more than the weather. It will take courage to object to a white man's use of the phrase "nigger" or "coon"—and all the other signs of racial contempt.

But if "we" want to head off the impending demise of democratic society, "we" had better not stick together. You and I had better go our separate ways and look at the problems that confront us.[12]

As the events following Ward's death unfolded, national attention shifted to the Apollo 10 mission. As the nation broke barriers in space, the Davises revisited all-too-familiar racial boundaries.

Within a month, another all-white jury in Michigan found another white policeman innocent in the shooting death of another African-American man during the Detroit riot of 1967. This verdict raised serious questions nationally about the role of racial prejudice in the justice system in 1969. The mother of the African-American teenager killed in what came to be known as "the Algiers Motel incident" expressed her view that "the jury refused to believe the facts. All whites stick together. I didn't think they would find him guilty."[13]

Soon, however, the civil rights movement would move off the nation's front pages and out of the forefront of its consciousness. In June, the University of Michigan was engulfed in protests against increased American military involvement in Vietnam. The movement for civil rights soon took a back seat to such campus protests. The movement did continue, expressing itself in myriad efforts for improvement of local conditions, as it had most of the time since 1865. In these local efforts, leaders of the civil rights movement built upon the gains made in the previous decade and confronted efforts to erode those gains.

"YOU START TO FEEL PART OF THAT HISTORY"

When William King moved back to Haywood County in 1972, it seemed unlikely that he would play a direct and public role in emancipation efforts. King was the same age as John Davis, Elisha's son, and, like him, had grown up without an awareness of the harsh realities of racial etiquette in the South.

But whereas John Davis lacked this awareness because he had been protected from it, King was unaware because he accepted things as they were. Like Robert McElwee and Elisha, Casher, and Thomas Davis, King had been brought up to accept the caste restrictions placed upon him. He minded the business of his family and his immediate African-American community. A high school student at the time of the movement in Haywood County, its meaning came to him only along the dual paths of fear and humor. The movement's political significance escaped him. He was among those high school students who were fearful of reprisal if they participated in the political activity in the county at the time:

> We were sort of kept out of things. I can remember the night the sheriff got killed, Jones killed him. When that happened we all had to go in the house. My mother specifically said, "Don't go outside for nothing." All of the lights were down and everybody was quiet. You could see she was edgy. I remember saying, "Why does she keep walking to the door?" I didn't know that a black man had killed the sheriff until a week or so afterwards, when we heard somebody talking about it.
>
> There was a comical part about the deputy [who had been with Hunter when he was killed]. They said that when he heard the shot, he hit the road and was running. When a car come by to offer him a ride, he said, "No thanks, I'm in a hurry," and he kept going. A lot of people laughed about that after-wards—to ourselves, not to them.

King's family, in the 1950s, participated in a tradition of economic subordination that extended back to Reconstruction and that had incorporated the McElwees in Haywood County. That tradition included the ritual of "settling" and the status of indebtedness. King remembered the meetings of his father with their landlord in the back of the house at the end of each year. Every time, the balance of accounts, money earned and money owed, was nearly even.

It was because of okra that King's mother decided to withdraw the family from that tradition. King's father's landlord, like the McElwees' landlord, encouraged the planting of okra. The crop required a great deal of work on the part of an entire family. The King family had many boys, making the Kings profitable tenants for a landlord. Okra yielded substantial income, and, as an incentive to their tenants to stay on, landlords were more generous with income from this crop. For Robert McElwee, as we have seen, okra as a cash crop signaled improvements in the status and opportunities of a sharecropping family. King's father saw okra the same way and put his sons to work on a new crop. To King's mother, however, okra was a chain that bound her sons to another man's land and to an economy that held out little opportunity for her children. At his mother's insistence, King's family plowed up the okra crop, left the farm, and moved to Brownsville for the better education available there. The Kings moved at about the same time that the McElwees left the land and Haywood County. Both families completely severed their link to a vanishing sharecropper economy.

It was in the U.S. Army that King finally became aware of the difference in race relations that migration and the movement had made for African Americans such as the Davises and McElwees. King had won an athletic scholarship to Murray State University in western Kentucky but learned of it too late to attend. To escape sharecropping and a lack of alternatives, King joined the army. There he met African Americans from urban areas and the North. They had a very different attitude toward racial equality.

> I had people to explain to me from somewhere else exactly what was happening here. I could hear people talking a language that I didn't even understand about things that they got in high school. The only thing that we ever had was a building trade. These other kids had auto mechanics, and these were southern kids. In the North, those kids could have probably come down here to teach school. When I came back, I think that my whole attitude about the South, about people, about black folks, white folks, school, and the whole thing had changed.

Sometime after his return to the county, King entered politics to protest the construction of a highway right through the predominantly African-American fairgrounds neighborhood, an area that had been established by McElwee's 1880s legislation. King's initial effort instructed him in basic civics. He learned what a petition was from his former high school teacher and how public meetings were conducted. When the time came for the hearing, King was extremely nervous: "I only went to the courthouse to pay taxes, get a license plate, or to pay fines. Now I was going to talk to a board. I prayed before I went, 'Lord, I'm going to the land of the pharaoh. Please guide and deliver me.' Man, I was nervous." Although many factors in addition to King's modest efforts may have played a role, the road that he and others protested was not constructed.

King's effort to block the construction of the road gave him notoriety that was still alive several years later. At that time, two Catholic nuns came to the county to begin a community organization, JONAH (Just Organized Neighborhood Area Headquarters). In these nuns' efforts, history was repeating itself. The abolitionist movement had continued after emancipation, as freedmen's aid societies developed schools in the 1860s. One hundred years later, the civil rights movement continued in a host of local community organizing efforts. Like the schools for freedpeople, JONAH initially was led by white church women from the North. Broadly speaking, the intentions of the two nuns, Attracta Kelley and Pat Siemans, had much in common with those of the Freedmen's Bureau agents and the teachers they recruited to West Tennessee—to conduct schools and to assist the freedpeople in implementing their new freedoms. The two nuns began their work by looking for leaders of previous reform efforts and learned of King's petition drive a few years earlier.

JONAH's belief statement, which Kelley and Siemans formulated along with the group's members, expressed the continuing goal of emancipation:

> The underlying philosophy of JONAH is one of deep belief in the liberating power of the Gospel. We believe that no one can give liberation and dignity to another—it can only be experienced and taken for oneself. We believe that through the power of the Spirit of God, a community can act upon its own liberation, and be transformed into a new people. We believe in the power of new life and transformation and therefore our hope is determined.
>
> JONAH attempts to enflesh these beliefs through organization and maintenance of community-based groups among low and moderate income peoples. JONAH focuses on grassroots leadership development because we see that our American society basically ignores the potential of those who have not been empowered for self-determination. JONAH tries to build an organizational strength that can address, influence and change some of the unjust social, political, economic, cultural and religious institutions and systems that deny full human dignity to all peoples. Many times JONAH's efforts can only be resistant to the values and attitudes that perpetuate unjust systems. However, JONAH believes that a people made aware of their own potential can deeply impact the future direction of local, national and global justice.[14]

As part of developing grassroots leadership for JONAH, Kelly and Siemans instructed King in the history of the civil rights movement. Kelly took King and others to the Highlander Center in East Tennessee, where Septima Clark had begun working with the Citizenship Schools. Some of these schools had reached Haywood County in 1960. King met Clark at Highlander:

> That was an experience! That lady, she's one of those people that just capti-
> vates you! She found out that I was from Haywood County. She said, "I
> remember Haywood County." She started telling me about setting up Free-
> dom Schools in the county. Then she was telling us about some of the expe-
> riences she had. She just captivated you by those stories and experiences.[15]
> After you listen to some of the history, then you start to feel a part of it. You
> start feeling like an organizer.

"WE STOPPED AT EQUAL"

King was elected to the county commission in 1982. He joined three other African Americans on the commission at the time. They included Roy Bond, his former high school principal, and C. P. Boyd.

King also staffed the Brownsville JONAH office, which was located in the courthouse square. A long, steep flight of fifty-nine stairs led to JONAH's second-floor office. The faded lettering on the door and on the window overlooking the square read, "Joe Sternberger, Attorney." Ironically, JONAH's office once had housed the attorney who had contested Samuel McElwee's parents, and many other African Americans, for their land. Now the space was being put to a very different purpose.

King worked to expand the political participation of African Americans in the county, drawing on the changed roles of African-American elected officials and African-American organizations. JONAH, for example, managed to increase the number of African Americans on the school board. Since the 1970 selection, the county commission had maintained two African Americans—the same two men, Odell Sanders and W. D. Rawls—on the school board. JONAH attempted to have Sanders replaced:

Odell had gotten old and the stuff was passing him by. He was just there. So what we were saying was, "Let's use him for counseling and put a young person there who has the expertise to deal with the problems we have now." We tried to get them to replace Odell Sanders. The white commissioner over there told us, "The man [Odell Sanders] is doing his job, there is no reason for moving him. He's a pillar of the community." That's what they were saying about Odell.

Failing to get Sanders replaced, JONAH began to pressure the county commission to expand African-American representation on the school board from two members to three. Eventually, a vacancy occurred, and the county commission acceded to JONAH's demand for a third African American.

They didn't want to fight it then, because that only made three blacks, and there were seven board members. The chair voted only on ties.

We stopped at equal. We got 65 percent of the kids in the schools that are black and 35 percent of them are white. So we asked why can't it at least be equal on the school board. Now if we want to do it proportionately, according to the proportion of kids in the schools, we got to have more representation. But our whole concept was to make it even and that happened.

The new school board member had a pivotal role in JONAH's subsequent effort to bring the school breakfast program to the county, despite the objections of school officials:

The school superintendent said, "There is no way we can have a school breakfast program. There is not enough time. Kids get to school at different times." We showed him that there was enough time and how long it takes. It takes about fifteen minutes. He said, "We didn't have anybody to cook it." That we were going to have to use volunteer teachers to come in to do it. That they would have to hire extra folks in to administer the breakfast. We showed where if the people come in fifteen minutes earlier, the kids could eat. They were going to be there anyway. We went through all the pros and cons. He still said no.

Failing with the school superintendent, JONAH continued its efforts to establish a school breakfast program in the county through another route, the Reverend Tom Averyheart, the newly appointed school board member. State regulations permitted a school board to begin a breakfast program, so Averyheart took the initiative to bring the matter to the board, bypassing the superintendent. His motion to begin the program failed for lack of a second. Averyheart then went to the Tennessee Department of Education. He passed along to them the information on the eligibility and need of Haywood County's schoolchildren, along with the petitions that JONAH had assembled. The state officials sent the letter and information back to the superintendent, who was sufficiently embarrassed to support the measure. Averyheart subsequently lost his position on the school board. According to King, "They called him a radical and said he wasn't working with the school board. They organized against him."

When Reverend Averyheart came up for reappointment, the court-house was packed with folks. We had petitions. We said, "He is a pillar of the community. He's a church member. He's been on the board. He's doing his job. So why move him? He's done so much for civil rights, brought the community together," and all this other stuff they had said about Odell [Sanders] one year before.

I was on the commission then. It was my first year, and it was the first thing that I did. We got three votes. Only the black commissioners voted for Reverend Averyheart. The others never opened their mouths. Somebody made a recommendation that another guy, a black man, be the seventh member of the school board, and all the white commissioners voted for it.

Averyheart was kicked out. That was the price he paid for the school breakfast. If he had've just played along and not said anything, went along with the system, he would be there now. You pay for those things. We knew that the cost of the school breakfast was losing that school board member.

But we did hang on to the third board member. What they found out is that, "Yes, we can work with three members." It's a better working condition. You don't have JONAH breaking down your door and get all of this bad publicity and have legal services to come over here for every kid that gets in trouble.

THE BIGGEST WIN

JONAH continued to test the federal resolve to support the civil rights of African Americans, as Odell Sanders and others had done in the 1960s. In 1982, JONAH alleged that the county commission had intentionally discriminated against African Americans in a decision to elect all five county road commissioners in at-large elections. This violated the law. Congress in the 1860s and 1870s had passed laws to enforce the Fourteenth and Fifteenth Amendments to the Constitution. Similarly, in 1982, Congress had amended the Voting Rights Act of 1965 to prohibit the adoption of any practice that would dilute the vote of any identifiable racial group, even in the absence of evidence of intentional discrimination. Just as a century before, these federal measures provided local and state African-American political organizations grounds upon which to challenge their exclusion, unintentional or deliberate, from politics.

King recalls the lawsuit as the "biggest win" that JONAH ever had. The county lost a commissioner's district when the 1980 census showed a decline in population. The total number of districts went from ten to nine. Prior to 1980, each of the five road commissioners had been assigned two commissioner districts. With the decline to nine commissioner districts, the road commissioner districts had to be changed. Five could not be evenly divided into nine.

All they had to do was to draw five road commissioner districts and they would have had it. They never drew the line. They said, "Why not just do it at-large. We'll just elect them at-large." That meant you wouldn't have districts. You could get all the road commissioners from out of this white district over here, and there never would be a black. We had never won an at-large position. No way. A black could never win an at-large position in Haywood County.

We had a smart lawyer, Rob McDuff from Mississippi. He was right out of law school and had a lot of zeal. He was working for the University of Mississippi. We got the NAACP to come in on it. Legal Services was in on it. They were taking it on because of the Voting Rights Act's amendments.

The county commission planned to hold at-large elections for the two vacant positions of road commissioners in August 1982. The plan required a two-thirds majority vote among the twenty commissioners. At the time of the vote, April 1982, the commission had seven African-American commissioners; enough to deny the motion the fourteen votes it required. The politics of the issue came down to straightforward arithmetic. If the commission voted along racial lines, the issue would not pass. The measure failed on the first vote. The commission voted again. The bloc of white votes held. The bloc of African-American votes chipped, losing one member. Roy Bond passed on the second roll-call vote. When the roll had been called, the vote stood at thirteen to six. Bond then voted for the measure and provided the needed fourteenth vote.

Bond explained his vote as the essence of politics: "Sometimes you have to join those who you are against. That's politics." He explained that to vote against the at-large election for road commissioner would have meant having no election at all for those positions, and he thought it was wrong to hold up a process like that. In addition, he reported that, before he voted, he had gained other commissioners' assurances that they would work with him to restore the road commissioners' vote to districts the following year. The county judge denied that any deals like that had been made.[16]

Having failed in the county commission, JONAH trekked to federal court. JONAH's lawyers showed that no African American had been appointed to any public position, board, or committee by the Haywood County Commission from 1960 to 1969. Since 1970, when the commission had selected Odell Sanders and W. D. Rawls for the school board, the commission had made 261 appointments. Thirty-six of them, only 14 percent, had gone to African Americans.[17] C. P. Boyd testified about the voter registration drives of 1959 and 1961 and the resistance of county officials. J. Morgan Kousser, a historian with a Yale Ph.D., offered evidence of the systematic disfranchisement of African Americans in the South during the nineteenth century. Kousser used McElwee's 1888 election and other events in Haywood County as examples of that process. JONAH alleged that the county commission, despite having African-American members at the time, discriminated against African Americans. The testimony of Kousser placed the current record of appointments and discrimination as part of a tradition of disfranchisement and restrictions of civil rights.[18]

JONAH's legal action succeeded. The federal judge in the case took note that Haywood County "has made substantial and commendable progress in race relations in the past few years." But, he continued, "The testimony in this case shows that the County has a history of hostile acts, inhuman treatment and deplorable examples of racial discrimination against black citizens."

The judge determined that the changes in road commissioner elections appeared to be racially motivated and threatened to dilute the voting rights of African Americans in the county, in violation of the Fourteenth Amendment and the Voting Rights Act of 1965, as amended. Therefore, he issued a preliminary injunction prohibiting the scheduled elections.[19] Once again, officials in Haywood County faced a federal court injunction to prevent their proposed action. The judge's injunction even included a preliminary finding that the county commission had discriminated with intent.

The judge's action and finding forced the county commission to reconsider its position on road commissioner elections. In January, lawyers for JONAH and the commission's attorney reached an agreement that ended the lawsuit. The commission agreed to draw up five road commissioner districts based on the 1980 census. JONAH agreed to let the county commission off the legal hook. The agreement did not assert intentional discrimination and stipulated that "discriminatory intent was never the subject of a final adjudication on the merits of this case."[20] As a temporary measure, the agreement provided the county commission authority to appoint two road commissioners until an election could be held.

JONAH then added one more condition, at which the county commission majority balked:

> After they redrew the districts, they had to make two appointments for the two commissioners who were supposed to have been elected. We said that one of those folks had to be Willie Ross. He was one of our members. He was a JONAH member. They said, "Find somebody else." They didn't want JONAH to have nothing to do with the settlement. The other guy we suggested was white. So we gave them one but they wanted us to name somebody else.
>
> We said that if you don't give us Willie Ross, then we are going to take you all right back to court. We were saying, "We don't want that

Fig. 21. Truly Mae Taylor, JONAH member who was plaintiff in the suit over Road Commission elections, in the Taylor Branch cemetery, 1992. Elbert Williams was buried here in an unmarked grave. Photograph by the author.

settlement you all are talking about if Willie can't be the road commissioner." They wanted that settlement, so they appointed Willie to the road commission.

But they tried to remove Willie afterwards, even when he got in. They said Willie had two jobs with the county, and there was a law on the books that said road commissioners could not draw two checks from the county. The reason that they had that law was because, in the old days, they had one guy who was road commissioner and he was a road superintendent. He was setting his own salary. He had been doing it for years and that's why they said they changed it.

But Willie was a road commissioner, and he drove a school bus. Willie said, "I'm not going to give up my school bus because there's some pension involved in it." So JONAH went back over to the county commission and got them to change the law to say you may draw two checks from the county if both of them are not for decision-making positions. You can be a road commissioner and drive a school bus, but you can't be a road commissioner and be the superintendent. So that meant that he could drive his bus and also be a road commissioner.

"IT MADE A BIG DIFFERENCE"

Robert McElwee came to Haywood County in 1983, after the controversies over the road commissioners and the new school breakfast program. He did not notice either of those political developments. He did notice changes on a personal level. He went out to the home of his former landlord and found that she had "passed." He also noticed the attention he received because he and his grandson, who came with him, were from California:

> My grandson, I carried him with me [to Brownsville] five years ago. I carried him with me in 1983 and I bought him a pair of shoes. The [white] lady asked, "Where are you from?" He said, "I'm from Mississippi." She said, "I thought you were." Later he walked up to the lady, caught her dress, and said "I'm just kidding. I'm from Los Angeles." You could see the change in her the way she did. "I knew it. I knew it." She just carried on. "This little boy here is from California." It made a big difference.
>
> The folks back there they eat you up. All they had to know is you are from California. If you are from California, they tote your watermelon to your car. That tickled me because I was born there, you know, and I know them. You go back there, they wouldn't let you carry a thing. One white boy, he said he wished my brother John and I could go to church with him. They want everybody to think things are really good.

McElwee also took special note that a slave block in Brownsville had been removed. That specific reminder of the time when African Americans had been bought, sold, and held as property was gone from his notice.

What McElwee did not know was that a reminder of his grandfather's career had also been removed from the courthouse lawn before anyone could notice. It happened so fast that few people had seen the marker go up and come down. In early January 1981, the Tennessee Historical Commission had approved a marker to commemorate the career and contributions of Samuel A. McElwee. The county historian, Morton Felsenthal, consulted with the county judge and notified the Tennessee Historical Commission

Fig. 22.
Disputed (and inaccurate) McElwee historical marker relocated from the Haywood County Courthouse to Fisk University, Nashville. Photograph by the author.

that the county would locate the marker in the courthouse or on its lawn, whichever seemed best. The marker contained several errors. It incorrectly recorded McElwee's dates of his death and his participation at the Republican party national conventions, in its brief accounting of his public career. Nonetheless, it was public notice of his political career, which had been all but forgotten:

Samuel A. McElwee
1858–1930

Born a slave in Madison County, Samuel McElwee began teaching school in Haywood County at the age of 16. He graduated from Fisk University and was elected to the Tenn. House of Representatives in 1883. Samuel McElwee served three successive terms in the legislature, promoting uniform education and justice. In 1885, led the state delegation at the Republican National Convention. Samuel McElwee moved to Nashville in 1888 after he was defeated for reelection by force of arms.

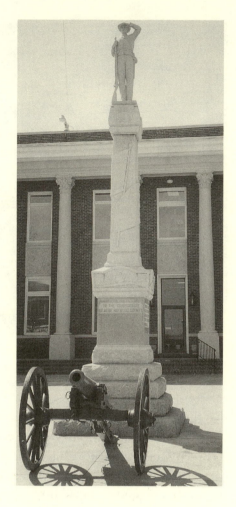

Fig. 23. Memorial monument of Civil War soldiers at the Haywood County Courthouse. Photograph by the author.

The county judge read the new marker when it was placed on the courthouse lawn in early April and immediately ordered it taken down. It was removed and placed in the basement of the courthouse. The Tennessee Historical Commission deputy director requested the assistance of the Haywood County Historical Society to relocate the marker. The society declined, judging it, "inappropriate to act . . . at this time. We would like more information on the background of Mr. Samuel McElwee, the decision to place the marker in Haywood County and how this marker came into being."[21]

After several years in the courthouse basement, the marker was removed and placed on the Fisk University campus. It stands directly across the street from the main entrance to the campus and from a statue of W. E. B. Du Bois. One hundred years after being on campus together, McElwee and Du Bois again met at Fisk. Now, however, McElwee stood far smaller in stature, figuratively and literally, than Du Bois.[22]

Changes the McElwees noticed on their visit to Haywood County suggested comparisons not only to the past, but also to their own present. When they first had arrived in Los Angeles, the city represented "heaven" or certainly a form of deliverance from the fear that they had known. By 1990, however, Robert McElwee was willing to engage in spirited discussion with his sisters about whether Los Angeles might not have become worse than what they left behind in Haywood County. His sister Julia took the firmest position in such discussions, arguing that things in California had become just as bad as those in West Tennessee. In particular, she felt that African-Americans needed better qualifications than white people did to get the same positions.

The differences in the various McElwees' positions were largely matters of degree, not substance. They all agreed, for example, that African Americans had more legal protections in Los Angeles than they had had in Haywood County. But they differed on the *degree* to which whites in Los Angeles had more protections than blacks. It amazed all of them to be living in a huge city with an African-American mayor, but they disagreed about what difference that mayor made. Robert McElwee generally saw more improvement in their lives in Los Angeles than his sisters did:

> Life's been pretty good to me here till it got to where I couldn't work. I got hurt. They had a tool at work they weren't supposed to let me work with. I fell with it and busted my fingers open. I went back the next day hoping to find the tool and throw it over behind the wall.
>
> I didn't know anything about suing or stuff like that. If I had sued them, I could have got a lot of money out of them. I didn't do that because they were so nice to me.
>
> I come from nice country and that's the way we were. There, if you made a friend, you threw up your hand. I don't care who he was. If you didn't know him, you met him and got acquainted with him.

Even Robert McElwee qualified the significance of the changes, including his ability to vote: "It's good to have the privilege of voting, but they are going to elect who they want anyway. I believe they got Tom Bradley bought in. I think Tom sort of minds the other fellows. I believe Tom Bradley can only go so far."

The police beating of Rodney King in 1991 shocked the nation and gave Robert McElwee another measure of the changes he has seen. This man who buried a lynch victim fifty years before thought King's beating "was real bad":

> He's lucky he's living. They beat him up pretty bad. It seemed to me it was a made-up job. He did what they told him. There were too many beating him. It's more of a racist thing, I think.
>
> Still things are better than back there in Haywood County. They could do what they wanted to back then. They can't do that now. You still have your rights here.

All the McElwees agreed that Los Angeles had grown more dangerous than it was when they moved there. They differed about the degree of danger. Robert McElwee was adamant about the basic danger:

> People out here, they are dying on the sidewalk, they step on your head and keep walking.
>
> Los Angeles ain't as good as when I came here. There are so many outside folk coming. You go out in the street and speak to one of them and they curse you out. When we first got here, you could lay a bike out in the yard and it would lay there a week. Nobody would touch it. Now, you go outside, you go to sleep in your yard and your head will be on the other side of the street in the morning.

The McElwees were unanimous in their opinions on one cause of the problems—drugs. "They use this dope and stuff and that makes them crazy." Robert McElwee went further, tracing the problem to the arrival of African Americans from other cities. The influx of African Americans from rural areas of the South ended, and, with the arrival of new urban migrants, drug use and violence increased.

Milmon Mitchell was equally adamant about the devastating impact of drugs in Michigan. In time, Mitchell had begun acquiring and renting property in Detroit. He was anxious, by the mid-1980s, to sell his property and leave the real estate business. Too frequently, renters set fires or caused other damage related to drug use. Mitchell also was working as a volunteer with the courts of Detroit to sponsor youngsters who were in legal trouble and thereby help them avoid incarceration.[23] As he approached the age of 90, Mitchell remained politically active. Most recently, he had supported efforts, which originated in Detroit, to gain reparations for African Americans for the violation of their rights while in slavery.[24]

Milmon Mitchell visited Haywood County in 1989. He stopped by to speak briefly with King. He learned, to his amazement, that African Americans not only voted but also, like King, served as elected officials in Haywood County. His mind retained the image of Brownsville as a Johannesburg, with white minority rule enforced by "legal" repression and violence. The existence of JONAH, with its multiple chapters in West Tennessee, reminded him of his own efforts to spread the NAACP through his staff of insurance agents. Mitchell's visit was cut short by a court date in Detroit involving his property and drug-abusing tenants.

In the lives and comments of the Davis family, drugs played a less salient role. The fear so pervasive in their lives in Haywood County lay far behind them. Of all the family, John Davis had the most direct and personal knowledge of the decay of the inner city and of the human spirit of people who lived there. He was working in a drug rehabilitation program in New York. His brothers and sisters worked in a variety of other occupations. They were blue-collar manufacturers, store owners, service workers, and teachers. One had served as president of her local chapter of the United Auto Workers.

The narrative of events in Haywood County that their father had partitioned among them had helped prepare them for challenges without miring them in the past. Eventually, shortly before his death, Elisha Davis was able to sit and talk humorously with his family about that terrible night in 1940. Emily Davis recalled a time about 1985:

> We sat there and laughed at my mother about it. My father said, "I told your momma just to put those guns in the bed and just to sit down. And the more I told her, the more she would get up. I just knowed that she was going to get both guns from under the covers and come out of there blasting."

He was more afraid of what momma was going to do than what they were going to do. He remembered momma coming bleating out of the house after them, "Now what are y'all going to do with him? Where are you taking him?" He said he was just trying to quiet her. He remembers her being louder than she said she was. She had a carrying voice. Daddy had a favorite expression that she was always "bleating" something out.

Likewise, the family recalls with humor that, although their Uncle Thomas fled to Nashville to escape the mob in 1940, he found new danger there. He took refuge with an old girlfriend, and that put him in danger of the wrath of his current girlfriend and future wife. Thomas eventually returned to Jackson, Tennessee, and was active in several associations, including the Urban League.

THE CONTINUING TASKS
OF EMANCIPATION

After a century and a quarter, JONAH, along with several other organizations, carried on the movement for emancipation in Haywood County. There were several impediments to this effort, functions of time and the unchanged economic position of African Americans. Young African Americans tended to leave the county in large numbers upon completing school— at about the age they would start to vote—to find employment in surrounding areas. African Americans who remained in the county had to be encouraged to register to vote and then to cast their ballot. Finally, voters had to be reregistered if they were purged from the registration lists for failing to vote in the past. King contrasted his work "of keeping black voters registered" with the previous efforts of others to "meet the qualifications and intimidation of registering." In ways of which King and his coworkers were less aware, they also were continuing the largely unrecorded efforts of the Union Leagues.

The increased number of African-American voters could make the difference in an election, if they participated and organized. King lamented that there was not enough of either participation or organization. For example, Ross had lost his position as road commissioner in a subsequent election:

"When the election came [1986], Willie Ross lost by about thirty-some votes because the district he was in was half white and half black, I think 51 percent white and 49 percent black. But the voting population was something like 32 percent black and the rest of them was white. There are no blacks on the road commission now. Willie was the only one we ever had."

The year 1986, too, almost saw the first African-American victory in a countywide election in Haywood County since the days of Samuel McElwee. Fred Sanders ran for sheriff in a field of four candidates. Many people still dispute the results of the election, referring to it as the "long count." Election results in nearby Memphis, with fifty times the population, were public before the Haywood County results that night. The election commission conducted its count out of public view. When the late results were finally announced, Sanders had lost the election by a narrow margin.

Two years later, in the August 1988 primary, C. P. Boyd waged another countywide campaign. He ran for state senator. His six-term incumbent opponent was leader of the remaining Bourbon faction of the Democratic party and had served as speaker of the state senate and lieutenant governor of the state for eighteen years. Boyd gained only 11 percent of the vote in a three-way race.[25]

The election marked a transition in the politics of the county. Thirty years after his first unsuccessful effort to register to vote, Boyd ran for office on a visionary, if not quixotic, platform. Boyd portrayed himself as "A Friend for the Poor." His platform advocated sweeping social changes, including home ownership, equal representation, a war on crime and drugs, jobs, public housing, better education, more support for the predominantly African-American Tennessee State University, relief for truckers, relief for farmers, prison reform, making Highway 64 a four-lane road, a system for AIDS control, care for the aged, adjustment of the "greenbelt tax" [a loophole benefiting large land-owners], lower phone rates, stronger family life, nuclear waste control, increased benefits for factory workers, teen pregnancy programs, and an end to racism.

In 1958, Boyd had protested the disfranchisement of African Americans that reached back seventy years. In 1988, his platform proposed a transformation of local, state, and national politics whose realization perhaps would come seventy years in the future. Nonetheless, in this election bid, Boyd represented a shift from the politics of protest to the politics of transformation.

Fig. 24.
Dr. C. P. Boyd's
Handbill from 1988
Election. Courtesy
of Dr. C. P. Boyd.

Between these two types of politics—between protest and transformation—lay the politics of portions. Once, as a member of the county commission, Boyd had participated in these politics in person. He had worked to increase the representation of African Americans in elected and appointed offices and to secure the allocation of a fairer portion of public services to African Americans. Boyd's efforts in the realm of portions were set back in 1990, when he lost his county commissioner seat. He gave up his safe district seat on the commission to run for the other seat in his district. His move, he hoped, would open the way for another African American to win the seat he had left. He expected to wage a difficult campaign and win another position, thus increasing the number of African Americans on the commission by one. Instead, he and the other African American both lost. The result was a net loss of one African American on the county commission and a decline in the politics of portions.

Boyd's losses suggested to King the need for organization and strategy in the conduct of local campaigns. In that connection, King spoke proudly of the change in the executive committee of the county Democratic party: "We took over the Democratic executive committee. Out of the thirty-six members, twenty-five are black, seventeen of them are JONAH members, and two of those are officers. One being the president and the other one being the treasurer. We deliberately did that."

King realized that such organized efforts still made white residents of the county anxious: "It's an awful threat to the whole power structure. Because the population here is mainly black, we could take over." He insisted that the goal of this organized political action was not the election of African-American officials. In fact, King said, he hoped to have more control over the caliber of candidates who ran for office—which might actually reduce the number of African-American candidates. King figured that one reason for the decline in African-American political participation was that some African-American candidates turned voters off: "There wasn't any reason to get hyped up about the election with the caliber of some of the people that we had running. They weren't saying anything." In contrast, some well-qualified African-American candidates were willing to run, and well-organized party support increased their chances of success in countywide elections. Despite organizations, white voters continued to vote as a bloc. More than twenty years after Odell Sanders first ran for elected office, the primary impediment to the success of African-American candidates was white voters' cohesiveness in backing white candidates.[26]

However affected the chances of some African-American candidates may be, organized action increased the accountability of all elected officials. Organized action could make the African-American community an important part of the population and of the electorate, enhancing its power: "In JONAH we are organized and have community meetings so that officials got to deal with all of us. We are going to keep them accountable. We won't let them get away with the kind of stuff they had been doing. We have become eyes now. We are watching. We can see and are not afraid to comment."

In this organized action King emphasized the politics of portions:

> What we want to know is, "How do we figure in?" Decisions being made on jobs, taxes, the whole agenda, "How do we figure in?" That's what we are saying. And they know it. We have candidate forums so people will have a general idea of what a candidate says, who he is, where he comes from, and what he stands for.
>
> It's not enough to say, "I'm going to treat everybody right." If you talk about God and if you believe in God, He commands you to do that in the first place. We expect the power structure to treat everybody right. Our thing is "What can you do for us? How do we figure in?" We say that all over the county.

The politics of portions means more than election of African Americans and accountability. These are but steps toward improved opportunities and conditions for people who are in greatest need in the county. The group in greatest need still, after one and a quarter centuries of emancipation, is the African-Americans. King judged that

> the average black man looks forward to getting out of here, to leaving. I have said this in court. There is nothing right now for a black man to stay for. There is no job for him. There is no security for his family. There is no recreation. As for as education, when you get out of high school, that's it. There is nothing to offer him. I have even told my own son that. I would love for him to come back here. But there is nothing for him to do. To come back and look at this is depressing. The role models themselves are not there any more. So this limits the future of our kids. Those kids who stay right here usually end up in trouble, end up on welfare, or end up doing nothing.
>
> A new factory just came about a month ago. They had to turn away over 60 percent of the folks that came out there to apply because they couldn't read a slide rule.
>
> We don't have people prepared to do those skilled jobs, and we will need them if we bring a factory in here. It's for us, the politicians, to prepare the workers. Just last year, the county commissioners managed to convince the board of education that we need an adult program in the county. Can you imagine, in 1990, an adult education program is just beginning?

AN ELECTION OF A CENTURY

The primary election on 4 August 1988 measured some of the progress of emancipation in Haywood County. Boyd lost his bid for the state senate in that election. However, for the first time in one hundred years, an African American ran for the seat in the Tennessee General Assembly formerly held by Samuel McElwee. Jean Carney had the qualifications and the community involvement that King spoke of as prerequisites for desirable candidates. She also had the backing of the Tennessee Black Legislative Caucus. The caucus organized the efforts of the fifteen African Americans who served in the General Assembly that session. For most of the time since Emancipation— that is, between 1896 and 1964—there had been no African Americans to caucus in the state legislature. Carney lost her election bid, 2,327 to 6,500. As decisive as that defeat was, her vote count had been unimaginably high for an African-American candidate in Haywood County since the elections of Samuel McElwee. Ironically, her total vote came within 150 votes of McElwee's totals in his three election victories.

Carney's bid marked several historic continuations. It had the link to McElwee's representation a century before. Carney played down that link: "I want to be elected on my qualifications, not on some racial division." She also was the first African American woman—indeed, the first woman—to run for that seat. The recent movement for civil rights in the county had made such a candidacy possible for the first time. Carney's effort made it easier for others to run for office. She had removed the disadvantages inherent in doing something for the first time. Her action formed part of the history of emancipation in the county. John L. Poston, Union League members in 1867, Samuel McElwee, Harriet McMurray, Hester Currie Boyd, Nann and Elisha Davis, the members of the 1940 Brownsville chapter of the NAACP, Elbert Williams, Bettye Douglass, the members of the Haywood County Civic and Welfare League, Odell Sanders, C. P. Boyd, JONAH members, William King, and countless others forged a chain of tradition. Each link was a person whose actions broke with the ways things had been done and removed some impediments to other new acts.

In the election in which Carney participated, there were some reminders of the past, as well as some harbingers of the future. She recounted a conversation with one African-American man, who complained about a campaign worker's attempt to buy his vote. Carney smiled with satisfaction as she repeated his response: "He told him, 'Those folks bought and sold my parents. They can't buy me.' He told me, 'I'm not a slave. I'm free.'"

Conclusion

The politics of emancipation, embedded in the events recounted here, encompass various forms of ongoing resistance to repression and subordination. This chapter examines these forms of resistance as the politics of protest and relates them to two other forms of the politics of emancipation—the politics of portions, what we call pluralism; and the politics of transformation. Though grounded in the events just discussed, this chapter offers generalizations about the politics of other forms of human emancipation as well.

THE ARTS OF RESISTANCE

Critiques and revisions of American democracy enhance our understanding of the mechanisms and forms of domination more than of the mechanisms and forms of resistance. The explication of domination leaves unanswered many questions about resistance undertaken to further emancipation. How is it that, over the course of more than a century, overt protest emerges time and again, despite strenuous opposition? An examination of emancipation efforts over time, such as we have conducted, suggests a simple answer: resistance continually emerges because it never stops. Some people, despite efforts to repress or subordinate them, maintain and express their sense of dignity and value. Such an answer raises a second question: how do people, economically subordinate and politically repressed, maintain their sense of dignity and value, when others deny them that sense? Once again, the examination of emancipation efforts over time suggests an answer. People find spaces in which to share and preserve their sense of dignity and value. In those spaces, they also share an understanding of their common condition of repression and subordination. What they share in those spaces is an alternative to what they are told and even to what they may say in public.

Given the circumstances of their repression, people like those described in this book may disguise their sense of having dignity and value, to avoid reprisals. They may decide not to protest some harm or injustice for other reasons. Such disguises and decisions form part of their ongoing analysis of the degree of freedom available to them at a given time, the risks entailed in acquiring more freedom, the benefits they have acquired, and the losses they may incur by protest. This history of emancipation efforts suggests that these forms of political analysis never cease, they only change. Circumstances change the stakes of politics and the places where they are practiced.

Opportunities for profound change can occur suddenly and last only briefly. The periods 1865–70 and 1959–65 drastically reversed political relations of the races in one county, in the South, and in the country. They were times when people could envision that democratic equality between the races might be established by providing African Americans full legal rights and improved services, such as education. On the other hand, the 1890s and, in Haywood County, 1940 were times of equally dramatic change. Violence eclipsed a vision of democratic equality and enforced the most repressive political race relations.

Times of dramatic change in democratic equality build upon the infrastructure of politics within a subordinate group—spaces where narratives preserve the group members' sense of having dignity and value. Such spaces include the family and may extend to kin, friends, churches, schools, and places of work. In times of public emancipation efforts, new spaces are created, such as the Union Leagues, the NAACP chapter, the Haywood County Civic and Welfare League, and JONAH. The new spaces permit members of subordinate groups to recognize, in the words of James C. Scott, "the full extent to which their claims, their dreams, their anger is shared by other subordinates with whom they have not been in direct touch."[1]

This infrastructure of resistance, its public and private spaces, is fundamental to the politics of emancipation.[2] From his mother and father, C. P. Boyd learned lessons taught by different—covert—forms of resistance. When emancipation efforts are covert, they are hidden in private spaces by design, in response to a careful calculation of the risks of resistance and the prospects of success. The choices that people make among emancipation efforts take into account the fact that a miscalculation, such as Elbert Williams's overt resistance, his "strong talk," could result in death. The "silence" around Williams's lynching is misleading. His lynching was discussed in confidence, in places where opinions and attitudes were not likely to be reported to those who might launch reprisals. At times such as 1940, politics involve people in potentially deadly activities for high stakes. In 1940, the McElwee and Davis families differed in their responses. The first maintained a profoundly defensive posture. The latter began a life of protest in exile.

Because the spaces of a subordinate and repressed group may foster resistance, they are not easily created and may have to be defended. The Union Leagues, the NAACP of 1940, the Haywood County Civic and Welfare League, and JONAH are indicative of the free spaces available in times of overt resistance and expanded opportunities for emancipation. In times of restricted freedoms, spaces like these are repressed. During Reconstruction, the school buildings of the freedpeople were used for meetings of the Union Leagues and were frequent arson targets, for example. When the Davis family hid in safe homes of friends, they discovered just how circumscribed space can become for those who resist domination. The bombing of Odell Sanders's home attacked another space of open resistance.[3] When public space for resistance is closed off, some people retreat to private spaces.

The harshest form of domination is the invasion of these private spaces, including the family, because such an act communicates that one cannot defend oneself or one's family members.[4] The Davis, McElwee, and King families fought hard to acquire land or to develop skills that would make them valued tenants, in order to enhance the security of their shelter, their private space. Ike Davis's dying words emphasized the importance of holding onto the land that he had acquired. Attaining a degree of self-sufficiency made one's private space less vulnerable to violation. Caste rules insured that these private spaces would never be perfectly safe. Elisha Davis and his family, for example, attained a high degree of economic self-sufficiency for African Americans at the time. Nevertheless, he was taken, illegally and against his will, from his home.

The McElwees had a private space within the family during the interregnum of emancipation. In the safe space of their family, stories of their great-grandparents passed on a tradition of dignity and self-worth dating back to slavery. In that safe space, they learned arts of survival as well. Ethel McElwee could still recite one cardinal principle of survival that goes back to the era of dirt roads: "You don't dust the white man. If the black man got a new car, he did not pass the white man. He did not pass him. You don't dust the white man." Like William King, the McElwees learned the art of speaking politely to white people and the wisdom of not speaking at all if it could be avoided.

Deference was a technique of survival. Because of its judicious use, some African Americans were given sanction by white authorities to protect themselves from "peckerwoods." Robert McElwee's brother John had the assistance of white people in extricating himself from the caste violation of bumping into a white woman. Likewise, Casher Davis earned an apologetic explanation of a beating of an African American from a white man who carried it out. The children of the Davis, McElwee, and King families were taught deference as a means of avoiding reprisals, not as an expression of inferiority. They learned that their subordination was the consequence of the mistaken judgments and character flaws of the people to whom they deferred, not their own. The deference they exhibited did not imply a denial of the injustice of their situation. Indeed, it reflected a clear-eyed assessment of the injustices they faced, including the probability of economic or violent reprisals for violating caste norms.

Deference combines a large measure of resignation with some measure of indignation. The combination varies among individuals at any given time. In 1940, Casher, Elisha and Nann Davis; Milmon Mitchell; Elbert Williams; and Robert McElwee all had different combinations of resignation and indignation. The combination varies, too, for the same persons as their circumstances change. The McElwees and Nann Davis recalled how their attitudes changed once they left Haywood County. William King described the change in his combination of resignation and indignation that came with military service. He returned from the service "knowing" some of what the African-American leaders of the county had learned by experience.

Resignation fostered positive interpretations of unavoidable circumstances, such as the burden of debt entailed in tenant farming. Of those interviewed for this study, Robert McElwee exhibited the greatest resignation to the conditions of tenant farming. Thus he was able to express both satisfaction in his work and confidence in the possibility of avoiding problems if safeguards were taken. Despite this resignation and satisfaction, however, he remained aware that some matters were neither right nor just, and he protested them.[5] To extricate himself from harm, he most often protested covertly. Thus, after cutting himself seriously, he threw the tool that injured him over the wall rather than sue his employer in Los Angeles. Similarly, he refused to participate in the NAACP in Haywood County because he calculated the risk of reprisal to be unacceptably high.

On the other hand, McElwee recounted at least two acts, two forms of overt resistance to his personal subordination. He would "talk crazy" at times, as when he refused to accept the provisions that a merchant had set aside for him that were different than what he had ordered. Again, he declined to defer to his landlord's three-year-old daughter and call her by a title, "Miss." These deeply political acts constituted overt resistance, precisely because, as domination escalates, it encroaches on the personal realm. McElwee's resistance indicated limits to the treatment he would accept and to the demands others could make of him.[6]

McElwee's acts of resistance suggest also that fundamental to the resistance was an ongoing economic struggle, in which he and his opponents probed for weaknesses and sought small advantages. McElwee took pride in not taking any of his landlord's peanut butter, despite being hungry, precisely because he was engaged in a contest over honor in the face of need. Other forms of resistance were covert. People recounted stories of tenant farmers hiding cotton bales from their landlords and secretly selling them for their own gain. This action provided income that helped families both subsist and escape the debt so characteristic of their condition. Such action challenged the landlord's unilateral definition of what was income and what was debt.

Another factor in the decision to make resistance overt or covert, public or personal, is structural. Evidence of a decline in the strength of a dominant group encourages subordinate groups to express their infrastructure publicly and elicits new emancipation efforts. The Union Leagues, the NAACP, the Haywood County Civic and Welfare League, and JONAH were all parts of a succession in the infrastructure of emancipation. Miscalculating the strength of the infrastructure of resistance, however, is dangerous. McElwee attributed Elbert Williams's lynching primarily to his mistaken belief that the

NAACP was strong enough to protect him from reprisals. Milmon Mitchell's determination to show local people that the NAACP was "no top-water organization" sprang from his intuitive sense of the need to show the strength of the infrastructure, to protect emancipation efforts.

When dominant groups are effectively restricted by law from repressive acts, the infrastructure of subordinate groups permits more effective public emancipation efforts. Such conditions existed in Haywood County in 1865–70, when state government enfranchised freedmen and supported the education of freed children. A similar configuration occurred in 1960 and 1961, when the Justice Department enjoined white bankers, merchants, and landlords from reprisals against African Americans who registered to vote. Things were quite different in 1940, when the federal government was divided between those "in the seat of government" and "those on the ground"; neither group had a particularly strong commitment to restrict violations of African-Americans' civil rights.

When law fails to restrict dominant groups, subordinate group members wisely forego public emancipation efforts, retreating to private spaces and engaging in those forms of resistance that carry fewest risks of reprisal. Such a period extended from the fraudulent election of 1888 to the voter registration efforts of 1959.

In registering to vote, Robert McElwee's sister, Homer Zell Hess, and her husband Sam conducted an act of public resistance. This resistance was undertaken after a lifetime of apparent conformity with caste and class restrictions and "success" in attaining the highest levels of self-sufficiency and positive self-regard available to them. Yet their resistance did not constitute a break with their pasts. It continued the calculation of stakes, the prospects for success and the risks of reprisal, that Sam Hess had displayed when he complained about the conduct of his white neighbor's sons.

All of this suggests that, as James C. Scott asserts, both domination and resistance occur in degrees.[7] The more menacing the power of domination, as in the election of 1888 or the repression of 1940, the more covert resistance becomes. At such times, larger numbers of people in subordinate groups will dampen their overt resistance.[8] However, they may take separate and circuitous routes to express their dignity and self-respect, as illustrated in African-American participation in the state and national expositions of the 1890s.

Dramatic public episodes of emancipation, such as the civil rights movement, are expressions of hope, within a subordinated community, that a significant minority within the dominant group is itself prepared to change. Such an expression of hope, like all resistance, reflects a calculation that a specific individual or set of individuals within a dominant group is prepared to recognize and ameliorate certain forms of domination. Resistance admits of degrees, and its hope of success depends on degrees of domination and changes in them.

EMANCIPATION WITHIN THE AMERICAN POLITICAL PROCESS

The account of emancipation that we have given here both confirms and contradicts American politics' democratic self-image. Robert Dahl defined the normal American political process as "one in which there is a high probability that an active and legitimate group in the population can make itself heard effectively at some crucial stage in the process of decision. To be 'heard' covers a wide range of activities."[9]

Dahl's paradigmatic description of American politics was published sixteen years after Davis's protest in 1940 and three years before the voting registration effort in Haywood County. It incorporates both, in a sense, and neither.

When we fit events like these two into Dahl's definition of the American political process, we obscure some of the undemocratic elements of that process. It may take years for some groups to be heard on some issues, for example. The exclusion of African Americans from political participation in Haywood County lasted seventy years. During that time groups took action but did not gain an effective hearing—an infrequent occurrence in normal American politics, if we accept Dahl's description of pluralism. On the other hand, for Haywood County's African Americans during that seventy-year period, politics consisted primarily of individual actions designed to win approval of employers and other "decision makers," so as to be heard or at least protected from harm. Political analysts often overlook such "normal politics" carried on by members of subordinated groups.

When we scrutinize the curious lack of success on the part of active and legitimate groups or examine how personal politics focuses on winning the approval of such authorities as landlords and employers, we see how frequently terror, repression, and economic subordination or reprisals are used in American politics. These obviously undemocratic strategies prevent groups from forming, disband pressure groups that have come together, and denigrate the status of groups of disfranchised people. A minority such as the Ku Klux Klan initially may use terror to control the political participation of another group. Later, occasional mob violence demarcates the boundaries of caste and enforces subordination. In the background, the majority, locally and nationally, makes its peace with this terror and subordination. Consequently, the voices of all groups in American politics are not "heard" equally. Moreover, some groups may not express their voices publicly and may remain mute for long periods of time. It is obvious from the events recounted in this book that, within the American system, political rights once given are not irrevocable. "Active and legitimate groups" may be heard and may act to revoke the democratic gains of other "active and legitimate groups" of a previous era. With the hindsight of history, we clearly see such a revocation during the transition from Reconstruction to the era of Jim Crow. In a hundred years, others may have a vantage point from which similarly to interpret the 1980s in relation to the 1960s.[10]

A retrospect of the post-Reconstruction era, and perhaps of our own, would suggest that the American political process does not accommodate the politics of emancipation well. Protest disrupts normal political processes that, to groups in power, appear adequate. Like the white leaders of Haywood County who in 1962 conducted discussions with black leaders, members of dominant groups often seek informal political channels to find out just what a protesting group desires. They have become much more accustomed to domination than subordinate groups have. The latter's desires include an end to exclusion, increased representation and participation, and general improvement of the status of group members.

The politics of emancipation encompasses but transcends the normal politics of pluralism. It includes three different forms of politics that are evident in the struggles we have recounted—the politics of protest, both overt and covert; the politics of portions, which most resembles pluralism; and the politics of transformation.

THE POLITICS OF PROTEST

As we have explained, groups and individuals practice the politics of covert and overt protest when they are restricted by law or practice from political participation or benefits that are provided to others. Covert protest, occurring in hidden places, provides the foundation for later emancipation efforts under changed circumstances. Overt protest by African Americans, springing from such hidden but free spaces, began almost immediately upon legal emancipation. In 1865, African Americans in Tennessee already were protesting their disfranchisement. When the rights conferred by legal emancipation were withdrawn, new protests began. Wells protested her assignment to a train's smoker coach, an assignment emblematic of the emerging order of Jim Crow in Tennessee. Wells gained access to the courts to voice her protest. Elisha Davis did not. Both protests were overt. Wells's came as the federal government began to remove itself from enforcing the civil rights of African Americans. Davis's protest came as the federal government hesitantly returned, under the prodding of several groups, to the arena of African-American civil rights.

C. P. Boyd's protest to Justice Department officials, and specifically to John Doar, marked a new epoch in federal opposition to segregation and to restrictions on legal emancipation. That protest began with the trial of a black man for the death of a white man, an offense that previously would have brought on a lynching. The reality most stringently enforcing the subordination of caste had been the lack of protection for a black person charged with the death of a white person. Such total disregard for the rights of people repressed the politics of overt protest and prevented other political expression. Comparing the lynching of Williams with the trials of Dodson and Jones, black men charged with the deaths of white police officers, suggests how race relations had changed between 1940 and 1960. These changes both stemmed from and encouraged at least one form of overt political protest, voter registration efforts.

THE POLITICS OF PORTIONS

The politics of overt protest entails demands for some public benefit or right that is being denied or otherwise withheld. When public benefits become available to groups, they then practice the politics of portions. They seek some greater degree of equality and a fairer share in representation and participation and in public benefits. In the events recounted here, this form of politics began early. The political rally in Brownsville in 1867 expressed the politics of portions, for example. Likewise, as early as the 1870s, dissatisfaction with the Republican party's appointment of African Americans to positions in the party and in government gave rise to breakaway movements. Such movements continued, resurfacing in places like Chicago when African-American voting patterns changed to favor the Democratic party.

Legal emancipation, despite its limitations, introduced the idea of providing public services to African Americans and distributing some portion of public benefits to them. For example, in the period from 1865 to 1870, the freedpeople made provisions for schools for their children. The allocation of public assistance was limited. As the Freedmen's Bureau education officer explained, developing services for the freed children was immensely difficult "while the white children were unprovided in this respect." Schools were provided for white children first. Then the benefits of the 1867 law "slowly extended to reach the colored people." Similarly, the Freedmen's Bureau's reports emphasized the schools of the benevolent societies rather than those initiated and conducted by the freedpeople.

With the restrictive legislation of 1870 and throughout the era of Jim Crow, African Americans pursued fair portions and sometimes protested unfair portions. African Americans and other supporters of schools for freed children found that the 1870 laws diminished public support for education and allocated to African Americans a far smaller share of what was left. McElwee expounded upon the disparate shares of public funds spent on white and black children. In the legislature he both protested existing allocations and pressed for a more equitable distribution to African Americans. Obviously, then, the politics of protest may continue within the politics of portions and support them. Several decades after McElwee's efforts in Nashville, African-American students such as William King understood that they received textbooks that had been used first by white children. As race relations were more rigid then, there was little overt protest concerning the inequitable distribution of resources.

The politics of portions calculates equality in a variety of ways. First, the politics of portions has meant simply that, in districts or services with a majority of African Americans, African-American representatives participate in decision making. It has not meant that African Americans are now present on governing bodies in proportion to their numbers. In Haywood County, as in the country generally, when the number of elected African-American officials has increased, the shift has resulted from the establishment of single-member districts where African Americans are in the majority. In Haywood County, no African American has yet won a countywide election, just as elsewhere very few African Americans have won at-large elections in places with a majority white electorate. In Haywood County and the nation, voting is still very much along racial lines. Consequently, the first degree of equality in the politics of portions is representation from districts that are overwhelmingly African American.

Gaining even this degree of equality, it should be remembered, required a return to the politics of protest. Lawsuits brought by Odell Sanders and JONAH challenged the system of at-large elections that had prevented the election of African Americans. These protests permitted African-American voting strength to express itself in the selection of African-American representatives. African Americans increased their portion of decision-making positions. Protest is still required. C. P. Boyd was a plaintiff in a 1992 lawsuit challenging the state's redistricting plans for the legislature, which he and others alleged would restrict African-American representation. New protests may garner more selection and representation of African Americans.

The second degree of equality in the politics of portions is a fifty-fifty split between the two races. In the case of the school board, for example, William King explained, "We stopped at being equal." He meant that it was sufficient that the board's membership be divided evenly between the two races, even though African-American children constituted a larger proportion of the total than white children. Another degree of equality would have been a school board with racial representation in accord with to the racial makeup of the school system's pupils.

The highest degree of equality in the politics of portions distributes a program's benefits according to need. American politics, in general, has an aversion to redistributive policies, which such programs resemble. The achievement of this form of program is more likely when the program's resources entail minimum direct and indirect costs to local government and existing programs. School breakfast programs, for example, are funded with state and federal funds. Haywood County officials accepted such a program only when protest over its absence seemed likely to produce more disruption than implementing it would.

The politics of portions assumes that an increase in representation of any group in the public arena also will increase the number of people likely to protest unfair portions of public benefits and to demand fairer shares for members of that group. The African-American state legislators of the 1880s exemplified this principle. Likewise, adding an African-American road commissioner was a necessary but insufficient step toward assuring better road maintenance in Haywood County's predominantly African-American residential areas. A school board with as many black members as white members was a board likely to improve opportunities for African-American teachers, school administrators, and pupils. It was also likely to pursue public programs, such as the school breakfast program, that would benefit more African-American than white children. Such changes only increase the likelihood of these outcomes; obviously, they do not guarantee them.

Samuel McElwee's legislative efforts well illustrate the difficulties of achieving higher forms of the politics of portions. He was the last African American to win a countywide election in Haywood County. He was able to get new, if very limited amounts of, resources allocated to programs of direct benefit to African Americans. His arguments for increased funding for African-American teachers, for example, emphasized the disparity between white and black students in the state's universities and urged closing the gap. But he was able to secure the establishment of a mental institution in West Tennessee that benefited both whites and blacks. In short, McElwee had more success in introducing a new program of benefit to white and black people than in eliminating a disparity between allocations of resources to the two groups. His legislation could touch upon class, as with new services for poor people, but not on caste. Ordinarily public programs would not be allowed that gave exclusive benefits to African Americans or gave them more benefits than whites received. Today's calls for improved social welfare programs build on this facet of the politics of portions. As a nation, we are more likely to support programs that benefit all citizens (universal health insurance, for example) or all members of a particular group (all people over sixty-five, say) than programs that benefit sets of individuals within groups (e.g., racial and ethnic minorities or those with low incomes).[11]

THE POLITICS OF TRANSFORMATION

The politics of protest and the politics of portions precede the politics of transformation[12] that emancipation entails. Protest and portions imply transformation of some elements of current practices, such as improved accountability of public officials and more competent administration of public programs. However great the change, race remains central to the politics of protest and portions. Race is less central in the politics of transformation. For example, race is neither a qualification nor a liability for public office in the politics of transformation.

The politics of transformation includes the desire to end the racial discrimination of the past. This preference expresses itself in the desire that public office be discharged without prejudice. As the NAACP members wrote to Sheriff Tip Hunter, "Please remember that as our sheriff, you are the one person we should be able to depend upon, to look to for protection and guidance and who is responsible for making this a safe community in which to live." C. P. Boyd's 1988 campaign platform set forth one vision of transforming politics.

It is difficult to overestimate the place of basic needs, such as security from physical harm, within the politics of transformation. For most of the history of emancipation, African-Americans received far less legal protection than whites. Lynchings went unprosecuted, for example, and African-American prisoners were not protected from lynch mobs while in the custody of law officials. McElwee was unable to secure passage of anti-lynching legislation during his six years in the Tennessee General Assembly. Nor did Congress ever pass anti-lynching legislation. Lynching represented a means of enforcing caste subordination that was beyond the law, beyond the politics of portions and protest, and even beyond the capacity of pluralist politics to address.

The extralegal status of lynching measured not only the degree of inequality within the politics of portions, but also the abuse of law by the white majority when power rested disproportionately in its hands. It was only when political power, and specifically the vote, came into the hands of African Americans that unpunished white-on-black violence decreased. In fact, the clearest effect of political emancipation has been the diminution among African Americans of fear of violence and intimidation designed to enforce caste restrictions. The quality of justice in cases of white-on-black violence is still suspect or clearly inadequate, as in the cases of Walter Ward in Niles, Michigan, and Rodney King in Los Angeles. Overt protests concerning the outcomes in these cases illustrate the impact of political emancipation, as Robert McElwee informed us. In contrast, under the rule of Jim Crow, African Americans won police protection by exemplifying compliance with caste restrictions and expectations and never by demanding to exercise their legal rights. Even then, that protection was good only against "peckerwoods," the lowest class of whites.

Blacks and whites both have clear but different stakes in the politics of transformation. McElwee's anti-lynching measures, for example, would have benefited white and black people by ending lawlessness. They would have benefited African Americans more, since lynching was more often directed at them. McElwee did not get his anti-lynching measure, because the white majority did not view African Americans as McElwee did. The majority was unwilling to protest acts against African Americans or to interpret their condition as the consequence of racial prejudice. Instead of being treated as brutal racial repression, lynching found various justifications in the white community.

The majority's justification of the condition of a subordinate group keeps society from progressing to the politics of transformation within political emancipation. Lynching illustrates this blockage, but so do poverty, homelessness, low income levels, inadequate education, high infant mortality, and a host of other social problems that are unequally distributed among groups of Americans. Some majority attempts to remedy these disparities may erode the position of a subordinate group, rather than transform society. The integration of the Haywood County High School illustrates this possibility. The construction of a new high school meant combining the student bodies of previously segregated high schools. This merger meant integrating the school staff, a move that threatened the jobs of African-American teachers and administrators. The change also presaged the loss of valuable school traditions, including pride in the virtues and resistance of African Americans. With all their shortcomings, segregated schools had provided African Americans with a space in which to preserve alternative understandings of their condition and to develop pride in their achievements. Transforming politics recognizes the virtues of a subordinate group and integrates the pride of a group, along with its members, into dominant institutions..

The narratives of this history of emancipation suggest a politics of transformation that envisions an integrated society in which the values and virtues of disparate traditions are recognized, valued, and, in that sense, assimilated. Such a politics envisions a day when people may be elected regardless of race, gender, or any characteristic other than the ability to carry out a set of transforming policies. That day will be marked by an openness to consider, and a willingness to implement, policies that redistribute resources and promote greater self-sufficiency in people across caste lines and regardless of class. The politics of transformation entails the promise of economic emancipation.

Integration and assimilation are means to the transforming politics of emancipation. Without a transfer of power and resources that incorporates the politics of portions, however, integration and assimilation may end by promoting inequality. They remove the appearance of segregation without dealing with inequality, caste restrictions, and their consequences. They herald a return to the period when Booker T. Washington urged African Americans to trust white people in politics as in other matters, without demanding a reciprocal expression of trust—that is, without some transfer of power and resources. The politics of transformation requires the majority to initiate steps to integrate institutions and assimilate new and different traditions within them. Steps beyond desegregation are best measured by steps that majorities take to change themselves. As the Niles, Michigan, columnist wrote so eloquently in the aftermath of Walter Ward's death: "It is the white community that must answer [what can be done]. Whites are the majority and the majority does rule, both legally and by sheer force of number. As long as a white 'we' excludes blacks, it is merely a question of time before ever more serious confrontations between the races occur."

Those confrontations delay the onset of a politics of transformation, naturally. Consequently, the politics of transformation awaits a breakup of the "we" of the white majority and the willingness of white voters and citizens to "look at the problems that confront *us*."

Redistributive measures to assist groups with small portions of resources and public benefits elicit protest more often than support from those with larger shares of resources and benefits. For example, Deputy Sheriff Buddy Sullivan complained bitterly when the FBI investigated the bombing of Odell Sanders's home but failed to investigate equally when a shot struck a white person's home. Whatever the merits of Sullivan's theoretical argument about "inequality," it ignored the way local practice insured whites better police protection than blacks. The use of federal programs and resources, in this as in most cases, redressed the inability or unwillingness of local authorities adequately to provide these programs or resources themselves. Charges of reverse discrimination, such as those made by Sullivan, subvert the politics of transformation. They signal the inability or unwillingness of some members of the majority to recognize the need for transformation and for a new distribution of resources. Over time, such charges allow the American political process to revert to some variant of the old unfair distribution of portions that gave rise to the protest. There is always hope that the reversion may not be complete and that some remnant, the "ineffaceable mark" of emancipation, may remain to support a succeeding politics of protest and portions. Certainly the events discussed in this book offer both hope for the politics of transformation and cause for worry about their success.

THE FULL EXTENT OF OUR DREAMS

Between dramatic periods of resistance and repression—times when we seriously consider transforming ourselves through political change—people of different groups collaborate and conflict within a politics of protest and a politics of portions. Emancipation presents itself in the form of particular issues, such as the provision of education and social services with some degree of equality to those eligible and those in need. The 1880s and the 1980s were times of protest over portions. Those periods may usher in interregnums of emancipation and declines in democratic practice. During such interregnums, the veil that Elisha Davis held is lowered again, not lifted higher. Veils become shrouds for the hope, the understanding, and the belief in individual dignity that are the foundations of emancipation.

In the midst of the civil rights movement, when many hands were once again engaged in lifting the veil, Martin Luther King, Jr., shared a dream of a day of freedom and of transforming politics. In that day, he said, all people, regardless of race, gender, religion, or other differences would be able, as God's children, "to join hands and sing, in the words of the old Negro spiritual, 'Free at last, free at last, thank God Almighty, we are free at last.'" King's words enthralled the nation, in part because they helped us understand how the freedom of some entailed the freedom of all. This speech provided a glimpse of a new dawn of freedom behind the veil of injustice to which we had become accustomed. Nann Davis remembered King's words: "Words like those touched you. They gave you a good feeling to keep going. I've been doing that ever since. Those kind of words will really keep you going, if you're any kind of person."

Notes

ABBREVIATIONS

BRFAL	Bureau of Refugees, Freedmen, and Abandoned Lands
CORE	Congress on Racial Equality
FSA	Farm Service Administration
IBWC	Ida B. Wells Collection, Special Collections, Joseph Regenstein Library, University of Chicago
JONAH	Just Organized Neighborhood Area Headquarters
LC	Library of Congress, Washington, D.C.
NA	National Archives, Washington, D.C.
NAACP	National Association for the Advancement of Colored People
SCLC	Southern Christian Leadership Conference
SHC	Southern Historical Collection, Univ. of North Carolina Library, Chapel Hill
TSLA	Tennessee State Library and Archives, Nashville
USJDFIO	U.S. Justice Department, Freedom of Information Office
WPA	Works Progress Administration

PREFACE

1. W. E. B. Du Bois, *The Souls of Black Folk* (New York: Bantam, 1989), xxxi.
2. Ida B. Wells, Diary, IBWC.
3. My dilemma is comparable to that of an anthropologist as Clifford Geertz discusses in *Works and Lives: The Anthropologist as Author* (Stanford, Calif.: Stanford Univ. Press, 1987), esp. 129–49. I have written as if the most important reviews are those that will come in the private spaces of the families depicted here. I have taken that standard as the most likely guarantee that I shall extend faithfully to a public audience the political discourse on emancipation that occurs in these private spaces. I have incorporated many insights of James C. Scott, *Weapons of the Weak: Everyday Forms of Resistance* (New Haven, Conn.: Yale Univ. Press, 1985). I have written this book as Scott might have if his primary audience had been the Malayan villagers who provided him the information for his book. Of course, such informants make up a very poor market, and the reason I write for the second audience of scholars is that they comprise a vast intellectual community, in which I hope there are some who want to share in emancipation and resistance.

INTRODUCTION

1. In its lack of African-American public officials, Haywood County resembled Tennessee as a whole. Between 1890 and 1964, in the entire state, 17 African Americans served as elected or appointed officials at either the state or local level. The majority of these 17 came from urban areas. Mingo Scott, Jr., *The Negro in Tennessee Politics and Governmental Affairs: 1865–1965* (Nashville, Tenn.: Rich Printing Co., 1964), 218–21.
2. For James Forman's account of his experience, see "Georgia May Hard Times," "Forgetting the People," and "Diary of Fayette," in Forman, *The Making of Black Revolutionaries: A Personal Account* (New York: Macmillan, 1972), 116–30, 130–37, and 137–45. See also Taylor Branch, *Parting the Waters: America in the King Years, 1954–63* (New York: Touchstone Books, 1988), 333–35. The most extensive treatment of the civil rights movement in Fayette County is the oral history by Robert Hamburger, *Our Portion of Hell* (New York: Links Books, 1973).
3. On the civil rights movement as a series of struggles for freedom, see Clayborne Carson, "Civil Rights Reform and the Black Freedom Struggle," in *The Civil Rights Movement in America*, ed. Charles W. Eagles (Jackson: Univ. Press of Mississippi, 1986), 19–32. For studies of local struggles and their relationship to the civil rights movement, see Stokely Carmichael and Charles V. Hamilton, *Black Power: The Politics of Liberation in America* (New York: Random House,

1973); William Henry Chafe, *Civilities and Civil Rights: Greensboro, North Carolina, and the Black Struggle for Equality* (New York: Oxford Univ. Press, 1980); Robert J. Norrell, *Reaping the Whirlwind: The Civil Rights Movement in Tuskegee* (New York: Knopf, 1985); and Jo Anne Gibson Robinson, *The Montgomery Bus Boycott and the Women Who Started It: Memoir of Jo Anne Gibson Robinson,* ed. David J. Garrow (Knoxville: Univ. of Tennessee Press, 1987).

For examples of the civil rights movement from the perspective of a person or an organization, see Branch, *Parting the Waters*; David J. Garrow, *Bearing the Cross: Martin Luther King, Jr., and the Southern Christian Leadership Conference* (New York: Vintage Books, 1988); Forman, *The Making of Black Revolutionaries*; and Clayborne Carson, *In Struggle: SNCC and the Black Awakening of the 1960s* (Cambridge: Harvard Univ. Press, 1981). There are also personal accounts of white civil rights workers—e.g., Mary King, *Freedom Song: A Personal Story of the 1960s Civil Rights Movement* (New York: Morrow, 1987). For an overview of persons and organizations in the movement, see Juan Williams, *Eyes on the Prize: America's Civil Rights Years, 1954–65* (New York: Penguin, 1987).

Some books examine the difference the civil rights movement made. See, e.g., Margaret Edds, *Free at Last: What Really Happened When Civil Rights Came to Southern Politics* (Bethesda, Md.: Adler and Adler, 1987); and Lawrence J. Hanks, *The Struggle for Black Political Empowerment in Three Georgia Counties* (Knoxville: Univ. of Tennessee Press, 1987).

Several studies have explored the years preceding the movement. See Steven F. Lawson, *Black Ballots: Voting Rights in the South, 1944–1969* (New York: Columbia Univ. Press, 1976); Doug McAdam, *Political Process and the Development of Black Insurgency, 1930–1970* (Chicago: Univ. of Chicago Press, 1972); and Aldon D. Morris, *The Origins of the Civil Rights Movement: Black Communities Organizing for Change* (New York: Free Press, 1984).

4. The second historical period of emancipation in Haywood County, the civil rights movement, began with the efforts of local African Americans to regain the right to vote. This second emancipation shared political characteristics with other social and liberation movements. A century of limited opportunity had given some African Americans, in the county and in the country, the education, psychology, and economic foundation to demand the political expression of their legal emancipation. This preparation distinguished the civil rights movement from Reconstruction. Reconstruction was restricted to legal emancipation, while the actual political participation of African Americans was limited. Eric Foner has written on the anatomy and politics of emancipation in his *Nothing But Freedom: Emancipation and Its Legacy* (Baton Rouge: Louisiana State Univ. Press, 1983), esp. 8–38 and 39–73. Overt emancipa-

tion efforts, Reconstruction, and the civil rights movement were all efforts to establish new forms of political and economic participation. These larger goals are still pursued and measure the place of the movement today.

5. I am referring to such scholarship as Morris, *Origins of the Civil Rights Movement*; J. Morgan Kousser, *The Shaping of Southern Politics: Suffrage Restriction and the Establishment of the One-Party South, 1880–1910* (New Haven, Conn.: Yale Univ. Press, 1974); Lawson, *Black Ballots*; Norrell, *Reaping the Whirlwind*; and McAdam, *Political Process and Black Insurgency.* Although Joel Williamson deals primarily with the turn of the century, his account ties Jim Crow to slavery and tenuously to the civil rights movement; see his *A Rage for Order: Black-White Relations in the American South Since Emancipation* (New York: Oxford Univ. Press, 1986).

6. Albert O. Hirschman, *Exit, Voice, and Loyalty: Response to Decline in Firms, Organizations, and States* (Cambridge: Harvard Univ. Press, 1970).

7. James C. Scott makes a similar point regarding Hirschman's discussion of exit, voice, and loyalty. When exit (defection to an alternative) is unavailable or costly, Hirschman argues, dissatisfaction will likely take the form of open complaints, anger, and demands. For our purposes, the form that voice takes will vary according to the capacity of power holders to severely punish open resistance. James C. Scott, *Domination and the Arts of Resistance: Hidden Transcripts* (New Haven, Conn.: Yale Univ. Press, 1990), 137, n. 3.

8. Charles Perrow distinguishes between broad resource mobilization theories and narrow approaches. Politics plays a less important role in the latter, which find their "agreeable imagery in economic theory." Perrow, "The Sixties Observed," in *The Dynamics of Social Movements: Resource Mobilization, Social Control, and Tactics*, ed. Mayer N. Zald and John D. McCarthy (Cambridge, Mass.: Winthrop Publishers, 1979), 192–211. For the premier example of the narrow approach, see John D. McCarthy and Mayer N. Zald, "Resource Mobilization and Social Movements: A Partial Theory," *American Journal of Sociology* 82: 6 (1977): 1212–41. See also Mancur Olson, *The Logic of Collective Action* (Cambridge: Harvard Univ. Press, 1965). Jo Freeman, ed., *Social Movements of the Sixties and Seventies* (New York: Longman, 1983).

9. Sara M. Evans and Harry C. Boyte, *Free Spaces: The Sources of Democratic Change in America* (New York: Harper & Row, 1986), viii and 17.

10. James C. Scott builds on the work of Sara M. Evans in describing the political nature of space and includes space in the internal politics of subordinated groups. James C. Scott, *Domination and the Arts of Resistance*, 65 n. 37, 183–84, 199–201, and 209.

11. One recent political science foray into social movement analysis borrows heavily from economic paradigms. One section of Robert H. Salisbury's "Po-

litical Movements in American Politics: An Essay on Concept and Analysis," *National Political Science Review* 1 (1989): 15–30, is headed "The Movement Market and Its Customers."

12. Robert A. Dahl, *Who Governs? Democracy and Power in an American City* (New Haven, Conn.: Yale Univ. Press, 1961), 293–95.

13. Sheriff Tip Hunter made this statement in Brownsville, Tenn., on 13 Aug. 1965, during a week of voter registration efforts that followed the enactment of the Voting Rights Act. "Brownsville To Be Tested by Demonstrations Today," *Memphis Commercial Appeal*, 14 Aug. 1965.

14. For a critique of the manner in which political scientists have examined social movements and a sociologist's effort to develop a model of political process in social movements, see McAdam, *Political Process and Black Insurgency*, 4–19 and 36–64.

15. John Gaventa presents a cogent assessment of community power studies in his *Power and Powerlessness: Rebellion and Quiescence in an Appalachian Valley* (Urbana: Univ. of Illinois Press, 1980). Also see James C. Scott, *Domination and the Art of Resistance*, 72–74.

16. George M. Frederickson, *The Arrogance of Race: Historical Perspectives on Slavery, Racism, and Social Inequality* (Middletown, Conn.: Wesleyan Univ. Press, 1988). James C. Scott, *Domination and the Arts of Resistance*, 220. I include social scientists among those elites. Joel Williamson also finds resistance within domination. He maintains that "the slave system was simply not tight enough to force blacks to become the Sambos they played." Williamson, *Rage for Order*, 15–29.

17. Charles E. Lindbloom, "Another State of Mind," *American Political Science Review* 76 (Mar. 1982): 16.

18. James C. Scott, *Weapons of the Weak* and *Domination and the Arts of Resistance*.

19. I borrow this euphemism from the title of a dialogue between two outstanding democratic educators, Paulo Freire and Myles Horton, *We Make the Road by Walking: Conversations on Education and Social Change* (Philadelphia: Temple Univ. Press, 1990).

20. Such a social science attempts to provide "an account of what a group is and what it might become, but also an historical analysis of the limits which are imposed both on the theory itself and on the members of the group." Brian Fay, *Critical Social Science: Liberation and Its Limits* (Ithaca, N.Y.: Cornell Univ. Press, 1987), 214.

21. James C. Scott, *Domination and the Arts of Resistance*, 136.

22. Clifford Geertz, *Local Knowledge: Further Essays in Interpretive Anthropology* (New York: Basic Books, 1983), 8.

23. James C. Scott, *Domination and the Arts of Resistance*, passim, and *Weapons of the Weak*, 284–89.

24. On going beyond texts to an analysis of socioeconomic conditions, see Kathleen M. Blee and Dwight B. Billings, "Reconstructing Daily Life in the Past: An Hermeneutical Approach to Ethnographic Data," *Sociological Quarterly* 27 (Fall 1986): 443–62. See also John W. Blassingame's discussion of the window that slave testimonies offer into "the hearts and secret thoughts of slaves" and the corresponding problem of sources. In Blassingame, *Slave Testimony: Two Centuries of Letters, Speeches, Interviews and Autobiographies* (Baton Rouge: Louisiana State Univ. Press, 1977), lxv, xxvii–xxx. Blassingame discusses the effect of caste on research methods. In our sort of study, the interpretation of events separates black and white groups and prompts concern about which side the researcher is "with." Which caste the researcher is "with" affects the narrator's ability to trust that the narratives will be accepted as valid.

25. James C. Scott, *Domination and the Arts of Resistance*, 160–61.

26. For an account of the civil rights movement in the county, emphasizing its relation to a 1940 program of the Farm Security Administration, see Richard A. Couto, *Ain't Gonna Let Nobody Turn Me Round: The Pursuit of Racial Justice in the Rural South* (Philadelphia: Temple Univ. Press, 1991).

27. On the effort to retrieve experience from deeds and other official records, see Blee and Billings, "Reconstructing Daily Life in the Past," 443–62. Gaventa uses this technique in *Power and Powerlessness*. See also Altina L. Waller, *Feud: Hatfields, McCoys, and Social Change in Appalachia, 1860–1900* (Chapel Hill: Univ. of North Carolina Press, 1988).

28. Yvonna S. Lincoln and Egon G. Guba, *Naturalistic Inquiry* (Beverly Hills, Calif.: Sage, 1985), 41; for the operational characteristics of naturalistic inquiry, see 39–43. Lincoln and Guba attempt a synthesis of methods and critiques and forego inquiry into epistemology. Yet the crosscurrents between their work and critical theory are evident.

29. This view of narrative is based on the discussion of the community of memory in Robert N. Bellah et al., *Habits of the Heart: Individualism and Commitment in American Life,* (Berkeley: Univ. of California Press, 1985). Bellah et al. rely heavily on Alasdaire MacIntyre. I too am indebted to MacIntyre's work on narrative in *After Virtue: A Study in Moral Theory* (Notre Dame, Ind.: Univ. of Notre Dame Press, 1981).

30. Gunnar Myrdal, "A Methodological Note on Facts and Valuations in Social Science," in Myrdal, *American Dilemma: The Negro Problem and Modern Democracy* (New York: Harper and Row, 1944), 1035–64.

31. W. E. B. Du Bois, "The Propaganda of History," in Du Bois, *Black Reconstruction in America, 1860–1880* (New York: Atheneum, 1962), 711–29.

32. Beginning in the 1950s, scholarship on Reconstruction changed more than in any other field of American history. See Michael Les Benedict, *The Impeachment Trial of Andrew Jackson* (New York: Norton, 1973), 192–202, and Bernard A. Weisberger, "The Dark and Bloody Ground of Reconstruction Historiography," *Journal of Southern History* 25 (Nov. 1959): 427–47.

CHAPTER 1. FREEDOM'S GAIN, 1865–1870

1. Election results can be found in Record Group 87, Tennessee Election Returns, TSLA. For background on the political factions, see Daniel Merritt Robison, *Bob Taylor and the Agrarian Revolt in Tennessee* (Chapel Hill: Univ. of North Carolina Press, 1935), 9.

2. Herbert Aptheker, *American Negro Slave Revolts*, 5th ed. (New York: International Publishers, 1983), 348.

3. Alrutheus Ambush Taylor, *The Negro in Tennessee, 1865–1880* (Spartanburg, S.C.: Reprint Co., Publishers, 1974), 1–11.

4. Herbert Aptheker, ed., *A Documentary History of the Negro People in the United States,* vol. 2: *From the Reconstruction to the Founding of the NAACP* (New York: Carol Publishing Group, 1990), 539. For a complete history of this period in Tennessee, see A. Taylor, *Negro in Tennessee*, 1–24.

5. According to the terms of the amendment, all men without the franchise, except those who had fought in the Confederate Army, would be subtracted from the population to be represented in Congress. Brownlow and the Radicals in the legislature had passed restrictions on the franchise for ex-Confederates in May 1866.

6. For a concise account of the dispute over voting laws, see Mingo Scott, *Negro in Tennessee Politics,* 8–16.

7. For an early and balanced overview of the Freedmen's Bureau, see Paul Skeels Pierce, *The Freedmen's Bureau: A Chapter in the History of Reconstruction* (Iowa City: Univ. of Iowa Press, 1904). For a more recent discussion, see George R. Bentley, *A History of the Freedmen's Bureau* (New York: Octagon Books, 1974). W. E. B. Du Bois esp. praised the Freedmen's Bureau, even at a time when Reconstruction was severely criticized. See Du Bois, *Black Reconstruction in America*, and "The Freedmen's Bureau," *Atlantic Monthly* 87 (Mar. 1901): 354–65.

8. F. S. Palmer to J. L. Poston, 15 Apr. 1867, in Record Group 105, BRFAL, Tennessee, Brownsville, 1867, E-3443, Box 52, NA.

9. On a local Freedmen's Bureau station in Louisiana that emphasizes the bureau's limited role in economic or political change, see J. Thomas May, "The

Freedmen's Bureau at the Local Level: A Study of a Louisiana Agent," *Louisiana History* 9 (Winter 1968): 5–19.

10. This and other contracts may be found in Record Group 105, BRFAL, Tennessee, Brownsville, 1867, E-3443, Box 52, NA.

11. On the transformation in the agricultural economy, specific to Haywood County at this time, see Robert Tracy McKenzie, "From Old South to New South in the Volunteer State: The Economy and Society of Rural Tennessee" (Ph.D. diss., Vanderbilt Univ., Nashville, Tenn., 1988).

12. Ibid.

13. The standard commission may be found in Record Group 105, BRFAL, Tennessee, Brownsville, 1867, E-3443, Box 52, NA.

14. Weston Goodspeed, *History of Tennessee: From the Earliest Times to the Present* (Nashville, Tenn.: Goodspeed Publishers, 1887), treats Poston's military service but says less about his political career in Haywood County. Goodspeed describes an influential Poston family of staunch Republicans in Crockett County, which at the time of the war was part of Haywood. Goodspeed, *History of Tennessee:*, 825, 839, 964. Poston's granddaughter Lillian Poston Jones, in *Some Poston Family Notes* (Memphis; Otis H. Jones, 1970), best traces the extensive political activity of this Republican family during and after Reconstruction. Jones's husband printed the work after his wife's death.

15. Goodspeed, *History of Tennessee*, 823–26. For a general discussion of white southerners who fought for the Union, see Richard N. Current, *Lincoln's Loyalists: Union Soldiers from the Confederacy* (Boston: Northeastern Univ. Press, 1992).

16. Foner, *Nothing but Freedom*, 39.

17. For this information I am indebted to Annie Laurie James, historian of Crockett County, Tenn. She led me to Jones, *Poston Family Notes*. More information is contained in Robert M. McBride and Dan M. Robinson, *Biographical Directory of the Tennessee General Assembly, 1861–1901* (Nashville: TSLA and Tennessee Historical Commission, 1979).

18. F. Kendrick, captain and acting sub-assistant commissioner for Memphis, to J. L. Poston, 12 Aug. 1867 and 20 Aug. 1867; in Record Group 105, BRFAL, Tennessee, Brownsville, 1867, E-3443, Box 52, NA. Nathaniel Leech to George W. Carlin, Nashville, 30 June 1868; in Roll 37, Letters Received, Assistant Commissioner, 1868–1869, Selected Records of the Tennessee Field Office, BRFAL, Manuscript Division, TSLA.

19. Leech to Carlin, 30 June 1868.

20. C. E. Compton to Maj. Gen. Howard, 30 June 1869. This and several other reports may be found in Henry Lee Swint, ed., "Reports from Educational

Agents of the Freedmen's Bureau in Tennessee, 1865–1870," *Tennessee Historical Quarterly* 1 (Winter 1942): 51–80 and 1 (Spring 1942): 152–70. The complete set of reports is in Record Group 105, BRFAL, Tennessee Superintendent of Education, 1867–70, School Reports, 1866–69, NA.

21. Swint, "Reports from Educational Agents," 152–58.
22. Ibid., 58.
23. Roll 37, Letters Received, Assistant Commissioner, Memphis Sub-District, 1868–69, Selected Records of the Tennessee Field Office, BRFAL, Manuscript Division, TSLA.
24. Newton's letter describes his experiences, which parallel those of civil rights workers a century later, in graphic detail. Isaac M. Newton to F. S. Palmer, 9 June 1868, enclosed in F. S. Palmer to G. W. Carlin, 6 July 1868; in Roll 37, Letter 730, Letters Received, Assistant Commissioner, Memphis Sub-District, 1868–69, Selected Records of the Tennessee Field Office, BRFAL, Manuscript Division, TSLA.
25. Ibid.
26. Report from Memphis Sub-District, Jan. 1868, in Record Group 105, BRFAL, Tennessee Superintendent of Education, 1867–70, School Reports, 1866–1869, Box E-3419, NA.
27. Compton's predecessor also had stressed the importance of colleges, universities, and normal schools for freedpeople and urged the bureau to support them as keys to developing educated leaders of the freedpeople. He noted the freedpeople's desire for teachers of their own race. D. Burt to Maj. Gen. O. O. Howard, 1 Nov. 1865, in Swint, "Reports From Educational Agents," 61.
28. C. E. Compton to Maj. Gen. O. O. Howard, 31 Dec. 1869, in Swint, "Reports From Educational Agents," 159.
29. Swint, "Reports From Educational Agents," 64.
30. R. C. Scott to J. A. Alden, 18 Jan. 1866, in Record Group 105, BRFAL, Tennessee Assistant Commissioner, Reports, Box 28, Reports of Outrages, Riots, and Murders, E-3394, NA.
31. J. L. Poston to F. S. Palmer, 26 May 1867, in Office of the Sub-Assistant Commissioner, vol. 137, Selected Records of the Tennessee Field Office, BRFAL, Manuscript Division, TSLA.
32. A. Taylor, *Negro in Tennessee,* 23.
33. See Mingo Scott, *Negro in Tennessee Politics,* 17–22. James S. Allen, *Reconstruction: The Battle for Democracy* (New York: International Publishers, 1937), 93–94. Eric Foner, *Reconstruction: America's Unfinished Revolution, 1863–1877* (New York: Harper & Row, 1988), 283–85.
34. Wayne F. Binning, "The Tennessee Republicans in Decline, 1869–1876,"

Tennessee Historical Quarterly 39 (Winter 1980): 471; Walter J. Fraser, Jr., "Black Reconstructionists in Tennessee," *Tennessee Historical Quarterly* 34 (Winter 1975): 365. For fuller discussion of the Union League in other parts of the South, see Michael W. Fitzgerald, *The Union League Movement in the Deep South: Politics and Agricultural Change during Reconstruction* (Baton Rouge: Louisiana State Univ. Press, 1989).

35. "Riot: The Fruit of Radicalism Blossoming in Brownsville," *Memphis Daily Appeal*, 15 May 1867. For data on some Republican orators of the day, see Walter J. Fraser, Jr., "Black Reconstructionists in Tennessee," *Tennessee Historical Quarterly* 34 (Winter 1974): 362–82.

36. F. S. Palmer to J. L. Poston, 25 May 1867, in Record Group 105, BRFAL, E-3443, Box 52, NA.

37. Fred S. Palmer to John L. Poston, 22 July 1867, and W. P. Carlin to Fred S. Palmer, 31 July 1867, in Record Group 105, BRFAL, E-3443, Box 52, NA.

38. W. P. Carlin to F. S. Palmer, 5 July 1867; F. S. Palmer to J. L. Poston, 20 July 1867; F. S. Palmer to J. L. Poston, 7 Sept. 1867; all in Record Group 105, BRFAL, E-3443, Box 52, NA.

39. Charles L. Lufkin, "A Forgotten Controversy: The Assassination of Senator Almon Case of Tennessee," *West Tennessee Historical Society Papers* 39 (1985): 37–42.

40. Stanley F. Horn, *Invisible Empire: The Story of the Ku Klux Klan, 1886–1871* (Cos Cobb, Conn.: John E. Edwards, 1969), 397.

41. Ibid., 413.

42. U.S. Congress, Joint Select Committee to Inquire into the Condition of Affairs in the Late Insurrectionary States, Report, 19 Feb. 1872, p. 7.

43. Tennessee General Assembly, Military Committee, *Report of Evidence Taken in Relation to Outrages Committed by the Ku Klux Klan in Middle and West Tennessee*, Extra Sess. of the 35th General Assembly, 2 Sept. 1872, pp. 31–32.

44. Smith's committee's finding was reported in U.S. Congress, Joint Select Committee to Inquire into the Condition of Affairs in the Late Insurrectionary States, *Report*, 19 Feb. 1872, 18.

45. Goodspeed, *History of Tennessee*, 823–24.

46. James Wall's testimony in U.S. Congress, Joint Committee on the Conduct of the War, "Report of the Sub-Committee to Investigate the Recent Attack on Fort Pillow," 38th Cong., 1st Sess., 5 May 1864, p. 34.

47. Testimony of Major Williams, private, Company B, 6th U.S. Heavy Artillery, ibid., 25. After Fort Pillow, many African Americans fought to "Remember Fort Pillow" and assumed that defeat meant certain death; James M.

McPherson, *The Negro's Civil War: How American Negroes Felt and Acted During the War for the Union* (New York: Pantheon, 1965), 216–23.

48. U.S. Congress, "Report of the Sub-Committee to Investigate the Recent Attack on Fort Pillow," 104–7.

49. J. S. Porter to F. S. Palmer, 10 Aug. 1868, in Office of the Sub-Assistant Commissioner, 3/23–9/29/1868, vol. 137, Selected Records of the Tennessee Field Office, BRFAL, Manuscript Division, TSLA.

50. A. Miller to F. S. Palmer, 13 Oct. 1868, in Office of the Sub-Assistant Commissioner, vol. 138, Selected Records of the Tennessee Field Office, BRFAL, Manuscript Division, TSLA. Miller's report details numerous specific instances of violence and intimidation at the time of the 1868 election:

> John Sherman, Sheriff of Haywood County, Tenn., states that . . . On or about the 27th of August 1868, Andrew Macklin, (colored) living in the Brownsville District, was assaulted while traveling on the highway, by a party of men, afterwards forced into a grocery and compelled to drink a toast to Seymour and Blair [Democratic candidates for president and vice president]; that a few nights after he was again badly beaten and his wife outraged; and the Justice of the Peace was afraid to issue warrants for their arrest.
>
> On or about the 1st of September 1868, Thos Grant and Benjamin Grant tied a colored man to a tree and whipped him severely with sticks; that the outrage was committed in day-light, and no action has been taken in the above case to bring the parties before the Court.
>
> On or about the 12th of September a party of freedmen were assaulted while on their way home from Brownsville and four of their number shot—one not expected to recover from his wounds; that on the same night a party of masked men committed outrages on freedmen and whites throughout the County, but he [Sheriff Sherman] does not know the names of any others, or the particulars.
>
> On or about the 15th of September 1868, Joseph Rook (white) came to the house of — Irvin (colored) and shot him; that he [Sheriff Sherman] arrested Rook and a trial was ordered on the 30th of September. On the night before the trial a party of masked men went to the house of Irvin and shot at him again, and told him if he appeared as a witness against Rook they would kill him. Since, Irvin has disappeared and his whereabouts are not known, and he is of the opinion that he has been killed. That on the 14th of Sept. 1868, he arrested Leon Wood, charged with

horse stealing and being one of the party that committed the above outrages; that he was followed by Sam'l Evans, and – Richards; that they
attempted to rescue the prisoner and would have done so had it not
been near the R. Road; that he stopped the cart and got aboard in time
to save himself.

51. Ibid. W. W. Bower, assistant commissioner for Tennessee, reported Miller's
    finding to Gen. O. O. Howard in his report of 28 Oct. 1868, in Record Group
    105, Tennessee Assistant Commissioner Reports, Box 22, NA.
52. Ibid.
53. F. S. Palmer to W. H. Bower, 21 Dec. 1868, in Roll 17, vol. 137, p. 134,
    Selected Records of the Tennessee Field Office, BRFAL, Manuscript Divi-
    sion, TSLA.
54. John A. Taylor, Diary, TSLA.
55. F. S. Palmer to J. S. Porter [telegram], 11 Nov. 1868; F. S. Palmer to
    Thompson, 9 Nov. 1868; both in Letters Received, Sub-Assistant, 23 Mar.
    1868 to 3 Dec. 1869, Roll 17, vol. 137, Selected Records of the Tennessee
    Field Office, BRFAL, Manuscript Division, TSLA.
56. A. Taylor, *Negro in Tennessee*, 73.
57. Binning, "Tennessee Republicans in Decline," 478.
58. The proclamation is quoted in A. Taylor, *Negro in Tennessee*, 100.
59. For accounts of the Klan's political impact, see George C. Rable, *But There
    Was No Peace: The Role of Violence in the Politics of Reconstruction* (Athens: Univ.
    of Georgia Press, 1984); Allen W. Trelease, *White Terror: The Ku Klux Klan
    Conspiracy and Southern Reconstruction* (Westport, Conn: Greenwood, 1971);
    and Everette Swinney, *Suppressing the Ku Klux Klan: The Enforcement of the
    Reconstruction Amendments, 1870–1877* (New York: Garland, 1987).
60. C. E. Compton to Gen. O. O. Howard, 15 July 1870, in Swint, "Reports
    from Educational Agents," 166–70.
61. Ibid., 159–66.
62. The precedent of normal school and college training for freedpeople, once
    established, was extended. LeMoyne Normal and Commercial School, begun
    in 1871, drew on a tradition that originated with camp schools established at
    Shiloh in 1862. Central Tennessee College developed a medical department
    that became Meharry Medical College, in 1876, and trained African-American
    men and women to be physicians. In 1882, the Colored Methodist Episcopal
    High School began classes in Jackson, Tenn., in Madison County, adjoining
    Haywood; it was the first secondary school for African Americans in Ten-
    nessee that was planned and staffed by African Americans. It later became
    Lane College. Cynthia Griggs Fleming, "A Survey of the Beginnings of

Tennessee's Black Colleges and Universities, 1865–1920," *Tennessee Histori-cal Quarterly*, 39: 2 (Summer 1980).

63. C. E. Compton to Gen. O. O. Howard, 31 Dec. 1869, in Swint, "Reports from Educational Agents," 161.

64. Ibid., 160. Andrew David Holt recounts the struggle to establish a state system of public schools after 1870. Generally critical of Brownlow and the Radical Republicans, whom he incorrectly terms "carpetbaggers," Holt ex-plains that the generally depressed nature of Tennessee's economy and the state's debt blocked public efforts to continue public support for schools. Ran-cor over the franchise for freedmen and the state debt, according to Holt, kept education low on the public agenda until century's end. Andrew David Holt, *The Struggle for a State System of Public Schools in Tennessee, 1903–1936* (New York: Teachers College Press, Columbia Univ., 1938), 3–30.

CHAPTER 2. FREEDOM'S DEMISE, 1870–1900

1. For the most complete biographical sketch of McElwee, see William J. Simmons, *Men of Mark: Eminent, Progressive and Rising* (Cleveland: Geo. M. Rewell & Co., 1887), 498–505. See another sketch in Northrup Henry Davenport, *The College of Life or Practical Self-Edu-cator: A Manual for Self-Improvement for the Colored Race forming an Educa-tional Emancipator and a Guide to Success, Giving Examples and Achievements of Successful Men and Women of the Race as an Incentive and Inspiration to the Rising Generation* (1895, rpt. Miami, Fla.: Mnemosyne Publishing, 1969).

2. *Fisk Herald* 5, no. 9 (May 1888): 9

3. Fleming, "Beginnings of Tennessee's Black Colleges," 203.

4. Binning, "Tennessee Republicans in Decline," 479.

5. Freeman had been an antebellum Whig and remained vehemently opposed to the Democratic party. Yet in 1866, in a conservative revolt against a radi-cal executive, he broke with Brownlow and led a group resignation of con-servative Republicans from the House of Representatives that left the body without a quorum and rendered Brownlow incapable of legislative action. In a special election to secure a quorum, a referendum on Brownlow's policies, Freeman ran for re-election but lost to a radical Republican in Haywood County. Binning, "Tennessee Republicans in Decline," 481.

6. Lester C. Lamon, *Blacks in Tennessee, 1791–1970* (Knoxville: Univ. of Ten-nessee Press, 1981), 49.

7. Swinney, *Suppressing the Ku Klux Klan*, 288.

8. A. Taylor, *Negro in Tennessee*, 103–5.

9. Ibid., 104–5.

10. Benjamin "Pop" Singleton, in Aptheker, *Documentary History of the Negro*, 723. See also Nell Irvin Painter, *Exodusters: Black Migration to Kansas after Reconstruction* (New York: Knopf, 1977), 108–17, 146–47.

11. Holt, *Struggle for a State System of Public Schools*, 11–13. A. Taylor, *Negro in Tennessee*, 261–64.

12. A. Taylor, *Negro in Tennessee*, 244–64.

13. In its party alignments, Haywood County seems to have differed from the rest of the South. In the common view of the South's political history, Republicans were placed in control by congressional and military Reconstruction after 1868 and by 1876 had been defeated in violence-marred elections. In Haywood County, however, as in Tennessee as a whole, Republicans retained majority status until 1888, although some local Republicans lost in the close elections of 1869 and 1874. In Haywood County, the 1874 election gave local Democrats temporary control of elected offices, as the 1876 election did in the southern states. But in Tennessee, virulent Democratic factionalism prevented the Democrats from using that control to consolidate power. In 1874, in Haywood County, Democrats defeated A. A. Freeman for the state legislature and narrowly missed carrying the county for their gubernatorial candidate. In 1876, however, Freeman regained his seat with about 60% of the votes—the same portion of county votes that went to Hayes, the Republican presidential candidate. At least two Democrats ran unsuccessfully in the 1878 and 1880 gubernatorial elections. Thus, although Democrats ended Reconstruction in Tennessee in 1869, they did not establish a party realignment or a solid Democratic majority until 1888. Haywood County was a bastion of Republican strength until that year.

14. Goodspeed, *History of Tennessee,* 964.

15. Holt, *Struggle for a State System of Public Schools,* 3–30.

16. Joseph H. Cartwright, "Black Legislators in Tennessee in the 1880's: A Case Study in Black Political Leadership," *Tennessee Historical Quarterly* 32 (Fall 1973): 276–78.

17. Ibid., 279.

18. Holt, *Struggle for a State System of Public Schools* , 25–30 and 16–17.

19. Cartwright, "Black Legislators in Tennessee," 273.

20. Daniel Merritt Robinson, *Bob Taylor and the Agrarian Revolt in Tennessee* (Chapel Hill: Univ. of North Carolina Press, 1935), 73–102.

21. Cartwright, "Black Legislators in Tennessee," 267.

22. Ibid., 269.

23. Ida B. Wells, *Crusade for Justice: The Autobiography of Ida B. Wells*, ed. Alfreda M. Duster (Chicago: Univ. of Chicago Press, 1970), 19.

24. Ibid., 20. See also *Chesapeake, Ohio & Southern Railroad Co. v. Wells* (Jack-

son, Tenn., 5 Apr. 1887), in *Tennessee Reports: 85 Cases Argued and Determined in the Supreme Court of Tennessee for the Western Division*, Apr. Term, 1887, p. 615. See also IBWC, Box 5, Folder 3.

25. No state or federal government representatives made oral arguments in the case. "United States v. Harris," *U.S. Reports* 106 (Boston: Little, Brown, 1883): 629–44; "A Civil Rights Decision," *New York Times*, 23 Jan. 1883, p. 2.

26. Wells, *Crusade for Justice*, 20. Wells's attorney, a white lawyer in Memphis, expressed his view that four of the state justices, acting from personal prejudice, decided "in face of all the evidence to the contrary that the smoking car was a first class coach for colored people." Wells, only 25, lost confidence in emancipatory efforts on several grounds. First, her initial lawyer, an African American, worked for the railroad and against her. Second, she was disappointed in the legal system. Wells, Diary, 11 Apr. 1887, p. 182; IBWC, Box 5, Folder 3.

27. Wells Diary, 18 Apr. 1887, p. 184; IBWC, Box 5, Folder 3.

28. Each southern legislature addressed the change in the legal status of African-American laborers. The new labor laws, referred to as Black Codes, generally preserved the socioeconomic subordination of African Americans in slavery while recognizing their new legal status. The stringency of these codes convinced national lawmakers such as Sumner that federal intervention was necessary to insure that state laws actually conveyed more of the promise of emancipation. See Du Bois, *Black Reconstruction in America*, 167–81, 192–97; Foner, *Reconstruction,* 199–201, 208–9.

29. Lamon, *Blacks in Tennessee*, 47.

30. A. Taylor, *Negro in Tennessee*, 42–44.

31. William Cohen, "Negro Involuntary Servitude in the South, 1865–1940: A Preliminary Analysis," *Journal of Southern History* 42 (Feb. 1976): 56. Randall G. Sheldon, "From Slave to Caste Society: The Penal Changes in Tennessee, 1830–1915," *Tennessee Historical Quarterly* 38 (1979): 461–71.

32. Cohen, "Negro Involuntary Solitude," 56.

33. Cartwright, "Black Legislators in Tennessee," 279.

34. Ibid., 281.

35. In Aug. 1886, Eliza Wood, an African-American woman, was in jail in Jackson, Tenn., awaiting trial on charges of poisoning her employer. The evidence against her was the presence of arsenic in the stomach of the dead woman, for whom she cooked, and a box of rat poison in Wood's house. A mob came to the jail and took Wood from her cell, apparently without resistance from the sheriff. The mob stripped her clothes off, hung her from a tree in front of the courthouse, and then riddled her naked corpse with bullets.

36. Ida B. Wells, Diary, 4 Sept. 1886, p. 126; IBWC, Box 5, Folder 3.

37. McElwee's speech, one of the few of McElwee's speeches available, is quoted at length in Simmons, *Men of Mark*, 502–4. This work also includes an assessment of McElwee by a Republican editor in Hopkinsville, Ky.: "A brilliant conversationalist and eloquent political orator; his countenance is pleasing and intellectual . . . the dogmas of philosophy and crudities of theology are impaled by his humor, and his wit is so boundless that it crops out often in his more serious utterances." Simmons suggested that "no colored man in the South ever rose as rapidly upon the rounds of the ladder of fame." Simmons, *Men of Mark*, 501. See also W. A. Reed and Alex Bontemps, "Brave Tennessean Forgotten By History," *Nashville Tennessean*, 13 Feb. 1971.

38. Simmons, *Men of Mark*, 502.

39. McElwee was in the company of James C. Napier and other African Americans who first had come to political power during Reconstruction and who regained political influence beginning in 1880. Ed Shaw raised the objection to McElwee's "Republican stump speech." McElwee was elected secretary of the committee to make the convention a permanent organization. Others on this nine-member committee were Napier of Nashville; T. F. Cassels of Memphis, who had preceded McElwee into the legislature; and W. F. Yardley of Knoxville—all very prominent men older than McElwee. Coverage of this two-day convention may be found in *Nashville Daily American*, 29 Feb. and 1 Mar. 1884, and *New York Globe*, 15 Mar. 1884. These papers published extensive excerpts from McElwee's speech.

40. *Fisk Herald* 1, no. 13 (Aug. 1884): 5.

41. Commentators praised McElwee's 1883 commencement address at Fisk, "The Genius of American Institutions"; *Fisk Herald*, 1, no. 1 (June 1883): 7.

42. *Fisk Herald* 3, no. 10 (June 1886): 11. *Fisk Herald* 1, no. 1 (June 1883): 7.

43. Herbert Aptheker, ed., *W. E. B. Du Bois: The Correspondence of W. E. B. Du Bois*, vol. 1: *Selections, 1877–1934* (Amherst: Univ. of Massachusetts Press, 1973), 33.

44. Louis R. Harlan, ed., *Booker T. Washington Papers*, vol. 2: *1860–89* (Urbana: Univ. of Illinois Press, 1972), 353.

45. William Jenkins to Booker T. Washington, 25 Apr. 1887. In Booker T. Washington Collection, LC.

46. *Fisk Herald* 2, no. 3 (Nov. 1884): 7. *Fisk Herald* 2, no. 10 (June 1885): 5. Wells wrote of her subscription: "I have, ever since I have known of [Fisk], had a craving that at times amounts to positive heart ache to go there and finish my education: the next best thing is to read of it." *Fisk Herald* 3, no. 5 (Jan. 1886): 5. On McElwee at Fisk, see *Fisk Herald* 3, no. 6 (Feb. 1886): 9.

47. Both Wells and McElwee knew William J. Simmons. Simmons was president of the National Baptist Convention, publisher of its newspaper, and

president of the state university in Louisville, Ky. Wells wrote for his publication. Simmons authored *Men of Mark*, profiling great African-American men.

48. Wells, Diary, 17 June 1887, p. 194, and 12 Aug. 1887, pp. 204–6; IBWC.

49. *Official Proceedings of the Republican National Convention, 1888.* (Minneapolis, Minn.: Charles W. Johnson, 1903), 227.

50. Ibid., 227–29.

51. Ibid., 229–30.

52. Cartwright, *Triumph of Jim Crow*, 90–91.

53. Robison, *Bob Taylor*, 103–31.

54. *Memphis Commercial Appeal*, 26 July 1884.

55. On Tennessee political party changes, see Robison, *Bob Taylor,* 132–57.

56. Cartwright, *Triumph of Jim Crow*, 96.

57. Republican State Committee to Leonidas C. Houk, 17 Nov. 1888. L. C. Houk Papers, Calvin M. McClung Historical Collection, Lawson McGee Library, Knoxville, Tenn. Houk, congressman from Knoxville, was the most influential Tennessee Republican in the federal government.

58. Kousser, *Shaping of Southern Politics:*, 108–9.

59. In 1869, a Democrat carried the county with 50.5% of the vote. This was the first election ex-Confederates could vote in and one in which the Republicans were divided. In 1874—the election marked by the Trenton Massacre—the Republican candidate carried Haywood County with only 50.2% of the vote. He lost the state, with only 35% of the vote.

60. The first new law required voters to re-register at least 20 days before every election. Local registrars applied this law rigorously to African-American men and far less rigorously to white men. The second law permitted two separate ballot boxes, one for federal and one or several for state offices. Ballots placed in the wrong box were disqualified. The boxes were identified in writing, with no symbols used. To further confuse illiterate voters, election officials moved the boxes during the course of the day. The third law provided for secret ballots and permitted election officials to assist any person eligible to vote in or before 1857 with their ballot. This seemingly progressive measure to safeguard the election process clearly aided white illiterate voters and impeded black illiterate voters. The fourth law strengthened enforcement of the poll tax. Even a $1 tax was prohibitive to black sharecroppers, whose annual income never exceeded $100. Kousser, *Shaping of Southern Politics*, documents the transition from illegal to legal disfranchisement in the southern states during this period.

61. For election votes in Haywood County, see Anne H. Hopkins and William Lyons, *Tennessee Votes: 1799–1976* (Knoxville: Bureau of Public Adminis-

tration, Univ. of Tennessee, 1978). The Democrats split again in the 1890s, permitting a Republican gubernatorial win in 1896. Robison, *Bob Taylor*, 203. This Democratic split increased pressure on the remnant of African-American political activity. A successful African-American candidate for the General Assembly was disqualified by the legislature for allegedly violating a state residency requirement for office. Gladys Murray Sherril, "Some Attempts at Black Endeavors: Jesse M. H. Graham and Other Blacks in Tennessee Politics, 1890–1900," master's thesis, Tennessee State Univ., 1974, 25–32. In Fayette County, Bourbon Democrats discarded votes in heavily African-American, Republican precincts. In 1898, the total votes cast in the gubernatorial election in Haywood County numbered fewer than before the Civil War; 99.5% of them were Democratic.

62. Gerald H. Gaither, "The Negro Alliance Movement in Tennessee, 1888–91," *West Tennessee Historical Society Papers* 23 (1973): 50–62. There were at least two violent incidents of action against organized African-American agricultural workers. See William F. Holmes, "The Arkansas Cotton Pickers Strike of 1891 and the Demise of the Colored Farmers' Alliance," *Arkansas Historical Quarterly* 32 (Summer 1973): 107–19, and William F. Holmes, "The LeFlore County Massacre and the Demise of the Colored Farmers' Alliance," *Phylon* 34 (Sept. 1973): 267–74. On the Colored Farmers' Alliance, see Floyd J. Miller, "Black Protest and White Leadership: A Note on the Colored Farmers' Alliance," *Phylon* 33 (June 1972): 169–74, and Jack Abromowitz, "The Negro in the Populist Movement," *Journal of Negro History* 38 (July 1953): 257–89. On lynchings in this era, see NAACP, *Thirty Years of Lynching*, (1919; rpt. New York: Arno Press and New York Times, 1969), 91–94, and Monroe W. Works, *Negro Yearbook: An Annual Encyclopedia of Negroes* (Tuskegee, Ala.: Negro Yearbook, 1932), 293.

63. On land-ownership and farming in Haywood County at this time, see McKenzie, "From Old South to New South."

64. *Fisk Herald* 1, no. 2 (Sept. 1883): 5, states that McElwee "will study law in connection with his grocery business in Brownsville." Harlan, *Booker T. Washington Papers*, 2: 353, states that McElwee operated a real estate agency in Brownsville.

65. S. A. McElwee to L. C. Houk, 19 Nov. 1888, Houk Papers.

66. Foner, *Nothing but Freedom:*, 11.

67. S. A. McElwee to L. C. Houk, 22 Nov. 1888, Houk Papers.

68. For the full text of this revealing letter, see ibid.

69. E. B. Stahlman to L. C. Houk, 26 Feb. 1889, Houk Papers: "He is able and active, and to my knowledge did very effective work in New York city, where he made a number of speeches, which were highly commended by those

who heard them. I speak of personal knowledge having been in New York at the time he was doing active work in that city."

70. J. C. Graham to L. C. Houk, 11 Feb. 1889, Houk Papers.

71. F. Looney, chairman, and R. D. Owen, secretary, Republican Committee of Gibson County, to L. C. Houk, Feb. 1889, Houk Papers.

72. J. A. Lester and W. J. Andrews to L. C. Houk, 22 Feb. 1889, Houk Papers.

73. Forty Republicans of Jackson, Tenn., to L. C. Houk, 22 Feb. 1889, Houk Papers.

74. Diplomatic posts in Liberia and Haiti had become "the Negro beat" by the time McElwee made his request. Norma Brown, *A Black Diplomat in Haiti: The Diplomatic Correspondence of U.S. Minister Frederick Douglass from Haiti, 1889–1891,* vol. 1 (Salisbury, N.C.: Documentary Publications, 1977), i.

75. On Sykes, see Cartwright, *Triumph of Jim Crow,* 247–48.

76. J. W. Brown to L. C. Houk, 17 Dec. 1889, Houk Papers.

77. Ike K. Revelle to L. C. Houk, 22 Feb. 1889, Houk Papers. For a profile of Ike K. Revelle, see L. D. Whitson, *Personal Sketches of the Forty-Fourth General Assembly of Tennessee* (Nashville, Tenn.: Southern Methodist Publishing House, 1885), 117–18. Whitson profiled only one of the five African-American legislators, Green E. Evans, in her sketches, omitting McElwee. On Poston and Revelle in the service of the Union army, see Goodspeed, *History of Tennessee,* 825. On a staunchly Republican family of the time, see Goodspeed's description of the Postons of Crockett County, 964.

78. In the 1870s there had been tensions between state Republican party officials and African-American leaders over patronage appointments, which the latter felt were too few, and over support for the Civil Rights Acts proposed by Sumner. Former Radical Republican governor and then U.S. Sen. William G. Brownlow, for example, had opposed these civil rights measures. Tensions surfaced again in 1888 at state and national levels. Moderate African-American Republican leaders, such as James C. Napier and McElwee, protested proposals to reduce the role of African Americans in the party. Eventually, African Americans lost access to all but meager patronage portions. Even these were difficult to obtain, and some set off violent reactions. See George B. Tindall, *South Carolina Negroes, 1877–1900* (Baton Rouge: Louisiana State Univ. Press, 1966), 255–59. A rarity, James C. Napier continued to obtain federal patronage appointments in post-Reconstruction Republican administrations. Cordell Hull Williams, "The Life of James Carroll Napier from 1845 to 1940" (Master's thesis, Tennessee State Univ., 1955). Nancy J. Weiss, "The Negro and the New Freedom," in *The Segregation Era, 1863–1954,* ed. Allen Weinstein and F. O. Gatell (New York: Oxford Univ. Press, 1970), 129–42.

79. On this shift in Tennessee, see Mingo Scott, *Negro in Tennessee Politics*, 87, and Cartwright, *Triumph of Jim Crow*, 89–99. On comparable developments nationally, see C. Vann Woodward, *The Strange Career of Jim Crow*, 2d rev. ed. (New York: Oxford Univ. Press, 1966), 67–110.

80. The Fisk *Herald* mentions McElwee two or three times a year during the 1890s. The notices grow shorter. See also his obituary in *Fisk Herald* 32, no. 2 (Dec. 1914): 17.

81. McElwee had served on a similar committee for the New Orleans Exposition, 1885, and actively had promoted fairs for African Americans during his time in the General Assembly.

82. Woodward, *Strange Career of Jim Crow*, 69–74.

83. John W. Burgess, quoted by Benjamin F. Shambaugh, "Review of John W. Burgess, *Reconstruction and the Constitution, 1866–76*," *Annals of the American Academy of Political and Social Science* 20: 2 (Sept. 1902): 130.

84. Herman Justi, ed., *Official History of the Tennessee Centennial Exposition* (Nashville, Tenn.: Brandon Printing Co., 1898), 193.

85. Ibid., 202, 204.

86. McElwee is not listed among the committee members at any of the major events at the building. He withdrew several months after Napier resigned as chairman of the executive committee. Gloria McKissack suggests that the extensive change in membership of the executive committee came with Napier's departure; McKissack, "Late Summer: Afro-American Nashville, 1890–1899," in *From Winter to Winter: The Afro-American History of Nashville, Tennessee,. 1870–1930*, ed. Bobby L. Lovett (Nashville: Tennessee State Univ., 1981), 103–34.

87. When a lynching in Memphis took the lives of three young men whom Wells knew, her newspaper, *Free Speech*, addressed the white community subtly but critically. In response, the office of the paper was ransacked, and she was threatened. She did not return to Memphis and began a formal effort to end lynching. See Wells, *Crusade for Justice* , 47–67, and Ida B. Wells, *On Lynchings: Southern Horror, A Red Record, and Mob Rule in New Orleans* , 1892, 1895, and 1900, rpt. New York: Arno Press and New York Times, 1969. See also David M. Tucker, "Miss Ida B. Wells and Memphis Lynching," *Phylon* 32 (Summer 1971): 112–22.

88. Wells protested spending money on "Afro American Jubilee Day" at the World's Fair while lynchings continued: "Even if the condition of our race was not so serious in this country, the whole thing is lacking in dignity, self-respect and judgment to say nothing of good taste." Wells, "The Reign of Mob Law: Iola's Opinion of Doings in the Southern Field," *New York Age*, 18 Feb. 1893; IBWC, Box 5, Folder 1.

89. Norma Brown, *Black Diplomat in Haiti*, 1: iii.

90. Elliott M. Rudwick and August Meier, "Black Man in the 'White City': Negroes and the Colombian Exposition, 1893," *Phylon* 26 (Winter 1965): 354–61. Wells, *Crusade for Justice*, 115–19. Frederick Douglass et al., *The Reason Why the Colored American Is Not in the World's Colombian Exposition* (n.p., 1893). William S. McFeely, *Frederick Douglass* (New York: Norton, 1991), 366–72.

91. Justi, *Official History of the Tennessee Centennial Exposition*, 196.

92. Ibid., 193.

93. Clarence Thomas is one contemporary spokesman of this conservative credo. Shelby Steele is another. This is not to suggest that they continued the tradition of Booker T. Washington. Far more than recent African-American conservatives, Washington was a progressive agent of change. In the face of rigid segregation, Washington used his position to gain resources with which to serve African Americans. The credo of contemporary conservative African Americans embodies a retreat from integration and justifies a decline in public resources and programs for African Americans and others with low incomes and inadequate opportunities for success. See, e.g., Shelby Steele, *The Content of Our Character: A New Vision of Race in America* (New York: St. Martin's Press, 1990). Comparing Frederick Douglass and later African-American conservatives, see Fredrickson, *Arrogance of Race*, 80–88.

94. Justi, *Official History of the Tennessee Centennial Exposition*, 202–3.

95. Ibid.

96. Ibid.

97. Quoted in Ridgely Torrence, *The Story of John Hope* (New York: Macmillan, 1948), 114–15. Later, Du Bois criticized Washington for this accommodationist philosophy. He became the most articulate opponent of the powerful Tuskegee machine. At the time, however, Du Bois wrote to Washington congratulating him on his speech, "a word fitly spoken." Aptheker, *Correspondence of W. E. B. Du Bois*, 39. Du Bois was then looking for a job, and Washington, in addition to having offered Du Bois a position teaching mathematics at Tuskegee, exercised enormous influence in the hiring of African-American college teachers; ibid., 38.

CHAPTER 3. FREEDOM'S SURROGATE, 1901–1940

1. Allen F. Davis and Mary Lynn McCree, *Eighty Years at Hull House* (Chicago: Quadrangle Books, 1969).

2. Chicago society was not so open that it encouraged interracial marriage, but the caste taboo was less rigid there than in the South. Interracial couples re-

mained somewhat alienated from both the white and the black communities of Chicago but were numerous enough to establish their own group, the Manassah Club, for mutual aid and recreation. St. Claire Drake, *Churches and Voluntary Associations in the Chicago Negro Community*, sponsored by the Works Progress Administration (Chicago: Univ. of Chicago, Institute for Juvenile Research, n.d.), 134. In 1882, Frederick Douglass had stirred criticism by his marriage to a white woman. He replied to his critics, "I am quite impartial. My first wife [who had died] was the color of my mother, and the second, the color of my father." Norma Brown, *Black Diplomat in Haiti,* vol. 1: iii. McElwee father's father had been white, and both of his wives were biracial.

3. *Fisk Herald* 19, no. 2 (Dec. 1901): 11. I have not been able to determine the specific lawsuit that took McElwee to Chicago. The amount of money involved, 4% of the net value of the railway companies, was substantial. At this time, Chicago was embroiled in "perhaps the most important and perplexing franchise problem yet considered by an American municipal legislative body." The company stockholders of the Union Traction Company went to federal court seeking an injunction to restrain the city council from declaring its franchise forfeited. McElwee had made a legal specialty of injunctions since his law school days. There was great public pressure for the city council to take action to improve services and to reform the practices of the street railway companies. In Apr. 1902, 84% of the electorate voted yes on a referendum proposing municipal ownership of street railways. H. A. Millis, "The Present Street Railway Situation in Chicago," *Annals of the American Academy of Political and Social Science* 20, no. 2 (Sept. 1902): 52–65.

4. *Chicago Broad Ax*, 17 Aug. 1901.

5. *Chicago Defender*, 10 Dec. 1910. Chicago had African-American newspapers, while Nashville did not. There, African Americans had to depend on the white press to include notice of them. McElwee's effort to start a newspaper in Nashville lasted little more than a year.

6. The literature on caste and class is extensive. One classic study is John Dollard, *Caste and Class in a Southern Town* (1937; rpt. Madison: Univ. of Wisconsin Press, 1988). My discussion is based on the synthesis offered in Drake, *Churches and Voluntary Associations*, 132–37. For a synopsis of caste and class analysis of American race relations, see Myrdal, *American Dilemma:*, 667–705. Myrdal, like Drake and Dollard, depended heavily on W. Lloyd Warner and the Univ. of Chicago school of sociology. George Fredrickson, *Arrogance of Race*, 154–71, draws on Max Weber for his concept of caste, which he qualifies as racial caste. In these treatments, caste is consistently a status separate from class structure and with less bearing on economic structure and status than class.

7. *Chicago Broad Ax*, 27 May 1905. *Chicago Broad Ax*'s scanty coverage of McElwee informs us that, in 1902 and 1903, he worked for the Mexican Mutual Planters' Company. Evidently, he traveled sections of the South, including West Tennessee and the Memphis area, encouraging African-American families to migrate to Mexico to work for the company. See *Chicago Broad Ax*, 27 Sept. 1902, 15 Nov. 1902, and 7 Feb. 1903. McElwee also addressed African Americans in South Haven, Mich., at an emancipation celebration on 3 Aug. 1903; *Chicago Broad Ax*, 8 Aug. 1903.

8. McElwee's mother-in-law, Georgianna Shelton, who had operated a Nashville boardinghouse and had helped save his family land in Haywood County, resided with him and his family in Chicago.

9. "Steve Green Liberated," *Chicago Defender*, 24 Sept. 1910.

10. "Attorneys William G. Anderson and Edward H. Wright Won One of the Greatest Legal Battles of their Lives," *Chicago Broad Ax*, 24 Sept. 1910.

11. "Mass Meeting at Quinn Chapel, Wednesday, Sept. 28th, 1910," *Chicago Defender*, 1 Oct. 1910.

12. "The Great Tidal Wave of Democracy Swept All Over the Country," *Chicago Broad Ax*, Nov. 12, 1910. "Protest of Republican Ticket, Switch to Democratic," *Chicago Defender*, Nov. 12, 1910, p. 1.

13. *Fisk Herald* 32, no. 2 (Dec. 1914): 17. "The Death of Atty. Samuel A. McElwee Occurred Wednesday Morning at 4 p.m. at his Residence, 3230 Forest Ave.," *Chicago Broad Ax*, 24 Oct. 1914. "Death Claims Samuel A. McElwee: Well Known Attorney, was Native of Brownsville, Tenn.—Was Member of Tennessee Legislature," *Chicago Defender*, 24 Oct. 1914. Ironically, the issue of the *Chicago Defender* that reported McElwee's death and achievements also reported the continuing racial exclusion policies of the American Bar Association.

14. *Nashville Banner*, 22 Oct. 1914. As noted above, McElwee's father was mulatto. The reference to no foreign blood indicates the manner in which the racism of the time discarded unwanted facts.

15. Harlan, *Booker T. Washington Papers*, 10: 222–23.

16. Ibid., 225.

17. Williamson, *Rage for Order*, 15–29, examines the "Sambo" and "savage" depictions. See also Fredrickson, *Arrogance of Race*.

18. Harlan, *Booker T. Washington Papers*, 10: 232–34.

19. In 1907, they had sold 39-1/2 acres and a month and a half later conveyed the remaining 56 acres to their grandson, with the proviso that they could remain on the land for the rest of their lives. By this time, 56 acres was larger than the farm average of about 55 acres. Although the number of African-

American land-owners had increased to more than 500, less than 3 in 100 African Americans in Haywood County owned land.

20. On this shift in African-American education, see James D. Anderson, *The Education of Blacks in the South, 1860–1935* (Chapel Hill: Univ. of North Carolina Press, 1988), 110–47. On Haywood County Training School, ibid., 142. See also Dorothy Granberry, "African American Education in Haywood County, Tenn., 1870–1970" (paper presented at the Local African American History Conference, Nashville, Tenn., 13 Feb. 1991).

21. Holt, *Struggle for a State System of Public Schools* , 101–2.

22. Granberry, "African American Education," 6.

23. I rely heavily upon the discussion of caste, class, and social equality in Myrdal, *American Dilemma*, 667–705, esp. 690–93. Myrdal himself depends heavily Robert E. Park, W. Lloyd Warner, and W. E. B. Du Bois.

24. In addition, biracial individuals were more likely to have been free before emancipation. For example, James C. Napier, McElwee's contemporary in Nashville, was a free man in Tennessee before legal emancipation. He, like others of biracial parentage, had greater opportunities for leadership during Reconstruction and later. Napier served as an agent of the Freedmen's Bureau and later became the most prominent African American in Nashville, as well as one of the most prominent African-American Republicans in the country. See Williams, "Life of James Carroll Napier," and Weiss, "The Negro and the New Freedom." Other African-Americans, such as Ida B. Wells, exercised leadership even if it was not given to them, because of their training. Williamson, *Rage for Order*, describes the constellation of sex, caste, and violence during this time.

CHAPTER 4. FREEDOM'S PURSUIT, 1940

1. W. E. B. Du Bois, "The Evolution of Negro Leadership," *The Dial*, 16 July 1901, 53–55.

2. W. E. B. Du Bois, "Of Mr. Booker T. Washington and Others," in Du Bois, *The Souls of Black Folk* (1903; rpt. New York: Bantam, 1989), 38, 42.

3. Ida B. Wells, *Crusade for Justice: The Autobiography of Ida B. Wells*, ed. Alfreda M. Duster (Chicago: Univ. of Chicago Press, 1970), 280–81.

4. See Wells, *On Lynchings* . For her work against lynching and other organizing efforts in Illinois, see Wells, *Crusade for Justice*. Her letter to Du Bois appears in Aptheker, *Correspondence of W. E. B. Du Bois*, 1: 55–56.

5. Elliott M. Rudwick, "The Niagara Movement," *Journal of Negro History* 42 (Fall 1957): 177–200. Torrence, *Story of John Hope* , 149–51.

6. For Wells on these events, see Wells, *Crusade for Freedom*, 321–28. For com-

mittee correspondence on Wells's exclusion, see Aptheker, *Correspondence of W. E. B. Du Bois*, 1: 147–50. The most detailed account is Charles Flint Kellogg, *NAACP: A History of the National Association for the Advancement of Colored People*, vol. 1: *1909–20* (Baltimore, Md.: Johns Hopkins Univ. Press, 1967), 22–29. Kellogg's summary of the Steve Green case differs in details from the newspaper accounts that I have relied on.

Green's case clearly influenced the formation of the NAACP. The organization looked to the courts to redress the violation of the civil rights of African Americans. Steve Green's case in Chicago provided some hope that the courts could act where legislatures and executives had not to curb the flagrant disregard of the constitutional rights of African Americans. Kellogg, *NAACP: A History*. For the NAACP's work against lynching, see Robert L. Zangrando, *The NAACP Crusade Against Lynching, 1909–1950* (Philadelphia: Temple Univ. Press, 1980). For an early defense of African Americans against a legally sanctioned lynching, see Richard A. Cortner, *A Mob Intent on Death: The NAACP and the Arkansas Riot Case* (Middletown, Conn.: Wesleyan Univ. Press, 1988). For NAACP and voting, see Lawson, *Black Ballots*, 17–54.

7. Editorial from Du Bois's *The Crisis*, cited in Drake, *Churches and Voluntary Associations*, 135. Neither Du Bois, Washington, nor their supporters extolled one or the other strategy exclusively. Du Bois, with his gift for pamphleteering, exaggerated the polarization of the two positions. Both men blended the two strategies. For example, Washington organized the most prominent African Americans into the National Businessmen's Association, even as he urged industrial training for African Americans and emphasized ties to the land. And Du Bois, writing in *The Crisis*, addressed a "talented tenth" of African Americans but constantly protested the deprivation of ordinary African Americans. Similarly, staff at Tuskegee, Washington's institution, had kept track of lynchings before the NAACP took up the issue. The differences between Washington and Du Bois primarily concerned where to begin in changing race relations. Washington's position demanded little change of white-dominated institutions, while Du Bois's demanded much.

8. Each of the two positions proposed to modify the class and caste structure of legal emancipation differently. Du Bois's position increased the distance between those at the top and those at the bottom of the African-American class structure. Castelike differentiations between comparable class positions within the two races remained but in diminished form. African Americans at the top of their class structure were discounted less when compared with their white counterparts. Washington's position maintained class and caste

distinctions but improved conditions at the lower end of the class structure, where most African Americans resided.

9. Wells assessed Washington's leadership for a group of white men who admired him: "A great many of us cannot approve Mr. Washington's plan of telling chicken-stealing stories on his own people in order to amuse his audiences and get money for Tuskegee." Wells, *Crusade for Justice*, 331.

10. Materials on early NAACP organizing efforts in Haywood County are in NAACP Administration Files, Group I, Box G-198, Brownsville Branch, LC.

11. On the Haywood County Farms Project of the Farm Security Administration (FSA) and its effect on later county change efforts, see Couto, *Ain't Gonna Let Nobody Turn Me Round*. On the influence of these projects on later civil rights efforts in the rural South, see Lester Salamon, "The Time Dimension in Policy Evaluation: The Case of the New Deal Land Reform Experiments," *Public Policy* 27 (Sept. 1972): 129–83. A history of FSA is Sidney Baldwin, *Poverty and Politics: The Rise and Fall of the Farm Security Administration* (Chapel Hill: Univ. of North Carolina Press, 1968).

12. National Association for the Advancement of Colored People, Jackson (Tenn.) Chapter, "Annual Report," 17 Jan. 1941, Milmon Mitchell Papers.

13. Ibid.

14. "Statement of the Facts in Brownsville, Tenn., Case," NAACP Administration Files, Group II, Box A-393, Tennessee Lynching—Williams, LC.

15. National Association for the Advancement of Colored People, Jackson (Tenn.) Chapter, "Report," 1940; Milmon Mitchell Papers. I obtained additional information on this event from the FBI and Justice Department through the · Freedom of Information Act: U.S., Justice Department, FBI, "Unknown Subjects, Negro Agitation," Brownsville, Tennessee, Violation of Civil Rights, Memorandum, 26 June 1940.

16. Milmon Mitchell to Walter White, 13 June 1940, Milmon Mitchell Papers.

17. "Statement of the Facts in Brownsville, Tennessee Case," NAACP Administration Files, Group II, Box A-393, Tennessee Lynching—Williams, LC.

18. Davis gave a sworn affidavit concerning these events the day he arrived in Jackson with Mitchell. Milmon Mitchell Papers. Both Elisha Davis and Nann Davis gave another, longer sworn affidavit concerning these events after arriving in Michigan. Debra Davis Papers.

19. Affidavit of Annie Williams, 11 Sept. 1940, NAACP Administration Files, Group II, Box A-393, Tennessee Lynching—Williams, LC.

20. Affidavit of Thomas Davis, 21 June 1940, Milmon Mitchell Papers.

21. Affidavit of Thomas Davis. See "'Lynch' Victim Widow Leaves for New York," *Memphis Press-Scimitar*, 26 June 1940; in Debra Davis Papers.

CHAPTER 5. FREEDOM'S DELAY, 1940–1954

1. On the mercenary aspect of lynchings, see Jessie D. Ames, *The Changing Character of Lynching: Review of Lynching, 1931–1941* (Atlanta: Commission on Interracial Cooperation, 1942).

2. Milmon Mitchell to J. L. LeFlore [telegram], 21 June 1940, Milmon Mitchell Papers.

3. B. Walker to Milmon Mitchell, 21 June 1940, Milmon Mitchell Papers.

4. J. L. LeFlore to M. Mitchell, 25 June 1940, Milmon Mitchell Papers.

5. On the formation of the Legal Defense Fund, see Ginna Rae McNeil, *Groundwork: Charles Hamilton Houston and the Struggle for Civil Rights* (Philadelphia: Univ. of Pennsylvania Press, 1983).

6. Walter White to William McClanahan, 1 July 1940, NAACP Administration Files, Group II, Box A-393, Tennessee Lynching—Williams, LC.

7. Ibid.

8. Zangrando, *NAACP Crusade Against Lynching,*, 3–21.

9. Jessie Daniel Ames made this report for the Association of Southern Women for the Prevention of Lynching (ASWPL). The International Labor Defense criticized her for ignoring the new mode of "quiet lynching." Walter White attempted to separate her and her organization from the Commission on Interracial Cooperation, of which ASWPL was part. This material is in Ames Collection, 3686, May 1940 correspondence, SHC. See also Jacquelyn Dowd Hall, *Revolt Against Chivalry: Jessie Daniel Ames and the Women's Campaign against Lynching* (New York: Columbia Univ. Press, 1979).

10. Zangrando, *NAACP Crusade Against Lynching*, 122–23.

11. M. Mitchell to Walter White, 1 July 1940, Milmon Mitchell Papers.

12. M. Mitchell to Rev. S. L. McDowell, 1 July 1940, Milmon Mitchell Papers.

13. Milmon Mitchell Papers.

14. NAACP Administration Files, Group II, Box A-393, Tennessee Lynching—Williams, LC.

15. M. Mitchell to Buster Walker, 23 July 1940, Milmon Mitchell Papers.

16. NAACP Administration Files, Group II, Box A-393, Tennessee Lynching—Williams, LC.

17. I. L. Newbern to Walter White, 9 July 1940, NAACP Administration Files, Group II, Box A-393, Tennessee Lynching—Williams, LC.

18. Marshall wrote, "The reason the FBI agents could not gather more information from Negroes was because they traveled around with Tip Hunter whom the Negroes knew to be the leader of the mob." Marshall to Office, Memorandum, 9 Dec. 1941, NAACP Administration Files, Group II, Box A-393, Tennessee Lynching—Williams, LC. Many years and several similar cases

later, Marshall wrote to FBI Director J. Edgar Hoover to express his distrust in FBI investigations of lynchings. Marshall explained to White, "I have . . . no faith in either Mr. Hoover or his investigators and there is no use in saying I do." Marshall also wrote to Attorney General Clark with his criticism of Hoover. Hoover responded that Marshall was untruthful and declined White's invitation for Hoover and Marshall to meet. J. E. Hoover to Walter White, 13 and 19 Jan. 1947, NAACP Administration Files, Group II-A, Lynching, 1940-47, LC. On Marshall's later conflicts with J. Edgar Hoover, see Carl T. Rowan, *Dream Makers, Dream Breakers: The World of Justice Thurgood Marshall* (Boston: Little, Brown, 1993), 115-23. On the obstacles facing the FBI's investigations of lynchings, see Howard Smead, *Blood Justice: The Lynching of Mack Charles Parker* (New York: Oxford Univ. Press, 1986).

19. J. Edgar Hoover to Mr. Tolson and Mr. Tamm, Memo, 14 Nov. 1941, USJDFIO, Serial 61-3176-18x11.

20. Documents of this investigation in USJDFIO, Serial 61-3176-18-5 and 61-3176-47. The reports indicated that the NAACP chapters considered more active and radical had ties to the colleges started with the aid of the Freedmen's Bureau—LeMoyne in Memphis, especially, and Lane College in Jackson.

21. Elisha Davis to Walter White, 25 July 1942, NAACP Administration Files, Group II, Box A-393, Tennessee Lynching—Williams, LC.

22. M. Mitchell to Roy Wilkins, 3 Aug. 1940, Milmon Mitchell Papers.

23. Mitchell sent the clipping to Thurgood Marshall, NAACP special counsel, on 16 Aug. 1940, Milmon Mitchell Papers.

24. Elisha Davis to Walter White, 19 Aug. 1940, Milmon Mitchell Papers.

25. Thelma Price recalls how her mother dealt with a difficult situation she encountered as a young girl while working for a white woman:

> She did cooking and cleaning. The white lady made her come in the back door even though she swept the front porch as well as the rest of the house.
>
> There was a rooster in the back yard, and every time my mother came to the house, that rooster would come and spur my mother's heel. So she complained to the white woman. But all the woman said was, "Don't worry, he'll get used to you." And my mother thought, "When? When is that rooster going to get used to me?" She couldn't quit her job, so she had to stay there and keep going through the yard with that big rooster chasing her, spurring at her heel.
>
> But one day, that rooster was about to spur her but she grabbed a piece of stove wood and hit him on the side of the head. He fell on his back

with his legs sticking straight in the air. And she thought, "Is he dead?" She thought he was dead. That rooster laid for half a day on the ground with his feet up in the air.

So the next day, when my mother came to the yard, that rooster was up, and it ran to the other side of the yard. He had no thought of spurring that day. And the white woman looked out and said to my mother, "Well, what's got into that rooster?" And my mother looked over at him and said, "I don't know." And the white woman said, "I guess he got used to you." And my mother said, "I guess so. I guess he just got used to me."

You see, my mother let him know that nothing that small would have control over her.

26. Newspaper coverage documented in NAACP Administration Files, Group II, Box A-393, Tennessee Lynching—Williams, LC. Clippings indicate coverage in Washington and Philadelphia, as well as Nashville.

27. Walter White to O. John Rogge [telegram], 3 Sept. 1940, Milmon Mitchell Papers.

28. The Davis family has the telegram from White on a plaque hanging on a wall in their home: "Have wired Federal Bureau of Investigation asking them have at Brownsville Sept. fourth and fifth agents to protect negro citizens who attempt to register. Have also wired Governor Cooper."

29. Davis sent this letter to Walter White, who used it to counter the assessment that Washington officials had received from Memphis. Walter White to O. John Rogge, 16 Sept. 1940, Milmon Mitchell Papers.

30. Elisha Davis to Walter White, 16 Sept. 1940, Milmon Mitchell Papers.

31. White nudged the federal authorities for accountable action, in Walter White to O. John Rogge, 16 Sept. 1940, Milmon Mitchell Papers.

32. Milmon Mitchell to Walter White, 9 Oct. 1940, Milmon Mitchell Papers.

33. Ibid.

34. T. D. Quinn to Elisha Davis, 14 Mar. 1941, Milmon Mitchell Papers.

35. Berge wrote McClanahan and Hoover that he had reviewed the case and determined that "the matter undoubtedly warrants presentation to a federal grand jury." Memo of Wendell Berge, assistant attorney general, to J. Edgar Hoover, 31 Mar. 1941. William McClanahan, U.S. attorney general, Memphis office, to Wendell Berge, assistant attorney general, 23 Apr. 1941. Berge again asked McClanahan to bring the case to a federal grand jury, in Berge to McClanahan, 2 Oct. 1941. All, USJDFIO.

36. The FBI file on the case includes a newspaper clipping reporting that U.S. Attorney McClanahan was waiting for the FBI report and thus action on the case was delayed. In November, agents reported to Hoover that, McClanahan had advised them "that no additional inquiry was deemed desirable or practical and upon receipt of this report he would request the opinion of the Department to ascertain if, in the view of the information developed, there were any violations of Federal statutes." N. B. Fletcher, 28 Nov. 1940, Memo, USJDFIO. Again on 18 Oct. 1941, Memphis office FBI agents informed Hoover that, in light of their difficulty in finding a witness, McClanahan had suggested that their efforts "be held in abeyance." USJDFIO.

37. Of course, McClanahan did not elaborate on the dual standard of justice. The suspects in the shootings of the white men were arrested, tried, and convicted. William McClanahan, U.S. attorney, Memphis office, to Thomas J. Dodd, Jr., special assistant to the attorney general, Criminal Division, 2 July 1940, USJDFIO.

38. Memo, Victor W. Rotnem, chief, Civil Rights Section, "Re: Tip Hunter et al.—Civil Rights and Domestic Violence," for the file, 23 Dec. 1941. Memo, J. Edgar Hoover, "For the Attorney General," 17 Nov. 1941. All, USJDFIO.

39. Memo, Thurgood Marshall to Office, 9 Dec. 1941, NAACP Administration Files, Group II, Box A-393, Tennessee Lynching—Williams, LC.

40. Memo, Victor W. Rotnem for the files, "Re: Tip Hunter et al.—Civil Rights and Domestic Violence," 23 Dec. 1941, USJDFIO.

41. Thurgood Marshall to Wendell Berge, 30 Jan. 1942, NAACP Administration Files, Group II, Box A-393, Tennessee Lynching—Williams, LC.

42. Milmon Mitchell to Francis M. Biddle, 16 Feb. 1942, Milmon Mitchell Papers.

43. Milmon Mitchell to Thurgood Marshall, 17 Feb. 1942, Milmon Mitchell Papers.

44. Davis moved his family to Niles with limited help from the NAACP. White responded to Davis's appeal for financial support, renewed in Nashville when they participated in the rally. The national appeal yielded $140, which White sent to Davis. Davis wrote appreciatively to White and explained that he would get his family and move them to Niles. He expressed his intention never to return to Brownsville to live, citing his mother's advice "never to come back there anymore, as I am alive and it would be best to stay away." Elisha Davis to Walter White, 24 Sept. 1940, NAACP Administration Files, Group II, Box A-393, Tennessee Lynching—Williams, LC.

45. L. B. Nichols to Tolson, memo, 4 Oct. 1947. D. M. Ladd to R. A. Tamm, memo, 2 Oct. 1947. D. M. Ladd "To the Director," memo, 26 Sept. 1947.

See also Hoover to Tamm, 30 Sept. 1947; Tamm to Hoover, 1 Oct. 1947; and D. M. Ladd to Hoover, 8 Oct. 1947. All, USJDFIO. See also Rowan, *Dream Makers*, 115-23.

46. On the expanded black electorate at this time, see: McAdam, *Political Process and Black Insurgency*; Oscar Glantz, "The Negro Vote in Northern Industrial Cities," *Western Political Quarterly* 13 (Dec. 1960): 999–1010; Thomas R. Brooks, *Walls Come Tumbling Down: A History of the Civil Rights Movement, 1940–1970* (Englewood Cliffs, N.J.: Prentice-Hall, 1974); and Ralph J. Bunche, *The Political Status of the Negro in the Age of FDR*, ed. Dewey Grantham (Chicago: Univ. of Chicago Press, 1973). On the South's electoral changes at this time, see Harvey Lee Moon, *Balance of Power: The Negro Vote* (Garden City, N.Y.: Doubleday, 1949), esp. 174–96; and Luther P. Jackson, "Race and Suffrage in the South Since 1940," *New South* 3 (June–July 1948): 1–26.

47. Elisha Davis to Thurgood Marshall, 3 Jan. 1953, NAACP Administration Files, Group II, Box A-393, Tennessee Lynching—Williams, LC.

48. Debra Davis Papers.

CHAPTER 6. FREEDOM'S RENEWAL, 1955–1965

1. The migration made it more difficult for African Americans to keep land they owned. When a land-owner died without a will, her or his lands were divided equally among the heirs. With children and grandchildren scattered around the country, determined speculators or others often could find one heir who was willing to sell her or his claim to their inheritance. This would lead to a partition sale to determine the market value of the land, such as the one through which the McElwees lost their land.

2. The McElwees' Aunt Minnie had a husband who regularly traveled to West Tennessee recruiting workers for California farms. Possibly his trips were related to the work that Samuel McElwee did in Chicago for land-owners in Mexico. Roy Bond recalls his father telling him that McElwee recruited farm workers for land-owners in California.

3. Granberry, "African American Education," 6.

4. "Haywood County Man Attacks Negro," *Nashville Tennessean*, 1 Oct. 1959.

5. On the relation of the Haywood County Farms Project and other federal programs to local civil rights movements, see Couto, *Ain't Gonna Let Nobody Turn Me Round:*; Richard A. Couto, "A Place to Call Our Own," *Southern Exposure* 9 (Fall 1981): 16–22; Richard A. Couto, "Sick for Justice," *Southern Exposure* 6 (Summer 1978): 73–76; and Salamon, "Time Dimension in Policy Evaluation," 129–83.

6. In 1961, direction of the Citizenship Schools was transferred from Highlander Folk School to the SCLC. Many leaders of the new movement—e.g., Rosa Parks—were NAACP officers or members. The NAACP's past successes, esp. in *Brown* v. *Board of Education*, led southern states to harass its members, just as Haywood County officials had threatened to do in 1940. Septima Clark, for example, was fired as a teacher in South Carolina because she would not relinquish her NAACP membership. After her firing, she began working with Highlander's Citizenship Schools. On the Citizenship Schools, see John Glen, *Highlander: No Ordinary School, 1932–1962* (Lexington: Univ. Press of Kentucky, 1988), 158–66, and Carl Tjerandsen, *Education for Citizenship: A Foundation's Experience* (Santa Cruz, Calif.: Emil Schwarzhaupt Foundation, 1980).

7. Boyd says California CORE chapters helped. The records of CORE's Chicago chapter are in the Chicago Historical Society, where Box 1, file 2, contains data on the chapter's work in Haywood County. By the end of 1961, the Freedom Rides had eclipsed Haywood County in CORE's priorities.

8. For coverage of this incident and trial, see *Brownsville States-Graphic*, 31 July 1959; 7 and 14 Aug. 1959; and 9 and 16 Oct. 1959.

9. 'Haywood Suit on Rights Filed," *Nashville Tennessean*, 31 May 1960.

10. Events in Haywood County at this time were the "most important of these early cases and the one in which the FBI demonstrated most clearly its reluctance to get involved in civil rights enforcement," according to Kenneth O'Reilly in *"Racial Matters": The FBI's Secret File on Black America, 1960–1972* (New York: Free Press, 1989), 52.

11. "Rights Agents Visit Haywood," *Nashville Tennessean*, 14 June 1960. "Kefauver Halts Haywood Fight," *Nashville Tennessean*, 15 June 1960.

12. "Negro Preacher Fined in Brownsville Case," *Nashville Tennessean*, 23 June 1960.

13. Charles V. Hamilton, *The Bench and the Ballot: Southern Federal Judges and Black Voters* (New York: Oxford Univ. Press, 1973), 30.

14. Branch, *Parting the Waters*, 333–35. Anthony Lewis labeled Doar's work in Haywood County imaginative, in *Portrait of a Decade: The Second American Revolution* (New York: Random House, 1964), 113.

15. *Brownsville States-Graphic*, 23 Dec. 1960.

16. "Hymn Bolsters Hungry Pastor," *Nashville Tennessean*, 17 Nov. 1961; "2nd 'Freedom' Group Member Under Arrest," *Nashville Tennessean*, 16 Nov. 1961.

17. "Michigan White Students Leave Haywood County," *Nashville Banner*, 6 Feb. 1961.

18. *New York Times*, 26 Jan. 1961.

19. John Wilder, quoted in "West Tennessee Food Seen Kennedy Bid for Sup-

port," *Nashville Banner*, 19 July 1961. Wilder was a large Fayette County farmer who became state senator and lieutenant governor. "U.S. Pays Grocery Bill for Fayette, Haywood Negroes," *Nashville Banner*, 18 July 1961. "Free Food Handouts Result in Squabble," *Nashville Banner*, 14 July 1961.

20. Branch, *Parting the Waters*, 387.

21. Press Release, "Report of the Attorney General to the President on the Department of Justice's Activities in the Field of Civil Rights," 29 Dec. 1961; President's Office File, Civil Rights General, 1961, Box 97, John F. Kennedy Library, Boston, Mass.

22. James Arnold Baxter, "Charles Allen Rawls, 'A Portrait,' 1907–1977." Master's thesis, Tennessee State Univ., 1982.

23. Press Release, "Young NAACP Woman Continues Parents' Work in Tennessee," NAACP Administration Files, Group I-A, Branches, Tennessee, Haywood County, LC.

24. NAACP, Haywood County Branch, "Dear Merchant," 19 July 1961. NAACP Administration Files. Group I-A, Branches, Tennessee, LC.

25. The entire letter is in NAACP, Haywood County Branch, to Taylor Hunter, 4 Aug. 1961, NAACP Administration Files, Group I-A, Branches, Tennessee, LC.

26. While the Civic and Welfare League cooperated with the NAACP chapter, others discouraged participation in the NAACP. Rumor had it that the principal of the African-American high school had threatened to expel any students who participated in the NAACP Youth Council. Ironically, the principal had been a member of the NAACP in 1940 and a friend and correspondent of Elisha Davis. To many in this period, he seemed resistant to change. Memo, Mildred Bond to Mr. Current, 29 Mar. 1962, NAACP Administration Files, Group I-A, Branches, Tennessee, LC.

27. Sam Hess, Homer Zell McElwee's husband, slept well the night they registered: "Mother [Homer] stayed up worrying. I went to bed and slept. I had done nothing wrong. Our landlord, he didn't mind our registering. He was a Jew. We was on thirds." Hess was continuing a tradition of courage. He could remember his father hiding a man from a mob. His father placed the fugitive in the center of several cattle and covered him with hay to attract and keep the animals' attention. In his own life, Hess had gone as far as any African-American man could go in defending himself. The sons of his white neighbor shot gravel, with slingshots, at his house and his horse. Hess asked them to stop, but they did not. He then spoke to their father, again without success. Finally, he went to a deputy sheriff. Hess recalls that the deputy informed the white neighbor, "Sam Hess don't bother nobody. His kids don't bother nobody. Don't bother him." Hess concludes, with some pride, I got

the law on them. Now more than twenty years after that incident, he rested easy after registering to vote. Nann Davis was a member of the Hess family.

28. The 1955 lynching of one such northern teenager who had little knowledge of southern racial etiquette, Emmett Till of Chicago, galvanized the African-American community at last. Fourteen-year-old Till's uncle stood up in court to identify the two men who had come to his cabin and taken Till away: "Thar he." His actions emboldened other African-American witnesses to parts of the lynching to come forward and testify as well. And if African Americans found some voice, white Americans found some conscience. Till's lynchers found it difficult to attain legal assistance. Medgar Evers, a World War II veteran, had been NAACP field secretary for less than a year when Till was lynched. He found witnesses and evidence for the prosecution, and, this time, law officials acted. They put the two men on trial to face witnesses who testified to their crime. The precedent of African-American witnesses testifying against white men being tried for a crime against an African American cracked the line of caste subordination. It did not break it, though. The all-white male jury deliberated little more than an hour and found the defendants not guilty. The jury reasoned that the prosecution had not proven the identity of the body. Juan Williams, *Eyes on the Prize,* 39–57.

29. Mark Stern, "Calculating Visions: Civil Rights Legislation in the Kennedy and Johnson Years" (Paper delivered at the annual meeting of the American Political Science Association, Washington, D. C., 1991), 11.

30. "Officers Grope for Key to Blasts" *Memphis Commercial Appeal,* 18 May 1960. For a description of armed vigilance at this time, see the comments of Jesse Cannon, Jr., M.D., in Couto, *Ain't Gonna Let Nobody Turn Me Round,* 40.

31. "Officers Grope for Key to Blasts," *Memphis Commercial Appeal,* 18 May 1966.

32. "Haywood County Is Puzzled by Difference of 2 Shots," *Memphis Commercial Appeal,* 14 July 1965.

33. "Judge Denies Haywood Order," *Memphis Commercial Appeal,* 6 Aug. 1965; "Rights Protest Set for Brownsville," *Memphis Commercial Appeal,* 7 Aug. 1965; "Police Disarm Prison Guard," *Memphis Commercial Appeal,* 8 Aug. 1965.

34. "Brownsville To Be Tested by Demonstrations Today," *Memphis Commercial Appeal,* 13 Aug. 1965.

CHAPTER 7. FREEDOM'S EXPRESSION, 1965–1990

1. Abigail M. Thernstrom, *Whose Votes Count? Affirmative Action and Minority Voting Rights* (Cambridge: Harvard Univ. Press, 1987), criticizes single-member districts as a means of increasing the number of African-American elected

officials. A particularly stinging review by Laughlin McDonald, "Review of Abigail M. Thernstrom, *Whose Votes Count? Affirmative Action and Minority Voting Rights*," *Southern Changes* 11 (Nov. 1989): 21–23, charges that Thernstrom ignored the history of civil rights in America.

2. Oddly, this African American's name was Ballard, the same as that of the attorney driven out of town after his 1940 appearance in Haywood County Court. "Negro to Serve on Haywood Jury," *Nashville Banner*, 23 May 1961.

3. Exhibit 25, "Appointments to Public Positions and Public Committees and Boards by the Haywood County Commission, by Race and Year, from 1960 to 1981, *Taylor* v. *Haywood County*." JONAH Records, Brownsville, Tenn.

4. *Sanders et al.* v. *A. S. Rose et al.*, "Memorandum Decision and Judgment," in the U.S. District Court for the Western District of Tenn., Western Division (24 Oct. 1969).

5. "To the Citizens of Haywood County from Brownsville–Haywood County Board of Education," *Brownsville States-Graphic*, 4 July 1969, and "Why You Should Vote for the Sales Tax," *Brownsville States-Graphic*, 11 July 1969.

6. Harold Cruse portrays this dilemma of integration and its ensuing impact on African-American leaders and institutions nationally, in *Plural But Equal: A Critical Study of Blacks and Minorities and America's Plural Society* (New York: William Morrow, 1987).

7. Table 1 suggests that the two votes represented parallel constellations of issues, including race. The precincts that voted for Wallace in largest proportions voted for the sales tax in a similar fashion. In the four largest precincts of the county, where Wallace gained 48% of his total vote, the sales tax acquired 66% of its support. These precincts had predominantly white voters. In three precincts with a preponderance of African-American voters, not only did Wallace receive the lowest percentage of votes in the county, but also the sales tax was rejected by the largest margins. The election results revealed differences between white and black voters and between white voters in rural areas and those in or around Brownsville.

8. Exhibit 25, "Appointments to Public Positions and Public Committees and Boards by the Haywood County Commission, by Race and Year, from 1960 to 1981, *Taylor* v. *Haywood County*." JONAH Records, Brownsville, Tenn.

9. John felt that his father chose the time to tell each child carefully, sharing information first with women rather than men "because the emotional responses, the psychological response would have been very, very different." John was thirty years old "when he told me the story—not the whole story, but his version, his short version, of the story. I was *thirty!* My impression is

that he thought finally you are mature enough that I can lay this on you and that you will handle it the way I think you should."

10. "Form Task Force to Cool Tensions," *Niles Daily Star*, 21 May 1969.

11. "Attorney Cites Niles Leadership Void," *Niles Daily Star*, 3 June 1969.

12. *Niles Daily Star*, 24 May 1969.

13. *Niles Daily Star*, 11 June 1969, carried news of the jury decision. The Detroit riot, the Algiers Motel incident, and the subsequent trials and hearings have been described extensively. See John Hersey, *The Algiers Motel Incident* (New York: Knopf, 1968).

14. JONAH Records, Brownsville, Tenn.

15. Several excellent studies trace the relation of Highlander to the civil rights movement: John Glen, *Highlander*, esp. 158–66; Tjerandsen, *Education for Citizenship;* and Aldon D. Morris, *The Origins of the Civil Rights Movement: Black Communities Organizing for Change* (New York: Free Press, 1984). For an oral history of Septima Clark, see Cynthia Stokes Brown, ed., *Ready from Within: Septima Clark and the Civil Rights Movement* (Navarro, Calif.: Wild Tree Press, 1986). Highlander's methods resembled and preceded the belief system of JONAH. See Horton and Freire, *We Make the Road by Walking.*

16. "Commissioner's Vote Risks His Constituency," *Memphis Commercial Appeal*, 21 Apr. 1982.

17. Exhibit 25, "Appointments to Public Positions and Public Committees and Boards by the Haywood County Commission, by Race and Year, from 1960 to 1981, *Taylor* v. *Haywood County.*" Exhibit 26, "Appointments by the Haywood County Commission to Public Positions, Boards, and Committees By Race, Year, and Position. *Taylor* v. *Haywood County.*" Both in JONAH Records, Brownsville, Tenn.

18. Kousser, *Shaping of Southern Politics.*

19. *Truly Mae Taylor et al., Plaintiffs*, v. *Haywood County, Tenn. et al., Defendants.* U.S. District Court for the Western District of Tenn., Eastern Division, Civil Action No. 82-1138.

20. Rob McDuff to JONAH, 3 Jan. 1983. Consent Order Granting Final Relief and Dismissing Case, *Taylor* v. *Haywood County, Tenn.* Both in JONAH Records, Brownsville, Tenn.

21. Herbert L. Harper to Jere Williamson, Jr., 10 Apr. 1981. Tennessee Historical Commission Files, Nashville, Tenn.

22. It is surprising, and appalling, that a bust of Nathan Bedford Forrest, who never served in the Tennessee legislature, or in state government, faces the door of the House of Representatives in the state capitol building.

23. On Detroit's problems in the 1980s, see Ze'ev Chafets, *Devil's Night.*

24. On recent efforts to gain reparations for slavery, see *In These Times*, 11 Oct.

1989. For earlier discussions of reparations, see James Forman, *Black Manifesto* (Richmond, Va.: Richmond News Leader, 1969), and Boris Bittker, *The Case for Black Reparations* (New York: Random House, 1973). See Mark Tushnet, letter to the editor, *In These Times*, 1 Jan. 1989.

25. Results taken from *Memphis Commercial Appeal*, 5 Aug. 1988.

26. In May 1992, the Rural West Tennessee African-American Affairs Council, brought suit against the State of Tennessee and several of its officials to protest the legislative redistricting plan of 1992 and to prevent its implementation. At the heart of the lawsuit was an allegation of racially polarized voting patterns. Election results from Haywood County and five adjoining counties make clear that whites vote as a bloc for white candidates far more cohesively than black voters do for black candidates. C. P. Boyd was a plaintiff in the suit. *Rural West Tenn. African-American Affairs Council, Inc.*, v. *Ned McWherter et al.*, U. S. District Court, Western District of Tenn., Western Div., Memphis, 15 May 1992.

CONCLUSION

1. James C. Scott, *Domination and the Arts of Resistance*, 223. The political use of space and its importance to social movements directed toward the emancipation of African-American men and women, white women, workers, and others is the central focus of Evans and Boyte, *Free Spaces*.

2. James C. Scott, in *Domination and the Arts of Resistance*, e.g., 115–16, 131–39, 192–227, discusses the infrapolitics of subordinate groups. He explains, for example, that racial and cultural barriers actually encourage the construction and continuation of separate spaces and traditions, some of which support the infrapolitics of subordinate groups. So the almost total segregation of Christian churches permits African Americans an interpretation of scripture that emphasizes liberation and deliverance. Scott observes that the political life of subordinate groups continues "at the very perimeter of what authorities are obliged to permit or unable to prevent." Under segregation, for instance, schools provided a political life, the construction of which white authorities and their African-American appointees could not block. Thus, William King recalled stories of Sheriff Jack Hunter's death that it was better not to repeat, at the time, to white people. Concerning the continuity of this infrapolitics with emancipation movements, see Scott's concluding chapter on the first public declaration of what he calls "the hidden transcript." Scott pays less attention to the evolution of this political infrastructure over time, but such attention allows us to see how resistance efforts—the voter registration effort of 1940, say—become part of the political infrastructure of subordinate groups.

3. Ibid., 65, points out the provocative nature of subordinate groups' space for public discussion. Scott cites Sara Evans's work to illustrate how the provocative nature of separate space continues even within a group seeking expanded emancipation—e.g., women seeking space separate from men (pp. 65, 148). See Sara M. Evans, *Personal Politics: The Roots of Women's Liberation in the Civil Rights Movement and the New Left* (New York: Vintage, 1980).

4. James C. Scott *Domination and the Arts of Resistance*, 37. Scott makes the point that covert resistance takes place "off stage" (p. 4). He suggests a hypothetical range of sites established by slaves where they could discuss their status in their own terms and not in those of their masters (125–26). Several historical accounts of slavery also emphasize resistance and the role of space, including family. See, e.g., Aptheker, *American Negro Slave Revolts*; Herbert G. Gutmann, "Schools for Freedom: The Post-Emancipation Origins of Afro-American Education," in *Power and Culture: Essays on the American Working Class*, ed. Ira Berlin (New York: Pantheon, 1987); John W. Blassingame, *The Slave Community: Plantation Life in the Antebellum South* (New York: Oxford Univ. Press, 1979). Such space, Scott emphasizes, could not be taken for granted. It was "created by people who fought to create it" (*Domination and the Arts of Resistance,* 123). When Willie Jones shot Sheriff Jack Hunter, he resisted an extreme form of domination.

5. James C. Scott, *Domination and the Arts of Resistance*, 72–80, discusses how injustice can seem like one form of justice and how that which is inevitable tends to appear natural. Clearly, if forms of domination are viewed as just and natural, the grounds for resistance are undermined and the repression of resistance appears legitimate. This is the nub of the discussion of false consciousness, explaining why oppressed and subordinate people seem not to act in their own interest or to resist. Scott critiques the concept of false consciousness and asserts that resistance is continuous, though varying in form (covert and overt) and degree. Resistance varies with individual and group calculations of the risks of reprisal, the prospects of success, and the importance of the issue at hand (90–96). Our history of emancipation efforts supports his view.

    Ibid., 51, cites Du Bois's suggestion, made at the beginning of the 20th century, that racial domination, with its double life of caste and class, fosters among African Americans "a double life with double thoughts, double duties, and double social classes." Eventually this duality, said Du Bois, "must give rise to double words and double ideals, and *tempt the mind to pretense or revolt, to hypocrisy or radicalism.*" Moving from the psychological to the social, Du Bois then suggested that each individual fell into one of two groups— those given to revolt or pretense (radicalism) and those given to accommodation. This dichotomy parallels that between self-regarding and self-sufficient groups that we treated in chapter 3, and between voice and loyalty, discussed in our introduction. Scott suggests that individuals simultaneously embody both terms of the dichotomy, one covertly and the other overtly. Whether radicalism or accommodation is expressed, according to Scott, depends on circumstances. In 1901, African Americans in Chicago, such as Samuel McElwee, lived in circumstances much more favorable to the expression of indignation and radicalism than their counterparts in the South, such as Sam McElwee's father and son. Rather than being a dichotomy, however, these positions are more likely to fall along a continuum, with a given individual combining elements of each type in varied ways.

6. Scott refers to actions such as "talking crazy" as "strange theater." He treats them as calculated acts overtly expressing resistance while reducing the risk of reprisal. The second act of resistance is an example, however private, of an act of defiance, a public refusal in the teeth of power. It implies the deeply personal nature of domination and resistance. Ibid., 21, 93, 203.

7. Scott relies on Barrington Moore's work to suggest a gradient in the interrogation of domination continually conducted by subordinate groups. What such groups ask for and how they ask depends on their perception of the circumstances of domination; they choose the forms and content of their demands strategically, so as to make gains and avoid reprisals. Thus the forms and content will vary with circumstances; witness the differences between Haywood County voter registration efforts in 1940 and in 1959. Ibid., 92.

8. Ibid., 3.

9. Robert A. Dahl, *A Preface to Democratic Theory* (Chicago: Univ. of Chicago Press, 1956), 145.

10. The events recounted in this book may be interpreted by some as being compatible with the pluralist paradigm proclaiming the sufficiency of American democracy. Others may understand these events, as I do, as an anomaly. The events, I believe, violate the tenets of the dominant, pluralist view of American democracy and require a change in its terms. In particular, my discussion of domination and resistance fundamentally contradicts dominant explanations of the emergence of groups and of their competition for political influence. The experience of domination and resistance, far from being merely a puzzle peculiar to Haywood County, is shared by women, laborers, and other groups of people who experience subordination sometimes or regularly. This is the politics of our everyday lives that pluralism has not visited and cannot explain well, because of its avoidance of the phenomenon of unjust and illegal domination. On the critique of pluralism, see Gaventa, *Power and Powerlessness:*, and James C. Scott, *Domination and the Arts of Resistance*, 70–107.

The debate between pluralists and their critics recalls the defense of a paradigm, within the analysis of Thomas Kuhn, *The Structure of Scientific Revolutions* , 2d ed. (Chicago: Univ. of Chicago Press, 1970).

11. William Julius Wilson is a prime exponent of social welfare policies that address class but not caste; see his *The Truly Disadvantaged: The Inner City, the Underclass, and Public Policy* (Chicago: Univ. of Chicago Press, 1987), 140–64.

12. I am indebted to James MacGregor Burns and his discussion of transforming leadership for both the term and the concept, "the politics of transformation." See Burns, *Leadership* (New York: Harper and Row, 1978).

Bibliography

I. PRIMARY SOURCES

A. Manuscripts

Atlanta, Ga. Martin Luther King, Jr., Archives. Southern Christian Leadership Conference Papers. "Citizenship Schools."

Boston, Mass. John F. Kennedy Library.

Brownsville, Tenn. Haywood County. County Clerk's Office. Records.

Brownsville, Tenn. Just Organized Neighborhood Area Headquarters (JONAH) Office. JONAH Records.

Brownsville, Tenn. Willie Mae Holloway. Personal Papers.

Chapel Hill, N.C. University of North Carolina Library. Southern Historical Collection. Ames Collection.

Chicago, Ill. Chicago Historical Society. Congress on Racial Equality. Records.

Chicago, Ill. University of Chicago. Joseph Regenstein Library. Special Collections. Ida B. Wells Collection.

Detroit, Mich. Milmon Mitchell. Personal Papers.

Indianapolis, Ind. Debra Davis. Personal Papers.

Knoxville, Tenn. Lawson McGee Library. Calvin M. McClung Historical Collection. L. C. Houk Papers.

Nashville, Tenn. Tennessee State Library and Archives. Manuscript Division. Bureau of Refugees, Freedmen and Abandoned Lands. Selected Records of the Tennessee Field Office.

———. Tennessee Centennial Exposition. Records.

———. Tennessee Election Returns.

———. Taylor, John A. Diary.

Washington, D. C. Library of Congress. National Association for the Advancement of Colored People. Administration Files. "Brownsville Branch" and
"Tennessee Lynching—Williams."

————. Booker T. Washington Collection.

Washington, D. C. National Archives. Bureau of Refugees, Freedmen and Abandoned Lands. Record Group 105: Tennessee, Brownsville; Tennessee Superintendent of Education, 1867–1870; Tennessee Assistant Commissioner Reports,
Reports of Outrages, Riots, and Murders.

B. Interviews

Unless otherwise noted, these interviews were conducted in person by Richard
Couto. Copies of all interviews are in the possession of the author.

Black, Ethel McElwee. Los Angeles, Calif., 14 Sept. 1990.

Boyd, , Currie P., Ed.D. Dancyville, Tenn., 17 Dec. 1987. Brownsville, Tenn.,
13 Apr. 1990. Nashville, Tenn., 24 Apr. 1991. Stanton, Tenn., 17 June 1991.
Dancyville, Tenn., 8 July 1991, interviewed by Veronica Lucas. Dancyville,
Tenn., 21 Oct. 1991, telephone interview.

Cannon, Jessie, Jr., M.D. Stanton, Tenn., 14 Mar. 1978.

Cannon Jessie, Sr. Stanton, Tenn., 13 Mar. 1978 and 18 Dec. 1987.

Carney, Jean. Stanton, Tenn., 14 Mar. 1978. Brownsville, Tenn., 18 Dec. 1987.
Ripley, Tenn., 4 Aug. 1988.

Davis, Casher. Niles, Mich., 30 Sept. 1987, 28 Oct. 1989, and 24 June 1991.

Davis, Evelyn; Joseph Davis; Mary Davis; John Davis; Nancy Davis; and Debra
Davis. Niles, Mich., 28 Oct. 1989.

Davis, Mrs. Thomas. Jackson, Tenn., 18 Dec. 1987.

Davis, Nann Hess. Niles, Mich., 30 Sept. 1987, 28 Oct. 1989, and 24 June 1991.

Douglass, Bettye. Stanton, Tenn., 18 Dec. 1987. Stanton, Tenn., 9 July 1991,
interviewed by Veronica Lucas.

Ford, Julia C. McElwee. Los Angeles, Calif., 14 Sept. 1990.

Hess, Homer Zell McElwee, and Sam Hess. Brownsville, Tenn., 13 Apr. 1990.

King, William. Brownsville, Tenn., 13 Apr. 1990. Memphis, Tenn., 26 Mar. 1991.
Stanton, Tenn., 17 June 1991. Stanton, Tenn., Jan. 8, 1992, telephone interview.

McElwee, Robert. Los Angeles, Calif., 13 and 14 Sept. 1990. Los Angeles, Calif.,
15 Mar. 1991, telephone interview.

Mitchell, Milmon. Nashville, Tenn., 1 Nov. 1989.

Price, Thelma Shell. Jackson, Tenn., 19 Dec. 1987.

Rice, Earl. Stanton, Tenn., 13 Mar. 1978. Brownsville, Tenn., 17 Dec. 1987.
Ripley, Tenn., 4 Aug. 1988.

Rice, Tom. Stanton, Tenn., 13 Mar. 1978.

Sanderlin, Tom. Stanton, Tenn., 12 Mar. 1978.

Taylor, Truly Mae. Brownsville, Tenn., 25 Mar. 1991.

C. Newspapers and Periodicals

Brownsville (Tenn.) States-Graphic. Consulted at the Tennessee State Library and
Archives, Nashville.

Chicago Broad Ax.

Chicago Defender

Fisk Herald, Fisk University, Nashville, Tenn.

Memphis Avalanche. Consulted at the Tennessee State Library and Archives, Nashville.

Memphis Commercial Appeal

Memphis Daily Appeal. Consulted at the Tennessee State Library and Archives,
Nashville.

Nashville Banner. Consulted at the Tennessee State Library and Archives, Nashville.

Nashville Daily American

Nashville Tennessean

Niles (Mich.) Daily Star

D. Government Documents

State of Tennessee. General Assembly. Military Committee. "Report of Evidence
Taken in Relation to Outrages Committed by the Ku Klux Klan in Middle
and West Tennessee," extra session of the 35th General Assembly (2 Sept.
1872). Tennessee State Library and Archives, Nashville, Tenn.

U.S. Federal Bureau of Investigation. Records Pertaining to the Violation of the
Civil Rights of Elbert Williams. U.S. Justice Department. Freedom of Information Office.

U.S. Congress. Joint Committee on the Conduct of the War. "Report of the Sub-
Committee to Investigate the Recent Attack on Fort Pillow." 38th Congress,
1st Session (5 May 1864).

U.S. Congress. Joint Select Committee to Inquire into the Condition of Affairs
in the Late Insurrectionary States. Report. 19 Feb. 1872.

U.S. Justice Department. Records Pertaining to the Violation of the Civil Rights
of Elbert Williams. Freedom of Information Office.

II. SECONDARY WORKS

A. Books

Ames, Jessie D. *The Changing Character of Lynching: Review of Lynching, 1931–1941*. Atlanta, Ga.: Commission on Interracial Cooperation, 1942.

Anderson, James D. *The Education of Blacks in the South, 1860–1935*. Chapel Hill: Univ. of North Carolina Press, 1988.

Aptheker, Herbert, ed. *W. E. B. Du Bois: The Correspondence of W. E. B. Du Bois*. Vol. 1: *Selections, 1877–1934*. Amherst: Univ. of Massachusetts Press, 1973.

―――. *American Negro Slave Revolts*. 5th ed. New York: International Publishers, 1983.

―――, ed. *A Documentary History of the Negro People in the United States*. Vol. 2: *From the Reconstruction to the Founding of the NAACP*. New York: Carol Publishing Group, 1990.

Baldwin, Sidney. *Poverty and Politics: The Rise and Fall of the Farm Security Administration*. Chapel Hill: Univ. of North Carolina Press, 1968.

Bellah, Robert N., Richard Madsen, William M. Sullivan, Ann Swidler, and Steven M. Tipton. *Habits of the Heart: Individualism and Commitment in American Life*. Berkeley: Univ. of California Press, 1985.

Benedict, Michael Les. *The Impeachment Trial of Andrew Jackson*. New York: Norton, 1973.

Bentley, George R. *A History of the Freedmen's Bureau*. New York: Octagon Books, 1974.

Bittker, Boris I. *The Case for Black Reparations*. New York: Random House, 1973.

Blassingame, John W. *Slave Testimony: Two Centuries of Letters, Speeches, Interviews and Autobiographies*. Baton Rouge: Louisiana State Univ. Press, 1977.

Branch, Taylor. *Parting the Waters: America in the King Years, 1954–1963*. New York: Touchstone Books, 1988.

Brooks, Thomas R. *Walls Come Tumbling Down: A History of the Civil Rights Movement, 1940–1970*. Englewood Cliffs, N.J.: Prentice-Hall, 1974.

Brown, Cynthia Stokes, ed. *Ready from Within: Septima Clark and the Civil Rights Movement*. Navarro, Calif.: Wild Tree Press, 1986.

Brown, Norma. *A Black Diplomat in Haiti: The Diplomatic Correspondence of U.S. Minister Frederick Douglass from Haiti, 1889–1891*. Vol. 1. Salisbury, N.C.: Documentary Publications, 1977.

Bunche, Ralph J. *The Political Status of the Negro in the Age of FDR*. Ed. Dewey Grantham. Chicago: Univ. of Chicago Press, 1973.

Burns, James MacGregor. *Leadership*. New York: Harper & Row, 1978.

Carmichael, Stokely, and Charles V. Hamilton. *Black Power: The Politics of Liberation in America*. New York: Random House, 1973.

Carson, Clayborne. *In Struggle: SNCC and the Black Awakening of the 1960s*. Cambridge, Mass.: Harvard Univ. Press, 1981.

Cartwright, Joseph H. *The Triumph of Jim Crow: Tennessee Race Relations in the 1880s*. Knoxville: Univ. of Tennessee Press, 1976.

Chafe, William Henry. *Civilities and Civil Rights: Greensboro, North Carolina, and the Black Struggle for Equality*. New York: Oxford Univ. Press, 1980.

Chafets, Ze'ev. *Devil's Night: And Other True Tales of Detroit*. New York: Random House, 1990.

Cortner, Richard A. *A Mob Intent on Death: The NAACP and the Arkansas Riot Case*. Middletown, Conn.: Wesleyan Univ. Press, 1988.

Couto, Richard A. *Ain't Gonna Let Nobody Turn Me Round: The Pursuit of Racial Justice in the Rural South*. Philadelphia: Temple Univ. Press, 1991.

Cruse, Harold. *Plural But Equal: A Critical Study of Blacks and Minorities and America's Plural Society*. New York: William Morrow, 1987.

Current, Richard A. *Lincoln's Loyalists: Union Soldiers from the Confederacy*. Boston: Northeastern Univ. Press, 1992.

Dahl, Robert A. *A Preface to Democratic Theory*. Chicago: Univ. of Chicago Press, 1956.

———. *Who Governs? Democracy and Power in an American City*. New Haven: Yale Univ. Press, 1961.

Danto, Arthur C. *Narration and Knowledge*. New York: Columbia Univ. Press, 1985.

Davenport, Northrup Henry. *The College of Life or Practical Self-Educator: A Manual for Self-Improvement for the Colored Race, forming an Educational Emancipator and a Guide to Success Giving Examples and Achievements of Successful Men and Women of the Race as an Incentive and Inspiration to the Rising Generation*. 1895. Reprint. Miami, Fla.: Mnemosyne Publishing, 1969.

Davis, Allen F., and Mary Lynn McCree. *Eighty Years at Hull House*. Chicago: Quadrangle Books, 1969.

Dollard, John. *Caste and Class in a Southern Town*. 1937. Reprint. Madison: Univ. of Wisconsin Press, 1988.

Douglass, Frederick, et al. *The Reason Why the Colored American Is Not in the World's Colombian Exposition*. N.p., 1893.

Drake, St. Claire. *Churches and Voluntary Associations in the Chicago Negro Community* (U.S., Work Projects Administration, Institute for Juvenile Research, Univ. of Chicago, n.d.). Available in the Library of the Chicago Historical Society, Chicago, Ill.

Du Bois, W. E. B. *The Souls of Black Folk*. 1903. Reprint. New York: Bantam, 1989.

————. *Black Reconstruction in America, 1860–1880*. 1935. Reprint. New York: Atheneum, 1962.

Eagles, Charles W., ed. *The Civil Rights Movement in America*. Jackson: Univ. Press of Mississippi, 1986.

Edds, Margaret. *Free at Last: What Really Happened When Civil Rights Came to Southern Politics*. Bethesda, Md.: Adler and Adler, 1987.

Evans, Sara M. *Personal Politics: The Roots of Women's Liberation in the Civil Rights Movement and the New Left*. New York: Vintage Books, 1980.

Evans, Sara M., and Harry C. Boyte. *Free Spaces: The Sources of Democratic Change in America*. New York: Harper & Row, 1986.

Fay, Brian. *Critical Social Science: Liberation and Its Limits*. Ithaca, N.Y.: Cornell Univ. Press, 1987.

Fay, Brian, Eugene O. Golob, and Richard R. Vann, eds. *Louis O. Mink: Historical Understanding*. Ithaca, N.Y.: Cornell Univ. Press, 1987.

Fitzgerald, Michael W. *The Union League Movement in the Deep South: Politics and Agricultural Change During Reconstruction*. Baton Rouge: Louisiana State Univ. Press, 1989.

Foner, Eric. *Nothing But Freedom: Emancipation and Its Legacy*. Baton Rouge: Louisiana State Univ. Press, 1983.

————. *Reconstruction: America's Unfinished Revolution, 1863–1877*. New York: Harper & Row, 1988.

Forman, James. *The Black Manifesto*. Richmond, Va.: Richmond News Leader, 1969.

————. *The Making of Black Revolutionaries: A Personal Account*. New York: Macmillan, 1972.

Freeman, Jo, ed. *Social Movements of the Sixties and Seventies*. New York: Longman, 1983.

Frederickson, George M. *The Arrogance of Race: Historical Perspectives on Slavery, Racism, and Social Inequality*. Middletown, Conn.: Wesleyan Univ. Press, 1988.

Garrow, David J. *Bearing the Cross: Martin Luther King, Jr., and the Southern Christian Leadership Conference*. New York: Vintage Books, 1988.

Gaventa, John. *Power and Powerless: Rebellion and Quiescence in an Appalachian Valley*. Urbana: Univ. of Illinois Press, 1980.

Geertz, Clifford. *Local Knowledge: Further Essays in Interpretive Anthropology*. New York: Basic Books, 1983.

————. *Works and Lives: The Anthropologist as Author*. Stanford, Calif.: Stanford Univ. Press, 1987.

Glen, John. *Highlander: No Ordinary School, 1932–1962.* Lexington: Univ. Press of Kentucky, 1988.

Goodspeed, Weston. *History of Tennessee: From the Earliest Times to the Present.* Nashville: Goodspeed Publishers, 1887.

Hall, Jacquelyn Dowd. *Revolt Against Chivalry: Jessie Daniel Ames and the Women's Campaign against Lynching.* New York: Columbia Univ. Press, 1979.

Hamilton, Charles V. *The Bench and the Ballot: Southern Federal Judges and Black Voters.* New York: Oxford Univ. Press, 1973.

Harlan, Louis R., ed. *The Booker T. Washington Papers.* Vol. 2: *1860–89.* Urbana: Univ. of Illinois Press, 1972.

Hamburger, Robert. *Our Portion of Hell.* New York: Links Books, 1973.

Hanks, Lawrence J. *The Struggle for Black Political Empowerment in Three Georgia Counties.* Knoxville: Univ. of Tennessee Press, 1987.

Hersey, John. *The Algiers Motel Incident.* New York: Knopf, 1968.

Hirschman, Albert O. *Exit, Voice, and Loyalty: Response to Decline in Firms, Organizations, and States.* Cambridge: Harvard Univ. Press, 1970.

Holt, Andrew David. *The Struggle for a State System of Public Schools in Tennessee, 1903–1936.* New York: Teachers College Press, Columbia Univ., 1938.

Hopkins, Anne H., and William Lyons. *Tennessee Votes: 1799–1976.* Knoxville: Univ. of Tennessee, Bureau of Public Administration, 1978.

Horn, Stanley F. *Invisible Empire: The Story of the Ku Klux Klan, 1886–1871.* Cos Cobb, Conn.: John E. Edwards, 1969.

Horton, Myles, and Paulo Freire. *We Make the Road by Walking: Conversations on Education and Social Change.* Philadelphia: Temple Univ. Press, 1990.

Jones, Lillian Poston. *Some Poston Family Notes.* Memphis, Tenn.: Otis H. Jones, 1970. Available in Crockett County Library, Alamo, Tenn.

Justi, Herman, ed. *Official History of the Tennessee Centennial Exposition.* Nashville: Brandon Printing Co., 1898.

Kellogg, Charles Flint. *NAACP: A History of the National Association for the Advancement of Colored People.* Vol. 1: *1909–20.* Baltimore, Md.: Johns Hopkins Univ. Press, 1967.

King, Mary. *Freedom Song: A Personal Story of the 1960s Civil Rights Movement.* New York: Morrow, 1987.

Kousser, J. Morgan. *The Shaping of Southern Politics: Suffrage Restriction and the Establishment of the One-Party South, 1880–1910.* New Haven, Conn.: Yale Univ. Press, 1974.

Kuhn, Thomas. *The Structure of Scientific Revolutions.* 2d ed. Chicago: Univ. of Chicago Press, 1970.

Lamon, Lester C. *Blacks in Tennessee, 1791–1970.* Knoxville: Univ. of Tennessee Press, 1981.

Lawson, Steven F. *Black Ballots: Voting Rights in the South, 1944–1969.* New York: Columbia Univ. Press, 1976.

Lewis, Anthony. *Portrait of a Decade: The Second American Revolution.* New York: Random House, 1964.

Lincoln, Yvonna S., and Egon G. Guba. *Naturalistic Inquiry.* Beverly Hills, Calif.: Sage, 1985.

MacIntyre, Alasdaire. *After Virtue: A Study in Moral Theory.* Notre Dame, Ind.: Univ. of Notre Dame Press, 1981.

McAdam, Doug. *Political Process and the Development of Black Insurgency, 1930– 1970.* Chicago: Univ. of Chicago Press, 1972.

McBride, Robert M., and Dan M. Robinson. *Biographical Directory of the Tennessee General Assembly, 1861–1901.* Nashville: Tennessee State Library and Archives and the Tennessee Historical Commission, 1979.

McFeely, William S. *Frederick Douglass.* New York: Norton, 1991.

McNeil, Ginna Rae. *Groundwork: Charles Hamilton Houston and the Struggle for Civil Rights.* Philadelphia: Univ. of Pennsylvania Press, 1983.

McPherson, James M. *The Negro's Civil War: How American Negroes Felt and Acted During the War for the Union.* New York: Pantheon, 1965.

Mills, C. Wright. *The Sociological Imagination.* New York: Oxford Univ. Press, 1959.

Moon, Harvey Lee. *Balance of Power: The Negro Vote.* Garden City, N.Y.: Doubleday, 1949.

Morris, Aldon D. *The Origins of the Civil Rights Movement: Black Communities Organizing for Change.* New York: Free Press, 1984.

Myrdal, Gunnar. *An American Dilemma: The Negro Problem and Modern Democracy.* New York: Harper and Row, 1944.

Nash, Christopher. *Narrative in Culture: The Uses of Storytelling in the Sciences, Philosophy, and Literature.* London: Routledge, 1990.

National Association for the Advancement of Colored People. *Thirty Years of Lynching.* 1919. Reprint. New York: Arno Press and the New York Times, 1969.

Norrell, Robert J. *Reaping the Whirlwind: The Civil Rights Movement in Tuskegee.* New York: Knopf, 1985.

Official Proceedings of the Republican National Convention, 1888. (Minneapolis, Minn.: Charles W. Johnson, 1903)

Olson, Mancur. *The Logic of Collective Action.* Cambridge: Harvard Univ. Press, 1965.

O'Reilly, Kenneth. *"Racial Matters:": The FBI's Secret File on Black America, 1960– 1972.* New York: Free Press, 1989.

Painter, Nell Irvin. *Exodusters: Black Migration to Kansas after Reconstruction.* New York: Knopf, 1977.

Pierce, Paul Skeels. *The Freedmen's Bureau: A Chapter in the History of Reconstruction.* Iowa City: Univ. of Iowa Press, 1904.

Rable, George C. *But There Was No Peace: The Role of Violence in the Politics of Reconstruction.* Athens: Univ. of Georgia, 1984.

Robinson, Jo Anne Gibson. *The Montgomery Bus Boycott and the Women Who Started It: Memoir of Jo Anne Gibson Robinson.* Ed. David J. Garrow. Knoxville: Univ. of Tennessee Press, 1987.

Robinson, Paul, and William M. Sullivan, eds. *Interpretive Social Science: A Second Look.* Berkeley: Univ. of California Press, 1987.

Robison, Daniel Merritt. *Bob Taylor and the Agrarian Revolt in Tennessee.* Chapel Hill: Univ. of North Carolina Press, 1935.

Rowan, Carl T. *Dream Makers, Dream Breakers: The World of Justice Thurgood Marshall.* Boston: Little, Brown, 1993.

Schrag, Calvin O. *Radical Reflection and the Origin of the Human Sciences.* West Lafayette, Ind.: Purdue Univ. Press, 1980.

Scott, James C. *Weapons of the Weak: Everyday Forms of Resistance.* New Haven: Yale Univ. Press, 1985.

―――. *Domination and the Arts of Resistance: Hidden Transcripts.* New Haven, Conn.: Yale Univ. Press, 1990.

Scott, Mingo, Jr. *The Negro in Tennessee Politics and Governmental Affairs: 1865–1965.* Nashville, Tenn.: Rich Printing Co., 1964.

Simmons, William J. *Men of Mark: Eminent, Progressive and Rising.* Cleveland: Geo. M. Rewell & Co., 1887.

Smead, Howard. *Blood Justice: The Lynching of Mack Charles Parker.* New York: Oxford Univ. Press, 1986.

Steele, Shelby. *The Content of Our Character: A New Vision of Race in America.* New York: St. Martin's Press, 1990.

Swinney, Everette. *Suppressing the Ku Klux Klan: The Enforcement of the Reconstruction Amendments, 1870–1877.* New York: Garland, 1987.

Taylor, Alrutheus Ambush. *The Negro in Tennessee, 1865–1880.* Spartanburg, S.C.: Reprint Co., Publishers, 1974.

Thernstrom, Abigail M. *Whose Votes Count? Affirmative Action and Minority Voting Rights.* Cambridge: Harvard Univ. Press, 1987.

Tindall, George B. *South Carolina Negroes, 1877–1900.* Baton Rouge: Louisiana State Univ. Press, 1966.

Tjerandsen, Carl. *Education for Citizenship: A Foundation's Experience.* Santa Cruz, Calif.: Emil Schwarzhaupt Foundation, 1980.

Torrence, Ridgely. *The Story of John Hope.* New York: Macmillan, 1948.

Trelease, Allen W. *White Terror: The Ku Klux Klan Conspiracy and Southern Reconstruction.* Westport, Conn.: Greenwood, 1971.

Waller, Altina L. *Feud: Hatfields, McCoys, and Social Change in Appalachia, 1860–1900.* Chapel Hill: Univ. of North Carolina Press, 1988.

Wells, Ida B. *Crusade for Justice: The Autobiography of Ida B. Wells.* Ed. Alfreda M. Duster. Chicago: Univ. of Chicago Press, 1970.

————. *On Lynchings: Southern Horror, A Red Record, and Mob Rule in New Orleans.* 1892, 1895, and 1900. Reprint. New York: Arno Press and the New York Times, 1969.

Whitson, L. D. *Personal Sketches of the Forty–Fourth General Assembly of Tennessee.* Nashville, Tenn.: Southern Methodist Publishing House, 1885.

Williams, Juan. *Eyes on the Prize: America's Civil Rights Years, 1954–65.* New York: Penguin, 1987.

Williamson, Joel. *A Rage for Order: Black-White Relations in the American South Since Emancipation.* New York: Oxford Univ. Press, 1986.

Wilson, William Julius. *The Truly Disadvantaged: The Inner City, the Underclass, and Public Policy.* Chicago: Univ. of Chicago Press, 1987.

Woodward, C. Vann. *The Strange Career of Jim Crow.* 2d rev. ed. New York: Oxford Univ. Press, 1966.

Works, Monroe W. *Negro Yearbook: An Annual Encyclopedia of Negroes.* Tuskegee, Ala.: Negro Yearbook Publishers, 1932.

Zangrando, Robert L. *The NAACP Crusade Against Lynching, 1909–1950.* Philadelphia: Temple Univ. Press, 1980.

B. Articles

Abromowitz, Jack. "The Negro in the Populist Movement." *Journal of Negro History* 38 (July 1953): 257–89.

Binning, Wayne F. "The Tennessee Republicans in Decline, 1869–1876." *Tennessee Historical Quarterly* 39 (Winter 1980): 471–84.

Blee, Kathleen M., and Dwight B. Billings. "Reconstructing Daily Life in the Past: An Hermeneutical Approach to Ethnographic Data." *Sociological Quarterly* 27 (Fall 1986): 443–62.

Carson, Clayborne. "Civil Rights Reform and the Black Freedom Struggle." In *The Civil Rights Movement in America*, ed. Charles W. Eagles, 19–32. Jackson: Univ. Press of Mississippi, 1986.

Cartwright, Joseph H. "Black Legislators in Tennessee in the 1880s: A Case Study in Black Political Leadership." *Tennessee Historical Quarterly* 32 (Fall 1973): 265–84.

Cohen, William. "Negro Involuntary Servitude in the South, 1865–1940: A Preliminary Analysis." *Journal of Southern History* 42 (Feb. 1976): 31–60.

Couto, Richard A. "Sick for Justice." *Southern Exposure* 6 (Summer 1978): 73–76.

————. "A Place to Call Our Own." *Southern Exposure* 9 (Fall 1981): 16–22.

————. "Participatory Research: Methodology and Critique." *Clinical Sociology Review* 5 (1987): 83–90.

Du Bois, W. E. B. "The Freedmen's Bureau." *Atlantic Monthly* 87 (Mar. 1901): 354–65.

————. "The Evolution of Negro Leadership." *The Dial*, 16 July 1901, 53–55.

————. "The Propaganda of History." In Du Bois, *Black Reconstruction in America, 1860–1880*, 711–29. 1935. Reprint. New York: Atheneum, 1962.

Fleming, Cynthia Griggs. "A Survey of the Beginnings of Tennessee's Black Colleges and Universities, 1865–1920." *Tennessee Historical Quarterly* 39 (Summer 1980): 195–207.

Fraser, Walter J., Jr. "Black Reconstructionists in Tennessee." *Tennessee Historical Quarterly* 34 (Winter 1975): 362–82.

Gaither, Gerald H. "The Negro Alliance Movement in Tennessee, 1888–91." *West Tennessee Historical Society Papers* 23 (1973): 50–62.

Glantz, Oscar. "The Negro Vote in Northern Industrial Cities." *Western Political Quarterly* 13 (Dec. 1960): 999–1010.

Gutmann, Herbert G. "Schools for Freedom: The Post-Emancipation Origins of Afro-American Education." In *Power and Culture: Essays on the American Working Class*, ed. Ira Berlin, 260–97. New York: Pantheon, 1987.

Holmes, William F. "The Arkansas Cotton Pickers Strike of 1891 and the Demise of the Colored Farmers' Alliance." *Arkansas Historical Quarterly* 32 (Summer 1973): 107–19.

————. "The LeFlore County Massacre and the Demise of the Colored Farmers' Alliance." *Phylon* 34 (Sept. 1973): 267–74.

Jackson, Luther P. "Race and Suffrage in the South Since 1940." *New South* 3 (June–July 1948): 1–26.

Lindbloom, Charles E. "Another State of Mind." *American Political Science Review* 76 (Mar. 1982): 9–21.

Lufkin, Charles L. "A Forgotten Controversy: The Assassination of Senator Almon Case of Tennessee." *West Tennessee Historical Society Papers* 39 (1985): 37–42.

McCarthy, John D., and Mayer N. Zald. "Resource Mobilization and Social Movements: A Partial Theory." *American Journal of Sociology* 82: 6 (1977): 1212–41.

McDonald, Laughlin. "Review of Abigail M. Thernstrom, *Whose Votes Count? Affirmative Action and Minority Voting Rights.*" *Southern Changes* 11 (Nov. 1989): 21–23.

May, J. Thomas. "The Freedmen's Bureau at the Local Level: A Study of a Louisiana Agent." *Louisiana History* 9 (Winter 1968): 5–19.

Miller, Floyd J. "Black Protest and White Leadership: A Note on the Colored Farmers' Alliance." *Phylon* 33 (June 1972): 169–74.

Millis, H. A. "The Present Street Railway Situation in Chicago." *Annals of the American Academy of Political and Social Science* 20: 2 (Sept. 1902): 52–65.

Myrdal, Gunnar. "A Methodological Note on Facts and Valuations in Social Science." In Myrdal, *An American Dilemma: The Negro Problem and Modern Democracy*, 1035–64. New York: Harper and Row, 1944.

Perrow, Charles. "The Sixties Observed." In *The Dynamics of Social Movements: Resource Mobilization, Social Control, and Tactics*, ed. Mayer N. Zald and John D. McCarthy, 192–211. Cambridge, Mass.: Winthrop Publishers, 1979.

Rudwick, Elliott M. "The Niagara Movement." *Journal of Negro History* 42 (Fall 1957): 177–200.

Rudwick, Elliott M., and August Meier. "Black Man in the 'White City': Negroes and the Columbian Exposition, 1893." *Phylon* 26 (Winter 1965): 354–61.

Salamon, Lester. "The Time Dimension in Policy Evaluation: The Case of the New Deal Land Reform Experiments." *Public Policy* 27 (Sept. 1972): 129–83.

Salisbury, Robert H. "Political Movements in American Politics: An Essay on Concept and Analysis." *National Political Science Review* 1 (1989): 15–30.

Shambaugh, Benjamin F. "Review of John W. Burgess, *Reconstruction and the Constitution, 1866–76.*" *Annals of the American Academy of Political and Social Science* 20: 2 (Sept. 1902): 130.

Sheldon, Randall G. "From Slave to Caste Society: The Penal Changes in Tennessee, 1830–1915." *Tennessee Historical Quarterly* 38 (1979): 461–71.

Swint, Henry Lee, ed. "Reports from Educational Agents of the Freedmen's Bureau in Tennessee, 1865–1870." *Tennessee Historical Quarterly* 1 (Winter 1942): 51–80 and 1 (Spring 1942): 152–70.

Tucker, David M. "Miss Ida B. Wells and Memphis Lynching." *Phylon* 32 (Summer 1971): 112–22.

Weisberger, Bernard A. "The Dark and Bloody Ground of Reconstruction Historiography." *Journal of Southern History* 25 (Nov. 1959): 427–47.

Weiss, Nancy J. "The Negro and the New Freedom." In *The Segregation Era, 1863–1954*, ed. Allen Weinstein and F. O. Gatell, 129–42. New York: Oxford Univ. Press, 1970.

Wolin, Sheldon S. "Paradigm and Political Theories." In *Paradigms and Revolutions: Appraisals and Applications of Theories Kuhn's Philosophy of Science*, ed. Gary Gutting, 160–91. Notre Dame, Ind.: Univ. of Notre Dame Press, 1980.

C. Unpublished Works

Baxter, James Arnold. "Charles Allen Rawls, 'A Portrait,' 1907–1977." Master's thesis, Tennessee State Univ., Nashville, Tenn., 1982.

Granberry, Dorothy. "African American Education in Haywood County, Tenn., 1870–1970." Paper presented at the Local African American History Conference, Nashville, Tenn., 13 Feb. 1991.

Lovett, Bobby L., ed. "From Winter to Winter: The Afro-American History of Nashville, Tennessee, 1870–1930." Unpublished ms. Photocopy. Nashville: Tennessee State Univ., 1981.

McKenzie, Robert Tracy. "From Old South to New South in the Volunteer State: The Economy and Society of Rural Tennessee." Ph.D. diss., Vanderbilt Univ., Nashville, Tenn., 1988.

McKissack, Gloria. "Late Summer: Afro-American Nashville, 1890–1899." In "From Winter to Winter: The Afro-American History of Nashville, Tennessee, 1870–1930," ed. Bobby L. Lovett, 103–314. Unpublished ms. Photocopy. Nashville: Tennessee State Univ., 1981.

Sherril, Gladys Murray. "Some Attempts at Black Endeavors: Jesse M. H. Graham and Other Blacks in Tennessee Politics, 1890–1900." Master's thesis, Tennessee State Univ., Nashville, Tenn., 1974.

Stern, Mark. "Calculating Visions: Civil Rights Legislation in the Kennedy and Johnson Years." Paper presented at the annual meeting of the American Political Science Association, Washington, D. C., 1991.

Williams, Cordell Hull. "The Life of James Carroll Napier from 1845 to 1940." Master's thesis, Tennessee State Univ., Nashville, Tenn., 1955.

Index